Islands of GENIUS

of related interest

Different Minds
Gifted Children with AD/HD, Asperger Syndrome, and Other Learning Deficits
Deirdre V. Lovecky
ISBN 978 1 85302 964 6

The Myriad Gifts of Asperger Syndrome
John M. Ortiz
ISBN 978 1 84310 883 2

The Girl Who Spoke With Pictures
Autism Through Art
Eileen Miller
Foreword by Robert Nickel MD
Illustrated by Kim Miller
ISBN 978 1 84310 889 4

Islands of GENIUS

The Bountiful Mind of the Autistic, Acquired, and Sudden Savant

Darold A. Treffert

Foreword by Daniel Tammet

Jessica Kingsley Publishers
London and Philadelphia

First published in 2010
by Jessica Kingsley Publishers
116 Pentonville Road
London N1 9JB, UK
and
400 Market Street, Suite 400
Philadelphia, PA 19106, USA

www.jkp.com

Copyright © Darold Treffert 2010
Foreword © Daniel Tammet 2010

Library of Congress Cataloging in Publication Data
A CIP catalog record for this book is available from the Library of Congress

British Library Cataloguing in Publication Data
A CIP catalogue record for this book is available from the British Library

ISBN 978 1 84905 810 0

Printed and bound in the United States by
Thomson-Shore, 7300 W. Joy Road, Dexter, MI 48130

Dedicated to Kim and Fran Peek, who share the same shadow,
and from whom I have learned as much about matters of the heart
as I have about workings of the mind

In Memoriam
Kim Peek 1951–2009

Contents

Part 1 *The Mind of the Savant*

Part 2 *The World of the Savant*

Part 3 *Significant New Dimensions to Savant Syndrome*

Part 4 *Training the Talent: "I've Got a Son or Daughter Who…"*

Part 5 *Our Journey Has Just Begun*

Foreword

Savant syndrome is a rare and remarkable condition. Once sidelined by researchers, savants are now at the forefront of scientists' attempts to understand the immense and fascinating complexities of the human mind.

Darold Treffert, a Wisconsin psychiatrist, writer, and lecturer, is also the world's leading expert on savant syndrome. Over the course of five decades, he has in his many roles helped transform the public's view of "differently able" minds. As an advisor to the Oscar-winning movie *Rainman*, Dr Treffert brought global attention to the extraordinary abilities of the savant. In his writings and online presence via the Wisconsin Medical Society savant syndrome pages, he has worked tirelessly to express, explain, and clarify a phenomenon that continues to fascinate the general public and the media as much as ever before.

A savant is an individual with exceptional ability in one or more fields that co-exists with some form of disability. Many, though not all, are—like myself—on the autistic spectrum. It is this evocative mix of talent and limitation that I think so many people find particularly compelling. But proper awareness should be accorded to the human reality of both these attributes; neither the savant's difficulties nor his gifts ought ever to be trivialized.

This is what, in my view, makes Dr Treffert's work unique and so important. He understands, as he argues in this book, that savants' abilities go far beyond doing large sums or remembering a great deal of factual information. Savants, he acknowledges, can be highly creative. His profiles include those who have won awards for their paintings, written poetry and best-selling books, and produced whole albums of original music.

As Dr Treffert also makes clear, savants are not simply "nerds," "geeks," or "bumbling professors." The numerous challenges they face are often significant and enduring. He is correct to highlight the hugely important role played by the savant's family in their intensive ongoing care and education.

I had the pleasure of meeting Dr Treffert in person in the summer of 2004, during filming for the documentary *Brainman*. It was at this time, at age twenty-five, that I was first diagnosed with Asperger syndrome—a mild, high-functioning form of autism. It was Dr Treffert who confirmed in our interview that I was also a "savant." Naturally, this meeting made a great impression on me and we have corresponded regularly ever since. When my own first book, the memoir *Born On A Blue Day* was published in 2006, Dr Treffert kindly agreed to write the foreword for it. His many ideas and insights proved particularly inspiring and helpful to me in the preparation and writing of my next book, *Embracing the Wide Sky* (2009).

As Dr Treffert mentions in his profile of me for this book, I am currently at work on my third book—a novel. Many are surprised to hear this. Perhaps this is because they have never heard of an autistic person who writes literary fiction. In my memoir I describe how, as a child, I read mostly non-fiction—encyclopedias and dictionaries were my favourites—rather than fiction titles. But people change, and that also includes savants. Scientists now know that the brains we are born with are not "fixed" at birth, as once believed, but continue to change throughout our lifetime. It is how I have learned to look people in the eye when I talk, or to understand body language, or to tell funny jokes. The savant is not, as often assumed, a prisoner of his condition.

What can savant syndrome teach "normal" minds? Plenty. As we read through this book's many beautifully written profiles of the world's best-known savants we discover that they have far more in common with the "average" person than not. Too often scientific and media discussions of the condition focus on the differences between savant and non-savant minds, to the exclusion of the many significant similarities. Savant abilities are neither the result of supercomputer-like mental processing, exhaustive rote learning, or genetic quirks. Rather they are the result of distinctly human qualities: passion, dedication, enthusiasm, love.

Few people would or should want to learn to recite Pi to 22,514 decimal places, draw landmarks in breathtaking detail, or remember the contents of 12,000 books. Everyone is different. By refusing to gawp at these feats, preferring instead to focus on the person behind them, Dr Treffert sends out the message that it is the creative, imaginative processes at the root of such abilities that matter most. Only by considering the context of savants' lives can we more fully and properly understand the gifts that they possess.

Thanks in good part to the immensely valuable and enlightened work over nearly fifty years of Dr Treffert, savants like myself now play an increasingly active role in the scientific research into their abilities. In many domains, they are making substantial contributions to the societies in which they live. Best of all, this deeper and more humane appreciation of the savant—in all his (and her) various manifestations—serves to enrich our understanding and respect for every kind of mind.

— *Daniel Tammet*

Preface

Kim Peek, the inspiration for the movie *Rain Man*, memorized 12,000 books. He is the Mt. Everest of memory with bottomless factual recall in multiple areas of expertise including history, geography, literature, music, sports, science and religion, to name only some. He became a living Google. But as a child, his parents were advised to put him in an institution. One doctor suggested a lobotomy.

Matt Savage, who couldn't stand noise or being touched as a child, very quickly mastered the piano at age 6½ and had his first CD of jazz composition at age eight. Matt is recognized worldwide now as "the Mozart of Jazz," a title conferred on him by the famous jazz artist Dave Brubeck. At age 17 he is the leader of the Matt Savage Trio, giving concerts around the globe. He recently recorded his eighth CD.

Leslie Lemke is blind, severely cognitively impaired and has cerebral palsy. Yet he played back Tchaikovsky's Piano Concerto No. 1 flawlessly after hearing it for the first time at age 14. Leslie, who has never had a music lesson in his life, is a musical genius.

After a 15-minute helicopter ride over London, Stephen Wiltshire, in a five-day drawing marathon, produced a spectacularly accurate four meter long sketch which captures with mind-boggling fidelity seven square miles of London—building by building, street by street, window by window. Diagnosed with autism at age three, he was described as a "rocket of young talent" by a leading art critic when his remarkable drawing ability "exploded" on the scene at age eight. Stephen was invested by Queen Elizabeth II as a Member of the Order of the British Empire and now has his own gallery in the Royal Opera Arcade in London.

These extraordinary people, and others like them described in this book, have savant syndrome, a rare but remarkable condition in which incredible abilities—

"islands of genius"—coexist side by side, in jarring juxtaposition, to certain disabilities within the same person.

I met my first savant in 1962. I was fascinated with that remarkable condition and how to explain it then, and I remain intrigued with this neuroscientific miracle and mystery still. This book is an account of my 47-year journey with these remarkable people, and their equally remarkable families and caregivers. It summarizes what I have learned along the way on this rare journey about the *mind* of the savant, which is where and why I began my inquiry. But it is also an account of a voyage into the *world* of the savant, because as I sought to find out more about the condition the savant has, I learned more and more about the person who has the condition. In so doing, and witnessing the belief, unconditional love, patience, optimism and hard work of those who care *for* the savant, but who also care *about* the savant as well, I have learned as much about matters of the heart as I have about circuits in the brain.

The movie *Rain Man* (1988), depicting Raymond Babbitt's many spectacular savant skills, brought a great deal of attention to savant syndrome and made the term "autistic savant" household words. Prior to that film this rare but extraordinary condition of savant syndrome remained in relative obscurity, except for an occasional "Gee whiz, look at that" magazine article or brief television clip.

Savant skills are spectacular and worthy of attention. But they deserve more than a passing "Gee whiz" glance, after which we return to a common denominator, diminutive, "the world is flat" view of brain capacity and brain function. This book will take you well beyond "Gee whiz" as you learn about these exceptional people with such special skills. And we need to go beyond "Gee whiz" because no model of brain function, including memory, will be complete until it can fully incorporate and explain this jarring contradiction of extraordinary ability and sometimes permeating disability in the same person. Until we can fully explain the savant, we cannot fully explain ourselves nor comprehend our full capacities.

From that time in 1962 when I met my first savant, I have felt that the paradox of genius and limitation within the same person, always linked with incredible memory, provides a unique window into the brain in terms of talent, intelligence, memory and perhaps creativity itself. I also felt, from the beginning of this most interesting journey, that savant syndrome holds vast implications for discovering and tapping the substantial and significant buried potential—an "inner savant" capability—that resides, I am convinced, within us all. This book explains how and why I have come to those conclusions.

Many of the savants you will meet in this book, and long remember, show the more typical combination of some underlying condition such as autism or other developmental disability with special talents and gifts, often at a spectacular level, grafted on to, or superimposed upon, that underlying disability. That is the type of savant syndrome seen most often and as stated, the implications of that circumstance in and of itself are vast. Indeed those were the type of savants I met early on this voyage with them.

But then, in the mid-1990s, I encountered my first cases of the "acquired" savant. These are instances in which previously normal (neurotypical) persons, with no particular prior special skills, unexpectedly and spectacularly show the emergence of savant-like skills, sometimes at a prodigious level, following some central nervous system (CNS) incident such as a head injury, stroke or progressive dementia. This circumstance to me points even more convincingly toward a reservoir of buried but untapped potential—an inner savant capability—within us all. Consider these instances:

- A 54-year-old construction worker, with no prior art interest or talent, survives a stroke and suddenly, very foreign to his earlier interests, becomes an accomplished poet, artist and sculptor.

- Twelve elderly persons with fronto-temporal dementia (FTD) show art or musical composition abilities, several at a prodigious level, as the dementia proceeds. No such interest or talent was evident before the beginning of the dementia process.

- A 54-year-old surgeon gets struck by lightning which he survives. After several weeks of mild memory impairment, he develops an obsessive interest in classical music which was not present pre-incident. He learns to play the piano but has a recurrent, intrusive, unrelenting tune in his head which he subsequently transcribes into a major sonata; he now performs professionally. His medical skills remain unaffected.

- A 40-year-old motivational speaker dives into a shallow pool and sustains a major concussion. When he recovers, he is able to play the piano and guitar, neither of which he could play pre-injury. He now composes movie soundtracks and makes his living performing professionally. There is no other residual from the concussion.

- A middle-aged woman has a stroke from which she fully recovered, except now she speaks with an unmistakable and precise foreign accent of a country she has never visited.

You will meet more of these intriguing cases as you read on. The ultimate challenge of course is how to tap such dormant potential without some CNS catastrophe, and later in the book some such techniques are described.

Then there are cases of what I call "sudden" savant syndrome. These are instances in which there is a sudden epiphany of talent in neurotypical persons without CNS injury, and without any trade-off of other abilities for the newly acquired skills. For example a 30-year-old attorney who had been trying to learn to play the piano, suddenly, over the course of several seconds, abruptly "knows" the rules of music and plays like an accomplished musician to the absolute astonishment of himself and his friends. A similar epiphany occurs in another young man who suddenly could play guitar like a master musician with no need for formal training or lessons. He now performs professionally.

The bottom-line question, whether autistic, acquired or sudden savant, is "How do they do it?" Researchers have struggled mightily to answer that critical question in the 122 years since Dr. Down first described this baffling condition in 1887. Thus far definitive clues have been somewhat elusive. But the *Mind of the Savant* chapters that follow address that important question and summarize where we are at this point in time in explaining the autistic, acquired and sudden savant.

May Lemke has her explanation for how her foster son Leslie, with no musical training or lessons whatsoever, does it. On the *60 Minutes* program *Genius* in 1983 that so many people remember, she explained Leslie's special musical gift this way: "Well, I think that a part of the brain, the musical part, was left by itself—because the brain was damaged—but I think that that part of the brain was left perfectly healthy and beautiful, just so Leslie could get a talent—and he got it." As you will see, May's explanation, while not phrased in very scientific terms, is quite an accurate one. Studies outlined in some of the following chapters document a process in the savant of recruitment, rewiring and repair in one area of the brain to offset damage in some other area. Researchers call that "paradoxical functional facilitation," a fancier term than May Lemke's certainly, describing a "compensatory," or perhaps instead a "release" phenomenon, as an example of newly recognized, and only recently appreciated, brain plasticity.

This is a particularly exciting time for making great strides in our efforts to explain savant syndrome better for several reasons. First, new imaging techniques and related technology allow us, for the first time, to study brain *function* rather than just brain *structure*. Such functional imaging gives a much clearer, more intricate, real-time glimpse into the brain at work through the unique and opportune window into the brain that savant syndrome provides.

Second, the availability of new cases provides sufficient numbers of these relatively rare persons for comparative group comparisons rather than having to rely on only anecdotal, single case descriptions. This book reports on those findings and those new cases. It also explores how prodigy and genius, with their manifestations of exceptional talent, relate to savant syndrome.

Third, savant syndrome has always raised questions about how much hidden brain potential, and memory capacity, might lay buried and dormant within each of us. Through the years people have wondered that if persons with savant syndrome can recruit and utilize undamaged brain capacity to compensate for dysfunction or injury somewhere else in the brain, might there be such an untapped reservoir of brain capacity within us all? This question has been given even more impetus, urgency and possibility with the discovery of the "acquired savant" in the past several years.

"Acquired" savants are normal (neurotypical) persons who, having previously shown no particular special savant skills or abilities, suddenly, *after* a head injury, stroke, or other brain disease or disorder, develop art, music or math skills, for example, sometimes at a prodigious level. These cases heighten the possibility that savant capabilities—a little *Rain Man* perhaps—might be buried, but dormant, within us all. If so, it also presents the related question as to how one might access such dormant potential without having a head injury, stroke or other central nervous system catastrophe. This book addresses those questions based on new cases, new findings and new techniques.

Fourth, there is the curious but compelling phenomenon that prodigious savants particularly seem to "know things they never learned." Leslie, for example, who has never had a music lesson in his life, and cannot read music because he is blind, innately and instinctively seems to know the "rules of music" according to professional musicians who have met and listened to him. An experienced music professor said about Matt, "He seems to know things that are beyond his own existence." Other prodigious savants, without exposure or training, also innately "know" the rules of music, art, mathematics or calendar calculating. They seem to come with software—the music, math or art chip—factory installed. As you will see, that same innate knowledge resides in and then surfaces in prodigies and geniuses.

The capacity to know or remember things we never learned is what I call genetic memory. It is the genetic transmission of knowledge. Do we all have such knowledge or inherited capacity, installed perhaps as backup systems in case of injury, to be uncovered only with such damage? Was Carl Jung right in his idea of a collective unconscious—traits, beliefs, customs and talents—residing in us from birth and carried forth genetically from our ancestors? Scientists in the recently emerging field of epigenetics have suggested that epigenes may be the "software" that programs and directs the more rigid DNA "hardware" in the cell and they could be the formulating and transmitting mechanism for the genetic knowledge and memories that prodigious savants (and prodigies) seem to innately possess and manifest.

Therefore new savants, new techniques and new insights make this an exciting and opportune time for better understanding this extraordinary condition and exploring all of its profound implications not only for savants, but for all of us as well.

Finally I wanted to provide in this book an important part missing in my earlier book, *Extraordinary People: Understanding Savant Syndrome* (Treffert 2006a). That part might be called a "So Now What?" section. In it chapters provide ideas and suggestions for parents, teachers and others looking for specific advice on how best to approach these special people when they encounter them. They outline particular techniques to help "train the talent" to full advantage and potential with all of the accompanying gains for the savant overall. For that task I have enlisted three experts in music, art and math who share strategies and techniques that have worked for them in such enhancing and actualizing efforts.

So this book is not just about savants. It is also about the buried potential that savant syndrome, particularly the newer findings of "acquired savant" and "genetic memory," suggests may reside within us all. Newer technologies allow us to explore that possibility further, and such efforts are already underway. Those new findings have demonstrated that the brain is a much more malleable structure throughout life than conventional medical wisdom has suggested. Savant syndrome provides convincing proof of brain plasticity—the capacity of the brain to rewire and restructure itself after damage whether by genetic, injury or illness processes. And with brain plasticity comes a much more optimistic view of the central nervous system's capacity to repair and restore itself, and all the enormous implications and positive ramifications such a view entails in the rapidly expanding field of neuroscience.

I have learned a great deal about the brain and its marvelous, awesome capacity on this journey with savants, all of which is of intriguing *scientific* interest. But, along the way, I have learned equally as much about matters of compelling *human* interest—the power of love, optimism, patience, belief, tenacity, support and acceptance in helping to shape and fully achieve human potential in whomever and in whatever proportion it exists. I have also learned some things about myself from these extraordinary people, and because of them, I have wandered into areas of inquiry and introspection I probably would never have explored except for this voyage.

Perhaps reading this book will have the same effect on you. Certainly herein you will learn something about both the mind of the savant and the world of the savant, and in so doing come to an even greater appreciation of the specialness of these extraordinary people and their exceptional talents. But I hope this book will also trigger in you inquiry and introspection regarding the implications savant syndrome has for determining, and perhaps better accessing, buried and dormant potential within each of us.

Massive as human brain capacity seems to be, and as intricate as brain function is, we know so very little about either. Our journey of exploration has just begun. But new technology and techniques, and ever more serious study of savants, prodigies and geniuses can propel us along much further than we have ever been in better understanding both the brain and human potential.

I hope you find this journey into the mind and world of the savants exciting and revealing not only about them, but also about each of us and our possibilities as well.

INTRODUCTION

Sightseeing on an Incredible Journey

My extraordinary journey with savants began on July 2, 1962. It was a Monday, my calendar-calculating savants tell me now. It was my first day on the job as a very new psychiatrist.

I was, in fact, the new doctor in town. I had just completed my residency in psychiatry at University Hospitals in Madison and had joined the staff of Winnebago Mental Health Institute near Oshkosh, Wisconsin. I was assigned the responsibility of starting a Children's Unit there. It was on that unit, 47 years ago, that I met my first savant.

This newly established children's program consisted of 30 patients age 18 and under, drawn from the 800-plus patients who were hospitalized at Winnebago at that time. These were children and adolescents with severe mental handicap, most often with a diagnosis of autism. All had severe disabilities.

But four of these troubled youngsters immediately captured my special attention. I have never forgotten them. They launched this remarkable voyage into the mind and its marvelous intricacies and capabilities.

One adolescent boy had memorized the bus system of the entire city of Milwaukee. John knew each and every route from origin to end, which caused one bus driver to comment that "You know more about these routes than the drivers." He often walked around the unit with a cardboard cutout fashioned like the destination window one sees on the front of a city bus. John had jotted innumerable street names on a paper, scroll-like device that he could turn and change the destination as he wished, just as the bus changes its destination as it moves along its route. (I recently did a 47-year follow-up on this lad, now in his sixties, and you will learn in Chapter 29 how he put his marvelous memory skills to a very worthwhile and productive purpose.)

Another boy with autism, mute and severely cognitively disabled, could glance at a 500-piece jigsaw puzzle, *picture side down*, on the table in front of him and then put it together with the precision, motion and rhythm of a sewing machine just from seeing the geometric shapes. No picture was required.

A third youngster was a walking this-day-in-history almanac. He quizzed me each morning about what, to my memory, had happened on that day in history. I would try to bone up the evening before, anticipating my daily quiz. I usually failed compared to his vast reservoir of facts connected with that date.

Another little guy could make basketball free throws with mechanical, pitching-machine-like accuracy. He would put his feet in exactly the same position on the free throw line, hold the ball in exactly the same way and use exactly the same trajectory each time. Since the distance from the free throw line to the basket always remained the same, by using the same obsessive-compulsive motion to toss the ball in that same trajectory, the basketball went in each time just as it should. (I was reminded of this lad this past year when an autistic teenager in Rochester, New York, playing in the final basketball game of the season for the first time, made six three-point shots in four minutes. "Hot as a pistol," he said. That video clip startled, captured and touched an entire nation as his teammates hoisted Jason to their shoulders and the crowd stormed the court. The coach cried. And so did many viewers.)

I was struck by the jarring juxtaposition of these "islands of genius," as I called them, immersed in and surrounded by a sea of otherwise permeating and severe mental handicap. How can that be? How is that possible? How do they do it? What might that suggest about brain function overall and hidden potential, perhaps, within each of us? I asked myself those questions then, and continue to ask myself those important questions still.

Interestingly, Dr. J. Langdon Down (1887), over a century earlier, was also struck, just as I was, by the paradox of deficiency and superiority occurring in the same individual in some of the patients he had seen during his 30-year career as a physician at the Earlswood Asylum in London. Dr. Down, who is best known for having described a form of mental retardation that now bears his name—Down syndrome—had spent 30 years working at Earlswood and had seen literally thousands of children and adults with various forms of developmental disability and mental retardation. In 1887 Dr. Down reflected on his long career, and the patients he had seen, in a series of lectures to the Medical Society of London.

In a portion of those lectures—*On Some of the Mental Affections of Childhood and Youth*—Dr. Down (1887) shared with his colleagues some extraordinary patients he had seen who had, as with me, especially caught his eye. One such patient built exquisite ships and copied complicated texts verbatim but could not understand a single sentence of what he had copied. Another boy had memorized *The Rise and Fall of the Roman Empire* verbatim. He could recite it forward or backward. Other children remembered dates and past events; one child could remember the address of every candy shop in London and tell the date of his every visit. Another could recite the arrival date of all the children at the institution; another knew the address of every resident.

Arithmetical genius was evident as well. One 12-year-old boy could multiply three-digit figures by three-digit figures with perfect accuracy as quickly as the number could be written down. "Lightning calculating," Dr. Down called it. There also were musical islands of genius in Dr. Down's caseload, just as exist now. One boy, after attending an opera, would come away with perfect recollection of all the arias. Still another of Dr. Down's patients had perfect appreciation of passing time with no reference to a clock. There are such precise timekeeping cases now as well.

All in all there were ten such conspicuous patients that Dr. Down had seen in his 30 years of clinical practice. The now regrettable term "idiot" was at that time an accepted scientific term for mental retardation for persons with IQ below 25. But these ten individuals had striking areas of knowledge and ability standing in such sharp contrast to overall handicap. So Dr. Down coined a new term for them. He combined the word "idiot" with the French word *savoir* (meaning "to know") and named the condition "idiot savant." For understandable reasons, that term has been discarded now and savant syndrome substituted.

Following the encounter with the four "savants" on my unit, I began to research the literature on what was known about this extraordinary, striking condition at that time. That's where I encountered Dr. Down's work. I found that between 1887 and 1962, there were only a few scattered case reports in the entire world literature on that topic. Interestingly in all these reports the skills reported narrowed generally to only five areas: art, music, calendar calculating, lightning calculating and mechanical or spatial skills. And almost all of the reports were in males. Even Dr. Down had commented on the absence of females in this unusual circumstance. But in all the reports there was mention of massive memory always accompanying the abilities or skills. A type of memory, though, that Down called "verbal adhesion" because there seemed to be no comprehension about the vast stores of knowledge in that massive memory.

As I continued to work on the unit, I followed up on my interest in savant syndrome and was intrigued with its relationship to autistic disorder particularly. My interest in autism had been kindled very much earlier, actually, while in medical school even before my residency in psychiatry. That interest evolved because of the valuable opportunity I had during those years to meet and interact with Dr. Leo Kanner, the "godfather" of autistic disorder. It was Kanner, at Johns Hopkins, who first named, and so accurately described, early infantile autism in a classic article published in 1944. His description of this puzzling disorder has never been surpassed in clarity, accuracy and sensitivity. Dr. Kanner was in Madison as a visiting professor for a semester and that is where I had an opportunity to listen to and learn from him.

Remembering Kanner's (1944) description of early infantile autism, I was impressed and intrigued by this baffling disorder when I encountered it in these handsome children on my unit that were so preoccupied, so distant, so uncommunicative, and so withdrawn into a mystical world of their own. Some would watch whirling tops or spinning tricycle wheels for hours on end. Others had peculiar but powerfully obsessive rituals and routines. Some toe-walked in a peculiar gait or would spin down the hall. Few made eye contact at all and none sought affection, nor did they give such. Some showed all those signs and symptoms since birth. Others had developed normally, were animated and talkative, only to suddenly, and dramatically, regress into their virtual silent isolation. I could walk on the unit and be entirely unnoticed nor acknowledged. This was so different from the units with Down syndrome children that I had visited in other settings during my training on which those youngsters would literally swarm and reach out for, and latch on to, happily and affectionately, anyone visiting their units.

At the time I began my work on our Children's Unit there was a very cruel notion floating about in the scientific and lay literature blaming "refrigerator mothers" for this devastating condition called autism. But the mothers of the autistic children on my unit looked, to me, just as warm, caring and concerned as all other mothers I had met along the way. I didn't see any "refrigerator mothers." So I set about doing a epidemiologic study on infantile autism (Treffert 1970), locating all the cases that I could in Wisconsin at that time. I located 270 such cases producing an incidence of about 4.5 cases per 10,000 children, the same incidence as reported in England and several other studies at that time.

In that study, somewhat to my surprise, I found that both the ages and educational level of the parents of the children with early infantile autism were significantly higher than those of the children in the study with other forms of developmental disability. I say "to my surprise" because I thought that perhaps the similar findings Kanner (1944) had reported might have been because of the nature of his Johns Hopkins' referral base compared to my more rural sample. But it turns out that in both Kanner's population and mine, both older age and higher educational level were factors in separating out early infantile autism from other forms of autistic disorder or other developmental disabilities. Those findings have been replicated recently in a similar epidemiologic survey of autistic spectrum disorder in Wisconsin (Maenner, Arneson and Durkin 2009).

Suffice it to say, beyond those variables, I found no evidence whatsoever of the coldness and aloofness embodied in the cruel "refrigerator mother" stereotype among the mothers of the children on my unit. And all my subsequent contacts with parents of children with autism, through my many years of clinical practice in which I have had the opportunity to meet and get to know them, have revealed instead the same abundance of love, warmth, care and concern as any other group of parents anywhere in the world.

In 1964 the superintendent of Winnebago left that position to move to a similar position in Hawaii. I was planning to leave Winnebago also to return to the Northwest to the state of Oregon where I had interned. But the superintendent position interested me because the whole mental health movement in the United States was undergoing a tremendous revitalization at the time, propelled along by the interest and impetus of President John F. Kennedy and the US Congress for increased visibility and funding for mental health programs nationwide. Some of that special funding was available in Wisconsin, and at Winnebago. As a result the Children's Unit was gaining a great deal of respect within the state, and nationally as well.

So I stayed at Winnebago and in May, 1964 I accepted the superintendent position in an "acting" capacity. That acting capacity eventually morphed into tenure of 15 years. But even though I was busied with the superintendent duties for the whole hospital, I maintained a special and steady interest in the Children's Unit. However, my research interest in savant syndrome, while still alive, was preempted in substantial degree by many other priorities.

Enter serendipity

In June, 1980 Leslie Lemke and his foster mother May Lemke came to Fond du Lac, Wisconsin, where we were living, to give a concert in the Little Theater at Goodrich High School. It was Foster Parent Recognition Month in Wisconsin, and May and Leslie had been invited to give a concert to honor May for her heroic and inspirational efforts as a foster mother in caring for Leslie. Leslie was born prematurely and given up for adoption at birth by his birth mother. He developed the blindness of prematurity and then severe glaucoma. As a result he had to have both of his eyes surgically removed in the first six months of life. He developed some complications from that surgery and was an extremely ill little boy. The Social Service Department of Milwaukee County called May Lemke because she had developed a respected reputation based on the exceptional skill and love she had shown in caring for handicapped children as a nurse and governess.

May Lemke was 52 years old when that phone call came. She had already successfully raised five children of her own. But Social Services sent Leslie to May, in search of a loving, hospice-like arrangement, cautioning May that Leslie was probably going to die. "You can send Leslie here," May said, "but he is not going to die." And he surely didn't. May taught Leslie how to swallow. She strapped him to herself, literally, to teach him how to walk. And she would put his hands over hers on the piano she had gotten for him at about age eight or nine and she would play some simple English tunes for him, and, in that way, with him. Leslie learned to play and sing some of those same simple tunes.

I wasn't at that concert. But my daughter Joni was. She came home that night bounding into the house announcing, "Dad, I just saw a miracle. It's a marvelous miracle." "What did you see?" I asked. "I saw this young man, severely cognitively impaired, who has never had a piano lesson in his life, playing from memory all sorts of classical, religious and popular music like a skilled piano virtuoso." Joni then told the story of how May and Joe Lemke had watched (and Leslie listened to) a television movie—*Sincerely Yours*—which has Tchaikovsky's Piano Concerto No. 1 as its theme song. May and Joe went to bed but May awoke in the middle of the night to hear some beautiful music coming from the living room where they had watched the movie. She went to investigate and there was Leslie, playing flawlessly from beginning to end, that concerto on the piano, having heard it for the first time that evening.

I told Joni that is miraculous, but it is also a condition called savant syndrome.

Attending that concert was a television station crew from Green Bay. They brought the tapes to me as the local mental health expert because they too were amazed by what they had seen and wondered if there was some explanation for this remarkable phenomenon. I told them indeed Leslie's musician skills are truly amazing, and again, that it is a condition called savant syndrome. There happened to be some reporters from the wire service in that meeting as well and they carried the story on the Associated Press (AP) wire that day about May and her remarkable foster son Leslie. There was immediate affection for, and interest in, Leslie and May across the entire United States. That Christmas season Walter Cronkite closed his *CBS Evening News* program one night with these words: "This is a season that celebrates a miracle, and the story belongs to the season. It's a story of a young man, a piano and a miracle."

Other television programs picked up the story. *That's Incredible* did a very touching story that many persons who viewed it still remember warmly. Then there was *Donahue*, *AM Chicago* with Oprah Winfrey, *The Morning Show* with Regis and Kathie Lee, and many, many other television programs, concert appearances and a multitude of stories in the print media.

In October, 1983 *60 Minutes* broadcast a program called *Genius*. It featured three savants—"a musician, a sculptor and a wizard." As I travel about lecturing on savant syndrome even today so many people in the audience remember that program, and they particularly remember Leslie and May. They often ask, "Whatever happened to Leslie Lemke?" I answer that question in Chapter 7 in this book.

Watching that *60 Minutes* program was Dustin Hoffman. He was "moved to tears" by that handicapped lad and his astonishing abilities. It was then he decided to play the savant in that remarkable movie about savant syndrome—*Rain Man*.

The 1988 film, *Rain Man*, won four Academy Awards and in its first 101 days did more toward educating the public about savant syndrome and autism than anything else that had happened in the 101 years since Dr. Down's original lecture on that topic. The tremendous appeal and wondrous success of that film made "autistic savant" household words. Because of my involvement with the *60 Minutes* program, and because I was working on the *Extraordinary People* (Treffert 1989) book at that time, the executive producer of *Rain Man* called and asked if I would be willing to review the script because Hollywood wanted the film to be accurate (as Bill Cosby would say: "right") and they wanted it to be sensitively done so as not to offend family and caretakers of people with disabilities. As it turns out their wishes in that regard were very genuine. The movie, while not based on the story of a specific savant, created a composite savant in the character of Raymond Babbitt which is remarkably accurate and sensitive. The making of that movie, and its messages and impact, are described in more detail in Chapter19.

Rain Man put savant syndrome prominently on the national and international radar screen. Interest in and visibility of savant syndrome accelerated markedly, including interest in Alonzo Clemons and his work, the remarkably gifted sculptor in the *60 Minutes* piece.

Enter the "acquired" savant

Alonzo was the first acquired savant I ever met. The phenomenon of the acquired savant was an intriguing discovery, as you will see, which has influenced the route of my journey with savant syndrome so drastically and significantly because it suggests so forcefully the hidden potential that I am convinced resides within us all.

Alonzo Clemons was not born a savant. Instead his spectacular sculpting abilities emerged after a childhood fall and brain injury. Alonzo, from that time forward, could look at a picture of an animal in a magazine, or see an animal at the zoo, and then sculpt that animal, in about an hour or so, using the oil-based clay which he molds so quickly and artistically with his gifted hands. He puts the finishing touches on carefully, using just his fingernails as the final tools. The result is a perfect replica of the animal, each muscle and tendon shaped exactly as it was seen by Alonzo on his first, and only, glance at the subject. Almost magically a two-dimensional picture is transformed into a three-dimensional sculpture. How can he "know" how to do that? Alonzo does not have to return to the picture or revisit the zoo to view his subject. That first image is frozen into his memory with the fidelity of a digital camera or the freeze frame on a video camcorder.

But my first meeting with Alonzo had another lasting impact on my savant syndrome journey as well.

Alonzo had his world premier as an artist on Monday, May 19, 1986 in Denver, Colorado. The highlight was the unveiling of a life-size bronze sculpture *Three Frolicking Foals*. Thirty other bronze pieces by Alonzo were featured as well. The First Interstate Bank of Denver, City Center Associates and Driscol Gallery sponsored the event. The Driscol Gallery had contacted me to see if I could suggest a charity or foundation to which some of the proceeds from sales at this event could go in order to further research and education about savant syndrome. As a result a special fund was set up in the Wisconsin Medical Society Foundation for just such a purpose and the Clearinghouse for Information Regarding Savant Syndrome was established.

Beginning in 1987 this clearinghouse distributed printed articles and other educational materials, including some videos, to interested persons and agencies at their request. Interest was steady, but inquiries were limited because there was no consistent method of making the clearinghouse widely known.

Enter the Internet

In the fall of 1997 a savant syndrome website was established at the Wisconsin Medical Society in Madison, Wisconsin. While it took some time to be incorporated into the major search engines, that website—www.savantsyndrome.com—has exploded with activity, particularly since streaming video was added in the fall of 2006. Presently the website receives more than 700 visitors each day or over 5000 per week, compared to a fraction of that amount at the beginning. The number increases each year.

The inquiries come from many different persons: students, from grade school to graduate school, whether doing term papers or PhD theses; researchers from diverse specialties from around the world; teachers looking for illustrative materials for their classes from elementary schools to medical schools; journalists and broadcasters seeking reliable information for magazines, books, radio, television or film. And most poignantly, requests come from concerned parents seeking advice and help for their child, adolescent or adult loved one. Those inquiries usually begin with "I've got a son or daughter who . . ." It is those requests that are most difficult to respond to because they point up so vividly the shortage of individualized resources for evaluation, and more importantly, for help in "training the talent" which can be so valuable in maximizing potential in persons with autism, other developmental disabilities or whatever the underlying condition.

The website has been a rich resource for learning about new savants from around the world—India, Indonesia, China, Japan, Australia, South Africa, Denmark, Germany, Hungary, Korea, The Philippines, Brazil, Iceland, Spain, Portugal, Canada, Mexico—just to name a few. What is striking, though, is the uniformity of the reports from wherever they originate. The same five general areas of skill—art, music, calendar calculating, lightning calculating and mechanical or spatial skills—all coupled with massive memory continue to dominate the condition wherever in the world it appears. Thus savant syndrome is a worldwide phenomenon, not unexpectedly, that cuts across the usual boundaries of geography, language and culture.

The website has also been a rich resource for learning about research being carried out not only in the United States, but also around the world. It provides instant access to new projects underway and the research findings from those studies, instead of waiting for what previously was a delay of 18 to 24 months for published results to surface in printed journals and to be exchanged in that more tedious manner.

The website has been a rich source of satisfaction as well. Grateful notes arrive frequently from parents and other caretakers who have not only found information on the website helpful, but also found optimism, reassurance, support and sometimes even inspiration from the various stories posted there.

The website has served another important purpose, however. Dr. Wilder Penfield (1978) was an important pioneer in brain research throughout his illustrious and trail-blazing career. Toward the end of his career he pondered an interesting question that had been posed to him: based on all his hours and hours investigating the brain, was there more to the "mind" than just the brain itself? That's a somewhat transcendental question, I suppose, but one that does occur when one investigates over time that marvelous piece of matter we call the brain. Dr. Penfield concluded, interestingly, that it seemed to him, after all those years of probing the brain, literally, there was more to the "mind" than the brain itself, even with its marvelous intricacy.

But what most caught my attention when Dr. Penfield reflected on his career was the hope he often expressed that his efforts might have helped recruit "fresh, new explorers," instilling in them the same vigor of curiosity and interest that had propelled him along in his stellar career. I harbor that same hope and I am continually on the lookout for "fresh, new explorers" as well. We do need them and I hope this book will also recruit some of those young persons.

Some of the emails or letters I receive from young people reflect that. A fifth grader wrote: "Thank you for your email answering my questions about savants… I have gotten interested in savants and will continue learning about them long after the completion of this project." A high school senior wrote: "I delivered my speech yesterday, and I got an A… I just wanted to thank you for helping me with the information. After doing so much research on savants, I have really been interested in studying genetics and now I actually plan on doing so next year at the University." A first year psychology college student from the United Kingdom writes: "I am hoping to specialize in neuroscience. I am doing a presentation and essay on savant syndrome in a few months… that is the sort of area I want to specialize in the future… your work is amazing and you are one of my greatest inspirations." Following my presentation on savants to incoming medical students in Milwaukee, several wrote that, while they had not been seriously considering psychiatry as a specialty, this intriguing area of study has tapped their interest in moving into neuroscience specialties.

But one of the most satisfying moments for me in these lectures was when two fourth-grade students came up to me after a presentation and one announced, "I want to be a scientist." His companion, a bright little girl, echoed: "And so do I." During that presentation in their classroom I was astonished by the unbashful enthusiasm with which these students bombarded me with questions—hands kept raising up all over the room—and I was likewise astonished by the depth and sophistication of their questions. The pay-off moment for me will be when these two students walk across the stage, one day, to receive their diplomas in neuroscience and enter the field as two of those "fresh, new explorers" that both Penfield and I heartily welcome.

The website has generated a great deal of interest in, and information for, journalists writing for newspaper and magazines from around the world. And it has done the same for a number of television broadcasts throughout the world as well. The initial flurry of activity after *Rain Man* produced appearances by savants, and often myself, on *Oprah, Dateline, Today, 20/20, Good Morning America, Larry King Live, CNN* and many other such programs. These shows do provide a good public information and education function, but the time limitations of many of those programs present problems in looking at savant syndrome, and the savant himself or herself, in any comprehensive way. So a number of television documentaries have looked at savant syndrome in greater depth either by examining individual cases, or at savant syndrome in more general terms using a number of persons with savant syndrome to tell the more complete story. Those I think that have been particularly good include *Uncommon Genius* (2000) by the Australian Broadcasting Company; a *What is Man* series (1999) by Japanese broadcasting companies; *The Many Faces of Genius* for A&E (2002) television. A three-hour program—*Beautiful Minds: Voyage into the Brain* (2006)—by Colourfield Productions of Dortmund, Germany is an especially comprehensive and in-depth review of savant syndrome, with outstanding graphics of the central nervous system and its relationship to the condition. Some particularly good programs on individual savants have also been produced including *Brainman* (2005), the story of Daniel Tammet, by Focus Productions of Bristol, England and a Swedish documentary—*Verklighetens: Rain Man* (2007)—based on the story of Kim Peek. Streaming video from these productions are available on the website at www.savantsyndrome.com.

Sightseeing on a less traveled path

I started this marvelous journey in 1962 when four patients on the Children's Unit at Winnebago startled me with their brilliant "islands of genius," so conspicuous and so jarring. Now I have met so many more of these extraordinary people. This has been an incredible journey for me personally and professionally. It has taken me into areas of inquiry into which I most likely otherwise would not have ventured. It has gotten me, a pretty traditional clinician and scientist, to think outside the brain. It has changed me as a doctor, and as a person, in many significant ways. I hope that sharing the information gleaned, the reflections upon, and the insights gained on this incredible journey will have the same effect upon you that it has upon me.

I have learned, for example, to be much more optimistic about that marvelous organ we call the brain and central nervous system overall. When I was in medical school I learned that if a liver, or heart, or skin cell is damaged or dies, the organ can regenerate itself and produce more such cells. But if a neuron dies, it can't regenerate and all that is left is brain damage. That's not so. Savant syndrome demonstrates impressively the tremendous plasticity of the central nervous system; the capacity to substitute an area of still intact neuronal cells to compensate for those damaged. This less pessimistic view of restorative central nervous system (CNS) function has tremendous implications not only for savant syndrome, but also for the rewiring and compensatory capacity of the brain in other conditions as well such as stroke, cerebral palsy and indeed autism itself. Now that we have tools to look at brain *structure*, not just brain *architecture*, we can see those compensatory processes at work *directly*. And it is a very encouraging sight.

I have also learned that savant skills are not frivolous. They deserve more than a "Gee whiz, look at that" superficial glance. Leslie's music is the way he communicates with us; music is his language. And for Alonzo Clemons, his sculpting is the way he communicates with us; his sculptures are his words. By seizing the opportunity to "train the talent" we can help the savant use his or her special ability as a productive conduit toward normalization that can ameliorate, to some degree, the "dis-ability" and in so doing increase language, socialization and daily living skills overall.

Also, I have witnessed first hand, through the families of savants, the incredible power that love, belief, determination, hope, patience, respect and unconditional positive regard can have in the lives of these persons they so value and appreciate. These are families that not only care *for* the savant, they care *about* the savant as well. That is a valuable lesson and role model for everyone in the healing professions because for us, also, it is not enough to care only about the condition the patient has, we need to care about the patient who has the condition as well. As such we naturally are as interested in the world of the savant, as we are in the mind of the savant.

This journey has changed my mind about creativity of the savant as well. Early on I was amazed at the incredible recall the savant had with his or her massive, literal memory capacity. That memorization ability in itself was astonishing. But I, like many others, thought that the savant's ability to recall, as remarkable as that was, lacked the flexibility to deviate, innovate or perhaps even create. But I was wrong about that. Savants, now that I have been able to follow them long enough, and have gotten to know them well enough, have shown me that they follow a quite predictable sequence that involves first, literal memory; then improvisation; and then finally creativity—forming something original and entirely new. And some of that creativity is truly spectacular, just as spectacular as the massive, literal memory itself.

Most of the savants I met early on this journey were born with those extraordinary capabilities. The skills themselves then emerged in childhood to everyone's astonishment, and we are their beneficiaries. But more recently the "acquired" savant has come to my attention. As explained above, these are instances in which savant-like skills suddenly and unexpectedly appear, sometimes at a prodigious level, following CNS injury or disease in previously "neurotypical" persons. This reservoir of dormant talent which surfaces only after some central nervous system injury or disease raises obvious questions about hidden capacities lying unused within us all. The more additional cases of this startling phenomenon that come to my attention worldwide, the more pressing the inquiry about them becomes because of the far-reaching implications such discoveries hold.

Then there is the question of how severely disabled, prodigious savants can possibly "know things they have never learned." While we are quite content to accept complex instincts and other signs of detailed knowledge in many animals or birds, for example, we have tended to limit discussion about the genetic factors we inherit to eye color, height, color of our hair, posture, along with, perhaps, certain other traits. But overall we tend to view ourselves as being born with a marvelous piece of hardware we call the brain and a huge blank disk. What we become, it has been assumed, is what we put on that blank disk as we experience and learn from our surroundings and relationships. But these prodigious savants, this journey has convinced me, demonstrate, as their extraordinary skills emerge, without lessons or training, that they indeed do know things they never learned. Such innate knowledge, without having learned it, is called genetic memory—the inherited, or innate, knowledge of the complex rules of music, art and mathematics, for example. Skilled professionals and teachers proficient in those areas of expertise tell me, after they have met some of these extraordinary people, that indeed that knowledge is present in the savant without training, without lessons and without formal education. They do indeed know things they never learned. "He transcends his own existence," one professor told me after hearing Matt Savage, at age nine, play like "the Mozart of jazz."

How much does such actual knowledge, or at least the software templates or scaffolding for those rules of music, art and mathematics, or even other areas of expertise, come "factory installed" in all of us? That is an important, transcendental question.

What I call genetic memory, some call ancestral memory. Carl Jung (1936) called it the "collective unconscious." Perhaps Jung was right. "Collective unconscious" is not an area into which I probably would have trod very far, if at all, were it not for some of the marvelous savants I have met along the way whose spectacular abilities and knowledge; surely because of their severe disabilities and difficulties learning, have to involve what I (and others) prefer to call genetic memory.

So many other questions leap up and intrigue me still. How do they do it? What is the difference between prodigy, genius and savant? Are we a series of multiple intelligences rather than a rather generic general intelligence? Because of an altered type of brain function, the savant often thinks visually and learns differently. We know that we can train the talent in the savant with different methods of teaching adapted to the unique islands of brilliance that exist in these special persons and the visual way in which they often perceive their giftedness. But might we be missing as well, even in the regular schools, some children who also learn differently because of the unique way their brain also visualizes, experiences and learns things? And how many savants might there be in homes, hospitals or communities whose special talents are still undiscovered?

Some say we use less than 10 percent of our brain capacity. Maybe that figure is more sensational than accurate. Is it possible though, as some very recent cases of hypermnesia (abnormally strong memory of the past) now suggest, that we do have the ability, and perhaps actually do record, *all* our daily experiences in a continuous fashion on our "hard disk" but simply lack the ability to recall those events and regularly access but a fraction of that data? Sodium amytal interviews I have done with patients, in which a sedative is used to help retrieve bured memories, and dreams we all have from time to time with unexpected and forgotten images of the past often intruding and passing by unexpectedly, suggest that might well be the case. Is the vast memory we marvel at in the savant not a matter of increased storage—that we might all possess—but rather a matter of access to those daily files? If so, are there ways to increase that access in all of us?

As you can see, this journey has taken me into some wondrous, and, for me, some unexpected places. It has changed my somewhat contemporary "the world is flat" view of the brain into a much broader view of brain function and brain capacity, not just in the savant, but in all the rest of us as well. Dr. Edward Sequin, writing about savants in 1866, nearly a century and a half ago, said: "To explain the physical and physiological mysteries of such human beings is beyond the present power of any known science" (p.443). A century later, in 1964, a discussant commenting on the case of the "calculating twins" presented at a scientific conference that year, noted: "The importance, then, of the idiot savant lies in our inability to explain him; he stands as a landmark of our own ignorance and the phenomenon of the idiot savant exists as a challenge to our capabilities" (Horwitz *et al.* 1965, p.1078).

A challenge to our capabilities? Indeed savant syndrome is that. But we now have new tools, that Dr. Sequin could never have even imagined, in our "present power of science" to investigate the "mysteries" of savant syndrome to where we are already better able to "explain" the savant at least in part. Savants are less and less a landmark of our ignorance about the brain, and its marvelous intricacy and capacity, than they were in 1964. This half-century journey of mine with these extraordinary people has been a marvelous odyssey into the mind, and the world, of the savant. I hope this trip and its findings, as I have recorded them, will instill the same wonder and awe about the brain as it has in me, and will cause you, just as it has me, to search further and further for the inner savant that, I am convinced, resides, to some degree, within us all.

PART ONE

The Mind of the Savant

CHAPTER I

What We Do Know: A Rare but Remarkable Condition

At the 1964 American Psychiatric Association Annual Meeting the amazing case of the "calculating twins," George and Charles, was presented. The calendar calculating ability of these identical twins—40,000 years backward or forward—astounded and intrigued the attendees. As mentioned earlier, one discussant, following the presentation, wisely remarked that "the importance, then, of the idiot savant lies in our inability to explain him; he stands as a landmark of our own ignorance and the phenomenon of the idiot savant exists as a challenge to our capabilities" (Horwitz *et al.* 1965, p.1078).

That discussant was correct on both counts. Until we can understand and fully explain the savant we cannot understand and fully explain ourselves since no model of brain function will be complete until it can incorporate and fully account for this dazzling juxtaposition of ability and disability in the same person. And savants certainly present a challenge to our capabilities. But beyond that, they also, in my view, provide an intriguing entree *into* the dormant potential within us all.

It has been 122 years since Down (1887) first described savant syndrome as a distinct condition. As the chapters in this book attest, there has been a great deal of progress in better understanding and appreciating this remarkable condition since that time. One of the most useful advances has been the substitution of the term "savant syndrome" for the regrettable term "idiot savant." Down did not intend that his newly coined term be degrading or insulting. At that time the word "idiot" was an accepted scientific term for a person with a very low IQ and did not have the pejorative connotation that term now carries.

I was concerned about that connotation and in my 1988 review article I suggested it was time to change the terminology from that archaic 1887 term to "savant syndrome" (Treffert 1988). I chose that term because "savant syndrome" includes "a range of abilities that occurs in several conditions" (p.563). That term is preferable to "autistic savant" because, as will be pointed out, not all persons with savant syndrome are autistic. Savant syndrome can be present with a number of other underlying disabilities. Today, I am pleased to say, there is general acceptance and use of the term "savant syndrome" for this extraordinary condition.

At the present time there is much we do know about savant syndrome and this chapter summarizes that body of information. Subsequent chapters will explore what questions remain unanswered, where we are, and where we are headed, in trying to lessen our "ignorance" about savant syndrome and to better tap the "challenge to our capabilities" inherent in savant syndrome.

Here's what we do know.

Savant syndrome is a rare condition

Savant syndrome is a rare but remarkable condition in which persons with developmental disabilities (including but not limited to autistic disorder), or other central nervous system injuries or diseases, have some spectacular "islands of genius" that stand in stark, jarring contrast to overall limitations. It is important to realize that savant syndrome is not a disease or disorder itself; rather it is an extraordinary condition *superimposed upon*, or coexistent with some other basic underlying condition and attendant disability.

In approximately 50 percent of the cases of savant syndrome, that underlying condition is autistic disorder. Savant syndrome occurs in as many as one in ten autistic persons.

That 10 percent figure comes from Rimland's (1978a) survey of 5400 children with autism, 531 of whom, based on parent reports, had special abilities in the typical skill areas seen in most savants: music, art, mathematics, calendar calculating or mechanical/spatial abilities. Hermelin (2001), however, based on her 20 years of study of savant syndrome, estimates that figure to be as low as "one or two in 200". Bolte and Poustka (2004) found 33 persons with savant syndrome out of a group of 254 individuals with "idiopathic autism" for a prevalence of 13 percent; of that number 30 percent had an IQ less than 70.

Howlin *et al.* (2009) reported 39 of 137 individuals with autism met their criteria for savant syndrome (28.5 percent) based on cognitive testing and parental reports. However, some of those individuals met the criteria for savant syndrome on the basis of cognitive test scores only which, in my view, is too liberal a definition. The differences in prevalence figures in various studies obviously depend on where one sets the criteria for "savant" abilities. As with hypertension, for example, if you lower the levels of systolic and diastolic blood pressure defined as "hypertension," more persons will qualify for that diagnosis. The differences in definition of savant syndrome in various studies argue for some standardized definition of "savant" abilities. I address that need, and how to achieve it, in later chapters.

My own experience over these years leads me to conclude, with respect to autistic disorder, that the 10 percent figure is really quite accurate if one includes the full spectrum of savant abilities as defined below. Rimland's (1978a) sample size of 5400 persons with autism is going to be hard to duplicate and his figure of 530 individuals with savant skills (10 percent) still seems to be the most reliable estimate.

But savant syndrome is not limited to autistic disorder as the underlying disability. In a survey of an institutionalized population with a diagnosis of mental retardation, Hill (1977) found that the incidence of savant skills was 1 per 2000 (0.05%). A more recent study (Saloviita, Ruusila and Ruusila 2000) surveyed 583 inpatient or residential facilities and found a prevalence rate for savant syndrome of 1.4 per 1000, (0.14%), more than double the 0.05 percent figure.

Mental retardation and other brain diseases and disorders, in the aggregate, are more common than autistic disorder, however, in day-to-day practice it turns out that approximately 50 percent of persons with savant syndrome have autistic disorder as their *underlying* disability and the other 50 percent have other disabilities as the *underlying* disorders. Thus *not all persons with autism have savant syndrome, and not all persons with savant syndrome are autistic.*

The fact that savant syndrome is always superimposed on some other underlying disability comes up often in many emails I get from students or others writing papers about savant syndrome in which they ask what is the "treatment" or "cure" for savant syndrome? In reply I point out that one doesn't seek to "treat" or "cure" savant syndrome as such. Rather any treatment efforts would be directed toward the underlying disability, whether that is autism, dementia or any other brain disease or defect. With respect to savant syndrome itself, efforts are directed to train the talent. In so doing, as will be pointed out in more detail later, maximizing savant abilities then serves as a "conduit toward normalization" with increased language, social and daily living skills as a deliberately intended by-product of focusing on and further honing savant abilities. One doesn't seek to cure savant syndrome, or take the special abilities away. Rather, by training the talent, those special skills become even more highly honed and, in so doing, generalize to better language acquisition, improved social abilities and increased daily living skills.

Savant skills typically occur in an intriguingly narrow range of special abilities

When one considers all the abilities in the human repertoire, is it rather extraordinary that savant skills generally narrow to only five particular areas of special expertise: music, art, calendar calculating, lightning calculating and mechanical and spatial skills.

Those five areas of expertise were present in Down's (1887) original ten cases, in Tredgold's (1914) more expansive description of savant syndrome, and in almost all reports of savant skills since that time. However, there is no formal "registry" of savants around the world so it is impossible to tabulate the relative frequency of particular skills. New cases of savant syndrome come to my attention almost daily from around the globe via the savant syndrome website (www.savantsyndrome.com). Many of those persons, and their families, are willing and eager to participate in research projects seeking to learn more, not just about savants, but about the interface between savant syndrome, prodigy and genius.

Such a registry of cases on a voluntary basis could provide insights into incidence of savant syndrome, the relative frequency of skills and outcome, for example. Other authors have ranked skills according to frequency but those vary from report to report. From my review of the literature on savant syndrome over these past 122 years, and from my experience with existing and new case reports, the five skill areas that are regularly reported would be ranked in the following order with respect to frequency: calendar calculating, music, art, mathematical and number skills and mechanical/spatial skills.

Calendar calculating

This skill, a remote and obscure ability in most persons, is in my experience the most frequently occurring savant skill either as a stand-alone talent or as an incidental accompaniment of some other music, art or mathematical ability. Most often calendar calculating is carried out by computing which day of the week a particular date, in the past or in the future, either did or will occur. For some savants this range of years backwards or forwards can exceed 40,000. While most often carried out using the present-day calendars, there have been reports of some calendar calculators using the Julian calendar or the Chinese calendar.

This curious skill extends in some calendar calculators well beyond just naming the day of the week at a point in time. For example, a computation might involve naming which years in the next 20 Easters will fall on March 27, or which years in the next 30 will February 9 be on a Friday. The Easter calculation is a particularly complex one and entails a very lengthy formula if written out. Such "reverse calendar calculating" goes well beyond memorization and does include some real calculation. Of course there are computer software programs now that can do that instantly, but calendar calculating savants seem to have that software "factory installed" at birth, or acquire it by unconscious absorption of the proper algorithm just from repetitive viewing of calendars.

Why calendar calculating ability, an obscure skill in most persons, is so frequently, almost universally, present in persons with savant syndrome is an important but as yet unanswered mystery. That question, including recent functional imaging findings, is explored in depth in Chapter 5 on medical mysteries.

Music

I would rank musical ability as the second most frequently reported skill. It is usually performance, and it is almost always accompanied by perfect pitch. Composing in the absence of performing has been reported, as has playing multiple instruments, as many as 22 or more. Almost all musical savants have a remarkable "literal" memory, which allows them to play back entire pieces after hearing them for the first time. A number of musical savants profiled in this book demonstrate the magnitude, and magnificence, of these musical islands of genius. Of special interest, discussed later, is the "musical triad" of blindness, mental impairment and musical genius—a rather rare combination of circumstances in an already rare condition—which occurs with a curious regularity throughout the history of savant syndrome.

Art

This skill is usually drawing, painting or sculpting. Extensive "literal memory" capacity exists with this skill as well. Usually a single exposure is sufficient after which exact replicas of scenes, or animals, for example, are produced in precise detail without further reference to a model. Compared to other artists, a number of distinguishing features characterize the savant artist: underlying disability; innate ability without teaching or training; talent which typically "explodes" on the scene at a very early age; obsessive preoccupation with the skill; prolific output of product on a continuous basis; and literal, eidetic-like memory with massive capacity in the area of expertise. In some savant artists the disability is severe and several are legally blind.

Mathematical and number skills

Typically this includes lightning calculating—rapid solution of complex multiplication or division problems, for example. Often there is an innate facility with prime numbers and square roots among savants with no idea or explanation as to "how they do it." Frequently this extensive calculating ability is seen with complete absence of other very simple arithmetic skills In the movie Rain Man, for example, Raymond Babbitt is able to instantly multiply numbers in his head ($4343 \times 1234 = 5359262$) and also give the correct answer for computing the square root of 2130 (46.15192304). Yet when asked how much money he would have left from a dollar if he spent 50 cents he says "about 70." Asked how much a candy bar would cost he says "about a hundred dollars." Asked how much a sport car would cost, his answer was the same, "About a hundred dollars."

Mechanical or spatial skills

These include the ability to construct complex models or structures with painstaking accuracy, or the ability to take apart, and then put back together, machines or other mechanical devices. It also includes highly developed navigation or mapmaking abilities. The capacity to measure distances or heights extremely accurately without reference to a measuring device has been reported, as has the ability to tell time with great precision without reference to a clock or any other timepiece. Many savants have an unusual interest in machines and motors. One boy in Wisconsin has memorized vacuum cleaner motor sounds and can identify the year, make and model just from hearing the motor run. Similar abilities have been reported in children who can identify washing machines by the sound of the motor, and, from those same sounds, tell when a motor is about to fail.

Other obscure skills

Certain other skills are reported less frequently, such as exceptional language (polyglot) abilities (Smith and Tsimpli 1995); unusual sensory discrimination in smell, touch or vision, including synesthesia; outstanding knowledge in specific fields such as neurophysiology, statistics, or navigation and subitizing (counting the number of items at a glance). In Rimland's (1978a) sample of 543 children with special skills, musical ability was followed in frequency by memory, art, pseudo-verbal abilities, mathematics, maps and directions and extrasensory perception.

About the time I think I have heard it all, however, come reports of a newly described skill such as "pinball wizard" (Kerbeshian and Burd 1986). In follow-up, a mother wrote to me about her 20-year-old son with autism "whose real talent seems to be pinball" which he now plays competitively. In 2008 he was considered fourth best in Canada and in the top 100 worldwide. In 2009 he competed in the world championship in Pittsburgh and placed fourteenth among top players from the United States and Canada.

An especially unusual skill in putting numbers to work, albeit illegally, was that of "Max the Bookie" as described in an *Atlantic Monthly* article titled: "One smart bookie" (El-Hai 2001). Bookmaking—taking bets on sporting or other events—is a form of gambling which is illegal in the US except for the state of Nevada. According to the article "police have seized nearly $700,000 from Max's house and bank accounts during a decade of repeated raids—a sure indication of his prowess as an oddsmaker." Taken before the court for these offenses, "Max has prevailed using a most unusual weapon: He is mentally retarded, an internal flaw counterbalanced only by his savant-like ability to channel a prodigious memory for numbers into his knack for taking bets." At trials in recent years psychologists, juries and judges all have concluded "that Max's disability renders him incapable of understanding the nature of his criminal acts." He then returns to his home and soon resumes his craft, only to be apprehended again at a later time with the same ultimate outcome.

Accounts of paranormal abilities, including extrasensory perception, have appeared in the savant syndrome literature through the years, and such reports come to the savant syndrome website from time to time from parents and other seemingly reliable observers. These particular skills of course are very difficult to assess and are highly controversial. Following publication of my 1988 review article on savant syndrome, I was criticized in a letter to the editor of that journal for even mentioning that some accounts, from parents to Rimland (1978a), included extrasensory perception abilities in their autistic children. Thus my merely reporting that there were such reports engendered censure from the scientific community. But reports of paranormal abilities in some persons with savant syndrome do continue to filter in periodically.

Reports of unusual athletic ability, particularly in golf, come to my attention as well. One of the earliest savants I met was a virtual "pitching machine" for making basketball free throws.

Generally a single special skill exists, but in some instances several skills exist simultaneously. Rimland and Fine (1988) note that the incidence of multiple skills appeared to be higher in savants with autism than in savants with other developmental disabilities. In both Stephen Wiltshire and Kim Peek, musical ability, including perfect pitch, surfaced quite unexpectedly to everyone's surprise and delight. And Matt Savage is as comfortable with his number and math skills, and memorizing roller coasters around the world, as he is with his prodigious musical abilities.

Whatever the skill, it is always associated with massive memory of a particular type: exceedingly deep but very narrow within the confines of the particular skill. Savant memory of this special type will be described separately in more detail below.

The skills tend to be right hemisphere in type

The special skills regularly seen in savant syndrome tend to be those associated with right hemisphere functions. These skills can be characterized as non-symbolic, artistic, concrete and directly perceived, in contrast to left hemisphere skills, which are more sequential, logical and symbolic, including language specialization. While "right brain" and "left brain" is a gross oversimplification of brain function, as if the two hemispheres operate entirely independently of each other, the fact is that the two brain hemispheres do specialize in certain functions, language being one such example.

In their book *Cerebral Lateralization*, Geschwind and Galaburda (1987) use the term "pathology of superiority" to describe compensatory growth leading to superior development of some portions of the brain as an accompaniment to and consequence of poorer development of other portions. These researchers also point out that superior talents of a right hemisphere type are often associated with learning disorders, and they note as well that "the remarkable talents of some autistic patients possibly represent further examples of the operation of this mechanism" (p.66). Today that is called savant syndrome. Likewise, they point out, "right hemisphere talents are common in dyslexics and their families" (p.15).

Narinder Kapur (1996) uses the term "paradoxical functional facilitation" (PFF) to describe the phenomenon where damage to intact brain tissue in one area of the brain brings about normal or near normal function in some other area of the brain which was operating earlier at a subnormal or abnormal level. In these instances the "restorative" capacity of the brain is actually a release phenomenon, of previously dormant or near dormant capacity, rather than the development of new abilities. Thus, within the construct of PFF, the right brain "compensation" seen in the savant secondary to left brain dysfunction taps dormant brain capacity in a "release" mechanism as opposed to developing entirely new compensatory capacities. Some specific examples of this PFF phenomenon are described in detail later in this book, particularly in Bruce Miller et al.'s (1996, 1998) fronto-temporal dementia patients and some other "acquired" savants. PFF also has broad implications for tapping the "inner savant," which is also addressed in detail in Chapter 23, altering and expanding views of brain plasticity immensely.

In short, in the savant the functions most often represented are those associated with the right hemisphere including art, music, "unconscious" calendar or lightning calculating and mechanical/spatial skills. The presence and enhancement of these skills is most likely due to left brain injury and right brain compensation dependent in part, at least, on paradoxical functional facilitation of right hemisphere capacities.

Savant skills are distributed over a spectrum of abilities

In general there are three levels of savant ability—"splinter skills," "talented" and "prodigious." These are distributed over a quantitative spectrum of ability which is, admittedly, at this point a subjective classification.

Most common are *splinter skills*, which include, for example, obsessive preoccupation with, absorption in, and memorization of, music and sports trivia, license plate numbers, maps, historical facts, birth dates, train or bus schedules, automobile makes and models, or any number of other obscure preoccupations such as with vacuum cleaner motor sounds, as mentioned above. These splinter skills are seen in as many as one in ten autistic children.

Talented savants are those persons with developmental or other disabilities in whom the musical, artistic, or other special abilities are more conspicuous and prominent than splinter skills. They are more highly honed and distinctive than splinter skills and typically occur within a single area of expertise. They are striking and noteworthy when seen in contrast to overall limitations.

Prodigious savant is a very high threshold term reserved for those extraordinarily rare individuals in whom the special skill is so outstanding that it would be spectacular even if it were to be seen in a non-impaired person. When present without a disability such exceptional talent would be ordinarily labeled "prodigy" or "genius." There are probably fewer than 100 *known* prodigious savants living worldwide at the present time who would meet that extremely high threshold of savant ability. But the World Wide Web continues to bring more such cases to attention from nations everywhere so that the *actual* number, rather than the *known* number of prodigious savants, is probably considerably higher.

In some media accounts of individual savants, stories will often use a phrase such as "this particular case is one of fewer than 100 known savants living worldwide at the present time," leaving out the critical qualifying word "prodigious." This is misleading because the "fewer than 100" estimate applies only to prodigious savants, not all savants.

This spectrum of savant ability is admittedly a subjective one. My hope is that over time there can be some more formal quantification of savant abilities. That would be more easily accomplished in measuring calendar calculating skills, or mathematical skills, than it would be measuring artistic or musical talent. Nevertheless such more formal quantification would provide more useful, more objective and more standardized assessments. As research on savant syndrome builds and intensifies, no doubt some such formal quantification can, and will, occur.

Whatever the special skill, it is always accompanied by prodigious memory

Whatever the special abilities, a remarkable memory of a unique and uniform type welds the condition together. Terms such as "automatic," "mechanical," and "habit" have been applied to this extraordinary memory. Down (1887) uses the term "verbal adhesion." Critchley (1979), in his book with the interesting title *The Divine Banquet of the Brain*, uses the terms "exultation of memory" and "memory without reckoning."

Tredgold (1914) terms such unconscious memory "automatic." Barr (1898) describes a patient with extensive echolalia and prodigious memory as having an "exaggerated form of habit (p.30)." Whatever one names that form of memory, it always includes certain characteristics: it is immediate; it is literal; it is automatic; it is very deep and extensive, but it is very narrow, generally limited to the confines of the special skill.

"Verbal adhesion" and "memory without reckoning" are apt terms in most cases since the savant often does not seem to have comprehension of that which was memorized so spectacularly. Down's patient could recite *The Rise and Fall of the Roman Empire* backward or forward, but he had no comprehension of the meaning of the book. In many savants the bits of memory, extensive and accurate as they are, seem to be both stored and recalled in an unconscious manner "without reckoning." There are exceptions, however. For example Kim Peek increasingly showed comprehension of the huge amount of data and entire books that he had stored. Kim was eventually able to connect those bits of knowledge from that huge database in a Google-like manner which is at times astounding, and steps ahead of those around him. Some examples of that are described in Kim's profile in Chapter 10.

The "unconscious," "automatic," or "without reckoning" memory seen in savant syndrome is consistent with what Mishkin and Petri (1984) refer to as a non-conscious "habit" formation rather than a "semantic" memory system. They propose two different neural circuits for these two types of memory: a cortico-limbic circuit for semantic memory, and a cortico-striatal circuit for habit memory which is sometimes referred to as procedural or implicit memory.

I will discuss these particular memory pathways and circuits in greater detail in Chapter 2.

Savant syndrome can be *congenital*—present at birth—or it can be *acquired*, following brain injury or disease later in infancy, childhood or adult life

Most cases of savant syndrome are associated with conditions which were present at birth such as autism or other developmental disabilities. In those instances the savant abilities are superimposed on, or grafted on to, the underlying disability which was present from birth (congenital). But there are other cases where savant abilities surface in previously non-disabled children or adults following head injury, stroke, or other central nervous system disorders (acquired). Such acquired savant abilities can occur in children, adolescents or adults, and a number of cases of acquired savant skills are described in more detail elsewhere in this book.

The fact that dormant savant abilities can emerge, or be released, after a head injury or disease in previously non-disabled persons raises enormous questions about the buried potential within us all. And it also raises the equally enormous challenge of how to tap those hidden abilities without injury, disease or some other CNS catastrophe.

The case of Nadia, a precocious and prodigious childhood artist reported in Selfe's (1977) book, has through the years continued to raise important questions about the persistence of savant skills, and whether there might be a regrettable "dreaded trade-off" of savant skills for language acquisition and other education efforts.

Nadia was a child with all the signs and symptoms of early infantile autism. At age six, she essentially had no usable language skills and demonstrated mutism, excessive slowness and withdrawal. She avoided both eye contact and physical contact. A complete medical and psychological examination in London at age five provided a diagnosis of autism. Nadia was obsessed with cutting paper into incredibly thin strips with stunning uniformity and precision.

Nadia's drawings, at age three, were phenomenal, not only in relation to her handicap but also in relation to any other child of her age or intelligence. Like other savant artists she needed to see an image or person only once and did not have to return to the original for reference. She drew with extreme rapidity and uncanny precision. Her drawings showed a superb sense of perspective, proportion and movement. She had an attractive and appealing style all her own. The inventiveness in her drawing along with the use of shading and shadows was striking.

Truly Nadia's gift was her drawing. But language, or the lack of it, was her deficit. Selfe (1977) postulates that the visual imagery used by Nadia was simply the initial language used by all of us when we are children. As we grow, language becomes shorthand for this visual reality and mental imagery which is then supplanted by language. In Nadia, Selfe proposes, the remarkable artistic talent was a compensatory method of offsetting her language deficit. Language was trade-off, the price to be paid, for the spectacular drawing ability.

Nadia entered a school for autistic children at age seven and language acquisition was given specific emphasis and effort. Nadia responded to this training and her language improved. But, regrettably, her special drawing ability vanished as a "dreaded trade-off," seemingly, for language acquisition. The case of Nadia has raised lingering questions as to whether there is, sometimes, maybe even often, a "dreaded trade-off" of precious savant skills with language training efforts and other education approaches.

In my experience, overwhelmingly, that is *not* the case and Nadia is the exception, not the rule. Occasionally a child, or even an adult, may lose some interest in a particular skill, such as calendar calculating for example, as he or she moves into other activities. If rehearsed regularly, however, the savant skills, whatever they might be, continue to flourish and even improve.

There have been some other reports of prodigious savants losing their talent, or their interest in some special skill later in life. Blind Tom lost interest in music, and performance, after the death of his master (see Chapter 6). Nadia's mother died about the same time as the educational effort to teach Nadia useful language skills began. Perhaps the loss of her mother was an important dynamic rather than language acquisition itself.

Regrettably the myth lingers that there is a "dreaded trade-off" of loss of savant skills as the price that must be paid for language acquisition and other educational efforts. That simply, fortunately, is not true. As you will see from many examples in this book, formal education efforts have *not* resulted in such a dreaded trade-off of special skills.

"Eliminate the defect or train the talent?"

Arthur Phillips was a special education teacher who in 1930 raised an important strategy question when teaching persons with special abilities: should one concentrate on "eliminating the defect" or "training the talent?" That question has been answered with overwhelming certainty as you will see from examples throughout this book: *train the talent* (Phillips 1930).

Savant skills are not frivolous curiosities or trivial talents. For many savants the special skill is their language and their best communication with the world around them. That's the good news. And there is more good news. Utilization of the savant skills helps increase language acquisition, socialization and daily living skills. In that sense it helps "eliminate the defect" to use Phillip's (1930) terminology. In my terms, utilization of savant skills provides a conduit toward normalization. The language, social and daily living skill gains occur without trade-off of the special abilities and those gains provide greater independence as well. Numerous examples of that welcome and marvelous transition follow.

Low IQ is *not* a requisite for savant syndrome

IQ levels in savant syndrome can range from below 40 to as high as 140. The majority of savants have IQ levels between 40 and 70; however as many as 25 percent have IQ scores above 70. Bolte and Poustka (2004) compared performance of 33 savant and 26 non-savant autistic subjects on the Wechsler Adult Intelligence Scale—Revised (WAIS-R). Full-scale IQ scores for the savants ranged from 38 to 128 with a mean of 83.3; the non-savant autistic control group IQ levels were somewhat lower (mean 71.4) but the difference was not statistically different. Interestingly, although not commented on in the article, the 33 subjects who had at least one savant skill were from a total of 254 autistic individuals, giving a prevalence figure of 13 percent. As an incidental finding, sex distribution in the savant group was 28 males and 5 females.

In some persons IQ can be in the superior range. Therefore while many persons with savant syndrome have IQ scores below 70, having an IQ above 70 does not "disqualify" someone from being a savant.

There are several reasons why savant syndrome is more often associated with low, rather than with average or above average IQ scores. First, certain of the developmental and other disorders underlying savant syndrome, including mental retardation, have limited intelligence as measured by IQ testing as an intrinsic element of the particular disorder.

Second, IQ tests rely heavily on verbal scale scores and many autistic persons, including those with savant syndrome, do poorly on verbal testing. They do better on performance scales but not sufficiently well to offset poor verbal performance. The result is a low IQ score even if overall functioning appears to be higher. This circumstance is called "functional retardation." In these instances individuals would have a normal or high IQ (if it could be accurately measured) but they function *as if* mentally deficient because of limited abilities in certain subscale testing or other behavioral traits or symptoms that prevent accurate measurement of IQ.

Third, IQ is one way, but not the only way, to measure "intelligence." In Chapter 7 on Leslie Lemke, who has a measured IQ of 58, I describe his ability to do parallel processing when asked to play a piano piece he had never heard before, accompanying someone rather than playing it back after hearing the piece. Such parallel processing is not consistent with an overall IQ level of 58. Rather that episode demonstrates that in the musical sphere—his island of genius—Leslie is highly intelligent.

Savant syndrome and the islands of genius within it argue forcefully that there are multiple "intelligences" in everyone. IQ measures what it measures (but only that) and it has produced a huge, useful database for some purposes. But in my view IQ is not a comprehensive measurement of "intelligence" overall. This conclusion is more than a semantic or academic one and it goes well beyond savant syndrome itself. The existence of "multiple intelligences" has profound implications for implementing more effective, individualized and targeted education efforts for all segments of the general population, not just persons with savant syndrome, as will be discussed later.

Males outnumber female savants by as many as six to one

From the time of the earliest reports, males have always outnumbered female savants in those accounts. Down (1887) comments: "All of these cases of idiot savants were males; I have never met with a female" (p.61). Tredgold (1914) in his classic chapter on savant syndrome, notes that almost "invariably" persons with savant syndrome were male, with female savants being very rare. In the approximately 15 cases that Tredgold comments on, either from his own observations or from case reports of others, he lists only two female savants, one with very advanced musical skills and the other with "astonishing quickness" for multiplication and division.

In a review article on savant syndrome Hill (1978) reports on 103 persons classified as savants in 63 publications. Of these, 89 were male and 14 were female, resulting in a 6:1 ratio among those savants. Rimland and Fine (1988) note a 3.25:1 male to female ratio in the 531 autistic savants they had studied. This is very near the same male preponderance in autistic disorder itself, which is generally reported to be 4:1 male to female.

Why is that so? Geschwind and Galaburda (1987), both Harvard neurologists, provide some answers to that question in their book *Cerebral Lateralization*. They point out that the human brain is asymmetrical even in fetal life. There is a natural, demonstrable and regular asymmetry that favors the left hemisphere, particularly the temporal lobe, in all humans. This exists not as a hereditary trait, but as a fundamental given in human anatomy. This same actual, anatomic asymmetry between the two brain hemispheres is reflected throughout the animal kingdom.

This innate asymmetry is easily documented and has been reflected in scientific literature for years under the term "cerebral dominance." This dominance is as much an actual anatomic one as a functional one. This hemispheric dominance is not a matter of an active, dominant, major hemisphere versus a passive, non-dominant minor one; rather each hemisphere is superior in certain functions. For example, the left hemisphere is generally dominant for language and the right brain specializes in skills such as spatial and musical abilities. This anatomic dominance is not limited to cortical structures but is reflected in some subcortical structures as well.

Because the left hemisphere develops later than the right in the fetus, the left hemisphere is exposed for a longer time to any prenatal influences that might be detrimental to it. One of those prenatal influences which can be detrimental is a male-related factor, circulating testosterone, which can slow cortical growth and impair neuronal architecture and assembly in the more vulnerable, longer exposed, left brain. Left brain injury from circulating testosterone causes an actual neuronal migration, enlargement of the right hemisphere and the shift of dominance to the right brain. In the case of the male fetus, at some point during periods of intra-uterine life, fetal testosterone levels can reach those of adult males. While the female fetus is also exposed to some testosterone from the maternal circulation, almost all of that is converted to estradiol in the placenta and it therefore does not have the same harmful effect on the developing cortex as circulating testosterone has in the case of a male fetus. Data on both animals and humans support the existence of hormonal effects on the cortex, including this male-related influence on the growth of certain cortical regions.

When this shift of dominance to the right brain occurs, that dominance favors talents associated with the right brain skills (the kind of skills in savants). This same process is seen, with the same disproportionate male:female ratios, in conditions such as dyslexia, delayed speech, stuttering, hyperactivity and indeed autistic disorder itself. It also accounts for the greater incidence of left-handedness in males in general.

Geschwind and Galaburda (1987) refer to this hormone-related switch in dominance as a "pathology of superiority" in which compensatory growth occurs in some portions of the brain as a result of poor development or actual injury to other areas of the brain. It should be noted that circulating testosterone affects the growth of many other tissues as well, including those of certain immune systems of the body, and this creates in males a disproportionate susceptibility to certain immune disorders.

In summary, high levels of circulating testosterone in the male fetus, and its detrimental effect on the later developing, more vulnerable left hemisphere of the brain results in a "shift to the right" of cerebral dominance with emergence of those skills typically associated with right brain abilities more often in male than female savants. These same changes account for as well the disproportionate male representation in other disorders associated with left brain dysfunction including some language and learning disorders as well as autistic disorder itself.

Savants can be creative

Some observers, while extolling the eidetic-like duplicative skills and massive memory of the savant, point out that savants, as a group, are not creative. In fact I was one of those observers who wrote just that in the first edition of *Extraordinary People* (Treffert 1989). There I raised the question "Is the savant creative?" I answered in this way: "In my experience, not very" (p.254).

I was wrong. Persons with savant syndrome can be, and are, creative.

What changed my mind? Some additional years of observation. In medicine there is a tremendous advantage in having a longitudinal "natural history" of each patient over time rather that a single "snapshot" consultation. I have had the opportunity and privilege of observing the "natural history" of savant syndrome in a number of such persons now and, in so doing, have seen a rather predictable and impressive pattern that can be summed up as *imitation* to *improvisation* to *creation*. Let me explain using Leslie Lemke as an example.

What often first catches attention is the savant's capacity to duplicate a piece of music or art, for example, with amazing fidelity. Leslie Lemke played back flawlessly Tchaikovsky's Piano Concerto No. 1 after hearing it for the first time and he will still play it back perfectly on request. Leslie's ability to *duplicate* what he has just heard is tested regularly in the challenge part of his concerts. The audience is always impressed.

At a 1989 concert a young girl played "Mississippi Hotdog" as a challenge piece. Leslie listened and then dutifully played it back exactly as he heard it. But toward the end of the exact repeat of the piece, he looked a bit restless, sat more erect and seemed even more excited and eager to play. As soon as he dutifully completed the playback, he launched into a five-minute *improvisation* that can best be described as "Variations on a Theme of Mississippi Hotdog." It was beautiful. It was skillful. He changed pitch and tempo demonstrating convincingly his innate access to the rules of music that other professional musicians have commented on.

Now Leslie is *creating* by composing his own songs including "Down Home on the Farm in Arpin" and a number of others. In one such piece he duplicates, by whistling softly as he plays, the songs of the birds he listens to with rapt and appreciative attention when he sits outside in the sun, which he so loves to do.

I have seen that same sequence of literal copying, to improvisation, to free form creation in other persons with savant syndrome. You will read about a number of these persons in the chapters about them. Matt Savage has traversed that same route from early literal playback of songs he heard, to jazz improvisation and creation of his own jazz pieces that now have world renown. Hikari Oe has composed a number of beautiful pieces for several CDs that have also been internationally distributed and appreciated. Thomas Bethune—Blind Tom—created a very complex piece depicting the battle of Manassas. It is a masterpiece by the account of many professional musicians.

So the savant *can* be creative.

These clinical impressions of creativity in savant syndrome have been bolstered by formal research as well. A study by Hermelin, O'Connor and Lee (1987) assessed musical inventiveness in five musical savants compared to six non-savant children who had musical training over a period of two years but had not yet been exposed to compositional or improvisational instruction. Five tasks measured "musical inventiveness." On those tests the savant group was superior to the control group. Similarly, on tests of musical competence—timing, balance and complexity—the savants were also superior to the control group. These researchers indicate that this study was consistent with earlier findings—that a series of separate intelligences, of which music is but one, exist in each person rather than a single, consistent intelligence that permeates all the skills and abilities of each person. Regarding music they concluded that savants were able to show some *creativity* and *improvisation* in addition to *mimicry*.

Another research project in which I participated with Hermelin, O'Connor and Lee (Hermelin *et al.* 1989) assessed improvisations by Leslie Lemke compared to a professional, non-savant musician after each had heard the same musical pieces. One was lyric (Grieg) and one a-tonal (Bartok). Leslie's improvisations were described as "virtuoso embellishments with a considerable degree of musical inventiveness and pianistic virtuosity" (p.452). That study concludes:

> both subjects' attempts at improvisation showed a high degree of generative musical ability, and what distinguishes them from each other is not so much a differential degree of musicianship but rather their own, different musical preferences as well as their respective personality characteristics. (Hermelin *et al.* 1989, p.452)

Savants can be creative. They often travel a trail of first duplication, then improvisation and finally creation of something truly their own. It is a well-traveled path that you will detect in many of the stories of savants that follow.

Savant syndrome is separate from prodigy and genius

It is popular these days to apply the diagnosis of high-functioning autism or Asperger syndrome to almost anyone generally considered to have been a prodigy or genius in the past. Names such as Mozart, Rembrandt, Einstein and others are bandied about, conjecturing that these persons were really persons with high-functioning autism rather than prodigies or geniuses. It is difficult enough to make a diagnosis of autism or Asperger's in day-to-day medical practice, with face-to-face interviews and testing, let alone trying to apply a postmortem diagnosis, sight unseen.

Suffice it to say that prodigies and geniuses do exist. They are not all savants. There is a critical difference in that prodigies and geniuses, unlike savants, do *not* have some underlying developmental or other disability. In addition, rather than having an island of genius, the exceptional skills and abilities of prodigies and geniuses are generally accompanied by high or exceptional performance in multiple areas of functioning compared to the very uneven performance levels of persons with savant syndrome.

Why is that distinction important? Because I get many emails from parents concerned that their child may be "autistic" since he or she reads at two years, or draws sensationally at age three, or hums back all the melodies he or she hears, or likes to line up railroad cars obsessively, or memorizes license plate numbers, or insists on routine or has certain recurrent rituals or fears. These parents look up "autism" on the Internet and are convinced, and frightened, that their child fits that profile. But not every child who reads early, likes to line up railroad cars, remembers songs, draws spectacularly, plays tunes prolifically and likes routine is autistic.

There is a wide variation in "normal" childhood behaviors, as any parent with several children can tell you. There is a wide range and overlap as well, between normal, gifted and talented, prodigy and genius levels in children. Such differential diagnosis requires skill and caution. While I support early identification of autism in youngsters so intervention can begin early, those efforts need to be balanced with sensible diagnostic caution lest parents be unnecessarily frightened and overwhelmed by premature or over-reaching conclusions. Diagnostic caution and watchful observation is the better path with young children unless the signs and symptoms of autistic disorder or some other developmental disorder are unmistakably certain.

One example of the importance of careful and cautious differential diagnosis is with hyperlexia. Some children simply read precociously. At age three instead of memorizing a book and "reading" it back, they are in fact actually reading. They are usually very bright, neurotypical children. Eventually their school classmates "catch up" as they too learn to read but at a later, more typical age. This is what I call hyperlexia group no.1.

Group no.2 are children on the autistic spectrum who have hyperlexia as a "splinter skill." Underlying that accelerated ability is autistic disorder as a disability with all the usual signs and symptoms of that condition.

Group no.3 are children who read exceptionally early and for a period of time have "autistic-like" symptoms, but they do not have autistic disorder. Over time the autistic-like symptoms fade without remnant. This, in my experience, is a rare form of hyperlexia but one where the long-term prognosis is very different from group no.2. Therefore when parents write me about their child with hyperlexia expressing their concerns that their child is showing some "autistic" behaviors, I urge a careful workup by a skilled professional or agency, and, depending on the diagnosis, careful observation over time. Some of the most grateful letters I have received from parents are those where their child was in group no.3, and, over time, everything turned out quite fine. I address hyperlexia, and my experience with this differential diagnosis, in more detail on the savant syndrome website.

Likewise, with respect to adults, not every absent-minded professor has Asperger syndrome. Instead, genius, sometimes with generous eccentricity, can exist without being "on the spectrum." The temptation to label all exceptional talents as autistic disorder or Asperger syndrome, rather than recognizing prodigy, genius or simply precociousness as distinct entities, needs to be resisted lest "diagnostic creep" errone-ously blurs the lines between these circumstances and voids all meaningful classifi-cation. When that occurs all those disorders lose their specificity and the spectrum engulfs us all.

The beginning of wisdom is to call things by their right names. To parents in search of early intervention and treatment for their child, labels don't matter and sometimes confuse. All they want is whatever is best for their child regardless of what particular diagnostic category clinicians place the child in. But from the re-search point of view, if we are ever to separate autism into its subgroups, which surely exist, and then target treatment specifically to each of those subgroups, precise clas-sifications do matter and our research efforts need to remain diligent to that reality. Then effective, targeted treatments will follow.

Parents, teachers and caregivers are a vital part of the equation

Innate talent, unusual brain circuitry, and obsessive repetition are biological parts of the savant syndrome equation. But the beneficial reinforcement and self-esteem that comes from the appreciation and praise that the savant gets from parents and others is a vital psychological part of the equation as well. This cannot be overstated. Just as Anne Sullivan, as depicted in the 1962 movie *The Miracle Worker*, was able to tap the tremendous, buried potential of Helen Keller with unwavering belief, encouragement, patience, appreciation, love and just plain hard work so there is always an Anne Sullivan type parent, relative, friend, teacher or therapist behind each savant who looks at strengths, not deficits, and pays more attention to abilities than to disabilities.

You will see the power of love, belief, optimism and hope in all of the savant stories that follow. Those stories convey that power more vividly than I can describe it here. As spectacular as the savant abilities are, equally impressive has been the unconditional positive regard of the families and others who certainly care lovingly for the savant, but they truly care about them as well, focusing not just on what the savant can do, but also on who he or she is. Their appreciation and accommodation to these special people and their special gifts provide a powerful, enviable role model for us all.

CHAPTER 2

How Do They Do It?
Some Earlier Theories from
Heredity to Quantum Theory

To anyone witnessing the extraordinary abilities of the savant, an obvious question looms up: "How do they do it?" When Morley Safer asked George that question on *60 Minutes,* his reply was simple: "I've got a good brain, that's how I do it." And that's true. He does have a good brain. Alonzo's answer was even more succinct: "God gives the gift." And many would agree that such spectacular talent is a gift from God. May Lemke answered the question with a longer reply, but really a neuroscientifically accurate one, as you will see, when she stated that while a part of Leslie's brain was damaged, another part was "left perfectly healthy and beautiful just so that Leslie would have a talent. And he got it!" He certainly did.

But the question "How *do* they do it?" requires further exploration because through the years there has been a tendency to give savants a fleeting "Gee whiz, look at that" glance and then return to studying more typical and traditional brain function with which we are more familiar and comfortable, leaving the savant unexplained. But savants are real. They do exist. Their incredible abilities are witnessed and documented. So it is not sufficient to view them as some sort of circus-like oddity, or dismiss them as the UFOs of neuroscience. For no model of brain function, including memory, will be complete until it can fully explain and account for the jarring juxtaposition of ability and disability existing side by side in the same person.

To leave the "How do they do it?" question unexplored is to accept a "world is flat" view of the brain, shortchanging by far its marvelous capacity and plasticity.

There is no single theory that can explain all savants. Investigators past and present have put forth a number of theories to explain the cause of this extraordinary condition. However, there are problems with these theories in that several merely describe savant characteristics, abilities and traits very accurately, but provide no explanation of cause. Others that do explore cause lack universal applicability to all savants. In fact none adequately addresses the fact that while savant syndrome does occur in persons with autistic disorder, it occurs with *other* developmental disabilities as well. Nor do theories linking savant syndrome to autism account for the phenomenon of the acquired savant.

In this chapter we will explore some proposed answers to the "How do they do it?" question put forward by various clinicians and investigators to date. In Chapter 3 we will look at an alternative theory, one which I favor, based on recent findings using newer imaging and other techniques that point toward a more universally applicable neurophysiological, neuropathological and neuroplasticity process that can account for this astonishing capability in both congenital and acquired savants. But before reviewing those newer findings in depth, let's study some of the other theories.

Eidetic imagery and visual image memory (photographic memory)

Some observers and researchers have proposed that eidetic imagery and/or visual image memory can explain certain savant syndrome abilities. These explanations stem from the fact that some savants, particularly those with calendar calculating or lightning calculating abilities, seem to "see" their answers as if projected on to a screen. Horwitz, Deming and Winter (1969), for example, described George and Charles, whom they studied closely, as having eidetic imagery. Sacks (1989), in describing those same twins, felt that they viewed the calendar dates as an "immense mnemonic tapestry, a vast (or possibly infinite) landscaping in which everything could be seen, either isolated or in relation" (p.200).

Stephen Wiltshire can store, recall and then draw an entire city with incredible detail after viewing it on a short helicopter ride. Alonzo needs to glance at an animal only once and then can, at any later time, recall a digital-camera-like image in his mind which he then sculpts into an exact duplicate of what he saw previously. Neither he nor Stephen use models or prior sketches in their work. A single glance, stored infinitely it seems, is sufficient. Is that eidetic imagery, or is it some other form of remarkable memory?

Eidetic imagery, in its pure form, is reserved for a very rare but specific memory function in which, after one has viewed an object or scene, an intensely strong visual image persists for a period of time immediately after the object is removed (Giray and Barclay 1977). *Visual image memory*, in contrast, is popularly referred to as photographic memory. This involves the ability to scan quickly and store, *for later retrieval*, vast amounts of very detailed information or images exactly as previously seen. Photographic memory, like eidetic memory, is also rare. The two terms are often used interchangeably but they differ considerably since eidetic imagery is an immediate, vivid, persisting after-image and photographic memory, while also vivid and exact, recalls images at a later time than when immediately viewed. While some researchers consider these two phenomena to be qualitatively different from each other, Gray and Gummerman (1975), after detailed study of data and theories in this area, conclude that eidetic imagery is only quantitatively different from visual image memory in that eidetic images are much more vivid.

Eidetic imagery can be present on a persistent basis in some forms of chronic brain damage; in those instances it is called palinopsia (Giray and Barclay 1977). Some researchers have found the occurence of that form of eidetic imagery to be as high as 50 percent in mental retardation based on organic brain damage, but other investigators, while confirming such an association, put the percentage at a much lower level. Suffice it to say that, in these cases and most probably in the savant as well, palinopsia, when present, is more a marker of brain damage than an explanation of savant abilities.

Through the years a number of other investigators describe eidetic imagery as being present in some individual cases (Treffert 2006a). But the most extensive study of the role of eidetic imagery and visual image memory in the savant was Duckett's (1976) systematic comparison of 25 developmentally disabled or mentally retarded individuals who showed savant abilities compared to 25 persons matched for age, sex, IQ and disability who did not display savant skills. Only two of the control subjects showed evidence of visual memory imagery, and only one savant and one control demonstrated eidetic imagery. Duckett (1976) concluded that both eidetic and visual image memory were infrequent in both groups, and certainly not universal, confirming her hypothesis that the skills of *all* savants *cannot* be explained by such mechanisms.

My observations are consistent with those findings. *Some* savants, such as Stephen Wiltshire, Alonzo Clemons and Richard Wawro, do have a form of vivid, later recall that could be classified as photographic memory, but that certainly is not the case with most savants. In others, eidetic imagery, when present, may simply be a marker of brain damage rather than an explanation for savant abilities. Rubin and Monaghan (1965) point out in a case report of theirs that eidetic imagery cannot be a universal explanation for savant abilities because the savant calendar calculator they studied was completely blind, and eidetic imagery is not possible in blind persons.

Heredity and savant syndrome: nature or nurture?

Rife and Snyder (1931) took on directly the issue of heredity and special skills in the savant. They are very critical of behavioral scientists of that time who espoused that "any normal, healthy child can be moulded to any desired pattern: artist, musician, recluse or social celebrity, craven or hero, fool or savant" (p.547). In short, they conclude, "nurture" is not a sufficient force to create savants, absent some genetic contributions of "nature."

They support their case for hereditary factors as being critical in the development of special savant skills in the study of 33 cases where musical, mathematical, artistic or mechanical skills coupled with phenomenal memory (savant syndrome) were present in developmentally disabled, institutionalized persons. By interview they were able to establish that *all* of the savants in their group had non-disabled relatives with skills similar to the savant.

Several cases were particularly interesting. In one case the person had developed mental handicap following spinal meningitis. Later impressive musical ability surfaced (acquired savant syndrome). This individual was interviewed at age 30 by these investigators: "The patient himself, in spite of his lack of mental ability, plays either classical music or jazz, with many variations. His ability is plainly inherent, and not the result of training" (p.555). This man had a sister who was a gifted violinist, a paternal grandmother who had unusual musical ability as a pianist, and two first cousins with exceptional musical ability. In another case a 19-year-old blind, severely handicapped man played the piano by ear: "He plays anything he hears and is said to have perfect pitch. He has a feebleminded brother who has no musical ability, and a normal sister, who, though blind, plays the piano and composes music" (p.558).

From these and the other cases studied, the researchers reached several important conclusions:

- Special savant abilities can develop in the presence of severe intellectual handicap *without* training or instruction.

- The special abilities are inherited independently of general intelligence and it is merely a coincidence when a person inherits both.

- When present in such persons these special abilities also "appear frequently in relatives of these patients" (p.558).

Henry Goddard (1914) proposes that savant skills are genetically determined and that if an individual with such skills was not handicapped by mental retardation or other similar disability, such a person would be a genius within the area of his or her skills (i.e. a "prodigious" savant if skills were at that level).

Brill (1940), in analyzing his case of a calendar calculator, Jungreis, expands the usual definition of behavioral heredity—constitution, talent and traits—to include a body of knowledge, instincts and intuitions inherited from ancestors, much as lower animals inherit instincts and adaptive behaviors (today these would be included in the broader definition of "genetic memory" discussed in more detail later). Brill states: "Our prodigies in a way resemble some of the lower animals insofar as they display in early life some instinctive knowledge like a prodigious memory" (p.724). In supporting this theory Brill (1940) points out that Jungreis's family "had supplied rabbis to their small community in Hungary for many generations, and his grandfather, also a rabbi, was considered a mathematical wizard.

Brill also points out that the mathematical prodigy Pascal had a long and eminent line of mathematical geniuses in his ancestry as well.

With respect to the nature/nurture argument regarding growth and development, Brill (1940) proposes two types of unconscious in each of us. Our *phylogenetic* unconscious is made up of instincts, traits and behaviors directly transmitted to each of us by our ancestry. Our *ontogenetic* unconscious, in contrast, is made up of our individual life experiences. With respect to savant abilities, Brill (1940) proposes that some person's life (ontogenetic) happenings can sometimes "kindle" the phylogenetic unconscious at which time some dormant, inherited phylogenetic abilities might emerge.

The nature/nurture argument has raged much more frequently in the study of genius than in the study of savant syndrome as such. Tammet (2009) explores this controversy in some depth in a section of Chapter 2, titled "Is Genius in the Genes?" in his book *Embracing the Wide Sky: A Tour across the Horizons of the Mind*. He concludes, and I agree, that "everyone is born with certain talents, which dedication and hard work help to realize. I broadly agree with the scientific consensus that says that high achievement is the result both of genetic and environmental factors" (p.56).

With respect to family history and savant skills, Duckett (1976) found special skills in some, but not all, of the relatives in the 25 savants she studied. Rimland (1978a) mentions that in his fairly large sample of autistic persons with savant skills, there was a tendency for those skills to run in families. But LaFontaine (1974) found only 1 family member with special skills in 23 relatives of 5 very carefully studied savants.

Young (1995) did interviews and standardized testing on 51 savants, which is the largest sample of persons with savant syndrome in any single study to date. In the group 41 of the savants carried a formal diagnosis of autism and the remainder had some other type of intellectual disability. As part of that study, family history was included where possible. Of the 51 savants in the group, 23 had family members who showed superior skills in savant-like areas.

In summary, with respect to heredity it can be said that special abilities and developmental disabilities can be inherited as separate characteristics. In some savants these two circumstances can occur together and a family history of special skills is contributory, but in other savants no such direct family history of special abilities can be documented. When prodigious special abilities are genetically transmitted without accompanying developmental disability, such persons would be prodigies or geniuses rather than savants. Psychological elements can and often do work as a nurturing force to kindle and accelerate special abilities that might otherwise remain dormant. But like eidetic memory, hereditary factors as a single theory cannot account for all savants.

Sensory deprivation

Attempts to explain savant skills by sensory deprivation fall into two categories: *social isolation*, such as solitary confinement or lack of social contact, or *sensory isolation* due to faulty sensory input from conditions such as blindness, deafness or perhaps autism itself. Viscott (1969) describes in great detail the case of Harriet, in which he proposed that early maternal deprivation and social isolation contributed causally to the special musical abilities this woman ultimately developed. As a child, according to Viscott, Harriet was kept in her crib day and night until age two: "The baby was ignored much of the time and with the exception of music was sensorily deprived" (Viscott 1969, p.498). Music eventually became a form of communication between Harriet and her mother, and a source of praise and reinforcement elsewhere in her life as well. Viscott delves deeply into the psychological importance of music in Harriet's life, and the reasons for her preoccupation with it, melding the social isolation and psychological factors to explain her prodigious musical ability.

Rubin and Monaghan (1965) report the case of a 16-year-old blind twin who had been a virtual crib baby for the first three years of her life. While there was some brain damage as well, these investigators felt the combination of social isolation in those early years, coupled with the sensory isolation from the blindness, were significant contributing factors to this person's savant characteristics and abilities.

Hoffman (1971) points out that persons in extreme social isolation sometimes carry out mental calculations or other rote memory exercises as their way of adapting to such a sensory-deprived environment, and proposes that that may be the mechanism by which savant skills develop in some sensory-deprived persons, whatever the cause of sensory deprivation.

Generally, however, theories based on sensory deprivation implicate a more biologically mediated process to account for the emergence of savant skills in persons who are blind or deaf, for example, or autistic. With blind and deaf persons the source of the sensory deprivation is obvious. For autistic persons, however, the source of the sensory isolation, and the biological reaction to it, are somewhat more complex.

Rimland (1978a), citing a number of his own as well as other studies, suggests that the autistic person, because of a specific biological defect, is locked into a very narrow, closed loop or circuit of sensory input and lacks the ability to connect to the rich associative network that most persons are able to access. This inability to "connect" to a wider source of input sets up a form of sensory deprivation and results in a very narrow, closed-loop band of super-intense, indistractible concentration. The savant then deals with only minute details in deep specificity. Being unable to broaden focus, the savant narrows attention and devotes intense mental energy to narrow preoccupations. The person becomes hypodistractible and overfocused on very limited items and processes.

Rimland describes this circumstance thus:

> The autistic child and the savant do not have the option of deploying their at-
> tention to the narrow (physical) or broad (conceptual) ends of the spectrum, as
> the circumstances require. The adjusting knob on their tuning dial has become
> loose with the dial set at the narrow band, hi-fidelity, physical-stimulus end of
> the range, so they are in effect locked into that attentional mode. (p.57)

In my view it may be that social isolation may be a contributing factor to some
savant capabilities or outcome in some cases, but it cannot be a universal contributor
or cause in all savants since so many of the persons with savant syndrome in this
book, in spite of extensive, indeed rich, social contacts through family, caretakers
and friends, still have developed savant syndrome.

With respect to sensory deprivation from biological causes such as blindness or
deafness, while some blind persons particularly may develop savant skills, especially
musical abilities as described elsewhere in this book, not all do. Likewise, while
the sensory deprivation of the type that Rimland (1978a) suggests may be opera-
tive, even causal, in persons with autism, not all persons with autism are savants.
Even more persuasive against this type of sensory deprivation being the underlying
cause of all savant syndrome cases is the fact that only 50 percent of persons with
savant syndrome are autistic and, therefore, would have this type of "autistic" brain
circuitry.

Concrete thinking and the inability to reason abstractly

The inability of the savant to think abstractly, with reliance almost exclusively on
concrete patterns of expression of thought, is well known and seen often in savants.
For some researchers, the inability of the savant to think abstractly has been viewed
as an interesting but incidental finding. However, others have defined concrete
thinking as the central defect in the savant and they propose that that phenomenon
explains the condition.

In their comprehensive five-year study of savant "L", Scheerer, Rothmann and
Goldstein (1945) conclude that the impairment in abstract ability was the central
defect present to account for the condition. "L" could not understand or use language
in a symbolic or conceptual manner, and was unable to comprehend ideas, words,
definitions or metaphors in any abstract sense. His speech was restricted to concrete,
situationally determined, conditioned responses of a mechanical, automatic type. His
skills included calendar and lightning calculating, extended retention of numbers,
the ability to spell words backwards or forwards orally or in writing, piano playing
with perfect pitch, and obsessive memorization and singing of opera in several languages. His IQ was 50. Neurological examination, electroencephalography (EEG),
pneumoencephalography and other laboratory examinations were normal. These
researchers concluded that the limitation to concrete thinking created a repertoire of

continually repetitive, narrow skills because "it is the only way he can come to terms with the world beyond his grasp" (p.33).

They expand on this thesis by noting that while on the surface the skills displayed by the savant seem miraculous, given the narrow outlets for the expression of these abilities, the abilities seem less astounding: "If any normal individual would be forced to indulge in nothing but L's memorial skills, he probably could accomplish the equivalent" (p.32). In that sense the savant becomes really good at what he or she does not *in spite* of a handicap, but *because* of that handicap.

Other researchers, including Nurcombe and Parker (1964) and Luszki (1966), also focus on the inability to think abstractly as being central to savant abilities. And this same finding surfaces again and again in descriptions of savants. It seems to be an almost universal symptom or trait. So it is probably best approached as that—a symptom rather than a cause, and a description of what occurs in savants rather than an explanation. As a theory, impaired abstract ability and a limitation to concrete thinking thus *describes* the savant, but does not *explain* him or her.

Compensatory learning, reinforcement, repetition-compulsion

Savants clearly enjoy what they do. Those abilities bring attention and approval from others, which acts as a tremendous motivation and provides a great deal of reinforcement of whatever the skill happens to be. Some investigators point toward that dynamic as being a central force in the development and continuation of savant effort. Others suggest that such efforts stem from a compensatory drive to offset other limitations, much as a deaf person compensates with increased visual awareness, and vice versa. Both of these are psychological, rather than biological phenomenon.

LaFontaine (1974) stresses positive reinforcement as a powerful motivator for the intense concentration, practice and skills seen in many of the savants she studied. Duckett (1976) emphasizes the fame that her savants received in the institutional setting. Hoffman and Reeves (1979) highlight that the tremendous attention and visibility savants receive by nature of their special abilities is immensely "socially reinforcing."

Finally, Sarason (1959) in his book *Psychological Problems in Mental Deficiency* points out that in all of the studies of savant syndrome until that time, the important role of parental influence on the child had been overlooked or minimized. Sarason (1959) feels that the influences the parents represented were far more than pure genetics, and that parent interaction and effort contributed psychologically very heavily in the discovery, emergence and nurturing of savant abilities in many children.

Certainly there is ample evidence of the tremendous, positive influence that parents or caretakers have on the development of savant abilities, and savant personalities. All one has to do is see May Lemke in action with Leslie to realize what a powerful, positive force she was in the nourishment of his newly discovered musical abilities. Ellen's parents did not see her preoccupation with opera and music as frivolous or insignificant; instead it was a special gift to be nurtured and appreciated providing tremendous positive reinforcement to Ellen. Tony's mother was not just his encouraging catalyst, she was his strongest advocate as well. And Richard's father celebrated the completion of each and every picture with the Polish equivalent of a high-five celebration between him and Richard that was a joyous, rewarding event for both the father and his gifted son.

I cannot emphasize enough the vital role that parents, caretakers, therapists and friends can play in discovering and nurturing savant skills, bringing those to full fruition, and, in that process, bringing the person with savant skills to full bloom as well. It is a delightfully pleasant, reassuring interaction and emergence to witness. The stories in this book amplify and verify that vital ingredient in the complex mosaic that is the savant.

But as important as these psychological factors—reinforcement, compulsion, repetition, compensatory effort and parental influence—are in helping to shape the final outcome with savants, they, by themselves, are not sufficient to explain the condition. For if they were, then why wouldn't every developmentally disabled, or autistic, or brain damaged person exposed to these same dynamics develop savant skills? Or why would savant skills occur in males so much more frequently than in females? Or why would some patients who live in the same unit, in the same facility, with the same staff, exposed to the same stimulation, develop savant skills and others not? The answer: because while these psychological components are an important ingredient in the development of savant syndrome, they are not singularly causal.

So, let's look elsewhere as well.

Weak central coherence, mind blindedness and the extreme male brain

In her book *Bright Splinters of the Mind*, Hermelin (2001) attempts to answer the question why are the majority of savants autistic? In her sample of about 50 savants, 80–90 percent were either autistic or had a diagnosis of Asperger syndrome. She and co-worker, Linda Pring, had proposed that the cognitive style of focusing on separate elements, rather than the whole picture, typical of autism itself, provided autistic savants with building blocks from which musical, calendrical, artistic, numerical and other typical savant skills could be built up and extracted. Based on a number of studies in which autistic children were compared to non-autistic controls, a theory of "weak central coherence" was formulated wherein autistic children tended to focus "attention on parts and details of information rather than on an integrated perception, cognition and memory. Thus those with autism do tend to 'not see the wood for the trees'" (p.45).

Hermelin (2001) describes this as a "from parts to wholes" strategy in a number of savants she studied. Savants also were attracted to any system that has rigid structure, repetition and regularity, such as the calendar. Thus the frequency with which calendar calculating is seen among savants. It is aided by an ability to incorporate, unconsciously, algorithms from that structure and regularity. This unconscious route to the whole, from intense focus on parts, can extend to other savant talents as well. Whatever the special ability, Hermelin concludes: "Overall, within the domain where they are talented, autistic savants appear to use the strategy of taking a path from single units to a subsequent extraction of higher-order patterns and structures" (p.175). This phenomenon is called "weak central coherence" and was deemed to be central to both autism and savant syndrome.

Baron-Cohen (2002) has been attempting to explain why autism is more common among boys than girls. He also approaches that question from a cognitive psychology standpoint, although somewhat differently from the "weak central coherence" theory mentioned above. He postulates that, on average, males have a stronger interest, drive and capacity to *systemize* and females have a stronger interest, drive and capacity to *empathize*. In persons on the autistic spectrum, he proposes, there is an exaggeration of the male profile, hence the term "extreme male brain" which Baron-Cohen applies to autism overall. Systemizing, Baron-Cohen (2002) explains, is the drive to construct or analyze a system and lends itself to identification of the rules or laws that govern that system. Empathizing is being able to imagine what someone else is thinking or feeling, and having an emotional response to that other person's feelings. The lack of empathizing also includes "mindblindedness" which, together with what Baron-Cohen refers to as "hypersystemizing," accounts for savantism, in his view. In his work, Baron-Cohen is also examining fetal testosterone levels to see if hormonal levels in some way may account for the male:female disparity in autistic spectrum disorders, with that disparity subsequently reflected in the "extreme male brain" with its interest in, and reliance upon, systemizing.

In savant syndrome there is ample evidence of systemizing, certainly, and from that, the capacity to form unconscious algorithms regarding music, art and mathematics, for example. But, as with concrete thinking and the inability to think abstractly, the weak coherence theory and extreme male brain theory more *describe* the savant than *explain* him or her. The "How do they do it?" question goes beyond descriptions of behavior, and attempts to address the origins—the causes—of those traits, behaviors and characteristics. Also, the extreme male brain theory of autism fails to address the fact that one out of four children with autism (and one out of eight with savant syndrome) are female. More importantly, the extreme male brain, as applied to savant syndrome, ignores the fact that only 50 percent of savants are autistic, the other 50 percent, including acquired savants, having other developmental disabilities or other types of brain injury or brain disease. So whatever theories are advanced to explain savant syndrome, those theories have to address, causally, both the congenital and the acquired savant.

A gene for savant syndrome?

Nurmi *et al.* (2003), using genetic exploration methods, were able to identify and separate a subset of persons with autism who shared savant skills from a much larger group of autistic persons who did not have such skills. They point out that as many as 20 genes may contribute to autism risk. Over-representation of certain genes on chromosome 15q11-q13 has been thought previously to perhaps contribute to autism risk.

But in this study 94 multiplex families (multiple affected members; mainly affected sibling pairs and their parents) were included; 21 families were identified as "savant skills positive" and 73 families were identified as "savant skills negative." Results showed "the subset of 21 savant skills positive families yielded significantly increased evidence for linkage to 15q11-q13" (p.861). The 73 families in which the individuals with autism had few or no savant skills showed no evidence of linkage.

Since savant skills are sometimes seen in autism as well as other conditions, the investigators point out that their results suggest that savant abilities and autism may be genetically related, but not exclusively so. They point out that Prader-Willi syndrome is due to a deletion on this same 15q11-q13 chromosome and some of the features of Prader-Willi (exceptional puzzle skills for example) overlap. They conclude

> These data could be explained by a gene (or genes) in the chromosome 15q11-q13 region that, when perturbed, contributes to predisposition to a particular cognitive style or pattern of intellectual impairments and relative strengths. Precisely how those skills are manifested in a given individual may be influenced by a variety of environmental, and possibly, "genetic" factors. (p.861)

The research team is careful to point out that the presence or absence of savant skills was by parent report only without specific testing for such skills and invited replication studies. Their conclusion that "these results may suggest the possibility that the 15q11-q13 locus that contributes to autism may also be relevant to savants who are not autistic" (p.862) is particularly interesting and challenging.

Ma *et al.* (2005) attempted to replicate those findings. Instead of parental reports, they used the savant skill factor (SFF) from the Autism Diagnostic Interview–Revised (ADI–R) to define "savant" for purposes of their study. There was a subgroup of 21 autism families out of a total of 94 families. Results "failed to demonstrate linkage to 15q11-q13" in their sample. However, a critical variable—the definition of "savant"— varies between these two studies, making it difficult to compare the results. Further studies should provide a more definitive answer to the role, if any, of the 15q11-q13 genetic aberrations.

"Quantum" processing and "entanglement"

In an article titled "We are all savants," Diane Powell (2006), a psychiatrist, describes her collaboration with artificial-intelligence expert Ken Hennacy to come up with what might be called a "quantum mechanics" theory of savant abilities. It proposes that there are two modes of information processing in the brain. The first is "classical" processing, of which we are consciously aware, which is "slow, linear and capable of handling only a limited amount of information. It solves problems by using abstract concepts, relies upon neural network connectivity and occurs in the neocortex" (p.17). In contrast, "quantum" processing is "extremely rapid, parallel and capable of handling exponentially more information than classical processing, but it operates outside of conscious awareness. It takes place in all brain regions and becomes more evident when classical processing is turned down or off" (p.17). The term "quantum" was chosen because it refers to "supercomputers" which use quantum mechanical principles to achieve "exponentially greater" computational capacities of most computers "because the quantum wave function of their subatomic particles will enable a vast sea of values to participate in calculations simultaneously, rather than sequentially" (p.1).

Powell cites functional magnetic resonance imaging (fMRI) findings in two studies in which autistic individuals and IQ-matched controls were given identical memory and attention tasks. According to Powell (2006):

> both groups performed at equal levels but they used different sections of their brains. The controls activated several areas of their left and right neocortices in an integrated fashion, whereas the autistic subjects preferentially activated a small portion of their right neocortex and/or both sides of their *visual* cortex. (p.16; emphasis in)

(This right-sided activation is interesting in view of left brain/right brain considerations in theories that follow.)

But Powell takes these savant syndrome circuitry and connectivity findings a step further, addressing what she calls a "Ghost in the machine" (p.17). Acknowledging that there have been reports of extrasensory perception capabilities, or "psi" capacities, in some savants, Powell (2006) puts forth the hypothesis that the quantum phenomenon known as "entanglement" might provide an explanation for reported "psi" capabilities in some savants:

> Physicists have found that two particles can be entangled, or capable of influencing one another instantaneously while separated at great distances.

Entanglement provides a means for consciousness to be coupled to other locations in space-time or for consciousness between individuals to be coupled—in
short, a mechanism for telepathic communication. (p.17)

While the "psi" phenomenon is certainly controversial, the idea that two levels of
information and memory processing occur in the human brain, one more conscious
and one subconscious, is consistent with other reports that use somewhat different
terms to describe these two quite different circuits for thought and memory. Of
these two methods of data processing, savants have much more access to, and reliance upon, such "without reckoning" circuitry and have less access to more typical,
conscious processing. In her discussion, Powell (2006) also suggests that suppression
of the influence of "dominance" from one area of the brain may release brain capacity
in other, non-dominant areas in persons with savant syndrome, whether congenital
or acquired. This brain area release and substitution phenomenon has been called
"paradoxical functional facilitation" by others (Kapur 1996) and presents itself as well
in some theories that follow.

CHAPTER 3

How Do They Do It? More Recent Findings: The Three "R's"— *Rewiring, Recruitment, Release*

After reviewing 122 years of reports on savant syndrome following Down's (1887) first description of this extraordinary condition, and now having had the opportunity to meet and to personally observe and interact with savants and their families since 1962, in my view any theory that can fully explain this unusual circumstance of juxtapositioned ability and disability within the same person must include and account for the following:

- While savant syndrome does occur in as many as one in ten persons with autistic disorder, it is not limited to persons with autism; it also occurs when some other developmental disorder, brain injury or brain disease is the underlying disability.

- Savant syndrome can be *congenital* (present from birth) or it can be *acquired* (later in childhood, adolescence or adult life following central nervous system (CNS) injury or disease).

- Savant skills range over a spectrum of abilities from splinter skill to talented to prodigious levels. Prodigious level skills represent a very high threshold and are exceedingly rare; persons with skills at this level, absent a disability, would be classified as prodigy or genius.

- Savant skills tend to be those associated with right brain specialization.

- Those special skills are always accompanied by massive memory of a particular type: exceedingly deep but very narrow.

- There is an approximately 6:1 preponderance of males to females.

- Savant abilities can be present in some persons with severe handicap in the absence of *any* formal training or instruction.

- A family history of special skills may or may not accompany the disorder.

- Measured intelligence levels in savant syndrome can range from moderate mental retardation to superior. Low IQ is not a requisite.

While perhaps no single theory can explain every instance of savant syndrome, a theory based on the brain's ability to *rewire* its intricate connectivity in certain circumstances, before birth or after, by either *recruitment* of capacity from some other area of the brain or the *release* of dormant capacity in some other area of the brain, most often the right hemisphere, does meet the required conditions above. And it does provide a likely explanation for savant syndrome in many persons with that remarkable condition.

Let me explain how I have reached that conclusion.

The specialized skills of the savant are often associated with right brain function

Since the beginning of my journey with savants in 1962 I have been intrigued by how consistently reports in the prior 100 years tended to narrow savant skills to only five areas: art, music, calendar calculating, lightning calculating and mechanical/spatial skills. This was striking to me, considering all the skills in the human repertoire. As a corollary, I also found it striking then, and still do today, how consistently the particular skills in the savant tend to be those associated with right hemisphere functions.

I concede that left brain/right brain is a gross oversimplification of central nervous system structure, and that there is ample cross-communication between the two brain hemispheres. Nevertheless, research does show that the two brain hemispheres do specialize in certain functions.

Restak (1984), based on a variety of studies involving split-brain research, cognitive and symbolic tasks, imaging (positron emission tomography or PET) techniques, autopsy and neuropathological dissections, sums up some contemporary conclusions regarding left brain/right brain function. First, the left brain is more involved than the right in language, speech and certain other motor skills. The right brain, in contrast, is generally more involved than the left in spatial tasks, visual-constructional skills and other abilities, such as artistic or mechanical ability, that do not depend as heavily on verbal ability. These are the charateristics of most savant skills. Second, regardless of the skill being tested, the strategy involved—cognitive or symbolic—also determines which side of the brain is being used. The left brain, for example, has more to do with functions that are sequential, logical, abstract and symbolic such as reading or speaking. The right brain, in contrast, is more involved with functions that use more simultaneous, intuitive, non-verbal and concrete strategies along with methods such as painting or constructing things (again such as most savant skills). Restak (1984) concludes that the division of the brain hemispheres into *symbolic-conceptual* (left hemisphere) vs. *non-symbolic, directly perceived* (right hemisphere) avoids many oversimplifications.

Left brain dysfunction has been demonstrated in autistic disorders

In reviewing the literature on savant syndrome, I was also intrigued by its close association with autistic disorders compared to other developmental disabilities. As I looked further into that association I noted that other observers had commented on the presence of left hemisphere dysfunction in autism itself, not just in savant syndrome. In his article on autistic savants, Rimland (1978b) comments on the nature and increased frequency of right brain skills in that population. He too noted the logical, verbal, rational, linear and *sequential* nature of left brain function in all persons, in contrast to the non-linear, spatial and intuitive and *simultaneous* nature of right brain function. In his view, the autistic savant demonstrated simultaneous, "high-fidelity" imagery and functions typical of right brain function, in contrast to left brain specialization. Tanguay (1973) likewise found the special skills most often present in autistic children were those associated with right hemisphere functions, and those absent were essentially left hemisphere activities.

Other early studies confirmed this clinical observation. Hauser, DeLong and Rosman (1975) analyzed the results of pneumoencephalograms on 17 patients with early infantile autism. Pneumoencephalography was the only technique available before computed tomography (CT) scans to study brain architecture meaningfully. Only 4 of the 17 patients had some savant abilities at a noticeable level, but it is interesting that 15 of the 17 patients did show abnormalities in the *left* temporal lobe and dilatation of the temporal horn in the *left* lateral ventricle of the brain. These researchers concluded

> The unusually frequent occurrence of left-handedness in our series also suggests that the major cerebral abnormality was left-sided and thus resulted in a "taking over" of some motor and language functions by the right hemisphere. It may be useful to think of the lesion under discussion as asymmetrically bilateral. (Hauser *et al.* 1975, p.681)

A 1999 PET study showed low serotonin synthesis in the left hemisphere of persons with autistic disorder and other studies have confirmed such left hemisphere deficits as well (DeLong 1999). Boddaert (2003) and co-workers demonstrated in five children with autism and eight controls that at rest and listening to speech-like sounds, the volume of activation was greater on the *right* side and diminished on the *left* among children with autism; the reverse pattern was found in the control group. Escalant-Mead, Minshew and Sweeney (2003) demonstrated an atypical pattern of cerebral dominance among persons with autism and early language disorder when compared with children with normal acquisition of early language skills.

Demonstrated left brain damage in some cases of savant syndrome

In 1980 I met Leslie Lemke and in 1986 complete neurologic examination, neuropsychological testing and imaging studies were carried out on him (Treffert 2006a). A CT scan showed marked left-sided abnormality especially in the left frontal lobe. There was of course evidence of the eyes having been surgically removed; the eye sockets showed some deformity along with deformity of the sinus area, both primarily on the left side. The left frontal area showed an area of atrophy consistent with either some previous vascular damage or residual damage from a previous brain abscess. There were areas of atrophy in the anterior and posterior portions of the left parietal lobe, and, to a minor degree, damage as well in the left and right occipital lobes of the brain.

Charness, Clifton and MacDonald (1988) report a case of a musical savant who, like Leslie Lemke, was blind, developmentally disabled and exceptionally musically gifted. He was severely cognitively impaired being virtually untestable on the standard Wechsler Adult Intelligence Scale instruments except for digit span. On the Vineland Social Maturity Scale, he showed a developmental level of a two-year-old child. Additionally he had a severe paralysis and spasticity of the right arm and hand. He also had grand mal epilepsy. A CT scan showed, like Leslie Lemke, left hemisphere damage. An EEG (electroencephalograpgy) showed slow wave and spike activity on the left.

Steel, Gorman and Flexman (1984) report that a CT scan on a 29-year-old male savant they examined was normal. IQ testing was 91, however, in contrast to the two savants above. Yet in spite of the normal CT scan, neuropsychological tests showed bilateral frontal lobe dysfunction with preserved posterior hemisphere abilities, the preserved abilities being "especially those of the *right* posterior regions" (p.76, emphasis mine).

Certainly not all savants show left-sided abnormalities on *static* imaging. In some cases, however, even though the static imaging studies are normal, neuropsychological testing does show left-sided impairment. Ultimately *functional* imaging is likely to be much more informative than static imaging with respect to left brain and right brain abnormalities in both autism and savant syndrome.

Demonstrated left hemisphere abnormalities in the "acquired" savant

As I continued my "How do they do it?" search I acknowledged that finding demonstrable left-sided brain abnormalities in *some* savants did not prove that this disruption applies to *all* savants. Yet I was intrigued when I came across a case report by Brink (1980) in which a young boy had suffered a gunshot wound to the *left* brain, which he survived. It left him with paralysis on the right side of his body, of course. But after that injury the boy developed savant mechanical skills which had not been present prior to the left brain damage. Following the injury, performance on language tests was very low in this child, and scores on performance and mechanical abilities were much higher. Brink (1980) concludes that "heredity, and an undamaged right hemisphere" were the underlying factors with "sufficient motivation, practice and reinforcement" (p.251) adding to the final clinical picture in this acquired savant.

Beyond that single case, the most powerful evidence for a left brain dysfunction and right brain compensation theory in savant syndrome comes from Bruce Miller's 12 patients with fronto-temporal dementia who developed savant skills when none was present before the dementia began (Miller *et al.* 1996; Miller *et al.* 1998). Almost all showed *left* anterior temporal dysfunction on single photon emission computed tomography (SPECT) imaging. The paradoxical functional facilitation that these elderly individuals demonstrated provided compelling support for right brain substitution of skills for left brain injury, whether those compensatory skills were from newly "recruited", still available brain areas or were instead dormant skills "released" from areas suppressed, until then, by dominance of the left hemisphere.

The relevance to savant syndrome of Miller's left hemisphere dysfunction findings in these elderly patients was reinforced by the finding that, when the same SPECT imaging technique was used in an autistic, artistic child with savant syndrome, left-sided abnormalities in the same location as the older FTD (fronto-temporal dementia) patients were documented (Hou *et al.* 2000). This finding led this research team to conclude: "*The anatomic substrate for the savant syndrome may involve loss of function in the left temporal lobe with enhanced function of the posterior cortex*" (p.29, emphasis mine)

Interestingly, in this autistic, artistic child the MRI was normal, and the left-sided brain abnormality was seen only with SPECT *functional* imaging. This is an instance which demonstrates, as suggested, that functional imaging may more informative than static imaging in persons with savant syndrome.

Memory, sex incidence and family history

This rewiring, recruitment and/or release process can explain some of the elements involved in savant syndrome. But it leaves the sex incidence, memory and hereditary factors still unexplained.

The 6:1 male:female incidence in savant syndrome is addressed in detail in Chapter 1. It too has left brain/right brain significance. In brief, circulating testosterone which reaches very high levels in the male fetus has a detrimental effect on neuronal tissue on the later developing *left* hemisphere, leaving the left hemisphere in the male fetus vulnerable for a longer period of time than the *right* hemisphere for any process that might be detrimental to it. Autistic disorder, in which savant syndrome is seen with considerable frequency, already has a 4:1 male:female ratio due to that same later developing left hemisphere vulnerability to circulating testosterone, so it is not unexpected that the incidence of savant syndrome would be higher in autistic disorders than some other developmental disorders.

The reasons for the particular type of automatic, unconscious, "without reckoning" memory so characteristic of savant syndrome are also mentioned in Chapter 1. In brief, the massive memory seen in savant syndrome—exceedingly deep but very narrow within its confines—is consistent with what Mishkin and Petri (1984) refer to as a non-conscious "habit" or "procedural" memory circuitry rather than a "semantic" or "cognitive" memory system. I propose that the same factors that caused CNS damage in some areas of the left hemisphere in the savant, simultaneously damage the cortico-limbic memory system (cognitive, semantic) leaving the savant to rely on the cortico-striatal (habit, procedural) memory circuitry.

With respect to heredity influences and family history, those are critical in the determination of what specific type and quantity of "talent" emerges from the brain areas involved in the rewiring, recruitment or release phenomena just described. In the case of the prodigious savant that reservoir of talent is huge. Prodigious savants, who often demonstrate incredible abilities very early in life without formal training coupled with severe disability and cognitive impairment, also provide the most striking examples of genetic memory—"people who know things they never learned." This phenomenon is described in detail in Chapter 4.

How do they do it? A biologic, neuropathologic explanation

A general neurobiologic theory for savant syndrome encompassing all of the above now follows.

The *general* mechanism that produces special abilities in savant syndrome, whether congenital or acquired, includes the *neurological* process of "rewiring" the connectivity within the brain by either (a) "recruiting" and substituting still available, still intact, unused brain capacity for those brain areas that have been damaged by a variety of developmental, traumatic or disease-induced processes or (b) "releasing" stored, dormant, brain capability from non-dominant brain areas which are freed up after the dominant brain areas have been damaged (release from the "tyranny of the left hemisphere").

The *specific* mechanism of rewiring, recruiting or releasing applicable to savant syndrome typically involves disruption of typical left hemisphere function from certain prenatal influences—such as detrimental hormonal effects on the cortex from circulating testosterone—or other injurious prenatal, perinatal or postnatal development in children and adolescents, or from later brain injury or disease in adults. These injuries produce compensatory right brain skills and abilities to offset left brain dominance. In addition there is, simultaneously, probably from those same detrimental factors, injury to the cortico-limbic (cognitive or semantic) memory circuits with substitution and reliance on (habit or procedural) memory circuits. This combination of left brain and cortico-limbic circuitry damage, with compensatory right brain skills and reliance on habit and procedural memory, produces the clinical picture that is savant syndrome.

That neurological, rewiring process (also called paradoxical functional facilitation) results in certain *cognitive* patterns including impaired abstract thinking, thought patterns locked within a narrow band, obsessiveness, practice and repetition. Constant practice can produce sufficient coding that non-cognitive or unconscious, "without reckoning" algorithms can be automatically developed.

Psychological factors, including recognition and praise from family and others, provide reinforcement of the special skill.

Genetic (family history) factors may influence the specific type of talent, and the size of the talent pool, that is present to draw upon in both congenital or acquired savant syndrome. In addition, genetic memory—the genetic transmission of knowledge—may also provide inherited templates, or actual knowledge itself, to account for the phenomenon of "knowing things they never learned" that is present in some savants.

Once savant skills are established, intense concentration, practice, compensatory drives, reinforcement and reward from family and others play a major role in developing and polishing those skills further.

In short, the principal causative process in all individuals with savant syndrome, whether congenital or acquired, and whether associated with autism or other underlying disorders, is a *rewiring* process that either *recruits* or *releases* dormant brain capacity and potential to offset damage or dysfunction in some other area of the brain. The nature of savant skills suggests that often that process represents right brain compensation to offset left brain injury although other patterns of offset can occur as well. This is basically a biological process, not a psychological one, although encouragement and reinforcement from family or others are important factors and can help propel the skills to higher and higher levels. The exact type of skills, and the size of the talent pool supporting them, are determined by genetic factors.

CHAPTER 4

Genetic Memory: How Do We Know Things We Never Learned?

"He seems to know things beyond his own existence." That's how one of his teachers summed up Matt's exceptional musical expertise.

In a similar manner professional musicians who have observed Leslie have been quizzically impressed that somehow Leslie, who has never had a music lesson in his life, and cannot read music because he is blind, innately knows the "rules of music" which he uses so adroitly in his playing and composing.

Likewise Alonzo has never had an art lesson, yet he instinctively has access to the "rules of art" which allow him to sculpt three-dimensional animals from only a brief glimpse at a two-dimensional photo, for example. Alonzo knew instantly how to armature his horse figures, by using some self-fashioned wires, to capture the real-life motion of his stallions. Armaturing is a skill that takes some artists years to master.

Then there is Jay. Jay is not a savant. Instead he is an extraordinarily gifted musical prodigy. By age five Jay had composed five symphonies. His fifth symphony, which was 190 pages and 1328 bars in length, was professionally recorded by the London Symphony Orchestra for Sony Records. On a *60 Minutes* program in 2006 Jay's parents stated that Jay spontaneously began to draw little cellos on paper at age two. Neither parent was particularly musically inclined, and there were never any musical instruments, including a cello, in the home. At age three Jay asked if he could have a cello of his own. The parents took him to a music store and to their astonishment Jay picked up a miniature cello and began to play it. He had never seen a real cello before that day. After that he began to draw miniature cellos and placed them on music lines. That was the beginning of his composing.

Jay says that the music just streams into his head at lightning speed, sometimes several symphonies running simultaneously. "My unconscious directs my conscious mind at a mile a minute," he told the correspondent on that program.

Where does Jay's musical genius come from? How did he know about cellos or how to play them at age three when he had never been exposed to them before? How did he instinctively, at age three, know the "rules of music" when he had never studied or learned them?

Some have said that Mozart, another musical prodigy, never really "composed" anything. Rather he simply wrote down that which was already inscribed on his soul.

Prodigious savants particularly, from my observations, "know things they never learned," or in the words of Matt's teacher, "know things beyond their own existence." How is that possible? Could it be that they innately "know" things they never learned because they in fact can "remember" things they never learned? And might such a reservoir of inherited "knowledge" exist in everyone, dormant perhaps, but present nonetheless?

I think so. I call it genetic memory. Some refer to it as ancestral memory.

Genetic memory is simply the *genetic transfer of knowledge* along with all the other physical characteristics, traits, instincts, talents, dispositions and behaviors that our genes carry forward in each of us from conception and birth. Genetic memory basically purports that none of us starts life with a blank disk which is only inscribed and filled later with knowledge and experiences gained from day-to-day living. Instead, genetic memory proposes that stored in each of us there is a generous amount of genetically inherited, factory-installed *software* for certain skills and abilities, along with considerable genetically transferred *knowledge* itself, unconsciously remembered.

In the prodigious savant, or in the prodigy, the amount of such software and knowledge is unusually prolific and advanced. In the prodigious savant particularly such innate access is so striking because it is seen in jarring contrast to overall limitations. In the prodigy it is so conspicuous because of its stark contrast to such abilities in peers. In both instances there is an exceptionally generous allotment of, or access to genetic memory.

Genetic memory is not an entirely new concept. Brill (1940) quotes Dr. William Carpenter who, in comparing Zerah Colburn's calculating powers to Mozart's mastery of music composition, defined these "congenital gifts" as "intuitions." He writes:

> In each of the foregoing cases, then, we have a peculiar example of the possession of an extraordinary congenital aptitude for certain mental activity, which showed itself at so early a period as to exclude the notion that it could have been acquired by the experience of the individual. To such congenital gifts we give the name intuitions; it can scarcely be questioned that like the instincts of the lower animals, they are the expressions of constitutional tendencies embodied in the organism of the individuals who manifest them. (p.719)

Carl Jung (1936) uses the term "collective unconscious" to define his even broader concept of inherited traits, intuitions and collective wisdom of the past.

Wilder Penfield (1978) in his pioneering book, *Mystery of the Mind*, also refers to three types of memory. "Animals," he states, "particularly show evidence of what might be called racial memory" (this was his term for genetic memory). He lists a second type of memory as that associated with "conditioned reflexes" and a third type of memory as "experiential." Those two latter types in my terminology would be called habit/procedural memory and cognitive/semantic memory.

In his book *The Mind's Past* Michael Gazzaniga (2000) states:

The baby does not learn trigonometry, but knows it; does not learn how to distinguish figure from ground but knows it; does not need to learn, but knows, when one object with mass hits another it will move the object. (p.2)

He goes on to state "the vast cerebral cortex is chock full of specialized systems ready, willing and able to be used for specific tasks. Moreover the brain is built under tight genetic control" (p.41). He concludes:

As soon as the brain is built, it starts to express what it knows, what it comes with from the factory. And the brain comes loaded. The number of special devices that are in place and active is staggering. Everything from perceptual phenomena to intuitive physics to social exchange rules comes with the brain. Each device solves a different problem...the magnitude of devices we have for doing what we do are factory installed; by the time we know about an action, the devices have already performed it. (p.170)

Gazzaniga (2000) then goes on to describe the specialized functions of the right and left hemisphere, using a multitude of split brain testing results.

In his book *What Counts: How Every Brain is Hardwired for Math*, Butterworth (1999) points out that babies have many specialized innate abilities, including numerical ones: "Babies will have had no opportunity to learn about these things: they seem to be built into the brain as part of the genetic code and they kick in as soon as the baby leaves the womb" (p.98). In other words they "know things they never learned." I would argue that such "knowledge"—genetic memory—extends to music and art as well as numbers.

Interestingly, Butterworth (1999) traces this inherited "number module" which is "encoded in our genome" to distant ancestors who lived more than 30,000 years ago. He cites the work of Marshack (1991) whose work on the "Lartet Bone" of that era concludes that markings on that bone kept track of phases of the moon. Butterworth then discusses reasons why ice-age ancestors would record lunar cycles. This is especially intriguing to me, beyond genetic numerosity itself, because as I point out in Chapter 5, in my mind at least there may well be a link between the calendar calculating that so many savants innately possess and interest in, and dependence upon, knowledge of lunar phases for planting and harvesting, and actual survival, in more ancient times. While that is certainly speculative, it seems to me *somewhere* in the past, calendar calculating had a much more utilitarian purpose than at the present time. Is it possible that the now seemingly obscure skill of calendar calculating seen so often innately in so many savants is knowledge "remembered" from an earlier time, and carried forward genetically from an era when knowledge of the lunar calendar had a specific and critical purpose? While not making that connection, Butterworth (1999) does provide important links between counting and lunar cycles in his writings.

Steven Pinker's (2003) book *The Blank Slate: The Modern Denial of Human Nature* focuses on what he termed "behavioral genetics" or what could be called hard-wired "human nature." He examines the nature versus nurture arguments with respect to innate behavioral traits and aptitudes. Pinker's "behavioral genetics" is an important, although controversial, area of inquiry, but it differs somewhat from what I am focusing on in this discussion. His focus is on "behavioral" genetics while I am focusing on what might be called "knowledge" genetics. Nevertheless his book, as indicated by its title, refutes the "blank slate" theories of human development and on that concept we are in complete agreement. We do not start life with a blank slate with respect to knowledge, intuitions and, I would suggest, even very specialized skills.

Marshall Nirenberg, from the US National Heart Institute, provides detailed insight into the actual DNA/RNA (deoxyribonucleic acid/ribonucleic acid) mechanisms for what he calls "genetic memory" in an article published in the *Journal of the American Medical Association* (Nirenberg 1968).

Keith Chandler (2004) ascribes the savants' ability "to remember things they never learned" to paranormal phenomena, and other writers have extended such abilities to include past life regression. But my view of genetic memory does not extend to nor include those phenomena or mechanisms. Instead I view genetic memory in a much more limited, strictly biological framework, even more narrow than Jung's "collective unconscious" construct. Let me explain.

It is generally accepted that we do inherit certain physical characteristics such as height, hair color, eye color, posture and even propensity to certain diseases, for example. It is also generally accepted that certain behavioral traits, and certain talents, can run in families. We see evidence of that all around us. Genetic memory simply adds inherited *knowledge* and even certain specialized *skills* to those items that can be transmitted to offspring through a complex mix of genes and chromosomes. Interestingly most people do readily concede that such complex knowledge or skills can be inherited in the animal kingdom. It is common knowledge that birds can demonstrate complex song patterns, or migration patterns, for example, without having "learned" them. They know those innately, and we readily accept that notion.

Applying the notion of genetic memory in humans simply proposes, as stated above, that we do not start life with a blank disk. Rather, in all of us, certain talents, skills and even inherited knowledge are embedded genetically at birth. To use

Gazzaniga's (2000) terms: "The brain comes loaded." A pool of such inherited skills, talents and areas of knowledge exist in all of us, distributed quantitatively along the lines of the usual bell-shaped curve, with prodigy and genius at the far end of that spectrum. Whether called "ancestral," "genetic" or "racial" memory, or referred to as "intuitions" or "congenital gifts," the genetic transmission or inheritance of sophisticated skills and knowledge is convincingly demonstrated, I believe, in the prodigious savant and child prodigies.

What I define as genetic memory does not include reincarnation, mysticism, existential ruminations, transcendentalism or paranormal phenomena. Indeed it is a concept even much narrower than Jung's "collective unconscious." Genetic memory is simply the biological transfer of *knowledge, templates and certain skills* along with the myriad of other inherited physical characteristics, instincts, traits and behaviors.

In discussions of "genetic memory," some argue that what a prodigy, or a savant, inherits is not specific music, art or mathematical knowledge or skills. Rather what is inherited are the music, art or mathematical "templates" or unconscious "rules" of those specialized skills. These templates serve as a ready-made and readily accessible scaffolding on which specialized skills are built with exceptional ease and speed. That may be and I am open to that alternative. I must say, though, from my observations of prodigious savants and prodigies, it appears to me that it is the actual knowledge itself within an area of special expertise that is inherited, not just the templates or scaffolding. It is this genetic memory—inherited knowledge and actual skills—that makes it possible for persons with exceptional talent to demonstrate so convincingly that they indeed do know things they never learned.

As discussed earlier, the acquired savant is a neurotypical person in whom new, special skills arise, sometimes at a spectacular level, following head injury or CNS disease, when no such skills were evident before illness or injury. Such cases raise the possibility of their being dormant brain capacity in all of us, perhaps as backup systems in case of CNS incident. In a similar manner I propose that we all have dormant inherited capabilities as well—specific knowledge and skills we "remember," genetically transmitted.

I just purchased a new computer. I know, because the salesperson told me, that there are a variety of software programs installed on the computer. If I use the proper keystrokes, those programs will be available and active. But I tend generally to use only those programs familiar to me, tailored to my specific needs. These are programs I have specifically learned to use and activated. But a whole cache of other programs are embedded on my hard drive; I just have to know how to tap them.

In a similar manner I think we all have considerable brain "software" and indeed specific "knowledge" which was factory installed genetically, but remains dormant and silent unless we access it. Instead we tend to use the same well-worn pathways and circuits on a regular basis because they serve us well and are familiar. Perhaps that dormant genetic memory is present also as a backup system just as is the case regarding dormant brain capacity in the acquired savant. If so, the challenge becomes how to access such buried potential without brain injury or other CNS incident or disease. That challenge is discussed in the chapters which follow.

The role of epigenetics

If genetic memory does exist, what might be the mechanisms involved for transmitting such knowledge, traits and skills? Epigenetics provides that mechanism.

In November 2007 PBS (Public Broadcasting System) aired an extremely informative NOVA program on epigenetics titled *Ghost in Your Genes*. It is the most informative source of information about epigenetics that I have encountered. That program is available now for purchase in DVD (digital video disc) format. The description of that DVD from station WGBH in Boston that produced the video provides a succinct description of epigenetics:

> In a provocative report from the frontiers of biology, NOVA explores new findings that call into question the long held belief that all inherited traits are passed on by our genes. The fast-growing field of epigenetics investigates hidden influences that could not only affect our health today, but that of our descendants far into the future. It now appears the environment we live in makes small chemical changes to our DNA without affecting the gene's overall makeup. In other words, epigenetics adds another layer to our DNA that acts as a control system of "switches." Variable life experiences, such as nutrition or stress, may trigger these "switches", turning genes on or off. *According to the new research, these subtle changes can then be "remembered" and passed on from generation to generation, altering the traits we inherit.* So the lives of your grandparents—the air they breathed, the food they ate, even things they saw—could possibly affect you, and what you do in your lifetime could, in turn, affect your grandchildren. NOVA delves into this fascinating new idea, interviewing top scientists in the field and following what could be a paradigm shift in the way we think about inheritance and our genes.

I have added emphasis to the above quote because it touches on genetic memory as pertinent to this discussion of savant syndrome and prodigy. A full explanation of epigenetics and its ramifications for better understanding "inheritance" is beyond the scope of this chapter. But I recommend viewing *Ghost in Your Genes* as the most efficient and effective way to understand how epigenetics applies to the mechanisms at work in genetic memory.

Essentially the epigenes work as "software" to modify the "hardware" genes, all the while doing so without changing the basic and unique structure of the more fundamental DNA itself. In other words, epigenes can mold and modify genes to carry traits, skills and actual knowledge, as a form of memory from past generations, without changing the basic DNA imprint that each of us indelibly carry. The NOVA program, by case examples, points out how "identical" twins, DNA-wise, can differ considerably in behaviors, and even with respect to diseases or longevity. One example explores two twins who, though identical and sharing many features in common, do not share autism in common. One twin is autistic and the other is not. The program also traces with precision, because of some meticulously kept records for generations, how famine, or particularly good crops, can affect children biologically, including lifespan and illnesses, generations later.

Perhaps an example will help explain how the epigenes (as software) can have an effect on the genes themselves (hardware) to imbed various subtle changes in those genes without disturbing the DNA imprint of the genes themselves. If you were to take a DNA sample from my skin, stomach and eye, you would find the DNA in each of those samples would be exactly identical. But something "programmed" the identical DNA to make quite dissimilar organs—skin, stomach and eye. That software programming influence was the epigenes.

In short, epigenetics provides the mechanism as to how subtle changes, beyond those we have traditionally ascribed to inheritance, can be transmitted. And I would include "remembering things we never learned" in that more subtle lexicon of things that can be inherited and transmitted genetically.

Some savants, especially those more high functioning, have been exposed to training in art, music or math. It is quite plausible then that they might well unconsciously inculcate algorithms to provide their access to the "rules" of music, art, math, or calendar calculating for example, without having been taught those rules explicitly. It is also possible that inherited "templates" have allowed them to inculcate unconscious algorithms of their skill much more quickly than most persons. But to account fully for the extraordinary skills and knowledge of the prodigious savant, such as Leslie, who has had no formal training whatsoever and is so severely cognitively impaired that such training would be almost impossible, one has to invoke the presence of genetic memory for a full explanation.

Bottom line: genetic memory exists. It provides a mechanism by which savants, and prodigies, can "know things they never learned." Genetic memory may also provide a reservoir of abilities from which some of the dormant skills surface in the acquired savant. Finally, genetic memory has vast implications regarding some of the "inner savant" which may reside within us all.

CHAPTER 5

More Medical Mysteries: Calendars, Cantors, Foreign Accents and Hypermnesia

Savant syndrome is a rare condition. Many clinicians, including child psychiatrists, can go through an entire career without encountering any such individuals. I have had the opportunity to meet many savants only because of my special interest in the condition. What has been very conspicuous and impressive to me however, given the rarity of the condition, is how the obscure and also rare ability to do calendar calculating appears with such an uncanny, almost universal frequency among savants. It is a mystery within a mystery.

Equally conspicuous is how often the triad of *blindness, autistic disorder* and *musical genius*, in itself a rare combination, occurs in savant syndrome. From the very early descriptions of savant syndrome, this unusual triad of ability and disability has been reported with unexpected regularity in many notable instances, including some of the cases reported in this book. Why should that triad occur with such frequency in an already rare condition such as savant syndrome? That mystery is deepened further by the finding of a link between visual impairment, musical genius and monumental memory, *without* autism, among a whole group of blind cantors in the Coptic religion. They present as a whole "choir" of such persons. They are not savants because there is no evidence of any particular mental disability (such as autism) in that group, but a clear link still exists, nevertheless, between the blindness, musical genius and massive memory.

Another "medical mystery" explored in this section involves the mind-jarring cases of foreign accent syndrome. I include it here, instead of in the acquired savant section, because language experts tend to explain this spectacular new foreign accent acquisition by indicating that it is only changes in rhythm, vowel production, pitch and stressing of certain syllables (prosody) that surface in existing language rather than the person adopting a whole new foreign accent as if that has been their life long native language. Others, including myself, are convinced from viewing these cases that such persons actually do have access to other languages, beyond prosody only, to which they have been neither earlier exposed nor taught. They have, in fact, adopted a whole new authentic accent in a language otherwise foreign to them. Therefore some other dynamics have to be at work, perhaps genetic memory. You can draw your own conclusions as you review the cases and findings in this dramatic condition.

The final condition to be explored here is hyperthymesic syndrome, or massive autobiographical memory. The question raised, based on some particular new instances of persons with nearly lifelong memory recall for everyday events, is whether or not there is a continuously running surveillance tape, as it were, within each of us all of the time. And, if so, are there ways to access those hours and hours and years and years of stored data?

Why calendar calculating?

In April, 2009 the documentary about Flo and Kay, identical twin autistic savants, was broadcast in the United States on The Learning Channel. I could tell that because the next morning my email box was full of messages from parents, teachers and clinicians informing me about other persons, both children and adults, who are able "to calculate the day and date just like Flo and Kay." That happens almost every time some documentary on savants airs in the United States or elsewhere.

After many years of observing and researching savant syndrome, there are a number of questions that intrigue me. Many of those are in this book. But one question that continues to puzzle me especially, because it is so constant and so conspicuous, is this: since calendar calculating is such an infrequent and obscure skill in most of us, why does it occur so regularly, predictably and almost uniformly in savant syndrome, especially in persons in which autistic disorder is the underlying disability? By my informal count, based on how often I encounter it, calendar calculating is the most frequent of savant skills. Hermelin (2001) states: "calendar calculation is probably the most frequently observed ability in savants" (p.78). Leon Miller (1989) found more than twice as many reports of calendar calculators than of either musically or artistically gifted savants. Saloviita *et al.* (2000) found calendar calculating to be the most common of exceptional skills in their research in Finland.

Some things we do know. There is regularity to the calendar and persons with autism are drawn to such organized structure. Some savants rely on *memorization* of calendars, being drawn to their regularity and predictability. In other cases savants study the calendar and form unconscious algorithms that permit them to do *calculations* over a span of 40,000 years backward and forward such as Horwitz *et al.* (1965) described. As I point out in Chapter 1, the ability to do "reverse" calendar calculating goes well beyond memorization alone and requires the use of complex formulas, albeit unconsciously in many instances. Formulas do exist that any person, including neurotypicals, can learn and with practice if interested, use to perform at least simple calendar calculating.

There have been many investigators who have addressed the "How do they do it?" question regarding calendar calculating. Some say it is math; some say it is memory; most say it is both.

I summarize that research in a chapter on calendar calculating in *Extraordinary People* (1989, 2006a) and Hermelin (2001) addresses that question in her book as well. I would sum up my answer to that question by saying that *calendar calculating skill in savants is a combination of either deliberately learned formulas or unconsciously inculcated algorithms plus massive memory plus compulsive practice.* In 2009 a study comparing "calendar calculating in savants with autism and healthy calendar calculators" confirms that general impression (Dubischar-Krivec *et al.* 2008). Those researchers found that autistic calendar calculators (ACC) did rely on rote memory for some calculations, but neither rote memory nor practice alone, nor together, could fully account for that special ability in autistic calendar calculators. To deal with future dates particularly, the ACC group also incorporated some method of calculating "calendar regularities for all types of dates" (p.7). Healthy calendar calculators, in contrast, relied much more heavily on formulas that included calendar regularities and much less on rote memory.

Thioux *et al.* (2006) studied a calendar calculating savant and concluded that two conditions were necessary and sufficient to explain that ability: (a) the presence of circumscribed foci of interests with a predilection for repeating behaviors and (b) the relative preservation of parietal lobe learning activities.

The cognitive profile in the calendar calculator with autism and multiple skills reported by Wallace, Happe and Giedd (2009) was consistent with a combination of "good memory, mental calculation, visuospatial processing as well as (implicit) knowledge of calendar structure and 'weak' central coherence" (p.1425), all of which contributed to the calendar calculating ability. Interestingly, on MRI this subject showed thickening of the superior parietal area of the cortex compared to a neurotypical control group. However, it should be noted that this particular savant had multiple skills including impressive art ability.

Cowan and Frith (2009) carried out fMRI imaging on two calendar calculating savants and demonstrated increased parietal *activation* during both mental arithmetic and date questions, but no parietal *thickening* on imaging. There were no other brain abnormalities on the brain scans of these two individuals. The research team conclude that memory alone was not sufficient to explain calendar calculation in all savants. Instead, "at least some calendrical savants, and maybe all, can calculate the answers to date questions" (p.1419). They put forth the explanation that "calendrical skills observed in savants result from intensive practice with calculations used in solving mental arithmetic problems. The mystery is not how they solve these problems, but why" (p.1417).

And indeed for me that is also the basic question. Why, considering all the skills in the human repertoire, does calendar calculating occur as a seemingly incidental, but almost universal, innate, "factory-installed" ability in so many autistic savants as well as in some acquired savants? When I asked Flo how she knows all those days and dates, she replied simply, "I've got that chip in my head." Asked the same question, George replied, "I've got a good mind. That's how I do it. It's fantastic I can do that!"

The more severe the disability, the more this special ability appears to be innate or factory installed. Take the example that Roberts (1945) describes. When tested the patient was a 27-year-old male with a paralysis that allowed only a movement of the upper lip for a "yes" and a smile for a "no" in reply to questions. Total vocabulary was one word: "buh" for bottle. The paralysis and other disabilities followed severe encephalitis at age six months with massive brain damage evident on pneumoencephalogram. Using this vestigial "yes" and "no" system, Roberts (1945) was able to demonstrate that this patient could name the day of the week for dates from 1915 to 1945. The patient knew his own age and was oriented to time and place. Roberts noted that the patient always looked at the ceiling when considering his answer and he concluded that the mechanism in this patient was eidetic imagery based on this individual's positive response on a test for eidetic imagery compared to four control subjects, none of whom demonstrated eidetic imagery.

Contrary to that finding, however, was a case presented by Rubin and Monaghan (1965). In this instance the patient was a 16-year-old blind, female calendar calculator which would rule out eidetic imagery as the mechanism in this particular person. The calendar calculating ability was quite narrow, covering only eight years. According to the report, "As far as the authors could discover, no calendar in Braille was available to R so whatever practicing that she did must have been entirely according to her memory of different dates" (p.483). They go on to conclude that any one case with savant syndrome such as theirs "*involves the interaction of a multiplicity of factors*" (p.485; empasis mine). Then there are the cases of calendar calculating in acquired savants such as Orlando Serrell or an eight-year-old boy following left hemispherectomy for a seizure disorder (Dorman 1991), described in more detail in Chapter 20.

From my observations, particularly of severely cognitively disabled savants, Flo's explanation that she simply possesses the calendar calculating chip, whether math, memory, or both, comes closest to explaining this very conspicuous but constant skill in many savants. If so, where did that "chip" come from, and why is it there?

Hermelin (2001) provides an abbreviated account of the history of the calendar from early times to the present. Sometimes lunar, and sometimes solar, "the structuring of time has always been a human preoccupation. Such a preoccupation in its extreme form characterizes the calendar calculator" (p.78). Beyond timekeeping, the sun and sowing and reaping seasons were a matter of life and death, literally, in very early times. Later the sun and moon provided the template for calendar production, with some corrections and alterations along the way resulting in the adoption generally now of the Gregorian calendar in most parts of the world. As I pointed out in Chapter 4 on genetic memory, Butterworth (1999) suggests that some evidence points toward ancestral attention to lunar phases as early as 30,000 years ago.

Could it be that the calendar calculating "chip" is derived innately from the predictable and constant rhythm of the sun and moon passed on through generations via genetic memory? Far out? Perhaps. I am not suggesting anything mystical, transcendental or some sort of engulfing but invisible cosmos. I am simply suggesting that, as discussed in Chapter 4 on genetic memory, we all come with much more factory-installed software than is generally acknowledged. We do not start life with a blank disk, and along with many other things we inherit, we also inherit certain kinds of knowledge and/or templates such as math, music, art and language "chips." To explain the constancy of calendar calculating in savants, it appears to me that many savants, if not all, have inherited a built-in calendar calculating chip which somehow many of them can access. To explain the almost uniform ability to carry out that otherwise obscure skill in so many persons with savant syndrome, perhaps genetic memory needs to be added to the math and/or memory + unconscious algorithms + obsessive practice equation.

A recurrent musical triad: blindness, mental impairment and musical genius

In the 1983 *60 Minutes* program *Genius*, Morley Safer called savant syndrome a "marvelous mystery." But a mystery within that mystery is the question why, in the already rare condition of savant syndrome, does the triad of *blindness, mental impairment* and *musical genius*—an even more rare combination of circumstances—appear with such conspicuous regularity in the history and present-day accounts of savant syndrome?

Historical accounts mention a number of cases. Tredgold (1914) mentions Trelat's case at Salpêtrière, a French mental hospital, of a woman who was blind, with mental retardation and great musical talent.

> Her voice was very correct and whenever she had sung or heard some piece she knew perfectly well the words and the music. As long as she lived they came to her to correct the mistakes in singing of her companions; they asked her to

repeat a passage, which had gone wrong, which she always did admirably. One day, Geraldy, Liszt, and Meyerbeer came to the humble singing class of our asylum to bring her encouraging consolations. (p.339)

The remarkable story of Blind Tom is recounted in Chapter 6. Blind Tom was the most prominent and highly paid worldwide black entertainer of the 1800s. Leslie Lemke, Ellen Boudreaux and Tony DeBlois, also described in this book, fit into this rare, but regularly occurring, exclusive group as well. Derek Paravicini is another well-known musical savant whose story is told in the book *In the Key of Genius* (2007) written by his long-time music teacher Adam Ockelford, Professor of Music at the University of Roehampton. Ockelford has had a sustained interest in the association between visual impairments, learning difficulties and exceptional musical abilities and needs, so much so that he was instrumental in establishing Soundscape, a school and performing art center in London specifically for persons with this combination of abilities and disabilities.

Miller (1989) first observed Eddie at a day program for people with multiple disabilities, all of whom were legally blind. Intrigued by a "truly precocious musical performance for a 5-year-old," Miller (1989) followed Eddie for the next four and a half years and summed up his impressions of Eddie, and savant syndrome itself, in his very detailed book about both.

On August 5, 2003 Brittany Maier was introduced to the viewers of *Dateline* in a program titled *Playing by Ear*. She was age 16 at the time. Brittany was blind from birth, with very limited verbal skills, but she is an outstanding pianist and, particularly, a composer. Brittany has her own website and her mother has established the Brittany Maier and Friends Foundation, which has now opened up a Music and Arts Center on Long Island specifically dedicated to teaching persons with disabilities who are very talented musically.

Kodi Lee is now an adolescent but from age eight onward he has been prominently featured in some news accounts and documentaries because of his exceptional piano and vocal skills. Kodi is energetic and engaging. He plays with enthusiasm, skill and verve. His parents have also set up a foundation. I especially like their mission statement: "Helping children one note at a time."

Rex Lewis Clack has had the distinction of having been on *60 Minutes* on three occasions as that program tracked his progress following his first appearance on that program at age eight. In 2008 a book about Rex and his mother's dedications and efforts with him titled *Rex: A Mother, her Autistic Child, and the Music that Transformed their Lives* was published (Lewis 2008). Both Kodi and Rex have their own websites which tell much more about them and their success.

Wen Kuei, in Taiwan, unintentionally touched an organ keyboard at age 12 at the Huei-Ming School for Blind Children where he had been a resident since age seven, immediately sparking his musical interest and accomplishment. Now he plays multiple instruments with ease, and takes great pride in teaching his also-blind classmates musical skills. He especially likes to play the violin. A very impressive and inspiring educational documentary titled *Capturing Dreams in the Dark* tells the story of Wen Kuei's impressive musical ability and progress.

There are other such musical savants with this rare triad of abilities and disabilities in the United States and around the world that come to my attention through the savant syndrome website with a curious regularity. Others have also written about the over-representation of blind children among those savants where music is their special skill. Charness *et al.* (1988) in his review of sixteen musical savants found this combination of abilities and disabilities, including blindness, to be present in seven of those individuals. Further, to date there have been 11 books published as biographies (listed in the Appendix) devoted solely to the inspirational story of a particular savant. Six of the eleven books were about musical savants, and four of those six books were about musical savants where the triad of blindness, mental handicap and musical genius was present.

There are three causes of blindness that occur most often in musical savants: retinopathy of prematurity (ROP, which was previously known as retrolental fibroplasia); septo-optic dysplasia (SOD, which is often associated with optic nerve hypoplasia—ONH); and Leber congenital amaurosis (LCA).

Retinopathy of prematurity was first described by Terry (1942). It is almost always associated with premature birth in a process by which portions of the vascular bed of the retina that are still developing proliferate extensively and wildly, outgrowing blood supply and forming fibrous tissue which ultimately detaches the retina from the back of the eye. In some instances, such as Leslie Lemke, glaucoma can result, necessitating removal of the eyes. In 1951 a clear causal association was made between excess oxygen given to premature infants at that time and the incidence of ROP. The excess oxygen apparently contributed to the wild proliferation of the retinal vasculature and developing neurons (interestingly, the retina is brain tissue and is the only place in the body where the brain tissue can be directly visualized). I discuss this process in much more detail in Chapter 13 of *Extraordinary People* (1989, 2006a) raising the question, as others have as well, whether that same damaging vascular/neuronal process might be occurring elsewhere in the still developing, vulnerable areas of the brain in the premature infant, producing some of the neuropathological changes in autistic disorder (Keeler 1958; Rimland 1964).

Septic-optic dysplasia is a developmental disorder which can include optic nerve hypoplasia, pituitary abnormalities and the absence or malformation of the septum pellucidum and/or corpus callosum. Leber congenital amaurosis is an inherited eye disorder of the retina with nystagmus and poor pupillary response.

In his *Focus on Music* series, Ockelford and his colleagues from the Institute of Education, Goldsmith's College (University of London) and the Royal National Institute of Blind People are carrying out studies to assess the impact of severe visual impairment, and its various causes, on musical development including savant syndrome. The SOD study by Ockelford, Pring, Welch and Treffert was published in 2006 and the ROP study by Ockelford and Matawa was published in 2009. The LCA study is underway at present.

In those projects questionnaires were completed by parents and other principal caregivers using information gathered from physicians, psychologists, teachers, therapists and other professionals. The sample included 32 SOD cases, 37 ROP cases and 32 fully sighted subjects.

The project also included observations of a sample of such patients engaged in musical activities at school, home or elsewhere; musicological analysis of some interactive sessions with teachers and therapists; and interviews with a sample of parents, teachers and other professionals.

A key interest in music was reported in 88 percent of the children with SOD or ROP (no statistical difference between these two groups) and 38 percent of the comparison group. The importance of music in terms of stimulation, comfort, understanding, communication, socialization was much higher in the visually impaired group compared to the normally sighted. In terms of absolute pitch (AP), none of the fully or partially sighted subjects had that ability. By combining the *Focus on Music* subjects with other children with ROP known to Ockelford, a cohort of 52 children was established. Of those 52 children with ROP, 54 percent, had absolute pitch; 12 of the 52 had cognitive impairments in addition to visual impairment and in this group 6 (50%) had AP. In contrast, 19 subjects with SOD showed only 4 persons (21%) had AP. These studies show that a child's level of vision is likely to have an impact on developing musical interests, motivations and abilities. They also demonstrate that different syndromes affect musicality in different ways including the presence or absence of AP.

Finally, they show that (as in the case of musical savants, for example) learning difficulties are not necessarily a barrier to exceptional musical development and this finding may have potential consequences for understanding of how different intelligences function and interrelate.

A number of studies have shown a disproportionately high incidence of cognitive, behavioral and autistic disabilities in children with ROP (Treffert 2006a). Keeler (1958) pointed out the frequent occurrence of infantile autism in patients blinded from ROP and also raised the question whether some vascular capillary process similar to that which occurs in the retina might be occurring elsewhere in the brain leading to the characteristic autistic symptoms seen in this group.

But in considering the relationship of ROP to autism and other developmental disabilities, including mental retardation, one has to consider the impact of prematurity itself, in a non-specific sense, on the still developing fetus at the time of birth. Willams (1958) reported that the incidence of serious mental defect in premature children is between 4 and 10 percent compared to the incidence of such disabilities in as high as 10–40 percent of children with ROP.

It has been of interest to me how many prodigious savants living today were prematurely born in the 1950s and, like Leslie, were exposed to excess oxygen before the causal association between ROP and excess oxygen was made. After that discovery, the number of cases of ROP fell precipitously, and now oxygen levels are monitored very strictly in all newborn nurseries. But the expert care given in specialized neonatal units nowadays permits premature infants of extremely low birth weight to survive and for some of those infants oxygen is necessary for them to survive at all. Consequently informed consent decisions are being made by parents regarding the use of oxygen to support life in these babies, weighing carefully the risks and benefits in these very frail newborns, including the risk of ROP. Cases of blindness due to SOD continue to appear as well with some indications that the incidence of that disorder may be on the rise for whatever reason.

Present-day cases of children and adolescents with savant syndrome where this triad of blindness, disability and musical genius exist can have either ROP or SOD as the cause of the visual impairment. Exactly what the biological connection is between those specific causes of blindness, the underlying developmental disability and musical ability, especially at the prodigious level, remains to be worked out. While it remains in part a mystery, studies such as those of Ockelford provide a sizeable enough sample of a rare condition that investigations can move beyond single, anecdotal reports, extraordinary and interesting as those individual reports are.

A "choir" of cantors

While not related to savant syndrome (because of the absence of a disability), there is another group of individuals where advanced musical ability, blindness and massive memory are intertwined in a remarkable and consistent manner. Through some correspondence after my earlier book (Treffert 2006a), it was brought to my attention that the liturgical chant of the Coptic religion, with its origin in ancient Egypt, is a very melodius but difficult and highly intricate one. Typically the only persons able to memorize and master that complex ancient liturgy were specially appointed and trained cantors, almost all of whom were blind. Therefore, since they were not written out, these liturgical masterpieces were handed down only by memory for over 20 centuries by these special musicians.

In a lecture on "The ancient music of the Coptic Church" given at Oxford in 1931, Professor Ernest Newlandsmith points out:

> this Coptic music has never until now been committed to paper (but has been handed down orally all through the centuries). The memory of the blind musicians who sing it is so astounding that vast as the range of the music is the slightest error in its performance is at once detected. Such a feat of memory is

little less than a miracle for although purely melodic, some of the hymns are often so extremely complicated that they would completely baffle a first rate opera singer. Several of the larger hymns take as much as twenty minutes to sing, and frequently there are pages of music to a single syllable of a word. (Newlandsmith 1931, p.4)

Gillespie (1964) states:

The cantor, vitally important in this liturgical drama, not only knows all the music destined for the choir (congregation) but that of the celebrant and deacon as well. The cantor is literally the teacher of church music. Following an enduring tradition that dates from Pharaonic times, the Coptic cantor is customarily blind and all chants are therefore committed to memory. (p.16)

The cantors are trained at the Saint Didymus Institute for the Blind, a branch of the theological seminary of the Coptic church.

Later in the book I write about "normal" savants, neurotypical persons who have some savant-like skills and capacities. As such persons, these blind cantors, with their advanced musical and memory capacities, without disabilities, add an interesting dimension to the complex interrelationship between diminished vision and musical genius. If, as in the case of the prodigious musical savant, one adds disability to that mix of blindness, musical ability and massive memory, unraveling and understanding the mystery of the prodigious musical savant who is blind and mentally impaired becomes all the more interesting and challenging.

Foreign accent syndrome

Foreign accent syndrome (FAS) is a rare but dramatic condition in which persons, following head injury, stroke or other CNS disease, begin to speak with the foreign accent of a country they have never visited, or with a regional dialect decidedly different from that prior to the CNS incident. Some news reports go even further beyond "accent" to describe instances where a person suddenly is fluent, after injury, in an entirely new language, again from a country or part of the world he or she has never visited.

While reports on FAS began as early as 1919, a report by Monrad-Krohn (1947) has received considerable visibility. He describes the case of a 30-year-old woman who was struck by a bomb fragment in 1941 with severe left brain hemisphere damage which left her with an altered rhythm and melody to her speech suggesting a German accent. This woman had spent her whole life in Norway, never having visited any foreign country. Because of her German accent at a critical time in World War II, she was ostracized by her Norwegian community.

Garst and Katz (2006) report that "since that famous case approximately 40 individuals with FAS have been described in world literature. Reported accent changes include Japanese to Korean, British-English to French, American-English to British-English and even Spanish to Hungarian" (p.10). In the past several years examples of this relatively rare condition have come to prominence in the daily news, whether in print or on TV. On September 18, 2007, for example, the London *Evening Standard* newspaper carried an account of a nine-year-old boy from York who had severe meningitis with a brain abscess which required surgery. When this lad emerged from a coma he was unable to read or write and his memory was also affected. But when he did begin to speak, gone was his Yorkshire accent. It had been replaced by "the Queen's English." Speech has now returned to normal except for his new, persistent accent. That same article also refers to the case of a Czech racecar driver who was knocked unconscious in a speedway accident. The *Daily Mail* reported on September 14, 2007, that when he regained consciousness "although the 18-year-old Czech knew only the most basic English phrases, he was conversing fluently in the language with paramedics." After full recovery, however, that fluency disappeared to where now this fellow struggles "to make himself understood in English."

Nick Miller, Lowit and O'Sullivan (2006) report a case of a woman from Tyneside, Britain who spoke with an accent common to the region where she had lived her whole life. She did not have any extended visits to foreign countries, and had never learned a foreign language. At age 60 this woman had a subarachnoid hemorrhage from an aneurysm of the right anterior communicating artery. There was a period of "stuttering and slurred" speech but when that cleared the woman "spoke with a foreign accent generally heard as Italian or occasionally Eastern European" (p.388). Recovery was otherwise uneventful except for some mild memory defects both before and after the CNS hemorrhage. At follow-up four years later, speech, except for the new accent, was fluent and intelligible.

In 2008 a research group from McMaster University in Ontario, Canada (Naidoo *et al.*) published a case report of a 50-year-old woman who had lived her entire life in southern Ontario with her only trip out of the country being a vacation in Florida. She suffered a left hemisphere ischemic stroke. When her speech fully returned she had a "Newfoundland" accent, much to the surprise, and consternation, of her family and others who knew her.

Foreign accent syndrome is more dramatic when seen visually rather than when described verbally. A number of broadcast TV programs and documentaries have shown cases of FAS "live and in color." A number of those have then been posted on YouTube. They are dramatic and they are convincing. Perhaps it is these graphic documentations that account for the heightened interest currently in this otherwise rather obscure and rare condition.

The speech and language scientific literature, including the articles above, generally conclude that foreign accent syndrome can be explained by changes in the prosody of language—the rhythm, stress and intonation of speech, especially involving vowel production, pitch and stressing of certain syllables. The *Journal of Neurolinguistics* (Gurder and Coleman 2006) devoted almost an entire issue to FAS. It provides a good summary of the present-day science of that condition.

What does foreign accent syndrome have to do with savant syndrome? FAS is important in the context of this book because, while not a savant skill as such, the sudden onset of a new ability following CNS injury is similar to the unexpected emergence of music or art ability, for example, in the acquired savant. It also touches on the phenomenon of genetic memory. Some have proceeded much further afield than that (too far for me), invoking reincarnation or a paranormal phenomenon of some sort for FAS, especially in those cases where the person suddenly not only appears to have a foreign accent, but also is fluent in the alternative, newly surfaced language. There is even a name for the latter—xenoglossy—written about quite extensively by Stevenson (1974) using hypnosis to demonstrate some of his cases.

I include FAS in these "medical mysteries" because it may be that the speech and language specialists are correct in that what is perceived as a foreign accent, is in fact simply the residual effect of damage to the language areas of the brain producing certain speech structure and prosody changes that sound like a foreign accent. And yet, some of the clips I have seen show the person using whole new terms in the newly acquired accent ("pretty frock" instead of "party dress" for example) which extend beyond pitch, rhythm and stressing of syllables. I confess I am not expert in this area, but could it be that some of these cases involve tapping "genetic memory" from a prior relative fluent in another language, either from living elsewhere or language study? I am not suggesting reincarnation or anything mystical or magical. Nor am I suggesting that there is a universal language "out there" in space or else residing within all of us. I am suggesting simply that the scientific phenomenon of genetic memory, accomplished through epigenetics as described elsewhere in this book, might be a consideration in some of these cases. That notion at least deserves some further inquiry.

Autobiographical memory: a continuous tape within us all?

Brad Williams is a radio reporter for station WIZM-AM in La Crosse, Wisconsin. Several years ago he learned about a woman in California who was being studied by researchers at the University of California-Irvine with a condition they had named "hyperthymestic syndrome"—exceptional autobiographical memory for everyday events. Brad and his family then realized that Brad's unusual recall which had for years startled them, but just was taken for granted by Brad, was in fact a very rare condition and not "just Brad." Brad is now one of the seven persons worldwide who meet the criteria of that California group for hyperthymestic syndrome or "unusual autobiographical remembering" (Parker, Cahill and McGaugh 2006).

Brad Williams has a diary-like recall of ordinary, daily events that most everyone else would have discarded or relegated to memory storage not ordinarily accessible. Except for memories before age five, or days that were singularly uneventful, Brad can, according to his brother Eric, "within reason, remember what happened every day of his life." Eric has been videotaping his brother's unusual memory skills for a number of years and has now completed a film, *Unforgettable*, documenting his brother's special ability. A huge collection of family photos and other trivia saved through the years is available to verify the accuracy of Brad's memory for his individual life or family events, and of course there are ample reference sources to provide the correct dates for comparison to Brad's recall of the dates of historical events. Give Brad a date, and he can usually tell you what happened on that day in his daily life, and if significant, what happened on that day in history. In short, he can recall both the trivial and the monumental.

Brad is not a savant; he has no disability. He lives a very normal life, loves radio broadcasting and is the pronouncer for the Wisconsin State Spelling Bee each year. He has no explanation for how he manages to have this massive recall with such clarity. It is "just there" and has always been a part of him. He can recall events on demand. The memories are not intrusive nor a burden. I had the opportunity to meet and quiz Brad as part of the filming of the documentary on him and his performance was indeed impressive.

The idea that his memory was exceptional first occurred to him in eighth grade, when he was 12 years old. There was a "memory expert" at school that day who asked for some volunteers. The expert had written a 12-digit number on the blackboard and asked the students to memorize it. He then asked Brad to turn his back to the blackboard and say out loud *every other number* from *back to front* of that memorized line of numbers. Brad did so easily and the memory expert said that was the first time anyone had been able to do that. Brad's actual memories of everyday life, though, began much earlier. He remembers lighting a match from a matchbook while sitting on the couch when he was two years old, alone in the living room. And he remembers his mother coming in from the kitchen at that very moment to see what he was doing.

I quizzed Brad about the date of certain historical events, such as the Pan Am flight 103 crash. He remembers that was December 21, 1988 and he was bowling that night. He indicated the last episode of *Cheers* was on a Thursday, May 20, 1993 and the first episode was on September 30, 1982. As I recited many dates, he gave the significance of that date along with his activities. Given some random dates with no particular historical events involved, he was able to tell where he was and what he was doing that day. May 2, 1982, however, was a "blank" day with no particular historical or personal significance. Brad can calendar calculate, which was a skill he learned in one of his college classes. He bases his calculations on the fact that the calendar repeats itself every 28 years.

At the present time Brad is one of seven persons actively involved as a subject in the neuropsychologic and imaging studies on hyperthymestic syndrome at UC-Irvine. While none of those seven persons has savant syndrome, autobiographical memory, sometimes at a spectacular level, does occur in persons with savant syndrome. When quizzed, Flo and Kay remember, for example, that they had pork chops, mixed vegetables and a baked potato on January 10, 1994 and that the weather on March 13, 1993 produced the "no-name storm". They also remember that the *$10,000 Dollar Pyramid* TV program with Dick Clark, their hero, began its tenure on ABC Television on May 6, 1974. They remember the questions and answers for that first show and most of the programs that followed. They remember what Dick Clark was wearing that day, and each program thereafter. The accuracy of that recall can be checked because they have charted Mr. Clark's wardrobe for each program in a diary they meticulously maintain.

George also remembers the weather for each day of his adult life. Orlando Serrell, when tested by researchers at the National Institute of Mental Health (NIMH) in Bethesda, Maryland, was able to remember what he was doing, what he had to eat, and what he was wearing for many days *since* his accident. The fact that autobiographical memory can be "acquired" is particularly intriguing, particularly since it apparently only then involves memories going forward, and not retrospectively.

What makes Brad William's autobiographical memory especially significant is that it exists with no disability, or trade-off, for that particular skill. And if such memory can exist in Brad and others without CNS deficit, is it possible such autobiographical memory might exist in everyone as a continuous, effortless, surveillance-camera type recording stored somewhere in our brain, but with access generally limited because it is overshadowed by stored-with-effort semantic/cognitive memory "tagged" with some particular factual or emotional significance?

Several findings point toward that possibility. First, the noted neurosurgeon Wilder Penfield (1978) would probe the cortex of awake patients in search of epileptigenic foci which could then be surgically removed. He could do that with only the dura mater under local anesthetic and the cortex exposed because the brain itself has no pain fibers. When the probe was put on the parietal area, there would be muscle movement in a limb or other area of the body. When the occipital lobe was probed, the patient would describe flashes of light. When the probe was put on certain areas of the temporal cortex, however, extremely detailed and often emotionally laden memories would come flooding forth. Some patients relived vivid scenes from the past, including sights, sounds, smells and other sensations associated with those memories. Others heard specific pieces of music in exact detail. These were memories not accessible in the usual fashion, not just as a snapshot, but as if the patient were actually there. Penfield (1978) concludes from his work that the brain contains a permanent record of everything we experience, stored in the brain like a gigantic videotape containing a lifetime of recorded, but generally dormant memories.

Second, more recently Hamani *et al.* (2008) were using deep hypothalamic brain stimulation to treat a patient with morbid obesity. They observed that "quite unexpectedly that stimulation evoked detailed autobiographical memories" (p.119) which they describe in the article. EEG localization showed the deep hypothalamic stimulation in this patient "drove activity in mesial temporal lobe structures. This shows that hypothalamic stimulation in this patient modulates limbic activity and improves certain memory functions" (p.119).

Third, my work with sodium amytal interviews with some patients likewise produces a flood of buried, but vivid, memories when under the influence of the drug; once awake the patients have little recall of what they had "remembered" in the amytal interview. Often, however, when they are fully awake and I tell them which memories did surface, such a verbal reminder does "jog" their awake memory. Then they do recall, to their astonishment, things they thought they had truly forgotten. The amytal somehow released those otherwise buried memories.

Fourth, an experience with a patient whom I first met in 1962 provided me with some insight into my own quite routine, but very distant memories. The patient was the first savant I ever met. He had memorized the bus system of the city of Milwaukee. We recently met for lunch, as described in Chapter 29. He remembered each of the patients who were his peers on that unit, often recalling admission dates, birthdays, and other things about each of them. As he recited their names, surprisingly, I could remember them also—my mind having been "jogged" by my former patient. Then he reminisced about the staff on the unit. I could remember, and see, most of them in my mind as well. If you had asked me, before this encounter, to name the children and the staff on that original unit I simply would not have been able to do so. Yet, those names and faces were stored somewhere in my memory. It took some sort of tickler-file "tag" to get to them. There is nothing particularly remarkable about my performance in that regard. We all have had times when we have gotten together, at a class reunion perhaps, where various people remind us of things past and, sure enough, then we "remember." It's just that our record filing system and "tagging" function varies from person to person. But the fact that those memories can be resurrected with some "tickler" is simply a powerful reminder that they reside there, probably permanently.

Fifth, our dreams tell us that certain memories, sometimes significant and sometimes trivial, lie dormant until they surface, often to our surprise, in sleep. We have all had the "Where did that come from?" experience when we recollect a particular dream we happen to remember the next morning. Often there is a time-warp of events in those dreams with a surreal and unlikely morphing together of memories from different life stages. But the snapshots of memory themselves are accurate, whatever the order, though they are usually fleeting. Those memories, too, draw on an existent, but submerged, memory bank.

So is there a continuous surveillance camera-like record in our head of all our life experiences? Some of the above points in that direction. How complete that record is remains to be seen. But, as you will see later, there is no doubt ample storage space for that to be the case.

At this time there is no way to "transfer" whatever knowledge, wisdom and memories exist between persons directly like one might copy an encoded DVD to a blank disk using electronic or any other method. It's been said that when an old person dies it is as if a library just burned down. Gone are all the collective knowledge, wisdom and recollections of that person. Will there ever be a method to somehow transfer knowledge or memories *directly* between persons, other than verbally or visually, in some futuristic yet to be discovered electronic or science fiction fashion? I doubt it. But I did have the fantasy in medical school of somehow being able to funnel *Gray's Anatomy* directly into my brain by some sort of osmosis without the laborious learning and memorizing work entailed. But even if we were able to do that, would it be a good idea? What if someone other than myself was deciding which ideas and which information to infuse into my mind? I'll leave those scientific discoveries and ethical dilemmas to someone else. Meanwhile, I will continue to marvel at the miraculous power of memory, even forgiving the moments that memory fails me.

Extensive autobiographical memory seen in hyperthymestic syndrome, and some savants, coupled with the surfacing of such buried memories in all of us from time to time as outlined above, raises the question whether or not, as Penfield (1978) suggests, there is a continuous tape of all our life experiences within the brain's tremendous memory capacity. Like a huge library with a poor catalog filing system, our memories do appear to be stored there. What is lacking, it seems, is an adequate and readily available retrieval system.

PART TWO

The World of
the Savant

CHAPTER 6

The Genius of Earlswood Asylum and Blind Tom: Some Early Savants

Savant syndrome did not begin with Dr. Down's naming the condition in 1887. No doubt there have been savants, perhaps unrecognized or unheralded, for as long as autism and other developmental disabilities have existed. But the first formal account of savant syndrome to appear in the scientific literature was in the German empirical psychology journal *Gnothi Sauton* in 1783 where an entry documented the case of a remarkable lightning calculator, Jedediah Buxton, who lived in England from 1702 to 1772.

Jedediah Buxton had no formal education and was unable to write his name. He was described as having the mind "of a boy ten years old." He was once asked: "In a body whose three sides are 23,145,789 yards, 5,642,732 and 54,965 yards, how many ⅛ inches exist?" He gave the correct 28-digit answer five hours later and could recite it backwards or forwards. Asked how many times a coach wheel six yards in circumference would revolve when traveling the 204 miles from York to London, he gave the correct answer—59,840 times; it took him 13 minutes to reach that answer. Given a question of how many barleycorns would be required to reach eight miles, his answer of 1,520,640 assumes three barleycorns to the inch. Steven Smith, in his book *The Great Mental Calculators* (1983), describes Buxton and other "calculating prodigies" in colorful detail.

In 1789, Dr. Benjamin Rush, the "father" of American psychiatry (and also a signer of the Declaration of Independence), reported the case of Thomas Fuller "of such limited intelligence who would comprehend scarcely anything, either theoretical or practical, more complex than counting" (Rush 1789, p.62). However, when

Fuller was asked how many seconds a man had lived who was 70 years, 17 days and 12 hours old, he gave the correct answer of 2,210,500,800 in 90 seconds, correcting for the 17 leap years included.

Fuller's fascination with numbers began when he learned to count to 100, and he counted the hairs in a cow's tail: 2,872. Asked if a farmer had six sows and each sow has six female pigs the first year, and they all increase in the same proportion for eight years, how many sows would the farmer have then, Fuller gave the correct answer, 34,588,806, in ten minutes. Most of his counting was related to his work as a farm hand, such as counting the grains in a bushel of wheat or flax. Yet he could also do nine-digit multiplication and many other complex computations.

In 1887, Dr. J. Langdon Down gave a series of lectures in London reflecting on his 30-year career as a physician at the Earlswood Asylum. It was in those lectures, as mentioned earlier, that Down first described the ten cases that had especially captured his attention because of the remarkable juxtaposition of extraordinary ability and sometimes profound disability in the same person. It was in those lectures that he coined the now regrettable term, "idiot savant."

Following Down's description of savant syndrome, some other clinicians reported cases they had seen along the way in their careers. Dr. Arthur Tredgold (1914) devotes an entire chapter to savant syndrome in his textbook *Mental Deficiency (Amentia)*. In that very comprehensive, classic chapter, Tredgold describes many new cases of savant syndrome and makes some observations that have endured to this day. For example, he noted that the special skills in savants narrowed to only certain specific areas: increased sensory sensitivity to touch, smell, hearing or sight; drawing; pronounced sense of locality; music; and extraordinary capacity for arithmetic and calculations. He noted "phenomenal memory" as an integral part of the special abilities in these extraordinary persons. While most of his cases displayed art, music and mathematical abilities, he also documented one case of a polyglot, or language savant, a skill he called "the gift of tongues."

While there are exceptions, in general these areas of special skill and expertise are those noted in almost all savants to this day: art, music, lightning and calendar calculating and spatial skills, all combined with massive memory. Tredgold's comprehensive and colorful chapter on savants has been included in many of the newer editions of his textbook, which is still available to this day. That chapter continues to be included because it is so pioneering, and enduring, at the same time.

There is not room in this book to summarize all those early cases. But two such savants do deserve special description here because of their notoriety and fame in their time—James Pullen: The Genius of Earlswood Asylum, and Thomas Greene Bethune, most often referred to as Blind Tom.

The Genius of Earlswood Asylum: James Henry Pullen

One of the earliest documented, and most colorful, savants was James Henry Pullen, who came to be known as the Genius of Earlswood Asylum. Pullen spent 66 years of his life at Earlswood, near London, from age 13 until his death in 1916. During that time, because of his marvelous mechanical and drawing abilities, he became a national celebrity and his abilities are extensively documented by a number of observers of that time including Drs. Sequin (1866), Tredgold (1914) and Sano (1918). Even King Edward VII, when Prince of Wales, took a tremendous interest in this remarkable man and sent him tusks of ivory to encourage him in producing beautiful carvings. An article by Breathnach and Ward (2005) provides a very comprehensive account of Pullen's abilities and his disabilities.

James Henry Pullen was born in 1836, one of thirteen children, only three of whom survived to adult life. His brother William was also cared for in an institution and, interestingly, also had exceptional artistic skills. Pullen was deaf and nearly mute, combining primitive speech with sign language. At age five or six he was impressed by the small ships that his playmates tried to maneuver on narrow puddles in Dalston, his birthplace, and he became obsessed with making such toys. He became skilled in carving ships and reproducing them in penciled drawings. Until he was age seven he spoke only one word, "muvver." He later learned some monosyllabic words.

At age 14 he entered Essex Hall in Colchester, a forerunner of the Royal Earlswood institution. Essex Hall was a facility for people with learning disabilities. It was there, apparently, that Pullen's artistic talent emerged. At age 15 he was transferred to the Earlswood Asylum where he was described as "unable to give any intelligible answer, unless he could accompany his broken words by gestures." Dr. J. Langdon Down was the medical superintendent there.

At Earlswood, Pullen developed skills as a carpenter and cabinet maker, becoming a tremendous craftsman. He would work constantly in his workshop from morning until night, then, later still in the evening, would do drawings in dark, colored chalk. Dr. Sequin describes those drawings as

> most meritorious, and many of them, framed and glazed by himself, adorn the corridor and other parts of the asylum. One was graciously approved and accepted by the Queen [Victoria], who was kindly pleased to send the artist a present. And Mr. Sidney had the honor of showing some of them to the Prince Consort, no common judge of art, who expressed the greatest surprise that one so gifted was still to be kept in the category of idiots, or ever had been one. His Royal Highness was particularly astonished, not only by his copies of first rate engravings, but by an imaginary drawing made by him of the Siege of Sebastopol, partly from the illustrated London News and partly from his own ideas. (Sequin 1866, p.422)

Because of his expert craftsmanship, Pullen was given two workshops, and freedom to pursue his talents. Those two workshops became museums of his art for many years after his death. Royal Earlswood closed in 1997. The museum artifacts mostly went into storage, but some are now on display in showcases in a shopping centre in Redhill. A Royal Earlswood Museum Committee does still exist, and all paper records are held at the Surrey History Centre in Woking, Surrey.

Several of Pullen's model ships achieved particular fame. His Man-of-War was exhibited at the Fisheries Exhibition in 1864. It required a four-wheel trolley to move it and contained 42 brass cannons and 200 working pulleys to hoist sails. Pullen made all the parts himself, including a copper bottom, after designing the boat from a picture on a pocket-handkerchief. He included ivory from tusks donated by Edward, Prince of Wales, and, according to newspaper accounts, the bottle hanging from the side was the original one used in the launch.

But his greatest masterpiece was the *The Great Eastern*, a model ship for which Pullen fashioned every screw, pulley, anchor and paddle from drawings he made beforehand. The planks were attached to the ribs by wooden pins that numbered over one million. The model was 10 feet long, contained 5,585 rivets and had 13 lifeboats hoisted on complete davits. State cabins were complete with chairs, bunks, tables and decorations. The ship was constructed so that the entire deck could be raised to view the intricate detail below. Pullen spent seven years completing this complicated ship, and it attracted worldwide attention when exhibited at the prestigious Fisheries Exhibition in 1883 in England, where it won the first prize medal.

Dr. Sequin described Pullen, at age 19, as alternately wild and sullen. He never learned to read or write. As he grew older, Pullen was usually quiet and reserved, but there was another side to him as well. He was intolerant of advice, suspicious of strangers and, at times, ill tempered and violent. He once wrecked his workshop in a fit of anger, and, another time, erected a guillotine-like instrument over a door, hoping a staff member he particularly disliked might come through. He both impressed and frightened people with a giant mannequin in the center of his workshop, inside of which he would sit, directing movements of its arms and legs and talking through a concealed bugle fitted to its mouth. Pullen was remarkably sensitive to vibrations coming through the ground and devised an alarm system in his workshop, based on that sensitivity, which made him aware of any approaching visitor.

At one point I had seen a picture of Pullen dressed as a Navy admiral. I wondered how that had come about. Breathnach and Ward (2005) provide some insight in their article. Pullen had very limited social skills but he did join in some group activities, including playing drum in the Earlswood band, showing considerable inherent rhythm.

> He was free to come and go and he drank at a local inn. At the age of 28 he wished to marry a casual drinking acquaintance but the hospital board found him willing to accept, instead, a fictitious rank of navy admiral, supported by no more circumstantial evidence than a fictitious certificate and the gift of a resplendent admiral's uniform. (p.153)

Mystery solved. Dr. Tredgold (1914) sums up Pullen this way:

> His powers of observation, comparison, attention, memory, will and pertinacity are extraordinary; and yet he is obviously too childish, and at the same time too emotional, unstable, and lacking in mental balance to make any headway, or even hold his own, in the outside world. Without someone to stage-manage him, his remarkable gifts would never suffice to supply him with the necessities of life, or even if they did, he would easily succumb to his utter want for ordinary prudence and foresight and his defect of common sense. In spite of his delicacy of manipulation, he has never learned to read or write beyond the simplest words of one syllable. He can understand little of what is said to him by lip reading, and more by signs, but, beyond a few words, nearly all that he says in reply is absolutely unintelligible. (p.344)

The three doctors who knew Pullen best had differing ideas about Pullen's basic *dis*ability (they all agreed on his extraordinary *a*bilities). Dr. Tredgold concluded that Pullen had a "primary dementia accompanied by a defect in the central organ of hearing" (p.345). Dr. Sequin summed it up this way: "In short, he has seemingly just missed, by defect of some faculties, and the want of equilibrium in those he possesses, being a distinguished genius" (p.442). Dr. Sano concluded that if Pullen has simply been affected by sensory depriviation like Helen Keller, "deprived of sight and hearing, and yet able to acquire every kind of knowledge that enobles human understanding" (p.253), Pullen should have been able to advance much further, given the attention and notoriety he had experienced because of his tremendous skill as a craftsman. Instead, Dr. Sano points out:

> Pullen with both of his eyes wide open to the bright world of London, and his skilled ten fingers under complete sense control... could not absorb, digest or exteriorize the most ordinary sentence of politeness. To say, "I am very much obliged to you" was strange to him in grammatical arrangement as well as in social meaning. (Sano 1918, p.253)

Dr. Sano carried his analysis of the case of Pullen one step further. For him, the case did not end with Pullen's death. Writing in the *Journal of Mental Science* in 1918, Sano not only gives his view of Pullen's life, but also provides an exhaustive description of a postmortem examination of Pullen's brain. The brain showed only arteriosclerosis, not unusual at Pullen's age. There was a slightly larger than normal corpus callosum (the mass of fibers connecting the cerebral hemispheres) and a good preservation of the occipital lobes (the visual center of the brain). From this particular prominent connection between the occipital lobes and the cerebral hemispheres, Sano concludes that those pathways were "bound to have special capacity in the visual sphere of mental existence" (p.267). There was some lack of cerebral development which, Dr. Sano felt, was consistent with the mental retardation present. But while Sano (1918) did find such evidence to explain the retardation, he went on to say that any further explanation of Pullen's "character" was "not only to be found in his convolutions" (p.267).

Breathnach and Ward (2005) also pay close attention to postmortem brain findings, correlating some of Pullen's strengths and deficiencies with more modern-day knowledge about brain architecture and abilities. In summary they conclude:

> Newer methods of brain analysis are gradually adding to our enlightenment about pervasive developmental disorders and we are better informed when we come to consider with the gift of hindsight the enigma of patients like James Henry Pullen. His highly idiosyncratic artistic and technical skills combined with an explosive temper and difficulty in making social relationships indicate that he suffered from a pervasive developmental disorder and it is likely that he was an autistic savant. (p.155)

Dr. Sano, a century earlier, sums up his puzzlement and awe of Pullen by quoting Carlyle's *Hero Worship* to capture the magic and mystery of the savant:

Science had done much for us, but it is a poor science that would hide from us the deep sacred infinitude of nescience, whither we can never penetrate, on which all science swims as a mere superficial film. The world, after all our science and sciences, is still a miracle—wonderful, inscrutable, magique, and more, whosoever will think of it. (p.267)

Those words—"wonderful, inscrutable, magique and more"—do describe James Henry Pullen. Like the other savants before and after him, Pullen was a paradox of ability and disability. He captured the interest of kings, doctors and the public. He was proud, even boastful, but with good reason given his prodigious ability. He capitalized on that ability with tremendous motivation and became the recipient of equally tremendous reinforcement. He was original, one of a kind, not soon to be duplicated.

It is a tribute to his skill that in spite of relative obscurity in an institution, he won worldwide recognition.

Thomas Bethune—"Blind Tom"—A Marvelous Musician

BLIND TOM.
vright 1880, by John G. Bethune.

Thomas Bethune has been referred to as "Blind Tom" through the years, ever since he was an internationally recognized musical savant around the time of the American Civil War. He was considered at that time to be the greatest musical prodigy of the age. In fact he became the most celebrated black concert artist of the nineteenth century. Only recently, however, has his story and fame been resurrected and more widely disseminated. Tom, like Leslie Lemke exactly a century later, was blind and mentally handicapped, yet possessed an incredible musical genius that exploded on the scene early in life and then developed into an international presence and reputation. Based on the extensive descriptive accounts from various texts, periodical and newspaper accounts, one can conclude that Blind Tom was indeed a prodigious musical savant. At age 11 Tom played at the White House, and he launched a world tour at age 16. His vocabulary, according to Dr. Edward Sequin, who observed and then described Tom in his 1866 textbook on mental deficiency, was less than 100 words but his musical repertoire was over 7000 pieces. In Philadelphia, a panel of 16 outstanding musicians of that day signed this statement about Blind Tom:

> Whether in his improvisations of performances of compositions by Gottschalk, Verdi, and others, in fact in every form of musical examination—and the experiments are too numerous to mention—he showed a capacity ranking him among the most wonderful phenomena in musical history. (Southall 1999, p.8)

The story of this remarkable musical savant begins at a slave auction in 1850 when his mother, Charity Wiggins, was sold as a slave to General James N. Bethune, a prominent lawyer in Columbus, Georgia. Her twelfth (or some accounts say fourteenth) child, born in 1849, was included in the sale "for nothing" because he was completely blind and was thought, therefore, to be of no value. His new master named him Thomas Greene Bethune. On the general's Georgia plantation, Tom was allowed to roam the rooms of the mansion. He loved nature and was fascinated with sounds of all types—rain on the roof, the grating of corn in the sheller, but most of all music. Tom would listen intensely to the general's daughters practicing their sonatas and minuets on the piano. Sequin (1866) noted:

> Till 5 or 6 years old he could not speak, scarce walk, and gave no other signs of intelligence than this everlasting thirst for music, but at 4 years already, if taken out from the corner where he lay dejected, and seated at the piano, he would play beautiful tunes; his little hands having already taken possession of the keys, and his wonderful ear of any combination of notes they had once heard. (p.405)

There are several versions of the sudden discovery of Tom's musical talent. According to the family's account, one day when the Bethunes had company, one of the daughters entertained them by playing the piano. As she finished playing a difficult selection, lunch was served. After the group sat down to the table, the strains that the Bethune daughter had finished a few minutes earlier came from the supposedly empty parlor. The group rushed in to find the little blind boy, Tom, playing the piano, repeating the difficult piece he had just heard. Another version tells that before Tom was four, the Bethunes were aroused from sleep one night by the repetition of piano pieces that the daughters had played earlier in the day. Early in infancy Tom was fascinated and responsive to all sounds, musical and otherwise, which he reproduced even before he could speak and could sing harmony to anything the family would sing (these were all traits and skills of Leslie Lemke as well).

Like any slave child, Tom never attended school, and seemed incapable of learning in other areas. He was restless, explosive and required constant supervision. He seemed irresistibly drawn to the piano and without instruction whatsoever could listen to a piece of music and play it through note for note, accent for accent, without error and without interruption (just as Leslie Lemke does). At age five, Tom composed a song he called "The Rainstorm" based on experiencing a thunderstorm that day. Since Tom was able to repeat complex pieces after a single hearing, General Bethune hired professional musicians to play for the child and thus, by simply listening and faithfully reproducing what was just heard, an instant repertoire of concert quality was created.

Word of this "blind genius" spread, and in 1857, at age eight, Tom gave his first concert in Columbus, Georgia. It was a sellout, and the newspapers' reports were enthusiastic, so General Bethune and young Tom took to the road on a concert tour, performing almost daily. Tom is said to have earned as much as $100,000 in the first year of giving concerts.

Every note of every piece Tom heard (just as Leslie) was indelibly imprinted on his mind, and he was able to reproduce any piece from beginning to end without a moment's hesitation. His repertoire included Beethoven, Mendelssohn, Bach, Chopin, Verdi, Rossini, Donizetti, Meyerbeer and many others. One newspaper account lists his repertoire of over 7000 pieces and another reported that his memory was so accurate that he could repeat, without the loss of a syllable, a discourse of 15 minutes' length, of which he seemingly did not understand a word. Likewise, it was reported, he would sing songs in French or German, after a single hearing, not only rendering them in whatever language he heard them, but also repeating with precision the notes, style and expression. In addition to this phenomenal memory, Tom usually introduced himself and his pieces in the third person, a phenomenon often seen in savant syndrome where autism is the underlying disorder. Detailed descriptions of his concert stage behavior, such as those provided by Sequin (1866) and many others, are also characteristic of savant syndrome.

At age 11, in 1860, Tom played at the White House before President James Buchanan. Several musicians, who felt that Tom had tricked the public and the president, tested him at his hotel the following day. They played two completely new compositions. The first, 13 pages in length, Tom repeated from beginning to end without effort or error, and the second, 20 pages in length, he also played to perfection.

In her book *Blind Tom: The Black Pianist-Composer* Southall (1999) provides a year by year, almost concert by concert account of Tom's early performances in his teen years. Barbara Schmidt (www.twainquotes.com/archangels.html) also provides one such description:

> Not only could Tom perform world classics, he would astound his audiences by turning his back to the piano and give an exact replication—a reversal of the keys the left and right hand played. Musicians in the audience were invited to challenge Tom to a musical duet. Tom could successfully reproduce on the keyboard any piece of music a challenger would perform. And taking that feat one step further—Tom could play a perfect bass accompaniment to the treble played by someone seated behind him—heard for the first time as he played it. Tom would often push the other performer aside and repeat the entire composition alone.

In 1866 Tom began his European tour. At one concert, Tom listened to two pianos hammered noisily and simultaneously while a run of 20 notes was played on a third piano. Tom's ability to distinguish and reproduce those 20 notes flawlessly appeared to prove his absolute pitch capacity. There were always challenge portions of his concerts (just as with Leslie) where audience members would play pieces Tom had never heard before to see if he could reproduce them accurately, and of course he always did. One such challenge at a Macon Opera House concert is described by a piano teacher who played a "novel selection for the left hand with my right hand behind me." She assumed Tom, being blind, would "imitate me with both hands according to the piece." Tom instead "paralyzed us by playing it with his right hand behind him" (Kyle 1978). To this day I am wondering why Blind Tom put his right hand behind him." At his concerts another favorite feat of his was carrying three different tunes at the same time—playing "Yankee Doodle" in B flat with his right hand, "Fisher's Hornpipe" in C with his left, all the while singing "Early in the Morning."

Following the European tour, Tom again played to capacity audiences in the United States and there are many newspaper accounts of his concerts available as well as concert programs and posters announcing his appearances. A more detailed description of some of these concerts appears in Chapter 2 in *Extraordinary People* (Treffert 2006a). A piece in the *New York Times* (Sunday, March 5, 2000) recounts in detail some of the later years in Tom's life and the considerable Bethune family turmoil, much of it settled in rather heated court battles, over Tom's care and concert proceeds after the death of General Bethune. One report estimates Tom had earned over $750,000 for the Bethune family. After the death of General Bethune, the care of Tom was transferred to General Bethune's son John. After John's death in 1883, except for a brief series of concerts in New York in 1904, Tom spent the last 20 years of his life in semi-retirement until his death on June 13, 1908 in Hoboken, New Jersey. He was buried in Evergreen Cemetery in Brooklyn, but a commemorative headstone was raised for him in 1976 in his native town, Columbus, Georgia.

Now, almost a century later, the New York pianist John Davis has professionally recorded 14 of Blind Tom's original compositions on a CD entitled *John Davis Plays Blind Tom* (Newport Classics NPD85660). It was released in 2000 and I am listening to that remarkable collection of pieces as I write this note about Tom. Included are three gallops, a waltz, a polka, two marches and a nocturne. Also included are "The Rainstorm," composed by Tom when he was five years old (reminiscent of Leslie's "Bird Song"), and "The Battle of Manassas," Tom's most famous piece, reconstructing an eyewitness's account of that Confederate battle complete with notes to imitate cannon shots, troop train whistles and other battle sounds. John Davis states that this piece "is one of the great battle pieces of any period." The preamble to the original score has these sections and notations:

> Southern Army leaving home to their favourite tune of "The Girl I Left Behind Me"... the Grand Union Army leaving Washington city to the tune of 'Dixie'... the eve of battle by a very soft melody, then the clatter of arms and accoutrements, the war trumpet of Beauregard ... and then McDowell's in the distance, like an echo of the first ... the firing of cannon to "Yankee Doodle," "Marseillaise Hymn," "Star Spangled Banner," "Dixie" and the arrival of the train cars containing Gen. Kirby Smith's reinforcements ... the fighting will grow more severe and then the retreat.

Mark Twain was intrigued with Blind Tom and frequently, whenever he could, attended many of Tom's performances. A particularly good summary of Blind Tom, with many pictures with links to much more material on Blind Tom, can be found at www.twainquotes.com/archangels.html. There Mark Twain describes Tom thus:

> He lorded it over the emotions of his audience like an autocrat. He swept them like a storm, with his battle-pieces; he lulled them to rest again with melodies as tender as those we hear in dreams; he gladdened them with others that rippled through the charmed air as happily and cheerily as the riot linnets make in California woods; and now and then he threw in queer imitations of the tuning of discordant harps and fiddles, and the groaning and wheezing of bag pipes, that sent the rapt silence into tempests of laughter. And every time the audience applauded, when a piece was finished, this happy, innocent joined in and clapped his hands, too, with vigorous emphasis. (Twain 1869)

Twain called Tom an "archangel."

After Tom's death, noted Kentucky newspaper editor Henry Watterson wrote a touching tribute also quoted on the above website: "What was he? Whence came he, and wherefore? That there was a soul there, be sure, imprisoned, chained in that little black bosom, released at last."

While separated by a century in years, Blind Tom and Leslie share remarkably similar physical and mental limitations, similar prodigious musical genius and similar life stories with respect to their discovery, the unfolding of that incredible musical genius, and the musical zenith they both reached, each in their own era. Both were musical savants, and musical giants, in their own times. To listen to Leslie Lemke play some of Blind Tom's pieces, as he now does having listened to them played by John Davis, is a most amazing, reliving, inspiring experience. What a duo Leslie and Tom would make. What inspiring stories they provide. A century apart, Blind Tom and Leslie Lemke are linked timelessly together with their incredibly unique, shared gift of marvelous music.

CHAPTER 7

Leslie and May:
"Two Memorable People"

On the 1983 *60 Minutes* program *Genius* on savant syndrome that so many people still remember, Morley Safer called Leslie Lemke "a memorable man." And he certainly is.

But there is another memorable person in that story, May Lemke, "the woman who willed a miracle." This chapter is about both of them. It answers the question, "Whatever happened to Leslie Lemke?" based on my now 30-year opportunity to follow Leslie and his family. So I will provide that follow-up. Even before my first meeting with Leslie, May and Joe, Shirlee Monty was driving them to and from concerts at the very beginning of Leslie's musical journey around the world. In the second part of this chapter Shirlee provides some unique insights into this remarkable duo, especially May Lemke, in those early years.

"And sings my soul"—Leslie's gift

I'm not sure that Leslie Lemke has a favorite song among the thousands in his repertoire. But there are two songs that he sings very often and, it seems to me, that he sings with special feeling. Perhaps that's because the lyrics seem so especially applicable to him: "And sings my soul" from *How Great Thou Art* and "I was blind but now I see" from *Amazing Grace*.

Leslie is still blind, to be sure. But it seems his songs do emanate from deep within his soul, and it seems also they have produced a kind of internal "sight" that has enlivened his life, and enriched the lives of those around him, including mine. I have heard Leslie play and sing hundreds of times. But each time I hear Leslie play and sing now, I still stand in awe of his remarkable ability, and I continue to be touched and inspired, as so many also have been, by his unlikely story.

Leslie's story really begins in Monkwearmouth, North East England, a tiny fishing village where his remarkable foster mother, May Lemke, grew up. May had endured some traumatic circumstances during the World War I bombings in London. She was severely injured at age 14 in the explosion of a munitions factory that took the lives of many of her co-workers but miraculously spared her. Through sheer determination she recovered from her injuries and then began training as an apprentice nurse with a local physician. She had already learned some governess skills when, at age 12, she had responsibility for looking after her younger brothers and sisters. Some of the trauma, and triumphs, of May's early years are recounted in detail in Shirlee Monty's (1981) book *May's Boy: An Incredible Story of Love*.

In 1924 May left the tiny fishing village to take a very long trip—first to Canada and then to the United States—to meet her husband to be, an American soldier. He and May had met when May was helping entertain troops in dance events. May always loved to dance. After her fiancée was back in the United States, arrangements were made for May to emigrate and marry him. They settled on an 80-acre farm in central Wisconsin.

May had five children, three boys and two girls. She was a deeply religious, grateful and optimistic person—all 4½ feet of her. She maintained that optimism even through some difficult times including the loss—twice—of the house and farm buildings to fires. There was a divorce and May moved to Milwaukee.

In Milwaukee May began to work as a nurse-governess and quickly gained a reputation as an extraordinarily skilled and loving caretaker. In 1948 she married Joe Lemke whom she had met at a dance. Joe was a construction worker, age 44, who had never married. He and May fixed up the little cottage they bought on Pewaukee Lake and settled into a more relaxed lifestyle. It was just May and Joe and their little house on the lake.

But one afternoon in 1952 that lifestyle changed dramatically. May received a phone call from Milwaukee Social Services. The agency knew of her nurse-governess skills and excellent rapport with children. And besides, May had applied to be a receiving home for newborn children awaiting foster placement. So Social Services called May to arrange for May's first such placement. But this particular child, given up by his mother for adoption, was a desperately ill child with multiple disabilities. They were looking for a home, or rather for a sort of hospice setting, for this frail and failing child. They hoped May might provide a foster home for this little lad, if only a temporary one, given his fragile health.

That little child, whom they had named Leslie, had been born prematurely on January 31, 1952. Leslie developed retrolental fibroplasia, a type of blindness seen so often in premature children that it is called the retinopathy of prematurity (ROP). This is a condition in which the retina proliferates wildly and sometimes, as in Leslie's case, blocks the drainage in the eye producing a form of childhood glaucoma. Because of increasing pressure in the left eye, and fear that the eye might literally burst, it was surgically removed at age four months. Six weeks later the right eye required surgical removal for the same reason.

Following that drastic surgery Leslie was desperately ill, apparently because of some infections or other complications following the surgery. (A 1986 CT brain scan shows considerable left-sided abnormality, especially in the left frontal lobe, with some damage in the left parietal lobe, and some damage in both the left and right occipital lobes: these findings of clear left-sided brain damage are very significant as will be seen in subsequent chapters when discussing the "How do they do it?" question.)

Social Services warned May Lemke that Leslie was so ill he was likely to die. They asked if she was still willing to take Leslie into her home under those circumstances. "You can send Leslie here," May said, "but he is not going to die. He will not die," a vow witnessed by both of May's daughters, Pat and Mary.

Pat and Mary remember those early years when Leslie came to live with May and Joe. They remember Leslie being so tiny and frail, barely able to move, cry or even swallow. They recall May helping Leslie learn to swallow by carefully placing cereal on his tongue and stroking his throat to encourage him to swallow. May showered Leslie with an abundance of a mother's love. But she was also a physical therapist, nurse, mentor, tutor and 24/7 caretaker to this young lad, who was blind and handicapped in so many ways both mentally and physically. May Lemke became to Leslie Lemke what Anne Mansfield Sullivan was to Helen Keller.

In this loving atmosphere, Leslie managed not only to survive, but also to thrive, as documented in the notes from visits to the doctor in those early years. At age 2½ Leslie was sitting up and crawling. Notes in the medical chart indicate that Leslie could sing and speak some words clearly, but he seemed distant and preoccupied. Questions were raised by the doctor as to whether Leslie might be "slow" but he charted, cautiously, "opinion reserved" in that regard.

A neurologist examined Leslie at age three and noted spasticity in the arms and legs and difficulty walking. He also noted echolalia, a tendency to repeat phrases rather than initiate conversation. That echolalia was very pronounced, and quite dramatic at home; both daughters remember that when they visited their mom, sometimes Leslie would repeat verbatim an entire day's conversation in the exact tone and manner of everyone who had visited that day. On some days Leslie would be found under a bed strumming the bedsprings with his hands, as if they were strings on an instrument and simultaneously beating out rhythms on those springs with the soles of his feet and his elbows.

May tackled Leslie's difficulty in walking head-on. She devised a strap system by which she could, with him fastened to her, allow him to bear some gradual weight on his frail legs and in that awkward but dedicated manner begin to walk. Then, later, by holding on to the chain link fence along the path to the little cottage where they lived, Leslie learned eventually to propel himself along unassisted.

A doctor's note when Leslie was 5½ confirmed Leslie's ability to walk. He was also singing songs and could repeat the Pledge of Allegiance by memory. Again conversation was echolalic. The doctor noted Leslie showed "inexhaustible restlessness" (somewhat like his foster mother, May). Then he made a prediction that, fortunately, never came about: "Foster mother has done well, very well, with him but a time will come when institutional placement will be necessary." But because of May's love, dedication, ingenuity and determination, such institutionalization was never necessary.

At about age seven May got a piano for Leslie. Like the walking she taught him, she would put his hands over hers as she played some simple English tunes she knew. Soon Leslie was playing songs that he had heard. At age eight Leslie was playing other instruments, including bongo drums, ukulele, concertina and accordion. On a visit to the doctor that year the notes document that Leslie sang for the doctor, beat time to music with a tongue blade, and recited some rock and roll titles.

By age nine Leslie had learned to play the chord organ. Yet Leslie was still not conversant, using mostly echolalia and imitation. He needed help in dressing and the spasticity in his hands was such that he could not use eating utensils. Yet that disappeared when Leslie played the piano, much like the person who stutters in everyday conversation but has that stuttering disappear when he or she rises to give a lecture to an audience.

By age 12 Leslie was playing piano, his favorite instrument, and singing beautifully in the little cottage on Pewaukee Lake. Batman's Theme Song was his favorite and Mary remembers him playing that loudly and endlessly. He loved listening to music on television or radio and would do so for hours. The stations, though, were chosen by May and rarely did they include any classical music.

As described in the Introduction, when Leslie was about 14 years old, May and Joe watched a movie on television. Leslie could only listen to the movie because he is blind. The movie was *Sincerely Yours* starring Dorothy Malone and Basil Rathbone. May and Joe went to bed after the movie. About 2 or 3 a.m. May heard some music coming from the living room where the television was. She thought perhaps Joe had left the television on and went to check on that. To her amazement there was Leslie sitting on the piano bench playing flawlessly, from beginning to end, Tchaikovsky's

Piano Concerto No. 1, which was the theme song to the movie he had listened to. That night is when "the miracle came into full bloom," as Leslie's family describes it.

Interestingly, to this day, if you ask Leslie to play that piece you get not only a beautiful rendition of it, but also an introduction, verbatim, from the announcer's description for that film that evening: "Tonight's movie is *Sincerely Yours*, starring Dorothy Malone and Basil Rathbone. As he falls in love with the beautiful black-haired woman… And, now, the Sunday night movie is proud to present…" Leslie will play the entire concerto and end by repeating the announcer's words he heard that evening, in the voice and with the intonation with which he heard it: "And that's tonight's movie, *Sincerely Yours*." Then the piano, and Leslie, are silent.

Leslie had his first public performance at age 22 at the Waukesha county fair singing hymns and doing his Louis Armstrong and Tiny Tim imitations. "Incredible," the local newspaper said.

The 1980 Fond du Lac appearance was carried as an AP wire story as described in the Introduction. It was that December when Walter Cronkite closed his *CBS Evening News* program this way: "This is a season that celebrates a miracle, and this story belongs to the season. It's the story of a young man, a piano and a miracle." In January, 1981 *That's Incredible* did a very touching profile on May, Leslie and Joe in their little cottage so filled with song and joy. Then came *Donahue, The Morning Show* with Regis and Kathie Lee, *Oprah, Geraldo* and many other programs.

But it is the *60 Minutes* program *Genius* on October 23, 1983 that so many people who saw it remember so vividly and so affectionately. Wherever I go in the United States now, people recall that program and ask, "How is Leslie doing?" In the interview on that program, May describes in detail the night the "miracle came into full bloom" and Leslie then plays the concerto vigorously. At the end of the segment, May gives her idea of how such a miracle could happen, quoted earlier but worthy of repeating here: "Well I think that a part of the brain, the musical part was damaged—because the brain was damaged—but I think that part of the brain was left perfectly healthy and beautiful, just so Leslie could get a talent. And he got it."

Watching that program was Dustin Hoffman. He was "moved to tears" by this blind, handicapped lad playing so magically and it was then he decided he wanted to play the part of the savant in *Rain Man*.

After the *60 Minutes* program and the other television shows, Leslie became a celebrity. I accompanied him to some of those programs to explain savant syndrome and how Leslie's remarkable gift fit into that extraordinary condition. Each audience loved Leslie and was enthralled and inspired by him. Sometimes May would be on the stage, and at other times Mary would be there. Each show wanted to demonstrate Leslie's ability to play back any piece presented as a "challenge." I remember one television progam particularly. The producer asked what they might play as a challenge. I told them to choose whatever they wished, but be sure it was a short piece because, I warned, Leslie was going to play it from beginning to end, no matter about commercial breaks or any other time constraints.

In general, it seems, producers never really listen and they do it their way regardless of any advice. For this show they chose "Rhapsody in Blue." They got "Rhapsody in Blue," all the many minutes of it from beginning to end. The camera would fade away for commercials, and, on return, Leslie was still playing. Then another commercial break—and more "Rhapsody in Blue" flowed forth. Finally I saw the producer in the wings, hands folded, gazing upward, as if to say "Please, Lord…" As I said, producers never listen.

That same need to complete each piece surfaced at each of his public concerts as well.

Mary learned early on that for the challenge part of the concert, persons requesting pieces should *write* them out, rather than shout them out. Because, if requested aloud, each piece would have to be played in its entirety, in the order in which it was received, like a juke box storing pieces coin after coin. If the requests were numerous, the night was long until each request, in the order it was received, was fully played out.

In 1984 Leslie gave a command performance for Crown Prince Harald and Crown Princess Sonja in Norway. The eminent Norwegian pianist, Kjell Baekkelund, challenged Leslie with a piece he obviously had never heard, including a deliberate mistake. Leslie played it back with his usual precision, mistake and all.

Leslie's performances, whether live or on television, were always impressive and memorable. *60 Minutes* chose Leslie's segment as one to be included in the *25th Anniversary Special* in 1998, and a *People Magazine* anniversary issue, along with a *People Magazine* television special, included Leslie's story as well.

Ironically, as Leslie's memory expanded, May's began to fade with the progression of Alzheimer's disease. In 1985 May moved in with her daughter Pat for a period of time. Then she moved in with her other daughter, Mary, who was also caring for Leslie. "Daddy Joe" died in 1987. May continued to live with Mary and Leslie in Arpin, Wisconsin. Pat and Mary had promised May she would never be in a nursing home. And she never was. May died in Mary's arms on November 6, 1993.

There was some concern that Leslie might stop playing after his mother's death, as Blind Tom essentially did after Colonel Bethune died, as described in Chapter 6. But, marvelously, with Leslie, "the band played on." Leslie says, "Mom is in heaven now," and his music continues to flow forth.

I have miles of videotape on the many savants I have been privileged to know. But a two-minute clip of Leslie and May is my favorite. I was visiting in the village of Winnebago, Wisconsin where May's daughter Pat lives. May's Alzheimer's was advancing markedly. She sat in a corner, just staring downward, silently, which for May as I always had known her was most unlike her. It was sad. I asked May to come over and sit on the piano bench with Leslie, and asked Leslie to play something for his mom. He began the introduction to "How Great Thou Art." May's face began to light up, she looked at Leslie proudly, then looked upward and raised her hands in praise as I had seen her do so many times. Life returned, May was animated again, smiling and singing along. "How Great Thou Art." Indeed, how great Thou art.

Words don't do justice in describing that two minutes of revival. It is touching. Every audience I share that with, male or female, young or old, public or professional, student or faculty, is touched. Tears are copious. May brought Leslie to life, and now, in a fitting payback of sorts, in those few precious moments, Leslie brought May to life. What an inspirational scene of renewal.

The years since May's death have shown even more changes and improvement in Leslie. While Leslie's repetition skills have always been spectacular, as time has gone on he moved beyond mere repetition to improvisation. At one concert, a young girl bravely came forward and played "Mississippi Hotdog" as a challenge piece. Leslie listened patiently, then played back the piece faithfully. But near the end of the piece, one can see Leslie get a bit restless on the piano bench, and sit up more attentively. As soon as he had obliged with the literal playback, he launched into his improvisation and provided a beautiful four-minute concerto one could name, I guess, "Variations on a Theme of Mississippi Hotdog." He changes tempo and pitch, and makes other variations which show his remarkable grasp of the rules of music, rules he has at his fingertips, literally. Remember, though, Leslie has never had a piano lesson in his life. He seems to know things he never learned.

But there has been an additional step in Leslie's musical progress and growth. First came repetition—spectacular repetition. Then came improvisation—remarkable improvisation. Now Leslie is composing—creating—his own songs. At first they seemed very familiar from other tunes. But now they are truly original, like "Down on the Farm in Arpin," where he plays and sings about the out of doors and farm animals he so loves. Then there is "Bird Song" in which he whistles, or mimics, the songs of the birds he has heard in his yard, and weaves them in a marvelous way with the tune he has composed.

The improvisation and creativity show up in another way now. At the concerts Leslie still gives, the audience always request songs and Leslie seems, somehow, to know them all. But every now and then someone will try to stump Leslie by writing down a request that is either so obscure it is most unlikely Leslie has ever heard it, or sometimes it is simply an entirely fictional title. But Mary, nevertheless, dutifully asks Leslie to play the request even though the song is totally unknown to her as well. It might have a title like "23 rag skidoo" or some such other unidentifiable song.

"Do you know that piece, Leslie?" Mary asks.

"Yes, I know it," Leslie replies confidently.

"Can you play it?"

"Sure I can play it."

And a song begins. It is unfamiliar to everyone, but sounds quite plausible.

"Leslie, are you sure that's 23 rag skidoo?" Mary inquires.

"That's it," Leslie says definitively.

"Leslie, are you sure? Or are you making it up?"

"I'm making it up," Leslie will then confess.

But, made up or not, it is a wonderful, original piece the audience gets to hear. And "23 rag skidoo" is born.

Leslie's measured IQ on testing in 1986 was 58 verbal, and testing overall put him into the "moderately retarded range." But that IQ score seems at great variance with a most unusual precocious and genius-like ability Leslie demonstrated at a concert in Texas in 1997. This particular time Leslie, instead of being asked to play back a song he had never heard before *after* he heard it for the first time, was asked to instead play it *with* the person. The challenger pianist began playing. Leslie waited about three seconds and then began playing *with* her. What was happening was that Leslie was *taking in* what he had just heard, *processing* it, and then *outputting* it almost simultaneously with the pianist playing this piece, entirely new to him. To do that, Leslie was *parallel processing*; by the end of the piece there was only about a one-second delay between what Leslie was hearing, processing and then playing.

Such parallel processing is similar to the rare ability that some gifted translators demonstrate when, rather than waiting for the speaker to say a phrase and then stop, at which time the translator translates, the really skilled translator translates *simultaneously* as the speaker speaks. Such parallel processing capability in anyone requires a high level of "intelligence." While it may be that Leslie's IQ is measured at 58, his capacity to do this level of parallel processing demonstrates, to me, that IQ is measuring only one form of intelligence, one which we have named IQ. But in reality, I believe, based on my work with savants, that we are each made up of a series of intelligences, more accurately called "multiple intelligences" along the lines that Gardner (1993) and others have proposed. In my view IQ scores, or what is sometimes referred to as the "G" factor, or general intelligence, oversimplifies our much more complex multiple intelligence organization. Leslie, and all the savants, provide, in my opinion, convincing verification of the model of multiple intelligences with all its implications for better understanding, and better educating, ourselves and our children.

Leslie's remarkable abilities are better seen than described. A 1987 documentary *Island of Genius* was produced for public television by the Weyerhaeuser Corporation Foundation and is still available through the *Miracle of Love Ministries* and Mary Parker, May's daughter, now Leslie's care provider. Tapes of a 2003 concert in Appleton, and a 2007 concert in Pittsville, Wisconsin, are available as well and provide a more up-to-date look at Leslie and his remarkable abilities. A made-for-television movie of the Leslie Lemke story—*The Woman Who Willed a Miracle*—starred Cloris Leachman as May Lemke and won four Emmy awards. It is still commercially available.

Meanwhile Leslie plays on. The concerts are fewer now because travel is more difficult for both Mary and Leslie. But there is a continuous concert at home, usually just for an audience of one. But that doesn't matter to Leslie. For him, and for Mary, and for the rest of us, the band plays on, marvelously, and miraculously.

THE IRREPRESSIBLE MAY LEMKE

by Shirlee Monty

> And as He passed by, He saw a man blind from birth. And His disciples asked Him saying: "Rabbi, who sinned, this man or his parents, that he should be born blind?" Jesus answered, "It was neither that this man sinned, nor his parents, but it was in order that the works of God might be displayed in him."
>
> John 9:1–3

Actors have an expression called "striking the set." It means tearing down the set, the play is over, the project ended. It also means saying good-by to people; fellow actors and dear friends who have shared in a common task.

In a way, authors share in this strange way of life. We, too, move from project to project, immersing ourselves in other people's lives, searching their memories, sifting through their thoughts and feelings until one day we, too, must strike the set. The project is over. The book is finished.

Some projects are easier to walk away from than others. I guess I always knew it was going to be hard saying good-by to the Lemkes. Long before my book, *May's Boy*, was finished, my professional detachment had broken down and I realized that I loved this family: May, the four and one-half foot, effervescent little Englishwoman who was the heroine of the story; Joe, her quiet, soft-spoken husband, and of course, Leslie, their blind, severely mentally-handicapped and cerebral-palsied foster son, whose piano virtuosity had prompted the writing of *May's Boy*.

But after a year had passed, I felt that I had captured their story and it was time to strike the set. There was nothing more to ask. The project was finished.

As it was, the book had taken much longer than I had planned. I hadn't bargained for the frequent tours of May's garden to see how the tomatoes had grown and how lovely the peonies had turned. Or the impromptu concerts that Leslie waited to give after every interview. Or the many trips to the bank or the store since the Lemkes had no car.

"Leslie's been asking for bananas. I knew you wouldn't mind." And of course, I didn't mind. By then, I was hooked anyway. There was nothing I wouldn't have done for May Lemke.

In early June, I scheduled our last interview. I really didn't have any more questions. I didn't even take my tape recorder. I just wanted to share a cup of coffee or tea and reminisce a little...and say good-by...and tell them that I wouldn't be calling or coming over so often. I knew they'd miss me, too. Isn't it strange, I thought. I've only known the Lemkes a year and yet I can hardly remember not knowing them.

I thought back to the dozens and dozens of mornings I had drained May's coffeepot and tried to rekindle childhood memories of this 80-year-old woman who had lived through so much: World War I in England, working as a nurse-governess, coming to America as a young girl alone, raising five children on an isolated farm in central Wisconsin, meeting Joe Lemke and finally, taking in Leslie.

I tried to capture whatever it was that allowed her to take in a severely handicapped six-month-old infant at an age when most of us are beginning to savor the prospect of a peaceful and unencumbered retirement.

I tried to figure out Joe Lemke, who was a middle-aged bachelor when he married May. Even if May could accept Leslie, what about Joe? What kind of man would take in a blind, severely handicapped infant as his first and only child?

I had been totally consumed by the Lemke story for a year. When I was playing tennis or shopping with my girls, my mind often slipped away, and I saw May rocking Leslie, singing to him, and trying to get some kind of response from him.

"He was like a plastic doll," she had told me. "No response, no emotion, no nothing."

I saw her dragging her limp young son behind her, praying that he would imitate her movements and learn to walk, to even stand alone. And I tried to envision her face the first time Leslie played the piano, the night she fell to her knees, weeping and thanking God for "a miracle."

On that last afternoon together, we talked about Leslie's future, fantasizing our dreams for him. Mine was a concert on a beautiful Steinway piano in a magnificent hall. May saw Leslie performing in a lovely restaurant, walking among the people, playing all the songs they wanted to hear.

And then it was time to go. We said our good-bys and I slowly walked up the hill to my car, trying to think about several offers that had come my way, or whether I would rather try that column I had always wanted to write. *May's Boy* is finished, I kept telling myself. We have struck the set.

A few weeks later, my phone rang. It was Larry Stone, an editor at Thomas Nelson Publishers. He asked if I could bring the Lemkes to Anaheim, California for the Christian Booksellers' Association's Convention. They hoped that Leslie could perform a concert there to help promote our book.

I was very doubtful. "Larry, the Lemkes are in their eighties and Leslie is severely handicapped. He is blind and cannot even walk alone. They've only been away twice in the 32 years they've had Leslie." But I promised to ask.

When I called May, she said, "We'd love to. When do we go?"

I had never traveled with the Lemkes before. When I had taken May shopping or out for lunch, Joe always stayed at home with Leslie. I knew they were simple, unconventional people but nothing could have prepared me for the morning my husband and I picked them up to go to the airport.

May came running up the hill from their cottage in a long, billowing concert gown while Joe and Leslie followed along behind, tandem-style, wearing matching jogging suits. They carried three small canvas bags, labeled in big, black letters: Joe, May and Leslie. May also carried a garment bag adorned with a large, English flag.

All I could think of was how was I going to get this little group through the airport without every eye on us? When we finally reached the airport, the wheelchair was waiting for Leslie, I checked my baggage and we were directed to Gate 9-C.

"Leslie, sing 'California, Here I Come'," I heard May tell Leslie. She was looking up at the redcap, poised for his reaction.

I fell back to where my husband had already retreated and looked at him in desperation. "Lee, I don't believe this! What am I going to do?" "I don't know what you're going to do," he laughed, "but I'm going home!"

By then, Leslie's voice could be heard reverberating throughout the corridors and May was well into the story of her remarkable son, the first time he played the piano, all the things that God had done for him, and why we were going to California. A crowd had assembled and stayed with us, in varying numbers, until at last we were called for early boarding.

I hurried on the plane, ducked behind a book, and for a time, anonymity seemed to have been restored. However, as soon as we reached our altitude and loosened our seat belts, I was aware of some confusion across the aisle, in the Lemke quarters. May was getting out of her seat and struggling to get Leslie's hands on her shoulders. I was puzzled because I knew she had taken him to the bathroom before we left the cottage.

"Come on, love," May was saying. "Sing something for the people. I bet they'd like to hear you do Louis Armstrong." So Leslie sang "Hello, Dolly" as May led him down the aisle. On the way back, he sang "The Lord's Prayer," and I noticed that even the stewardesses had stopped their work to listen.

By the time we got to California, May was holding court. People were stopping at her seat, asking questions, requesting songs, writing down the name of the book and telling Leslie how wonderful he was. And I was beginning to relax and accept the fact that travelling with the Lemkes would never be normal, or dull, or predictable.

Not surprisingly, the Lemkes were a big hit in California; May, as well as Leslie. Her spontaneity, vivacity, warmth, sense of fun, and pride in Leslie all attracted as much attention and enthusiasm as Leslie's music.

Because of the Lemkes' success in California, we were sent on a series of promotional trips throughout the country: appearances on television shows, interviews, tapings, and concerts. At the end of six months, the Lemkes and I were inundated with requests for concerts and I suddenly found myself cast in a number of unfamiliar roles: travel agent, public relations person, promoter, speaker and travelling companion on a journey that was to last more than three years. And during that journey, I burrowed deeper into May Lemke's complex personality and uncovered a maze of new discoveries. I found that May was totally uninhibited, unintimidated by anyone and clearly unflappable.

When I first began accompanying the Lemkes to concerts, I saw that May would grow restless during the introduction, and if it seemed a bit long or flowery, she might dart up on the stage in mid-sentence and begin clowning around with the emcee.

At one such event, May ran under the emcee's arm, catching her wig, which went sailing across the stage like a frisbee. Everyone was appalled except May, who dashed over, retrieved it, pulled it on her head, adjusted it in front of the audience until they nodded their approval, and then it was on with the show.

After a few such encounters, I decided that, stage fright or not, I would introduce the Lemkes myself. My husband agreed to keep May in tow at the back of the church or auditorium until they were properly introduced. Of course, once released, May came flying down the aisle, dancing and chattering to the audience. Once she came waving her shoes in the air and calling out, "You'll have to excuse me, folks, but my feet are killing me!"

My immediate goal was to try to get some structure in these concerts. May's style was to tell Leslie to play whatever came to her mind at the moment; old English war songs, unknown hymns or foreign songs that most people had never heard of. My preference was a mix...classics, show tunes, familiar hymns...organized and listed before the concert.

What developed was a friendly kind of contest between us on stage. I would be standing at the mike, introducing "Amazing Grace," and May would slip behind me to the piano and whisper in Leslie's ear, "Where the Action Is," and of course, he always played her song!

May's spontaneity and sense of fun combined with Leslie's musical brilliance provoked a gamut of emotions in her audiences. Laughter would turn to tears, and seconds later, tears to laughter as May spun around the stage, telling stories, wiping Leslie's brow, dancing with her husband, being outrageous one minute, tender and poignant the next.

Coming from England as a young girl who had been an eyewitness to much tragedy and deprivation during World War I, as well as being disfigured herself, May never tired of talking about how wonderful America is, the lovely homes, the beautiful children.

During a concert in Oshkosh, Wisconsin, she spotted an American flag at the back of the stage. Running over, she dragged the flagpole to the piano, made a speech about this wonderful country that took her in and treated her so lovely, then asked everyone to stand and sing "God Bless America" while Leslie played. It was a poignant moment, indeed.

But I suspect the thing I loved most about May was her total acceptance of, as well as the special attention she showered on, handicapped youngsters. She insisted that room be left in front of the auditorium or church for wheelchairs and handicapped children. During the concert, she often left the stage to speak with them, ask for their requests, hold their hands and hug them. When she was on stage, their eyes would be riveted on May and they would be laughing, waving, clapping and having a wonderful time.

Then after the concert, when Leslie was playing informal requests and people surrounded the piano, May was always on the lookout for any handicapped youngster who may wish to hear Leslie. She would then ask people to step aside, wheel the youngster next to Leslie, introduce them and put their hands together, and ask Leslie to play their request.

As Leslie's presence became known, more and more requests came in for television tapings as well as live television appearances. Crews from *That's Incredible, 60 Minutes, 700 Club* and *PM Magazine* were among those who found their way to the tiny cottage on Pewaukee Lake and spent a day they were not likely to forget. May greeted her visitors with bear hugs and fed them fruit, English cheese and 7-Up, "but no ice. We don't drink anything with ice in England," she explained.

Of course, after all the preliminaries, the real show was Leslie, and May always seemed as awed by her talented son as her guests were.

"Isn't he wonderful?" she would say after a particularly difficult passage. "How about that from a boy who can't see, can't walk by himself, can't even eat by himself?"

But after a few numbers, it was time to "set up" and the camera crew faced the formidable challenge of trying to get lights, cameras, tripods, and sound equipment arranged in postage stamp quarters. There was always a shortage of electric plugs and extension cords, and while Joe would try to be helpful, May was running around, chattering about Leslie, showing awards and pictures, brewing tea, bringing out more food and telling Joe to behave himself! Since the cottage was old and antiquated, fuses would frequently blow under the onslaught of so much electrical equipment. Joe would grab a flashlight, duck under the kitchen table, lift a trap door and crawl into the dank basement while everyone waited for him to restore power.

May, in particular, was never still and hard to keep track of. Nor did she ever quite understand the intricacies of taping and the crew quickly accepted the fact that it was going to be a long day.

The host of the segment would get May arranged on the sofa for an interview, mike unobtrusively attached to her sweater. But at the first question, May would leap up to better dramatize her answer, and by then, the mike was halfway across the room!

She also interrupted when anything else was going on. In the middle of one of my interviews, I described Joe as a balance wheel. Forgetting that she had been instructed to be silent, May yelled, "And WHAT is a balance wheel?"

Kathy Bullock, former features producer for CBN, which taped several segments for the *700 Club*, described her reaction to May Lemke:

I remember her total lack of "star respect" that usually accompanies television crews when we come into home of persons not accustomed to the media. May is May and one quickly realizes that the world adapts to her, not vice versa.

I say this in complete affection. She was refreshingly oblivious to the "rules" of television. Talking when silence was necessary, walking around cords, cameras, and crew when shooting was underway, and generally living her life thriving on the attention.

I particularly remember one incident. About four hours into shooting, the crew had grown accustomed to May's spontaneous self-directing and had taken to instructing her before each scene to be quiet. May would hold out generally for about two minutes before she would begin shouting in "whispers" across the room. At one shot we were to shoot Leslie walking from his chair to the piano. The cameraman firmly, but gently, told May that she COULD NOT talk. She must be completely silent.

Tape was rolling, Leslie was responding perfectly, May was silent. But unable to resist the urge to talk she decided to move to another room. She quietly stood up. And "pink panther style" stalked across the room, carefully tiptoeing so as not to make a sound. Unfortunately, she stalked right in front of the camera. Apparently, she saw no harm in walking in front of the lens as long as she was quiet!

Our live television appearances were almost cut short when May received a letter, discussing makeup and apparel for each guest. It read: "All guests will be made up prior to the program. Please allow 20 to 30 minutes."

May called me, ready to cancel. "I go places the way God made me. I don't need all that fancy greasepaint to cover me up. I am one of God's servants. Who do they want me to be?"

I assured her that I wouldn't let them touch her, Leslie, or Joe, and throughout our many television appearances, I was always amused that May never submitted to a single smudge of powder or makeup. When the Lemkes appeared on the *Donahue* show, two psychiatrists were sitting in chairs being made up when May announced defiantly, "Well, nobody's touching any of us!"

May proved to be as intractable on television as she was during tapings and concerts.

Pat Robertson, president of CBN and host of the *700 Club*, recalled her appearance on his show. "I was warned to give May freedom when she appeared on our program... and that is what I did. That marvelous, vivacious little lady took over the studio to the delight of all of us and provided what was one of our greatest television programs."

When she appeared on the *PTL Club*, Jim Bakker suggested that she enter through the velvet curtains while the band played a rousing English tune. May not only swept dramatically through the curtains but danced and twirled until someone finally had to retrieve her and lead her to the couch where Jim was waiting for an interview!

And yet, the most touching moments that I recall weren't on the stage or in front of a camera, but in the most mundane places; a restaurant, airport, hotel room where May so often turned an ordinary situation into a "happening."

I remember sitting in Milwaukee's Mitchell Airport, waiting for our plane to Minneapolis, when three little girls, about four, six and eight, inched toward us and stood near Leslie, staring. When Leslie is not singing, his head slumps forward and he is nearly immobile. Finally, one of the girls looked at May and asked, "Is he dead?"

"Oh no, darling," May said. "He's not dead. But he's had both eyes taken out. And he's blind. Aren't you all lucky to have two beautiful eyes to see with? But this boy will never see and he can't walk alone, either. But God gave him a beautiful gift instead. He can play the piano and sing and he gives concerts all over the country. Now would you girls like to hear Leslie sing?"

The girls nodded in disbelief, and May asked Leslie to sing "Six Little Ducks." As Leslie sang, airport conversation gradually diminished until the only sound left was Leslie's voice.

When he finished, May said, "Now, is there something you would like to hear Leslie sing?" One of the girls asked if he knew "Jesus Loves Me." "Indeed he does," May said and Leslie sang "Jesus Loves Me." It was truly beautiful to see so many people stop and listen in awe to this gifted and yet so handicapped young man.

A few months later, we were waiting in the Los Angeles airport on our way back to Milwaukee and May was regaling a small group with stories about Leslie. Asked if he could sing without a piano, May said, "Of course, he can. Leslie, sing 'He Touched Me.'" The crowd swelled to 50 or 60 when halfway through the song, we were called for early boarding. As the steward pushed Leslie, still singing, through the ramp, the crowd burst into loud applause, which followed us all the way into the plane.

Another unforgettable happening took place in a hotel in LaCrosse, Wisconsin, where we were staying, prior to a concert the following day. We were having dinner in the hotel restaurant when one of the diners recognized Leslie and asked May if he could play a few songs. The manager consented so Leslie began to play requests while May ran from table to table chattering and telling them all about her remarkable son.

Other people began to drift in from the bar, the lobby, even from the street outside, until the room was jammed. May was finding people with birthdays, anniversaries, honeymooning couples, and in turn, Leslie would play the appropriate song.

At ten o'clock, I felt that we must leave, and as we walked out, Leslie, with hands on Joe's shoulders, sang "I Am a Child of God." The crowd rose, almost in unison, and gave Leslie a heartfelt and tearful standing ovation.

Another discovery concerning May's character was her generosity; in fact, almost a disregard for money. The Lemkes certainly lived a frugal life. In the four years that I knew May, she never bought a dress, coat, or shoes, despite all our travels and television appearances. They didn't own a car, didn't have drinking water, had none of the niceties that most of us take for granted. "We live just like Jesus," May offered one morning over tea. "We don't have much and we use what we have!"

She neglected to add that she also gives it away. She had a compulsion to tip anyone who did anything for her, appropriate or not. She once explained that it was because of Leslie. "Remember," she said, "when you have a boy like this, people have to do things for you. And you have to pay them."

She often tried to tip the pilot of the plane for "a nice trip and for bringing us home safely." She tried to give money to stewardesses, chauffeurs, the maitre'd in an elegant hotel, the girl at McDonalds. "Is that all?" she would ask. "Here, love. Keep a little for yourself. You can't make all that food for so little."

She once tipped a redcap whom she thought was wheeling Leslie, then discovered he was wheeling someone else. He tried to return the money, but May would have none of it. "No, you keep it, love. It's not your fault that I made a fool of myself!"

Instead of charging admission to Leslie's concerts, we took a Love Offering for the Lemkes. Frequently, May would forget what it was for and run off the stage and deposit some money in the basket.

On our pre-Christmas flights, she ran up and down the aisle handing out dollar bills to all the children. "Now children," she would announce, "Santa Claus is nice, but remember, Jesus Christ always comes first." Then she would ask Leslie to sing "Happy Birthday, Dear Jesus" and then the requests would begin.

I had taken May grocery shopping one morning when an elderly woman in front of us realized it was not senior citizen discount day and didn't have enough money for her groceries. As she began discarding a few things, May laid a $10 bill in front of her and said, "Here, this will take care of it." When the lady protested, May said, "Now money is to share with those who need it and today you needed it!"

I think I marveled the most, though, at May's patient and unending devotion to Leslie. It had baffled me when I wrote the book, and it continued to leave me incredulous.

When we drove home from a concert, May would rub Leslie's neck, or stroke his forehead, or hug him and say, "You know, love, you really worked for Jesus tonight," or "You sure made a lot of people think about God."

When the *PM Magazine* crew wanted to take some footage outside, May said, "No, it's too cold outdoors today. I don't want that boy to shiver!"

But on a lovely fall day, May allowed cameramen from *60 Minutes* to film Leslie walking along the fence by the cottage. It had been a long, tiring day and everybody was in a rush to finish, but May would not be hurried. She insisted that Leslie dress himself, a task that took endless patience and encouragement.

"A boy that is a famous singer has to learn to put his jacket on right, doesn't he, love?" she said as she gently prodded him. "Now, that's a good beginning. Put your arms through the sleeves. We must find out our own mistakes. That's how we learn, love. Now you're getting it."

Leslie got caught under his hood and couldn't find his way out. May gave him some assistance. "That's all right, love. We all make mistakes, don't we?" At last, Leslie was ready to go outside.

I noticed that May frequently asked, "Are you all right, love?" and Leslie would answer, "Yes, I'm all right, love." It happened so often that it was almost a litany. She told me that she does this so Leslie will always know she's around, where she is. "Remember," she said, "he can't see me. So he might get anxious if he doesn't hear my voice."

Toward the end, May's health and memory began to fail and she became more and more pensive during our talks in her tiny kitchen. "Isn't it funny?" she mused one afternoon. "It's as if God gave Leslie a trade. He can earn money just like any other man and take care of himself. Just think, a blind, mentally-handicapped and cerebral-palsied boy earning money for himself!"

Sometimes, in the midst of our conversation, she would get severe pains in her head or legs, and she seemed to turn to Leslie for solace. "Leslie, play a little tune for me. How about 'Golden Dreams' or 'My Reverie'?" We would sit silently, tears welling in May's deep set eyes, and somehow, it seemed to get her through the crisis.

Although the Lemkes lived to see their foster son appear on national television and perform in concerts throughout the country, May was denied her wish to "die onstage with Leslie, doing God's work." Instead, at the age of 84, with her health continuing to fail, May lived her last nine years under the care of her daughter in central Wisconsin, where she died of Alzheimer's disease in 1993.

Joe Lemke elected to stay in the tiny cottage on Pewaukee Lake where he and May had lived for 36 years and where he died in August of 1987.

When I last saw May, her memory had declined to the point where she couldn't remember me, the concerts, the book or a single event that took place during those four memorable years together.

However, she did leave me with one memory which I will always cherish. During her last winter in Pewaukee, May developed a persistent cough and severe chest pains. Concerned that she might have pneumonia, I finally convinced her to let me check her into a hospital.

I went to see her every day and one afternoon I was sitting by her bed, holding her hand, when she looked at me and said, "You know, Shirlee, I think my life is coming to an end. And I think that one of these days, God is going to have a little cottage ready for me and a cup of hot, boiling tea. And then He's going to call me home.

"But," she went on, "someday He's going to call you home, too. And when He does, I hope you'll stop by and visit me sometime. And we'll have a cup of hot tea together, just like old times."

Now that is something I'm really looking forward to!

CHAPTER 8

Alonzo: "God Gives the Gift"

Alonzo Clemons is a marvelous sculptor. His hands and fingers are his only tools. The precise images etched in his exacting memory are his only models. In galleries Alonzo's carefully crafted pieces are displayed side by side with the works of other artists without qualification or explanation. His bronze pieces are spectacular, not because they were done by someone with certain limitations, but rather because they simply are exceptional by any standard. Yet Alonzo has never had an art lesson in his life. He hasn't needed any.

Alonzo can look at a picture of an animal in a magazine and then magically sculpt a three-dimensional, perfect replica of that animal in 45 or 50 minutes. The oil-based clay that he so deftly uses is his language. One glimpse at the picture is sufficient; he doesn't need to return to it again. That picture is etched indelibly into his memory instantly with the accuracy of a freeze-frame on a digital camcorder.

He can do the same after a visit to the zoo. After a quick glance at one of the animals in the zoo, Alonzo will return home to sculpt that animal with perfect precision, each muscle and tendon poised exactly as he observed them. He is a virtual copy machine.

How does Alonzo do it? "God gives the gift" is his gentle explanation accompanied by an ever-present warm and contagious smile. Alonzo is one of the most mellow persons I have ever met. His joyous demeanor is infectious.

Alonzo is a prodigious savant. He is also what I call an "acquired" savant because Alonzo's special artistic gift emerged following a head injury he suffered as a child.

Alonzo was born in 1957. His mother says that Alonzo was a normal baby who seemed to learn very quickly. She thought he might have even been a precocious child. However, at about age three, according to his mother, Alonzo had a fall that left him with a brain injury that slowed his development precipitously, and left him with serious cognitive disability and very limited vocabulary and speech. He cannot read or write. His IQ has been measured at 40, but, as I point out in Chapter 28, whatever IQ measures, it does not measure the high-level skills and creativity that many savants, including Alonzo, demonstrate so spectacularly. Such abilities and imagination certainly are another component of "intelligence" and ought to be considered as such.

Besides Alonzo's extraordinary, literal memory for art, he shows other types of exceptional memory. On a trip back to the facility where he had spent some of his early years, Alonzo surprised the staff with his ability to recall the names of many of the residents on his unit from when he was there, along with many other details of his stay. And Alonzo loves music, especially classic rock from the 1950s. His recall of titles and artists is phenomenal according to those persons who know him.

Alonzo resided in a Colorado State Home and Training School from about age 10 to age 20. With the welcome national effort to move appropriate persons from institutions to placement in community facilities, Alonzo was able to move to a group home closer to his family. There he was also given the opportunity for employment which led, eventually, to his part-time job at the YMCA (Young Men's Christian Association) which has played such an important role in his overall development.

Throughout Alonzo's life, sculpting has been as much a force as it is a gift. For example while in one of the residential facilities some of the staff felt Alonzo's obsessive sculpting was getting in the way of learning language, other classroom subjects and even some basic living skills. So they took his clay away with the intent of using it as a reward for other behaviors designed for more overall growth including speech, school and social skills. That went on for some weeks. Then one evening the staff discovered, under Alonzo's bed, a whole menagerie of miniature sticky, black animals sculpted from the tar Alonzo had scraped from the school pavement with his fingernails.

Alonzo must sculpt. It is his language. It is his world.

For many persons their first introduction to Alonzo Clemons was his story as told on the October 1983 *60 Minutes* program *Genius* which also featured Leslie Lemke and George Finn, two other prodigious savants. On that program Alonzo continuously kneaded and shaped his clay into a beautiful colt even as he spoke with Morley Safer as the interview proceeded. "He can complete one of these horses in 45 minutes," Mr. Safer told the audience. And a beautiful horse it was.

The program also told of how Alonzo's works had earlier caught the attention of Pam Driscol, owner of the Driscol Gallery in Denver, Colorado. At that time Alonzo was getting most of the material for his pieces from pictures in magazines. Ms. Driscol suggested Alonzo's mother take him to the zoo where he could see some animals live and active. Alonzo's work immediately showed dramatic progress from static, relatively still sculptures to pieces full of life and motion. Instinctively Alonzo knew how to armature those clay figures to capture that motion and movement, a skill it takes most artists a great deal time to master. His life-size bronze piece—*Three Frolicking Foals*—conveys that excitement and vitality. It was commissioned by a corporation in Chicago for its office-building complex. It took Alonzo only three weeks to complete that impressive piece.

Following his introduction to the public, there was considerable visibility given to Alonzo and his exceptional works in the printed and electronic media. Other awards and fame followed as well. In May, 1984 for example, Alonzo's work was featured in the National Art Festival for the Handicapped in Washington, DC. There he had tea on the White House lawn and met Mrs. Nancy Reagan. He then went to San Francisco to appear on a television show and returned to Colorado where he showed his skills at a state fair. Finally in that busy month he participated in a benefit for handicapped persons in Kansas City, Missouri.

In May 1986 there was another milestone in Alonzo's career. The First Interstate Bank of Denver, and the Driscol Gallery of that city, sponsored the world premier exhibition of 30 of Alonzo's bronze sculptures. The highlight of the show was the *Three Frolicking Foals* piece mentioned above. I attended that world premier and I too was astonished. Alonzo loved the attention. He was so proud of his work and loved sharing it with others. Alonzo walked among all the exhibits beaming proudly. It was clear, though, that his greatest pride came from the life-sized *Three Frolicking Foals* piece. He loved doing that life-sized piece and it is his hope he can do more such large pieces if commissioned to do so.

Part of the proceeds from that world premier event went to the Wisconsin Medical Society Foundation to establish an information clearinghouse dedicated to raising awareness of, and providing education about, savant syndrome for the general public. That was the beginning of the program at the Wisconsin Medical Society

Foundation which today has now morphed into the very popular, and only, website in the world on savant syndrome—www.savantsyndrome.com—which is described in more detail elsewhere in this book.

After the world premier Alonzo's works gained even more national and international visibility. As a result Alonzo established in several years a reputation in the field as premier sculptor that ordinarily takes years and years to establish. His works sold for a variety of prices from $350 dollars to $5000 dollars. Art critics were enthusiastic about his sculptures, the public was astonished and the art world in general was appreciative, and proud, of the excellent quality of Alonzo's works.

I have had the rare chance to be together with Alonzo, Leslie Lemke and their families on several occasions. Once was at a camp for people with disabilities in northern Wisconsin. Leslie played the piano on a makeshift stage in the woods as Alonzo contentedly sculpted. Neither said much with words since music is Leslie's language and sculptures are Alonzo's vocabulary. Leslie's music and Alonzo's mellow smile blended beautifully. The campers were delighted and inspired by what they saw and heard. And so was I. What a rare opportunity to have two such remarkable persons sharing the same stage.

The second time I had the opportunity to be with Alonzo and Leslie together occurred in 1985 on *The Morning Show* with Regis and Kathie Lee in New York City. It was a live broadcast; no chance for editing. What was so especially valuable about that show was the time devoted to that segment. So many television pieces on savants are extremely limited timewise, usually only five or six minutes. In that clipped time one really never gets to know the savant, or his or her family members, in any depth. But this particular program devoted almost the entire hour to these remarkable savants and Alonzo's mother, Evelyn Clemons, and May's daughter, Mary Parker, who now cares for Leslie. As a result of having sufficient time, the audience got to see Alonzo take a square block of clay, and in 30 minutes sculpt that into a magnificent lifelike elephant, tusks and all. Alonzo used no model, just a freeze-frame, retrieved memory. The piece was finished. The audience was astonished by its beauty and accuracy. But Alonzo had another surprise for them. He showed them a horse and a colt he had completed in the 20 minutes he had waited in the green room before appearing on the program.

Soon it was Leslie's turn to play the piano. He had been sitting and quietly listening, tolerantly, to the chatter among us about him, and about savant syndrome. He began playing, and singing "You Light Up My Life." He dedicated the song to Alonzo, a person he knew but had never seen. Leslie is blind, but nevertheless sang about light. It was a very moving performance. Tears were plentiful. And the song touched Alonzo as well. Because some months later I received a beautiful bronze sculpture of a horse from Alonzo titled "You Light Up My Life." On his return home from New York, Alonzo had sculpted that piece and, in appreciation, dedicated it to Leslie. That piece has a treasured spot in my home.

There have been many other television or benefit appearances by Alonzo. The *Geraldo* program did a sufficiently lengthy broadcast on savant syndrome that the audience got to know Alonzo and Evelyn in some depth. Milwaukee County gives special recognition each year to industries that have been especially good about giving meaningful employment to people with disabilities. For several years the award gift was one of Alonzo's bronze sculptures. In 1998 the host group decided to invite Alonzo and Evelyn to come to the award ceremony in Milwaukee so the recipients could meet the sculptor in person, which made the award even more special to the recipients. Alonzo sculpted during the entire event, of course, and that as background made the evening even more inspiring and memorable.

There have been numerous documentary programs that have included Alonzo as well. Three television shows have been particularly informative. One was broadcast on the A&E *World of Wonder* program in 1997. It was exceptionally well done and won several media awards. A 2005 piece on Discovery Channel as part of the Canadian *Daily Planet* series was also particularly well done, not only portraying Alonzo's remarkable skills, but also summarizing in a concise yet comprehensive way present-day understanding and research on savant syndrome, especially the acquired savant. And *Beautiful Minds: Voyage into the Brain* by Colourfield Productions in Dortmund, Germany has an excellent segment on Alonzo and his remarkable talent as well. It provides a good update on his present life and progress.

In 1995 Alonzo moved to his own condominium in Boulder, Colorado where he still resides. His mother, who now lives in California, visits frequently. Some of the day-to-day management of Alonzo's affairs is provided by Nancy Mason, a family-recruited provider. Nancy also was instrumental in establishing Gifted Hands, Inc. as a resource for those wanting to learn more about Alonzo or purchase his works. Nancy is a very caring person who has helped Alonzo enormously in maintaining his independent living and continuing his art. She is immensely proud of him and his work, and has been a vital force in his progress overall.

The rooms in the condominium are full of Alonzo's sculptures, almost all of them animals. He has done some human figures but he prefers to do animals, especially horses or other large animals such as cows, steers, bears, elephants or giraffes. Some of his works are of dolphins, another large mammal. With respect to human figures, Nancy has observed that the innate chip that Alonzo so skillfully accesses for animal figures is not accessible for sculpting human figures. He will do persons, riding a horse for example, but not with the same ease or precision as the animals themselves.

Alonzo's work as a part-time janitor at the YMCA has played a very important role in his development overall. He was particularly intrigued with the weight-lifting equipment there and began to work out regularly. That led to his participating in power lifting—dead lift, bench press and squat—in Special Olympics after that event was added to the competition. He has a coach to help him with that skill, and recently won two gold, one silver and one bronze medal for his skills. In addition to the YMCA position, he also works a few hours per week at a company where he assembles certain items, showing considerable mechanical ability and interest, which is sometimes another savant skill.

As Alonzo's art skills have improved, so have his speech and vocabulary along with improved social and daily living skills. His special art abilities have worked as the "conduit toward normalization" which I described in Chapter 1. Alonzo is very proud of his increasing independence. While he may never be able to read or write, that has not worked as a deterrent to his progressive improvement overall and certainly has not detracted from his seemingly perpetual gentle demeanor which is so refreshing.

Alonzo has progressed to where he is not just a purveyor of art, but now a teacher as well. Alonzo loves to do demonstrations of his art in schools. These are events that Nancy arranges whenever possible. Alonzo's eagerness and enthusiasm for those events, and his comments thereafter, show that contributing in that way to the community that has been so kind to him is enormously fulfilling for him.

Alonzo continues to sculpt magnificently. His works have moved now from the Driscol Gallery in Aspen, Colorado to Gifted Hands, Inc. in Boulder, Colorado. His work continues to receive recognition and draw high praise. For example the Board of Directors of the Jewish Foundation for Group Homes established the S. Robert Cohen Achievement Award in 1986 to be given annually to the person or entity who "best exemplifies the spirit of the Jewish Foundation for Group Homes and its commitment to independent living." Each year the organization has chosen one of Alonzo's bronze works as the gift to the recipient of the award. That list of award winners is a very prestigious one. And certainly Alonzo's life story is an excellent and fitting example of a continual and successful move toward more and more "independent living" and a flowering of his humanity.

Alonzo's works can be seen online at www.artsales.com where he is listed as one of the artists. Gifted Hands, Inc. is now the official representative and contact point for information about Alonzo and his work. Gifted Hands can be reached via email at info@giftedhandsalonzo.com. A streaming video clip of Alonzo tells about him, and displays some of his works, at www.savantsyndrome.com in the profiles section.

CHAPTER 9

George: "It's Fantastic I Can Do That!"

George Finn remembers the weather for every day of his adult life. But there is one day, among those thousands of days, which he remembers especially well. "The day I hit a home run," he announces proudly. "That's a day I will never forget." And I am sure he won't because it seems, from listening to him, no other day even comes close.

I learned about that home run one day when George and I took a limo trip from New York City to a cable television station in New Jersey. We had appeared together on the *Joan Rivers Show* earlier that day and had another television appearance scheduled that afternoon on a local cable station. I don't remember the day of the week, or what the weather was like. But, of course, George remembers all those details.

I do remember the trip though because throughout the long ride George talked tirelessly about numbers, days and dates. He was absorbed and consumed with them. They were the centerpieces of our conversation. I heard about the home run a couple of times: George is so proud of that feat.

George is a calendar calculator. He can tell you instantly what day of the week a particular date will fall on for many centuries past or in the future. But he can also do the much more difficult task of inverse computing, calculating, for example, in which of the next 20 years will June 23 fall on a Tuesday or which years Easter will fall on March 27. George also remembers the weather for each day of his adult life. But he is baffled by simple arithmetic problems such as how much is 5 x 7. He guesses it might be 50.

Many people remember George Finn from the 1983 *60 Minutes* program *Genius* with Morley Safer on which he appeared as a calendar calculator—a "wizard"—along with Leslie Lemke the musician and Alonzo the sculptor. George bears a striking resemblance to Raymond Babbitt in the movie *Rain Man*. He also has many of the same habits and mannerisms. That is no coincidence because a number of scenes in that movie—calendar calculating, remembering the weather for days and years past, and computing square roots without being able to multiply 5 x 7 correctly—are based on George's real-life abilities.

The final scene with George in that *60 Minutes* program is particularly ironic. Just after having told Morely Safer that in the year 91,360 June 6 will be on a Friday, and then announcing that he would remember this day the rest of his life, George asks Mr. Safer, "What's your name again?"

George and his identical twin brother share this incredible calendar calculating ability. In fact their calendar calculating abilities are probably the most carefully documented and studied instances of savant syndrome reported in the scientific literature up until 1965.

In May, 1964 William A. Horwitz and his co-workers presented the remarkable case of "the calculating twins" to their colleagues at the annual meeting of the American Psychiatric Association in Los Angeles. That lecture was published as a scientific paper in the September, 1965 *American Journal of Psychiatry* (Horwitz *et al.* 1965). It was this report that first brought George to my attention.

The twins were born three months prematurely in December 1939. They were delivered by Caesarean section as of a set of triplets, two boys and a girl. The girl died within 12 hours. The boys were kept in an incubator for two months and there was a history of seizures during that period of time.

Developmental milestones were quite delayed. Both twins displayed head banging, head biting and destructiveness. Institutionalization was advised by a pediatrician when the twins were three years old, but instead both remained at home. Both twins studied an almanac that also contained a printed perpetual calendar. They later also played endlessly with a silver perpetual calendar that their father had brought them to replace the printed one.

The twins were admitted to Letchworth Village in New York State where they remained for 15 years. In 1963 they were transferred to a different facility. Both boys had an exquisite sense of smell and frequently would approach people and sniff them. They could pick up their own slippers and clothes by smelling them. Both boys showed almost constant rocking and swinging movements.

At age 24, when tested by Horwitz, the twins' IQs were between 60 and 70.

In his paper Horwitz provides extensive detail on the twins' ability both with calendar calculating and mathematics. Horwitz notes that the twins could not even add, subtract, multiply or divide simple digit numbers. Even with those limited arithmetic skills, however, given a particular birthday date, they would accurately tell you how many weeks there were until your next birthday or how many weeks had passed since your last birthday.

It was at the meeting in 1964 that a discussant observed that "the importance then, of the idiot savant lies in our inability to explain him; he stands as a landmark of our own ignorance and the phenomenon of the idiot savant exists as a challenge to our capabilities."

Four years later Horwitz *et al.* (1969) put forth their ideas on how to explain the remarkable calendar calculating abilities of the twins. George's range was seemingly unlimited; already then he was able to give a correct day for the date in the year 32,011. Neither boy knew the difference between the Gregorian and the Julian calendars (the changeover occurred in 1582) so that when testing went backwards in time there always needed to be allowance for the ten-day difference in the calendars. The authors surmised that the calculations were done by subtracting rapidly in multiples of 400, leaving the remainder in the present 400 year cycle as the correct answer.

Hamblin (1966) also describes the twins in some detail when she did an evaluation on them. They were 26 years old at that time, and were patients at the New York State Psychiatric Institute. Both twins told Hamblin that they did actually "see" numbers in their heads but they indicated they did not see whole pages of the calendar. Asked how they could do these calculations the answer was a simple one: "I've got a good head. That's how I do it."

Asked that same question 17 years later by Morley Safer on the 1983 *60 Minutes* program, George answered that question with even more energy and enthusiasm: "It's in my head. That's how I do it. It's fantastic I can do that!" And it truly is.

As mentioned above, George's ability with the calendar extends far beyond naming the day of the week in which a given date fell or will fall and extends to what is called inverse calendar calculating. For example, if asked in which months, in 2012, Wednesday will be the third day of the month, George can give an immediate answer. Other such questions might be on what months of the year 2012 does the first of the month fall on a Friday? Or in what years in the next 25 will April 21 fall on a Sunday? Again, answers are immediate and correct.

For all calendar calculators determining Easter is the most complex challenge. It is an extremely complicated and lengthy equation, even for a computer. In her article Hamblin points out that in 325 AD the Church fathers, following the First Council of Nicaea recommendation, decreed that Easter would fall on the first Sunday following the fourteenth day of the Paschal, or Easter moon, and that Paschal moon should be the first moon whose fourteenth day came on or after March 21. Since the moon's months is 29.53059 days long—the time it takes the moon to go through its phases—and since the Earth's month is 30 or 31 days, with 28 or 29 for February, the moon calendar and earth calendar are rarely in phase. Easter can turn up as early as March 22 and as late as April 25.

Yet even with the complexity of that computation, George can tell, without hesitation, which years in the next century Easter will fall on March 27, for example.

Horwitz *et al.* (1969) concludes that the twins' skill is a peculiar and unique kind of rote memory. Sacks (1989) concludes that they are viewing an "immense mnemonic tapestry" on which the twins literally could see a whole landscape of numbers from which they then simply read when giving the answer. Hamblin (1966) simply states she cannot explain the twins' skill. So perhaps, for now, George's explanation will have to suffice: "It's fantastic I can do that!"

On March 10, 1999 the television program *60 Minutes II* revisited George, providing Morley Safer an opportunity to see what had happened to George in the 16 years since their first meeting. George of course remembered exactly the day, and the weather, on which he and Morley had met in 1983. It was obvious on questioning that George's calendar calculating skills were undiminished. He knew, on questioning, that May 17, 1918 was on a Tuesday and he then listed the years from 1929 to 1996 on which that date would again fall on a Tuesday.

While his calendar calculating skills remained unchanged and undiminished, some very positive changes had occurred in his life in that 16-year time span. George was no longer living in a group home. He was living more independently in a shared apartment. He proudly announced to Mr. Safer, as he did to me on our ride to New Jersey, that he no longer required a guardian. At that time George was working as a messenger for an organization in New York City, navigating with ease the streets of that busy metropolis. George was as cordial and memorable in 1999 as in 1983.

For George, as with all savants, his special skills have served as a "conduit toward normalization." His exceptional skill is not silly or frivolous. Through the use of savant skills—"training the talent"—there is an increase in language ability, social aptitude and daily living skills on a road toward more independence.

Calendar calculating, an obscure skill in most of us, is a very common, almost universal ability among savants. Why calendar calculating? That is another mystery within savant syndrome, which I addressed earlier in Chapter 5.

My most recent contact with George was by telephone on Saturday, January 16, 2010. He immediately remembered me and our time together. He has moved out of the shared apartment into a house and he is extremely pleased about that. He is immensely proud of his work and his work record. He reminded me again that he is truly "on his own" with no need for a guardian. He wanted me to include him in this book so long as I promised to send him a copy.

But he has a new memory now that ranks right up there with the home run that he hit at the hospital. On August 14, 2003 there was a blackout in New York and he walked, "all by myself" all the way home, over the Brooklyn Bridge. It was a really "brave" thing to do he said—"It's a day I'll never forget." He reminded me again in our conversation that he always tells the truth. Telling the truth is incredibly important to George. "They call me honest Abe," George proudly says.

What a delightful, unforgettable person, with an unequalled lifelong calendar calculating ability that remains undiminished.

CHAPTER 10

Kim: "The Real *Rain Man*"

Kim Peek is the Mt. Everest of memory. There simply has not been anyone like him before among the memory giants of the past, and I doubt there will be anyone like him in the future. He was truly incredible, and one of a kind. His friends called him "Kim-puter."

Kim Peek memorized more than 12,000 books. Yes, memorized them. He would read a page in eight to ten seconds and then instantly commit that page, and all that followed, to his seemingly inexhaustible memory. Once fully scanned and stored, he would put the book upside down in the bookshelf—mission accomplished.

He could add a column of numbers on a page in the telephone book and give the mean of those numbers in an instant. He had encyclopedic knowledge in multiple areas of interest including world and American history, sports, movies, geography, the space program, actors, actresses, the Bible, church history, literature, classical music and Shakespeare to name some of them. He knew all the area codes in the country along with major city zip codes and all the television stations in the United States and their markets. He could identify most classical music compositions and tell the date when the music was written, the composer's birth date, place of birth and when and where the composition was first performed. He also memorized the maps in the front of telephone books so he was an onboard global positioning system for anyone driving him anywhere in the United States and Canada. Taxi drivers loved him; he provided them with directions to whatever the destination, whatever the city.

Kim read and memorized books so quickly because he was able to read two pages of a paperback book simultaneously, one page with the right eye and the other with the left. Somehow those two divergent images formed one lasting memory, which was stored as if on a hard disk with remarkable fidelity. I always kept waiting for the "disk full" message to appear, as I was convinced it surely would at some point. But it never did. Kim also demonstrated an unusual form of dyslexia wherein he could read a page turned sideways or upside down.

His father also described Kim's ability to "mirror read." Dad discovered this ability when Kim was skimming the front page of a newspaper that had inadvertently been placed on a mirrored dresser.

My first contact with Kim was by telephone. He asked me for my birth date, of course, and told me it was a Sunday, which it was, and reminded me that it was the evening of the first of President Roosevelt's fireside chats at a gloomy point in US history. He also reminded me that I would retire in 1998 when my sixty-fifth birthday would be on a Thursday, which it was. He also immediately named the area and zip codes for Fond du Lac, Wisconsin, gave me the call letters for the television stations from both Milwaukee and Green Bay that I could receive, which telephone company served my area at that time, my congressional representative and senators. He then gave me a brief history of senators from Wisconsin, some quite notorious, and some very progressive. He reminded me of the Green Bay Packer Super Bowl games, opponents and scores. He recalled the exact date and temperature of the famous "ice bowl" game along with the final score. He was right. I also remember those numbers because I was at Lambeau field in Green Bay that day, nearly frozen solid.

Kim was the inspiration for the movie *Rain Man*. In that movie Raymond Babbitt, an autistic savant, instantly and accurately computes square roots in his head. His brother Charlie remarks he "ought to work for NASA or something." It turns out that indeed NASA did involve Kim in one of their projects.

NASA was interested in Kim's brain scans because it hopes that by comparing and contrasting a wide range of neurotypical as well as other brain scans, it can eventually produce a comprehensive, high-fidelity, high-resolution three-dimensional anatomical model of the human brain using overlaying and fusing techniques to merge into a single model the imaging data obtained from multi-modality structural as well as functional CT and MRI scans on a wide variety of persons. Ultrasound is the only imaging system sufficiently small and portable that it can be used to monitor brain function of astronauts in space vehicles. NASA hopes that by overlaying ultrasound technology on detailed brain static and functional imaging, ultrasound can be made sufficiently sensitive to provide brain images rich enough to provide diagnostic information and permit tracking of brain function in space longitudinally over time during certain interventions and countermeasures. Thus the anatomic and functional imaging models will feed into ultrasonic methods of providing tracking and predictive tools.

Kim was born on November 11, 1951. It was a Sunday according to Kim He had an enlarged head, with an encephalocele—"a baseball sized 'blister' on the back of his head" which is how his father describes it—which later reduced spontaneously. Now only a thin layer of skull covered the area of the previous enecephalocele.

At age nine months doctors told the family Kim was "retarded" and they should put him in an institution and "get on with your lives." Another doctor suggested a lobotomy. But the family didn't follow any of that expert advice. Instead, they had Kim remain at home, a home lovingly provided him his entire life.

Mom and Dad read to Kim hour after hour moving Kim's finger along each sentence being read. By age 18 months Kim was able to memorize all the books read to him just with a single reading. Having committed the book to memory Kim would put it upside down on the shelf, so that no one would attempt to read it to him again; no need for that, the book was already in his memory bank. Then that book would go on the shelf upside down or backwards; it was already scanned.

At age three Kim asked what the word "confidential" meant. He was told kiddingly to look it up in the dictionary and he did just that. He somehow knew how to use alphabetical listings, found the word and then proceeded to read, phonetically, the word's definition. He was obsessed with numbers, reading telephone books and adding columns of telephone numbers. He enjoyed totaling numbers on license plates as well.

By age six Kim was reciting whole paragraphs verbatim from a book with the mere mention of its page number. By that time he had memorized the entire index of a set of encyclopedias. But when it came time to begin attending school, Kim lasted only a few minutes, according to his father, because of his hyperactivity. At that point the family was advised to consider a lobotomy for Kim to help with the hyperactivity. Fortunately, they declined.

Kim was home schooled after age seven with the help of some retired elementary school teachers as tutors. They met with Kim for twice-weekly, 45-minute sessions. He completed all high school requirements by age 14.

Kim did not walk until he was age four and continued to have problems with hand–eye coordination and balance. Even as an adult his father had to help Kim bathe, dress, button his shirts, brush his teeth and comb his hair. That kind of assistance was essentially a 24/7 responsibility that his father patiently carried on throughout Kim's life.

Kim had his first head X-rays in 1983 but they were not that informative because they were essentially only skull films. The first MRI was done in 1988, the same week that *Rain Man* premiered in Hollywood which Kim, his dad and Barry Morrow, the writer of the *Rain Man* script, attended. The MRI showed that Kim's head was approximately one-third larger than normal. Most striking was the total absence of the corpus callosum, the large connecting structure between the left and right hemispheres of the brain. Other connecting structures such as the left and right anterior and posterior commissures were missing as well. And there was extensive damage to the cerebellum, particularly on the right side.

Psychological testing in 1988 showed an IQ score of 87, with very wide discrepancy between the subtests of verbal and performance abilities, some falling in the mentally retarded range and others in the superior range of intelligence. The report concluded that "Kim's IQ classification is not a valid description of his intellectual abilities." I agree. IQ scores on many savants are misleading and are not valid descriptions of intellectual abilities. Kim's profile, and that of many savants, as I will point out in Chapter 28, argues, rather, for "multiple intelligences" within us all, rather than a single "intelligence" or G factor as it is called.

Final diagnosis from that testing was "developmental disorder not otherwise specified." A diagnosis of autism was *not* applied to Kim (a correct assessment in my view). Kim is not an "autistic savant" as he is often described. He does have some autistic traits and mannerisms, but those are superimposed on a developmental disability caused by his encephalocele and other unique brain architecture.

As Kim grew older, he attended a sheltered workshop where he helped with payroll calculations for other clients. He would tally daily production earnings for each client based on piecework, and do so in his head without benefit of an adding machine or calculator. He would also help distribute the checks. He remained very introverted at home, however, and if visitors came, Kim would often simply retreat to his room.

Kim did accompany his father Fran on some of his travels however. In 1984 they attended a meeting of the National Association for Retarded Citizens (The ARC) in Arlington, Texas. Fran was volunteer chairman of the communications committee, a field familiar to him since he was president of his own advertising company, Fran Peek Advertising, in Salt Lake City. Barry Morrow, a screenwriter from Los Angeles, attended the meeting also, at the invitation of the committee seeking his advice on how to increase national exposure of the organization through public service announcements and other public relations efforts. Mr. Morrow had earlier received some awards for his TV Emmy-winning programs *Bill* and *Bill II*, in which Mickey Rooney played the part of a cognitively impaired person in a sensitive and touching fashion.

Barry Morrow recalls his first meeting with Kim. It began with Kim abruptly and solemnly stating: "Think about yourself, Barry Morrow." It was a greeting that both surprised and intrigued him. Kim then astonished Mr. Morrow by correcting the zip codes on membership lists they perused. To Mr. Morrow's astonishment Kim was familiar with almost every author and book in the ARC's library. He quoted an unending amount of sports trivia and provided detailed driving directions for destinations almost anywhere in the United States and Canada. Having given his birth date to Kim, Mr. Morrow was told the day of the week he was born, the day of the week his birthday will fall on in the present year, and the day of the week when he would turn 65 and could think about retiring. The two of them then also discussed events of the Revolutionary War, the Civil War, World Wars I and II, Korea and Vietnam.

On the airplane ride home from that meeting Mr. Morrow jotted down "autistic savant" and remembers vividly thinking, "This is a character in search of a movie." He then wrote the original script for the movie *Rain Man*.

In the course of preparation for playing the part of Raymond Babbitt in the movie, Dustin Hoffman met with Kim and his father in February 1987. Fran Peek describes that "special" day at length in his book about Kim (Peek and Hanson 2008) and chronicles in detail Kim's encyclopedic memory feats as shared with Dustin Hoffman, including facts about British monarchs, the Bible, baseball, horse racing, dates, times, composers, melodies, movies, geography, the space program, authors and literature. Dustin Hoffman's parting remark to Kim, according to his father, was: "I may be the star, but you are the heavens." When Dustin Hoffman accepted his Oscar in March 1989, he opened his remarks with: "My special thanks to Kim Peek for making *Rain Man* a reality."

While Kim Peek was the inspiration for the movie *Rain Man*, it was not his life story. Certainly some of Kim's skills are seen as played out in the main character, Raymond Babbitt. But Raymond Babbitt is a composite savant. All of the skills seen—computing square roots, memorizing the phone book, counting the spilled toothpicks—are drawn from real-life savants. And along the way in the screenwriting, the decision was made to portray an autistic savant because autism had not been to that point depicted in any major film until *Rain Man*. And while Kim Peek did have some autistic mannerisms (as mentioned above), he did not have autistic disorder as his basic disability.

Although *Rain Man* was not the story of Kim's life, it did change Kim Peek's life in a major way. Kim no longer retreated to his room when company came. He was no longer reclusive at all. Instead, he and his father logged nearly three million airline miles and appeared in person hundreds of times each year on their mission to share Kim's skills and gifts with the audiences along with Kim's message of inclusion and appreciation of diversity. As a result of these appearances in which Kim would actively interact with the audience members, Kim became much more comfortable socially and developed escalating confidence. In the feedback received from this multitude of appearances there were continual comments about Kim's positive influence on children and parents in creating better awareness, recognition and respect for persons who are "different."

Kim regularly summed up his outlook this way: "Recognizing and respecting differences in others, and treating everyone like you want them to treat you, will help make our world a better place for everyone. You don't have to be handicapped to be different. Everyone is different."

Barry Morrow says it this way: "I don't think anybody could spend five minutes with Kim and not come away with a slightly altered view of themselves, the world and our potential as human beings."

Kim also made innumerable television appearances in the United States and other countries. He was also featured in a number of documentaries nationally and internationally. Focus Productions of Bristol, England has an hour-long documentary called *The Real Rain Man* which has been shown widely in the United Kingdom, United States and many other countries. That program features a very interesting on-camera interaction between Kim Peek and Daniel Tammet, two memory giants. A three-hour documentary *Beautiful Minds: Voyage into the Brain* has also been seen and distributed worldwide by Colourfield Productions of Dortmund, Germany. A Swedish film—*Verklighetens Rain Man*—is a particularly touching look at the relationship between Kim and his father.

As a result of all of this, Kim became much more outgoing, much more animated and much more comfortable in personal interactions. His factual recall base continued to expand, seemingly without limit. But along with that deepening spectacular recall, Kim showed increased evidence of *comprehending* what was in that massive databank. With that comprehension came the ability to connect those facts together, from that massive store, in a computer-like, search-engine manner. Kim became a living Google, which often emerged in creative, mind-dazzling wit and puns.

Throughout this book I mention the transition I have seen in many savants from *literal memorization* to *improvisation* to *creation* of something entirely new. In Kim's case that evolution was from massive literal memorization, to comprehension and improvisation in the form of puns, to creativity in the form of insights and wit. Kim developed extremely sharp wit. He was often two or three steps ahead of those around him, including his father, in that regard. It was sometimes moments, or even days, before the clever, creative meaning of some of his puns and witticisms dawned on those around him, including me.

For example, on being asked what he knew about Beethoven's Fifth Symphony, Kim uttered, "Churchill." Where did that come from? What's the link there? Left to explain, Kim points out the first four notes of Beethoven's Fifth—dah, dah, dah, dum—are also dot, dot, dot, dash. That's Morse Code for the letter "V." Winston Churchill is known for his victory speech and his frequent poses with the letter "V" for victory held high as formed by the index and middle fingers. Then Kim would recite portions of Churchill's speeches.

At one of his appearances an audience member asked Kim what he knew about Lincoln's Gettysburg address. "Will's house, 227 West Front Street. But he stayed there only one night. He gave the speech the next day," Kim responded. Indeed that was Lincoln's address in Gettysburg before his famous speech.

Kim's father has amassed a whole collection of these witticisms now; it is impressive and entertaining. It often required Kim's father, acting as a sort of decoder, to decipher Kim's rapid and extraordinary steps-ahead-of-everyone's wit.

In recent years another skill very surprisingly surfaced in Kim. Quite by chance Kim met Dr. April Greenan, Professor of Music at the University of Utah in 2002. Dr. Greenan is a Mozart scholar as well as a music teacher. In working with Dr. Greenan, Kim began to show some interest in piano *performance*, not just music *memory*. Kim was long been able to recognize almost any song he had ever heard just by hearing its melody, or even just seeing it on an album cover. He would then recall the name of the composer, along with the place of birth and birth date, followed by the place and date of death if deceased, and would name where and what date the piece was first played.

But his musical prowess didn't end there. While some motor coordination difficulties limited his ability to play music, he continued to make some progress in that regard. He also showed, to the professor's amazement, a remarkable, innate understanding of the organization, content, style and "rules of music" beyond the huge musical repertoire he stored so accurately.

That musical sophistication led to some interesting problems for his father, Fran. When he and Kim would attend symphonies Kim was sometimes troubled by musical mistakes during the performances based on his massive memory of the musical scores. Sometimes he would point those out to the conductor after the concert. This requirement for precision not just in music, but in words also, surfaced one time when Kim and his father were at a Shakespeare play. Near the end of the performance Kim shouted out, "Stop! Stop the play!" One of the actors asked what was the matter? "You missed some words in that last line," Kim shouted. The actor replied, "Well I didn't think anyone would notice. And further, I didn't think that anyone would have really cared." "Well, Shakespeare would have cared," Kim volunteered.

Since the MRI studies in 1988, more sophisticated imaging has been carried out on Kim including functional MRI and diffusion tensor imaging (DTI), new techniques described in more detail in Chapter 28. Through the measurement of water movement in neuronal tissue, DTI can demonstrate graphically connections *within* the two hemispheres, *between* the two hemispheres, and *between* the upper and lower level circuits in the brain. Kim's DTI demonstrates numerous connections between the two hemispheres, even with absence of the corpus callosum.

Studies are underway now as well with other persons with absent corpus callosum to compare and contrast those images with the brain imaging which accompanies Kim's particular repertoire of abilities and skills, Not everyone with absent corpus callosum has Kim's abilities. So these studies should be able to assess the significance of that particular CNS malformation in him, and should give further clues to the importance of the corpus callosum to CNS and brain function overall. Fortunately the collection of brain imaging studies on Kim is extensive and will continue to be available for further analysis over time.

Kim and his father have been very willing participants in various research explorations with Kim, some of which were carried out as part of documentary productions. His one-of-a-kind massive memory skills, coupled with his particular brain architecture as seen in structural and functional imaging studies, provide an excellent opportunity to compare and contrast Kim's unique skills and brain imaging with neurotypical, or other savant, brain architecture, circuitry and function overall

Kim and his father carried out their worldwide mission and message, about diversity and about caring, with tireless energy. Perhaps the pinnacle of Kim's lecture circuit was the appearance of him and his father at the respected and prestigious Oxford Union in Oxford which has hosted so many important persons in the past. Kim of course answered the students' questions on history, geography and other topics with ease. And, true to form, he told each person who inquired the day of the week when they were born, and the day they will turn 65 and "can retire." But one question was particularly touching to the audience. A girl asked, "Kim, are you happy?"

"I am happy just to look at you," he answered. So happiness and many other emotions were not foreign to Kim. He was full of emotion and expression.

Kim emerged from his introversion and isolation in an astounding and magnificent manner. Kim puts it this way: "*Rain Man* changed my life." Still, however, Fran was constantly working behind the scenes, of necessity as he always has, providing the day-to-day care Kim required. But he did so with untiring patience, and without complaint. Audiences were certainly always left with astonishment about Kim's memory skills. But they are always equally touched by the splendid example of love and care—unconditional positive regard—that was so evident between a father and his son, *both* extraordinary persons in their particular ways.

Fran Peek wrote his first book about his son, titled *The Real Rain Man*, in 1996. An updated version of that book, *The Life and Message of the Real Rain Man: The Journey of a Mega-savant* was published 12 years later (Peek and Hanson 2008). An article in the *Scientific American* magazine by Dr. Dan Christensen and myself titled "Inside the mind of a savant" provides more background on Kim, and, for those interested, it contains some of the actual MRI images on Kim as well (Treffert and Christensen 2005).

Kim's phenomenal, one-of-a-kind memory capacity is better seen than described. It is simply so massive it is almost beyond description. So I would invite you to view some of the video clips of Kim on the savant syndrome website at www.savant-syndrome.com and you will see immediately why it was that Barry Morrow was so impressed with Kim, the real Rain Man, and why the movie he inspired has touched so many.

Kim Peek *is* the Mt. Everest of memory. I doubt a person like him, with such unique and massive memory, will ever come along again.

There have been other famous cases in the past of persons with memory seemingly without boundaries. Dr. A.R. Luria (1968) described his patient "S" in great detail in his book *The Mind of the Mnemonist.* But "S" had no mental disability so by definition was not a savant. And, unlike Kim, "S" had to develop a formal system of forgetting each day to "clear the slate," like an overcrowded Etch-a-Sketch, to make way for the next day's memories. Kim did not need to do that. He just didn't forget, and somehow the "disk full" message never surfaced. I describe a number of other persons with "exultation of memory" in Chapter 5 of *Extraordinary People* (Treffert 2006a). But among all those mnemonists of the past and present, Kim Peek remains unique.

Kim always said, with love and pride, that he and his father "share the same shadow." And they do. Seeing them walking side by side reminds one of seeing Charlie and Raymond Babbitt in *Rain Man* walking side by side on their first meeting. Having the privilege of interacting with them in real life emphasized for me how much they did share the same shadow. And it was that "shared shadow" image that always left audiences so touched, and so inspired. It remains a shadow widely cast as a role model for all of us in our dealing with each other whatever our individual abilities or disabilities.

In April, 2008 Kim and Fran visited Wisconsin to keynote a Wisconsin Medical Society Foundation Dinner. They also did some other presentations including a lecture at the University of Wisconsin—Fond du Lac campus, meetings with two elementary school classes and then Grand Rounds at the University of Wisconsin Medical School. Having the chance to spend an entire week with them on that visit was a special privilege for me. And Kim and Fran left an indelible, warm and inspiring impression on everyone in Wisconsin who met them that week.

It turns out, though, regrettably that's the last time I would be with Kim in person.

Home for Christmas

About five o'clock on Saturday, December 19, 2009 I received a very sad phone call from Fran Peek. He called to tell me that Kim had died suddenly of a heart attack that afternoon. Kim had not been ill and he and his dad were looking forward to the holiday season. They had been opening Christmas cards earlier in the day and Kim liked them all, including the one my wife and I had sent. Kim had his 58th birthday in November and had been looking forward to many more.

There has never been, and I doubt there ever will be, another Kim Peek. His talents were unique, exceptional, and spectacular. And the story of the bond between him and his dad was inspirational. Their willingness to share both the skills, and the story, with so many appreciative audiences worldwide so unselfishly was their gift to us. Their travels to tell the story, and share the inspiration, left them 5500 miles short of three million air miles. Fran kept track and says that he and Kim had spoken, on that remarkable odyssey, to over 60 million people—half of them students—over these past 20 years.

Kim says "*Rain Man* changed my life." Kim, in turn, along with his father Fran, touched and changed our lives as well. As I told Fran the following day when I spoke with him again, "Kim went home for Christmas. Last night I looked up and saw a new star in the heavens. It shone brightly but it had a uniquely different shape than all the others. It was truly one of a kind. And Kim Peek was certainly one of a kind."

I posted notice of Kim's death on the savant syndrome web site. Since Fran Peek was not into email, I invited persons who wanted to send condolences in that manner to send them to me and I would forward them to Fran. There was an instant outpouring of hundreds of messages from around the world—Poland, India, China, England, United States, New Zealand, Venezuela, and all points in between. Some were from parents of handicapped children now determined to be the best parents they could be inspired by Fran's loyalty to Kim and grateful that Kim and Fran made the world a better place for families such as theirs. Others were from students who now looked at disabilities differently, or whose motivation to pursue successful careers in neuroscience was kindled by Kim and Fran's visit to their schools. Still others were from individuals on the autistic spectrum grateful that acceptance of being "different" was now more commonplace, and Kim's message about universal acceptance of differences had helped make the planet a better and more comfortable place for them.

If I had to condense the thousands of words in those messages to one word it would be: inspiration. I didn't count the number of times that actual word—inspiration—appeared in the messages, but it seemed to be present in almost all of them. Some messages were in Chinese which I couldn't read but one "stranger" from China was kind enough to interpret the text for me: "Kim Peek will live in our heart forever. Thank Fran."

Indeed Kim will live in our hearts forever. And, indeed, thank you Fran.

CHAPTER 11

Ellen: "With a Song in Her Heart"

Ellen Boudreaux was the first female savant I had the opportunity to meet. I remember that occasion vividly. It was on a visit to Ellen's home in 1986, when she was 29 years of age. Her parents had told me that Ellen was very time conscious and wanted things to occur *exactly* on schedule. That preoccupation began some years earlier when her mother had Ellen, who is blind, listen to the "time lady." There seems to be a digital clock running in her head ever since.

I was at the bottom of the stairs on the first floor talking with her parents. Suddenly Ellen came flying down the stairs from her bedroom, rushed into the living room and turned on the TV *exactly* at the moment Dan Rather opened his evening newscast with a friendly "Good evening." Ellen seemed relieved, and pleased.

Impeccable timekeeping without reference to a watch or clock is an astonishing skill in some savants. One of Dr. Down's original ten savants whom he described in his classic 1887 paper on savant syndrome was a 17-year-old boy with that ability. He was unable to use a clock or tell time in a conventional manner but he always did know the time with perfect precision when tested.

Ellen's highly developed sense of timekeeping surfaced at about age eight. To help Ellen overcome a fear of the telephone that she seemed to have at that age, her mother, Barbara, coaxed Ellen one afternoon to listen to the automatic time recording of the "time lady" which was available in those days. Ellen listened for about ten minutes and returned to her room where she mimicked what she had heard on the phone. She correctly understood the sequence of seconds, and when she came to "1 59 and 59 seconds," Ellen announced, "The time is two o'clock." The mystery is that, during the ten minutes she had listened, there was no change from one hour to the next, and there is no real explanation as to how Ellen knew to change the hour at the 59-minute, 59-second point. Obviously she had never seen a clock, nor did the house contain any Braille clocks. And neither the concept of elapsing time nor the workings of a clock had ever been explained to her.

Ellen's most astonishing skill is music. For me, that day, Ellen played an opera she had transposed to the piano after having listened to a recording of the live performance. It was impressive. Today Ellen plays the piano, guitar and the keyboard. She is the soloist with a rock and roll band—"The Diremakers"—which has become well known in her hometown area. With her multiple instruments and many musical interests she has developed a vast repertoire.

Bob Sylva, a reporter for the *Sacramento Bee* newspaper, summed it up this way in a January 18, 2001 article: "With a song in her heart, music is her bridge to the world. By any measure of musical virtuosity and genius, this is a remarkable performance. For Ellen, it's a form of child's play" (Sylva 2001, pp.E1, E5).

It is very hard to stump Ellen, as the newspaper writer found out in a flawless recollection by Ellen of a variety of tunes and styles ranging from the Supremes to "Dueling Banjos" (in which she plays both parts), to Ellen's tour de force orchestration of "Whole Lotta Love" and the Led Zeppelin "Appassionata" in which she replicates, remarkably, every voice, instrument and studio sound effect.

Ellen provides an example of the conspicuous and curious recurrent *triad* of *blindness + mental disability + musical genius* that occurs in savant syndrome with such striking regularity over the past 125 years, beginning with the story of "Blind Tom" in the 1800s (see Chapter 6). It would also include Leslie Lemke and Tony DeBlois (see Chapters 7 and 12 respectively) and of course Ellen herself. I have met a number of other savants with this striking combination of gifts and disabilities, and a number of others are documented in the literature since the nineteenth century. Why those three traits should be linked together with such relative frequency in a condition as rare as savant syndrome is a puzzling question explored earlier in Chapter 5. Suffice it to say, Ellen is a convincing example of that recurrent triad.

Ellen was born prematurely in 1957 and developed the blindness of prematurity (retrolental fibroplasias) following birth. Ellen developed slowly. When she was four months old, doctors confirmed what her parents suspected—Ellen was blind. But when Ellen was six months old her sister came running out to tell her mother that "the baby is singing." The cradle gym above the baby played Brahms' "Lullaby" and indeed Ellen was, at six months, humming that song with the same precision and rhythm that has characterized all of her music since that time.

In early childhood years Ellen listened, with her sister, to popular artists of the time—Frankie Avalon, Elvis Presley, Chubby Checker and Jerry Lee Lewis, among others. Now, 40 years later, Ellen can play all those "golden oldies" perfectly on the piano or guitar with all the musical introductions and embellishments intact, imitating the voices of Holly, Presley, Lewis and all the others.

Ellen was four years old before she walked. But once she began to walk, it was with a superior spatial sense. From the very beginning she was aware of large objects such as walls, fences and buildings from a distance of six feet or more and insisted on going to them and touching them. Her father noted that from those early years on, she has been able to walk in thick forests, new to her, without running into trees. She navigates her way by making a constant little chirping sound as a form, apparently, of her own personal radar.

At age 4½ psychological testing showed a score of 40 on the Vineland Social Maturity Scale which suggested an estimated IQ, at that time, of between 30 and 50. The family became determined to find the best educational and vocational opportunities for their daughter and enrolled her in the San Juan Unified School District in Fair Oaks, California. Ellen did extremely well in school and has proceeded through a series of steps in the special education program, including now adult special education programming. Speech therapy began in 1983 and progress in language development was impressive as well, with no sacrifice of her artistic skill.

Ellen's musical skill and memory are prodigious. Her interest in music, as mentioned previously, began as early as six months of age. At about age four, Ellen surprised her mother by picking out some tunes on a small electronic organ. At age seven, a teacher advised her parents to get Ellen a piano. They did and the music has poured forth ever since. Ellen now constructs complicated chords to accompany melodies she hears on the radio or the stereo. She has transposed the orchestra and chorus of *Evita* to the piano with complex, precise chords. She reproduces the crowd and mob sounds with intense dissonances using both hands. That rendition is an impressive, and lengthy, performance.

Ellen taught herself guitar by spending countless hours going up and down each string, memorizing the tones that each fingering produced and experimenting with chords. She is driven by and enamored of rhythm of any type, form or origin. She loves to improvise and after listening to almost any album, she will begin to play chords with it, improvising unusual but striking accompaniments. She will play what she has heard in one form such as jazz, then in another style, perhaps classical. She will transpose rock and roll to a waltz form in three-quarter time. She is fascinated with radio and television commercials and will immediately transpose those to the piano as well.

Time, like music, is a vital part of Ellen's life now. Precisely at the right time each day she listens—regularly, obsessively and without fail—to her favorite television programs, just as Raymond Babbitt did in the movie *Rain Man*. Those programs include speeches, Spanish language broadcasts, football games, every game of the Oakland A's baseball team, stock market reports and revival meetings.

Ellen has continued to grow and mature as a musician, expanding not only her repertoire of songs, but her repertoire of instruments as well. Vital to her progress has been the belief and support of her very loving family. Ellen is another convincing example that music, or any other special skill, can be used as a conduit toward increased socialization and better language acquisition, all without any trade-off of special skills. The wedding of her fascination with rhythm to her spectacular sense of time suggests some clear connection between those two traits. Those two abilities, linked as they are in Ellen, provide some support for the idea that music may be, as some have suggested, simply "unconscious counting."

In 1988 Ellen joined other students in a rock and roll band—"The Diremakers"—when she enrolled at an adult education center for the developmentally disabled in Sacramento, California to increase her exposure to music training. The band plays locally and has also performed at the California State Fair, for example, on a number of occasions. With the band involvement, Ellen became "quite the social butterfly," according to her sister, and has become much more verbal. That social and language progression has continued. Ellen increasingly enjoys being with people and especially loves to have visitors come to the home. Now instead of retreating into seclusion behind her closed bedroom door, as she once did, she readily extends her hands to meet the welcome guests.

Ellen continues to play daily with "The Diremakers," for which she is the main soloist. Ellen has done solo performances at the Ronald Reagan Library in Los Angeles, and has played with the band for a number of statewide appearances. Ellen continues to become more sociable, more outgoing and more independent. The 2001 *Sacramento Bee* article (Sylva 2001) describes Ellen this way:

> She loves music. No, that doesn't capture Ellen's total absorption of sound. She sucks in notes like particles of oxygen. She instantly processes melodies and complex rhythms, intonations and lyrics. She can hear a song once on the radio, store it in her vast database, and recall it years later. Play it with absolute fidelity and technical precision.
>
> She's a person of unfathomable depth. She's a daughter, and a sister. She's a valued friend and bandmate. Truly, at heart, behind that angelic demeanor, that sublime smile, what she really is is a raging rock star.

Her mother's description of Ellen, and her progress overall in even more recent years, extends beyond the extraordinary musical ability itself:

> Ellen has progressed, albeit slowly, from a shy, reclusive, touch-me-not individual, into an affectionate, outgoing person who loves to hug and who says, at the same time, "I love you." She is that rarity—someone who is almost always happy. When she wakes, she sits up in her bed and begins singing as she reads her Braille storybooks, smiling with pleasure.

When Ellen began singing years ago she did so softly and with her head down. Now, according to her mother, Ellen "holds her head high and projects her voice, which is naturally strong and one can hear her hit some of the highest notes, sometimes solo. Again this brings her the greatest joy and a wide smile."

While Ellen's vocal communication is often in short phrases or even single words, she can understand long instructions and will carry those out carefully. While there may be paucity of conversation, Ellen memorizes lengthy commercials that she hears on the radio and recites them back with absolute precision, pronouncing even the longer words correctly.

Given her somewhat limited verbal skills, surprisingly, a new fascination has recently surfaced in Ellen: *foreign* languages. Ellen enjoys listening to the local Spanish-language radio station and shows interest in other foreign languages as well. In preparation for a trip to France, Ellen's mother purchased some tapes in conversational French. When Ellen discovered those tapes she began to listen to them regularly and now each Friday evening has become the designated time, in her self-imposed schedule, to listen to those tapes intently, objecting if anyone intrudes. For a recent birthday her sister gave Ellen a series of CDs in basic German. Now Saturday afternoons are "German Talk" time.

When a TV crew from Japan filmed at Ellen's home, one of the crew members sang, shyly and softly, a folk song in Japanese. Ellen listened closely. When asked, Ellen played the song back on the piano. Then, when asked to do so, Ellen sang the song together with the somewhat reluctant Japanese soloist—in Japanese. Ellen's mother described that encounter this way:

> It was priceless and we were enchanted. I can't say how accurate her version was, but the very polite gentleman declared it to be "perfect." In any case it was fascinating to see how far she could go with this.

During the past several years, Ellen's family has made a very important and intriguing discovery: *the more we direct Ellen toward change, the better she responds.* In prior years Ellen was insistent that her daily life—days, weeks and months—be pre-set on a schedule which she would recite well in advance, for the entire year. Like many autistic persons she would become emotional or even defiant if there were variations. June was swimming; October meant four days at the beach north of San Francisco—no exceptions.

However, as the years passed she was slowly changing from her loner, touch-me-not autistic persona. There were three principal indicators of that:

1. Summer Camp

    In the spring of 2008 Ellen's sister Nancy and her mother decided to make a change from the summer camp Ellen had attended for 20 years near Sacramento to Enchanted Hills, which has a permanent home in the red-woods near the Napa wine country. It is a Program of the Lighthouse for the Blind in San Francisco. The goal of the camp is to encourage independence including having the campers move about as self-reliantly as possible. This involves encouraging cane usage, service dogs, mobility devices, guide ropes or even human guides to support this independence. Young counselors are assigned on a ratio of one for every three campers to guide, but not pamper the campers.

    On an advance Visitor's Day Ellen was given an arm-in-arm walking tour with the camp director and she seemed elated about attending her "new camp." On Registration Day her sister Cheryl provided moral support. Ellen was assigned to a tidy redwood cabin with three other blind campers. She made an immediate bond with them by playing Elvis Presley tunes on her guitar and some of the initial stress was eased for all four of them. Of course the family was apprehensive what might happen that week. Parents and caregivers are "on call" during the week, but no calls came indicating any problems.

    At the end of the week the family drove up the winding mountain road with some understandable apprehension as to how Ellen might have done that week. Their concern was short-lived when the director assured that "Ellen did fine!"

    As it turns out the staff and campers soon realized Ellen could play on the piano almost anything they asked from memory. So the donated grand piano that had been painted sky blue for the 4th of July celebration was rolled outside and speakers were set up. In the small lake beyond the deck, campers and crew drifted by and sang along with Ellen's John Philip Sousa repertoire or any other songs they requested.

    Ellen loved the camp and is already counting the weeks until she can return next time. From that experience the family came to the important realization that pushing Ellen outward from the long-established routines did not cause her to retreat into herself as she has always done in the past. Instead that change in routine had just the opposite effect of making her more outgoing and more independent.

2. Breakthrough on Braille

    Ellen did have some beginning Braille lessons many years ago. But for the past several years Ellen was encouraged to resume Braille lessons with the Society for the Blind. She meets with an instructor for 90 minutes each week for advanced Braille lessons where she has learned "contractions" and "brief forms" she never knew before. There has been a 400 percent improvement in her reading skills in terms of speed and confidence. At each lesson the instructor and Ellen read a book together. Then Ellen types out a story on her Braille writer, using some material from the story she just read, but also adding her own personal twist to her writing.

    Ellen's interaction with the Society is reciprocal. She appreciates very much what she has learned, and the independence and expansion of her vistas that the advanced Braille has provided for her. And the Society, in turn, has come to appreciate Ellen's exceptional musical talent which she shares liberally with them when she brings her keyboard along to special events playing everything from symphonies to rock and roll and anything in between.

3. Jazzin' with Beethoven

    Because Ellen's piano is at her sister Nancy's house where Ellen stays during the week, her mother bought Ellen a keyboard to use on the weekends that she spends with her mother. One of Ellen's favorite pieces is the final movement to Beethoven's Symphony No. 9, known and loved by audiences worldwide as the "Ode to Joy." Her mother ordered a video of that piece with Leonard Bernstein, four soloists, a large chorus and the Vienna Philharmonic orchestra. As Ellen listened to the video, she began to play along on her keyboard. The video was faulty and after a few weeks it began sticking and then quit playing altogether. Mother discarded the video and asked Ellen if she could play it by herself. To her mother's utter amazement, she not only did so, but also played the second video of the set, Beethoven's Piano Concerto No. 1 with Bernstein conducting the Vienna Philharmonic and playing solo piano. Ellen played the piece without pausing for intermissions and managed to top Bernstein's time by 15 minutes.

    But what happened next was even more intriguing. Each weekend she still loves to play those two works, but now with *jazz improvisation*. Now no two performances are ever alike.

    The first indication of improvisation came when her mother realized that Ellen's left hand was playing very dominantly, with almost a Latin beat during the concerto. The following week, the main theme of the "Ode" had evolved into exuberance, with each note played twice. Later new melodies crept in, sometimes to be repeated several times; other times the melody disappeared entirely. Each performance is unique.

Mother sums it up this way:

> When I watch and listen, I can't help remembering the battery of tests she was given at age four with the consensus designation of an IQ of 30 to 50 with the recommendation that she be institutionalized, as she would "never learn anything."
>
> How far we have come since that time.
>
> While music purists might decry Ellen's effrontery in jazzing up Beethoven, she has only the foggiest conception of who he was. When we watch her happy smile and occasional giggle while she plays, it is quite obvious that she doesn't play for Beethoven, or for us. She plays for her own pleasure. She will accept a bit of praise, but not too much, as that is not what matters to her.
>
> As her verbal communication remains limited and likely will be always, she cannot tell me what she is doing. So what goes on here? As a layman I cannot know, but I am grateful to have been a constant observer and sometimes participant in what seems to me to have been an awesome and often inexplicable journey.

The love, care, concern and pride that Ellen's family show toward Ellen every day is a powerful propellant in her continual progress, and an indispensable ingredient toward her happiness, her pride and her contentment. Has it been a burden for them? Ellen's mother puts it this way: "Sometimes when her sister Nancy and I are out and about with her, friends may comment that they could never have done it. Nancy and I exchange a smile that says 'But you don't know what you have missed!'"

CHAPTER 12

Tony: "Against All Odds"— *Magna Cum Laude* from Berklee

It's not easy to graduate *Magna Cum Laude* from the prestigious Berklee College of Music in Boston, Massachusetts. Only a few do. But Tony DeBlois, a blind, autistic, musical savant, did just that. It is an uplifting, against-all-odds story of Tony's incredible musical talent, his mother's indefatigable advocacy on behalf of her son and a school's willingness to focus on *a*-bility rather than *dis*-ability.

It was in fact some issues around Tony's admission to Berklee that first brought us together in 1989. I was an expert witness in an action Tony's mother, Janice DeBlois, had brought against Waltham Public Schools to permit Tony to attend summer school at the Berklee College of Music. At age 15, Tony had won a summer scholarship to Berklee based on his remarkable jazz talent. But, unlike other students at Berklee, Tony was blind, autistic and lacked a high school diploma. More importantly, the school district Tony was already attending was not at all sure that the Berklee experience was necessary, or fit in with his Individual Education Plan (IEP). Let me explain.

At age 15, Tony performed as part of The Music School at Rivers jazz ensemble at the Berklee College of Music High School Jazz Festival. Tony had been attending Rivers School part-time in an after-school program. Faculty from the Berklee College of Music were very impressed with Tony's performance at the festival, and awarded him a $500 scholarship to Berklee's five-week summer high school performance program. But there was a problem. The judges didn't realize at the time they awarded the scholarship that Tony was only 15 (the award was for 16-year-old students in the last year of high school). Nor did the judges realize that Tony was blind and autistic. Berklee had never had a 15-year-old, blind, autistic student in its school. But his mother, so understandably proud of the fact that Tony had won the scholarship, asked Berklee to give accommodation and special consideration to Tony's incredible talent. Berklee agreed to do so. A special audition was held and the school decided, then, based on Tony's talent and performance, to admit him to Berklee for the summer school session for which he had earned the scholarship.

However, the scholarship covered only portions of the tuition for the program and the special assistant Tony required. His mother requested that the summer program be covered by the school district as part of Tony's IEP. When the school rejected that idea, Janice put a hearing process into motion in the case of *Anthony DeBlois v. Waltham Public Schools* (BSEA No. 89–1764), which was put before the Massachusetts Department of Education's Bureau of Special Education Appeals.

The school system argued that it was already providing an appropriate education for Tony with "maximum possible development in the least restrictive environment" in that Tony was attending the Perkins School for the Blind as well as participating in after-school music studies at The Music School at Rivers just several miles away.

Because of my interest in musical savants, the attorneys representing Tony and his mother asked if I would write a report in this case, emphasizing the extra benefits that a program like the Berklee summer session would have for Tony. In support of that position I provided a report which read, in part:

> The musical gift that Anthony DeBlois shows is more than a curious and conspicuous talent. Like other savants, in his case it can be the conduit to further socialization, amelioration of some of his autistic symptoms and a mechanism to raise considerably whatever hindrances his basic mental handicap produce. While continual attention to the specific talent of the savant may at times seem optional, or even frivolous, it is through training that talent that the savant can move beyond the defect toward better attention to daily living skills, enhanced socialization, better communication skills, more interactive relationships, and even intimacy… [the goal with these special skills] is to patiently and creatively put them to good

use without fearing that in so doing, overall development will be harmed or impeded. Quite to the contrary, such skills become a mode of expression through which others can reach and interact with the savant, and consequently those skills lead to the development of other related skills and human communication. The skills serve as a window to the world for the savant, and they serve as a window to the savant for the rest of us. "Training the talent can diminish the defect"...

It is my opinion that whatever can be done to further the musical exposure, education, and advantage of Anthony DeBlois is not merely a fascination with his astonishing talent but rather a direct investment in furthering his overall development to allow him to reach his full potential and become as self-reliant and self-supporting an individual as possible in the least restrictive alternative living circumstance available to him. Increasing his exposure to music and other musicians, such as would be accomplished at the Special Summer Performance Program, is far more than a "cultural experience" but indeed is an extension of his special education experience to give him full advantage of using his very special skills to offset his otherwise very impeding handicap. I highly recommend the summer performance experience as the best investment of the summer months for him toward a full educational objective as an integral part of the best special education experience that can be provided to him.

Other persons testified at the hearing as well. One of his music instructors at Perkins stated that Tony's exceptional musical aptitude and skills would prepare him to perform professionally as a mature musician in five years either as a soloist or as a member of a group. He went on to say: "Tony has much to contribute to the world of music, and I strongly urge anyone who can to help give him this chance to fully develop his musical artistry."

In October 1989 the hearing officer handed down her decision, which ruled that the Berklee summer school program was a valid addition to Tony's overall special education program. She ordered the Waltham Public Schools to reimburse Janice for the tuition, transportation and personal assistant costs that she had already paid privately for Tony's involvement in that summer's special program.

The Berklee summer performance program was a turning point in Tony's life. John Laporta, one of the most influential jazz educators in the United States, took a special interest in Tony, given Tony's incredible jazz ability. At Berklee, Tony became much more social and talkative during that first summer's program. He was popular with the other students.

The next year Tony again attended the summer program at Berklee. Additionally, The Music School at Rivers Jazz Ensemble won a $1000 scholarship for the school to give to their most deserving student. Tony was awarded that scholarship, this time to attend Berklee's regular college program. With the help of the Boston Disability Law Center, Janice arranged that Tony's Individual Education Plan include full-time participation in the Berklee diploma program, pointing out that music was a true vocational path for her son. In June, 1992, at age 17, Tony DeBlois became a full-time student at Berklee College of Music.

The students at Berklee loved Tony. A 1991 *Today Show* segment showed one classmate saying, "He's one cool cat, that's all I've got to say" and another, "When he starts jamming here, it always works because he just starts it with so much energy, it's contagious." Another television program showed Tony as he received his diploma, *Magna Cum Laude*, from Berklee, his classmates cheering in the background. "You know how I feel? I feel proud," Tony says. And well he, his family and the Berklee staff should be. That momentous day, Tony also received Berklee's Fifty-Year Anniversary Medallion in recognition of his being the "most improved student." Quite an accomplishment for the first 17-year-old high school student Berklee ever admitted, and the first blind, autistic person at Berklee as well. I would give both Tony and Berklee, and certainly Janice as well, an A+ for that successful first.

But that mission accomplished was just the successful culmination of a number of other against-all-odds situations that Tony and Janice had faced throughout Tony's life. Tony was born prematurely on January 22, 1974. He weighed only *one pound, three-quarter ounces.* At that tiny size of prematurity, Tony had respiratory distress syndrome and needed to be given oxygen in order to survive, despite the known risk of blindness that could follow. Tony had to remain in the hospital until May of that year. He weighed five pounds, four ounces at that time. Unfortunately the retinopathy of prematurity (ROP) had robbed him of his vision. Some later medical testing at age nine, with EEG and CT procedures, showed that in addition to the blindness there was evidence of left hemisphere damage and dysfunction.

From the first moments that Tony was able to be at home, his mother noted Tony's affinity for music. He was calmed by music, and was distressed even by brief pauses between tracks of the albums which he listened to endlessly. When Tony was two years old, Janice bought a Magnus chord organ at a garage sale. Several months later Janice was startled to hear the theme song from *Lawrence of Arabia* coming from a nearby room. It was Tony playing that tune on his chord organ. By age three Tony was playing songs he had heard on the *Lawrence Welk* show as they came off the air, producing harmonies with his left hand and melody with his right.

There had been a number of moves for Tony and his family during his childhood years. But Janice always had in her mind the wish to bring Tony to Massachusetts because she had heard about opportunities for special education approaches to children with special needs in that state. In May, 1983 the family moved to Massachusetts and Tony entered the Perkins School for the Blind, where there was special attention to his musical abilities. That attention was fortified on June 23, 1987 when Tony also began to participate in an after-school music program at The Music School at Rivers County Day School Campus, a private preparatory school for grades 6 through 12. Tony began his studies at The Music School at Rivers with the help of Marshalls Corporation, St. Patrick's Church, and The Lions Club along with a collection taken at a church in which he played in New Hampshire. We took Waltham School Committee to hearing BSEA No. 88–1003 winning a settlement resulting in Waltham agreeing to pay for transportation and tuition for Tony's placement at The Music School at Rivers.

It was there that Tony began studying jazz piano with the director of the jazz program at the Music School at Rivers. And it was that school's jazz ensemble that competed in the 1988 Berklee College of Music High School Jazz Festival where Tony earned an Outstanding Musicianship Award. It was the following year, then, as described above, that Tony was "discovered" by Berklee and ultimately admitted to its program.

In 1991 Tony was featured on the *Today Show*, and it was in conjunction with that show that I visited Tony and his family for the first time at their home in Waltham. Tony was a very pleasant, outgoing 18-year-old boy. He maneuvered around the house and yard with impressive ease, considering his blindness. I played a recorded piece of music for him and he immediately played it back. Such literal replication is certainly remarkable. But what struck me particularly was Tony's ability to improvise, beyond literal reproduction. Conspicuous to me was Tony's ability to "feel" the music and interject emotion into, and extract feeling from, the music he played. He was not simply echoing what he heard, he was improvising on it, and "feeling" it as well.

As we chatted, there were some echolalic responses to questions, but conversation proceeded comfortably. Tony did have some problems with abstract thinking, but that hardly interfered. Tony's joy, enthusiasm and pride permeated the day. Tony's mother echoed that pride, justifiably, and her satisfaction with all that Tony and she were able to accomplish was evident as well.

Following the airing of that program on the *Today Show*, a Hollywood producer became interested in the story of Tony and his mother, Janice. That interest eventually culminated, in 1997, with the broadcast of a CBS Movie of the Week—*Journey of the Heart*—with Cybill Shepherd playing the part of Janice and Chris Demetral as Tony. Tony played the five songs on the soundtrack and he appeared briefly in the final scene of that film.

Tony has won numerous awards for his talents, and has been part of many radio and television programs. He has given many concerts in the United States and has been on tour in other parts of the world, including Singapore, Taiwan, Ireland, Africa and China. Tony now plays over 22 instruments including the organ, harpsichord, guitar, harmonica, handbells, violin, banjo, drums, trumpet, saxophone, clarinet, ukulele, mandolin and flute.

Tony has recorded six CDs: *Thank God for Life* (1999), *Four Thousand Years of Music* (1999), *Beyond Words* (2002), *Mercer, Mercy Me* (2003), *Thrice as Nice* (2004) and *Some Kind of Genius* (2005). On some of these Tony plays piano and does vocals as well. On others he also plays the saxophone or trumpet. Some tracks are solo; others include a jazz ensemble. Some tracks are well-known pieces, but many include Tony's own compositions and improvisations.

In 2005 an excellent book about Tony—*Some Kind of Genius: The Extraordinary Journey of Musical Savant Tony DeBlois*—was written by Janice DeBlois and Antonia Felix, and published by Rodale Publishing Company. It provides a very comprehensive look at Tony the artist and Tony the person, filling in many more of the details of Tony and Janice's journey than can be summarized above. Similarly, there is much more information about Tony on his personal website at www.tonydeblois.com.

There are a number of important storylines in Tony's journey: Tony's very survival with a birth weight of barely more than a pound; another instance of the fascinating triad of musical genius, mental handicap and blindness; his mother's advocacy on behalf of her son and her unyielding optimism regarding his future; Tony's progression as a skilled musician which is mirrored in his increased language, socialization and daily living skills; his graduation *Magna Cum Laude* after what seemed like an improbable and unlikely mainstreaming into one of the most prestigious music schools in the United States; the successful career he now enjoys as a musician and how "training the talent" made that possible; and the love and pride of a mother in her son propelling along her helpful advocacy and against-all-odds tenacity.

Like so many savants I have had the opportunity to get to know, Tony radiates the joy and pride in themselves that so many savants, impressively, share. That they can be so satisfied and content, even with sometimes daunting limitations, should provide an inspirational, yet humbling, perspective for each of us.

CHAPTER 13

Temple: "An Emergence Extraordinaire"

Dr. Temple Grandin is well known around the world. She has become an extremely valuable and articulate ambassador for raising awareness of, information about, and insight into autism and Asperger syndrome as she shares the story of her own "emergence labeled autistic," as she calls it, through the years. She is a fierce advocate for "training the talent" and provides a stellar example and role model of the success of that strategy for anyone with autism or Asperger syndrome.

Temple Grandin is also known equally well around the world as a leading animal scientist with special expertise on the design of animal handling facilities; she lectures and consults worldwide on this topic. One-half of the cattle in the United States are handled in equipment she has designed for meat plants. Temple obtained her PhD in animal science from the University of Illinois in 1989 and presently is a professor at Colorado State University in Fort Collins, Colorado. Her book, *Animals in Translation* (Grandin and Johnson 2005) was a *New York Times* bestseller and she has several hundred industry-related publications in addition to winning numerous industry awards.

Temple attributes much of her success as a livestock facility designer to her ability to think visually—*Thinking in Pictures* as she calls it in her very insightful and popular book on that topic (Grandin 2006)—coupled with an extraordinary ability to recognize and remember detail in tape recorder or hard-disk-like, digital image fashion. Her visual thinking patterns, abilities and memory are closely linked, she feels, to her autism. Mechanical/spatial skills, coupled with massive, literal memory of the type that Temple demonstrates, do occur in savant syndrome in some persons, along with the more frequently reported art, music and math skills.

Temple maintains a very active website on these animal science matters at www.grandin.com. That website is devoted to "help educate people throughout the world about modern methods of livestock handling which will improve animal welfare and productivity." She spends a great deal of her time lecturing, consulting, writing and doing research in this area of her special expertise.

In addition to her heavy schedule in that specialized vocational area, Temple has been equally engaged in sharing her story, and her expertise, about autism with audiences around the world. She lectures frequently at autism conferences and has written extensively on that topic as well as providing valuable insights and advice to parents, professionals and the public, based on the unique credential of her own personal journey with autism.

Temple Grandin first shared her story of autism in 1986 in her book *Emergence Labeled Autistic* (Grandin and Scariano 1986). Dr. Bernard Rimland captured the significance and mission of that book well in his Foreword:

> To my knowledge this is the first book written by a recovered autistic individual. It is an exciting book. The readers share the adventure of growing from an extremely handicapped child who appeared to be destined for permanent institutionalization to a vigorous, productive and respected adult who is a world authority in her field. (Grandin and Scariano 1986, p.7)

That first book about her personal journey with autism is a marvelous documentation of Temple's life from childhood to early thirties. It is both a subjective and objective account of that "emergence" because in addition to Temple's personal recollections, there are numerous verbatim entries by others gathered from letters, reports, notes and diaries of her mother, teachers, doctors and other significant witnesses to those early years. The book documents the symptoms of early autism—lack of language until age 3½, withdrawal, flatness, spinning, rituals, and exquisite super-sensitivity to touch, sound and other sensations. It also chronicles her struggles in elementary school, junior high and boarding school. It tells of Temple's discovery on the calming effect of the "magic device"—the cattle chute squeeze machine—that Temple modified to her own use at about age 18. The squeeze, or hug machine, had a calming influence on Temple at that time and that method of dealing with sensory overload continues to work for her to the present time as well.

In graduate school Temple switched her major from psychology to animal science, and the "rest is history," as the saying goes.

The final chapter, "Autistics and the Real World", in her first book gives 17 very specific, understandable and practical "hints, tips and pearls" for anyone dealing with autistic children, whether a parent, teacher or therapist. It provides easily applicable advice for dealing with the special interests, hypersensitivity, need for structure, fixations and many other unique needs that autistic children have. It is very practical advice from a real expert who has experienced the world of autism from the inside.

In 1995 Oliver Sacks published his popular book, *An Anthropologist on Mars: Seven Paradoxical Tales*, which contained a sensitive and eloquent description of Temple Grandin. In fact the book takes its title from Temple's description of herself: "Much of the time I feel like an anthropologist on Mars." Sack's perceptive and engaging description of Temple Grandin in that book brought her more and more into public visibility; many more articles and major television program appearances followed.

In 1996 Temple Grandin's book *Thinking in Pictures: And Other Reports from My Life with Autism* was published and became an immediate bestseller. That book was reissued in an expanded version in 2006. In the mean time, in 2004, her book *Developing Talents: Careers for Individuals with Asperger Syndrome and High Functioning Autism* (Grandin and Duffy 2004) was published. That book is particularly pertinent to "training the talent" as seen not only in savant syndrome, but also in Asperger syndrome and high-functioning autism as well. *Animals in Translation: Using the Mysteries of Autism to Decode Animal Behavior* (Grandin and Johnson 2005), representing a merging of Temple's two areas of expertise, has been widely distributed. That same year, a book co-authored by Temple Grandin and Sean Barron, *Unwritten Rules of Social Relationships: Decoding Social Mysteries Through the Unique Perspective of Autism* (Grandin and Barron 2005), was winner of the prestigious Foreword Book of the Year award. That work focuses on understanding and learning the social "rules" that often present such obstacles to persons with autism and Asperger syndrome.

In May, 2005 Temple presented the keynote lecture at the annual meeting of the Autism Society of Wisconsin, as she has done at so many similar conferences around the United States and the world. I had the opportunity to hear that lecture. At a time when there is considerable polarization between "traditional medicine" and "alternative medicine" approaches in terms of causation and treatment, fueled largely by the vaccine controversy, Temple brings a uniquely calming and uniting credential—the emergence from her autism—to the podium that provides an instant rapport with, and practical advice for, the attentive and appreciative audiences. Other "experts" sometimes are not quite so convincingly accepted by those same audiences because of the controversy and polarization.

But in her presentation Temple points out that there is likely no single cause for autism, but it is most probably a group of disorders rather than a single disorder.

She approaches the delicate topic of the use of medication pointing out that medication can sometimes be helpful with specific target symptoms, such as anxiety for example, as it has been in her own case. Then she appropriately points out that finding the right medication for the right patient in the right dose is a highly individualized clinical search. And she also wisely cautions that often only very low doses of medication are required and titrating to the proper dose level needs to be a very careful process. In her presentation she very convincingly bridges the traditional medicine versus alternative medicine controversy, pointing out that, properly applied, both can be useful depending on each individual circumstance.

Finally, if ever there was a person who can make a convincing case for "training the talent" and approaching each person individually, wherever he or she is on the autism spectrum, discarding labels and instead focusing on *a*-bilities rather than only *dis*-abilities, it is Temple Grandin. What a pleasant, optimistic, practical, believable, reliable and tireless ambassador she is for persons with, or interested in, autistic spectrum disorders everywhere.

That lecture was in essence the way she sees it. What a rich resource of understanding, empathy, practical advice and hope it was for the parents and professionals attending. Fortunately Temple has put those pearls of insight and activity into book form to spread her useful message further. I first learned about her most recent book on autism—*The Way I See It* (Grandin 2008b)—from some parents and teachers who wrote to me highly recommending it because of the first-hand information, knowledge and optimism they found in those valuable pages.

As the above demonstrates, Temple Grandin is on two main missions in her life, and she divides her time fully and selflessly between them. One is her extraordinarily successful vocational calling as an animal scientist. The other is her extraordinarily successful calling as teacher, role model, interpreter and mentor toward wider acceptance and better understanding about autism among parents, professionals and the general public with whom she interacts. Correspondingly, she has *two* websites to differentiate those activities: www.grandin.com is directed toward her animal science expertise and endeavors, while www.templegrandin.com highlights her activities, articles, books, videos, DVDs and speaking engagements regarding autism. That website also provides an in-depth "up close and personal" look at Temple's remarkable history and emergence to the present time.

Temple Grandin, throughout her writings and presentations, gives credit to some very important caring and understanding people in her life and, in turn, points out the very positive influence that those persons around the autistic individual (or savant) can have on that person. Temple gives credit to her mother and nanny, who worked hard to encourage her interest in art from a very young age. Temple credits that artwork as an important element in the development of her visual thinking skills.

Another very important and influential person in her life was her high school teacher, William Carlock. His philosophy is reflected in Temple's life, and in all of her writings and presentations. That teacher

> didn't see any of the labels, just the underlying talents. Even the principal had doubts about my getting through tech school. But Mr. Carlock believed in building what was within the student. He channeled my fixations into constructive projects. He didn't try to draw me into his world but came instead into my world. (Grandin and Scariano 1986, p.86)

Mr. Carlock has been very pleased by what has happened to Temple in her career and life. And his advice, which was so helpful to Temple, is good advice for everyone—parents, teachers, therapists—who have contact with autistic children:

> Temple has demonstrated without question, that there is hope for the autistic child—that deep, constant caring, understanding, acceptance, appropriately high expectations, and support and encouragement for what is best in him will provide a base, from which he can grow to his own potential. (Grandin and Scariano 1986, p.11)

Blueprints are essential in Temple Grandin's animal science work and she does those spectacularly. But her high school teacher's advice, which was so valuable to Temple, is also a "blueprint" for success with persons with autism, Asperger and savant syndrome. And in her autism awareness work, Temple Grandin draws such blueprints, for all those interested, spectacularly as well.

CHAPTER 14

Matt: "The Key of Genius"

Matt Savage, age 17, is already world famous in the music world. Not every musician gets noticed by the Arts & Entertainment section of the *Wall Street Journal*. But the October 29, 2008 edition of that paper carried an article about Matt and his music titled "The Musical Maturing of Matt Savage." The story paid him a very high compliment when it described him as "a phenomenally talented pianist and composer who demands to be taken seriously on purely musical terms."

Other musicians agree. Dave Brubeck, who heard Matt play for the first time when Matt was only eight years old, calls Matt "the Mozart of jazz." Matt has his own website now, a place "where genius and joy make a quantum leap." How accurate that is!

By age nine Matt was already the leader of the Matt Savage Trio, with his side-men world-class, adult musicians. He debuted at age 11 at the famed Blue Note jazz club in Manhattan. Matt is the youngest performer ever to have performed at that prestigious venue. The following year, at age 12, Matt debuted at Birdland. In 2003. at age 11, Matt was signed as a "Bösendorfer Artist," the youngest pianist and the only child to be so honored in the history of the Bösendorfer Piano Company, founded in 1828. Currently, Matt performs concerts and plays as jazz festivals in the United States and other countries. Matt has recorded eight audio CDs; donating a portion of the proceeds of those sales to autism research and support organizations. His most recent album, *Hot Ticket–Live in Boston*, was released to rave reviews in 2007. He signed a sub-publishing deal with Sony/ATC in 2008.

I first met Matt and his mother, Diane, in September, 2004. They had come to Appleton, Wisconsin, at our invitation, for "A-bilities Week," which focuses on strengths and talent in individuals with dis-abilities. Matt was the guest of honor for a special evening concert, and he performed as artist in residence in some of the Appleton schools during the four days we were privileged to have them in Wisconsin.

It was quite a week. Matt and his mother met with elementary and high school students in two separate appearances at those schools. What enthusiasm and inspiration Matt provided! The energized students were amazed at his abilities and were fully captured by his engaging personality. Matt particularly enjoyed the "audience challenge" part of the presentation where Matt would instantly improvise a piano piece to any word or subject suggested by the audience, such as a color, or an animal, or a feeling.

Matt involved the audience at the evening concert in the same manner, conveying instantly, musically, the meaning, tone and concept of whatever word was suggested. He served, masterfully, as his own master of ceremonies at the concert. He was entirely at ease, comical at times, but eminently serious with his music. He played a piece he had composed for his sister's birthday, and one dedicated to his grandmother. How he managed to get such mighty tones from his tiny hands is a mystery. Matt needed literally to stretch, or bend, or move the piano bench to reach both ends of the concert grand it was, so much bigger than he. But he masters that instrument, with his own compositions, impressively.

I had the chance to have lunch with him and his mother the day of the concert. He was as relaxed and engaging over lunch as he was on stage. As soon as we met he recognized "Treffert" as a palindrome, and proceeded to list a number of other palindromes and cited resources on palindromes where I could find, if I wished, the longest palindrome in the world. When I told him my date of birth, he paused for a bit and then announced that day was a Sunday. And it was.

I then learned that Matt was a world authority on roller coasters. He could easily name the longest, the highest, the fastest and the incline angles of roller coasters wherever they were located. But, in full disclosure, he admitted he prefers to learn about roller coasters rather than ride them. As he put it: "I'm a roller coaster studying freak, not a roller coaster riding person."

Matt is obviously very bright, articulate, well rounded and engagingly pleasant. His mother, who home schools both Matt and his younger sister, is justifiably proud of Matt, as well she should be. She has obviously done a great job as a mother and a teacher. Matt and Diane both cherish their rural lifestyle in New Hampshire and Diane has been very careful to balance Matt's stage life with his home life, choosing concerts carefully and sparingly, leaving plenty of time for family and farm.

Diane describes Matt as being different from other children, even from birth. He was very jumpy, never slept, and was very fussy. He would line up toys and do things repetitively. He had many mandatory rituals. He walked, and sometimes ran, on his tiptoes, turning his head sideways and waving his arms. He rarely played with other children and would often run away from any such interaction. Matt entered pre-school but was there for only two days when the school called his mother and said she should come and get him because they just couldn't handle him. "He was officially expelled from pre-school," as his mother describes it now.

But Matt had an extensive vocabulary because he was echolalic, repeating what words he had just heard. And he was very perseverative. He also was reading everything in sight because he was hyperlexic. It was obvious that Matt was highly intelligent, but he also was extraordinarily sensitive to sound, including any music whatsoever. He was also extremely sensitive to touch and didn't like to be held. He tried to avoid both sound and touch.

At age three, Matt was evaluated and given a diagnosis of pervasive developmental disorder (PDD), and possibly Asperger syndrome, with hyperlexia. The family provided Matt with most of the treatments recommended by DAN! (Defeat Autism Now!). One especially helpful treatment was auditory integration therapy, which lessened markedly his intense aversion to sound. With those treatments the family saw a steady improvement in language and socialization, and a decrease in frustrations overall. The fewer the frustrations, the less autistic Matt appeared over time.

Matt's hyperlexia turned out to be a useful tool. His mother describes it in this way:

We used his obsession with words and visuals to teach him things, even though he sometimes did not want to learn. If something was written on paper, Matt's personality just *made* him read the words. He might throw a tantrum or throw away the paper after having read it; however we would give him the paper again and again. And each time he couldn't help himself. He *had* to read it. We were able to reach him with written word when spoken word would not have been processed. Hyperlexia is a blessing, not a curse. It is a tool. It allows you to reach the child within.

But Matt was also intrigued with numbers, not just words. At age six he told his mother, "My head is full of math problems." So his mother bought some math puzzle books and he attacked those with the same enthusiasm as word books, solving the problems aimed at persons twice his age with ease. Matt continues, to this day, to be fascinated with numbers and math. He also loves geography. In April, 2004 he won the National Geography Bee state competition in New Hampshire and represented that state in the National Geography Bee Finals in Washington, DC.

Matt's musical ability appeared quite unexpectedly when he was about six years old. One evening Matt's parents were startled to hear "London Bridge" being pounded out, in an adjacent room, on a toy keyboard his mother had purchased for him. His mother then introduced him to the full piano and he learned to play "almost overnight." In six months he mastered a Schubert sonata.

Matt started to compose at age seven. At that time he was taking lessons from a classical music teacher. One day when the teacher pointed out an error in his playing a particular piece, he announced he liked his version better. So he began to compose his own music and has done so ever since.

After a year of classical music lessons, he was enrolled in the jazz program at the New England Conservatory of Music where he progressed quickly. One of his instructors commented that "Matt seems to know things that are deeper than his own existence."

His mother puts it this way: "Matt tells us the music is already in his head. He hears it, and he plays it. He knows he has to practice technique. But the music itself—it's already there."

To me Matt is an example of what I call genetic memory. In that sense Matt does "know things beyond his own existence." To use my words: Matt "knows things he never learned." He comes with the "music chip" factory-installed which accounts for what he describes, in his words, as "the music is already in my head." It is as if he simply transcribes, as was said about Mozart, "that which is already written on his soul." Genetic memory was discussed in more detail in Chapter 4.

Matt has had extensive media exposure because of his incredible talent. He has been on the *Today Show* twice. He was featured on *Late Night with Conan O'Brien* in 2006 and the *Late Show with David Letterman* in 2008. Matt's spotlight on a National Public Radio broadcast of the *Marian McParland's Piano Jazz Program* (mentioned below) provided two 27-minute interviews with good in-depth conversations along with generous portions of Matt's piano playing. A segment on CNN explored Matt's musical genius as well. And he has appeared in a number of documentaries.

Matt's performance schedule is a busy and varied one. In October, 2008, for example, he appeared at Shanghai Jazz in Madison, New Jersey, in a duo with internationally renowned Dutch bassist Joris Teepe. Then he appeared for two nights with his two New York based sidemen as the Matt Savage Trio at the Cachaça Jazz 'n' Samba Club in Greenwich Village. And the list goes on and on, around the United States and elsewhere.

Matt was invited to write the theme song for an AID 4 AUTISM concert in Atlanta, Georgia in May, 2009. Matt's song, "I'm Not Afraid," had the daunting task of combining the musical styles of all the AID 4 AUTISM performers, including rock, country, jazz, blues, classical, Latin, rhythm and blues, folk, dance and pop. According to the organizers, "Matt was selected because of his incredible ability to think unconventionally about music."

There are three excellent resources for more information about Matt Savage. First, there is his website at www.savagerecords.com. Second, there is an article by Steve Silberman titled "The key to genius" in the December, 2003 issue of *Wired* magazine. In that extensive piece, Matt is described as a "prolific composer and a skilled improviser. With the precocious abilities of a savant and the melodic imagination of a seasoned musician, he has dual citizenship in two countries of the mind" (Silberman 2003, p.228). Third, there is an excellent video clip of Matt from the *Beautiful Minds* program (Colourfield Productions of Dortmund, Germany). It can be readily accessed on the savant syndrome website at www.savantsyndrome.com in the profiles section.

Matt Savage and his incredible ability provide answers to some commonly asked questions about savant syndrome.

1.   **Can savants be creative?**

     Matt's story answers that question with a resounding "Yes." Indeed he certainly is creative. All one needs to do is to listen to his composition and improvisations. Matt has composed almost, *all* the songs contained on his albums.

2.   **Can savant abilities help foster better socialization and other skills and actually help minimize disability?**

     Matt's story answers that question also with a resounding "Yes." Matt's extraordinary musical ability has been the "conduit toward normalization" that I discuss in Part 4, "Training the Talent." It is remarkable, and inspirational, how far Matt has come from those early childhood days when he was traumatized by loud sounds and insisted that the house he lived in could contain no music. Now music has become his strength and his passion, propelling him to international recognition as a great jazz artist. At the same time, his musical savant skill has been a vital contributor to, and component of, his overall progress and development with diminution of his early disabilities.

3.   **As socialization, language and other skills increase, is there a risk that the special skills will disappear?**

     The answer to that question, as Matt so convincingly demonstrates, is a resounding and reassuring "No." Contrary to the concern raised by the case of Nadia in the past (Selfe 1977), with Matt there has been no "dreaded trade-off" of special skills for more general progress. Instead, his overall progress and musical progress have occurred in parallel with each other, with a corresponding diminution of behavioral problems or other deficits.

4. **How important are the family, teachers and others in discovering, nourishing, and propelling special skills along?**
    Matt, and his family, provide a convincing answer to that question as well. Family members, and sometimes others, are vital in discovering, and then nurturing the special abilities and skills that persons with savant syndrome possess. The unconditional love, belief, support, pride, cheerleading, tolerance and untiring patience that the family can provide are vital ingredients in the emergence, shaping and growth of the special gifts the savant displays. The love and pride that Matt's parents have in him shines brightly through. It has been a bottomless reservoir of trust, acceptance and validation for Matt, and serves as a brilliant and inspirational example for all parents of children with disabilities regarding the hope, optimism, faith, patience and good old-fashioned hard work that are a part of that loving formula.

    What Matt *does* with his musical talent is important to Mom and Dad. But more important, and shining through, is an appreciation for who Matt *is* as a person. Matt's mom smiles a lot. And it is infectious. Matt smiles a lot too. There is a joy in their interaction. And while Matt certainly does have a magnificent musical gift, that is not the only topic of his familiy conversation or interaction. They speak as much about the farm, the crops and the animals as they do about concerts and albums. They delight in the beauty of the seasons and the tranquility of fields and forests. Mom and Dad are careful to maintain a balance between Matt's musical life, and his family and farm life. And Matt maintains an eclectic outlook, likewise balancing musical life with life in general.

In September, 2009 Matt began a new chapter in his evolving career. He entered the freshman class of the prestigious Berklee College of Music in Boston. Matt enjoys the Berklee experience immensely and is benefiting from it enormously. A *Boston Globe* article of February 9, 2010 quotes one of his professors as saying, "As Matt's evolved on stage, his social life has grown too. He's learned how to talk onstage to the point that he's almost a ham." The *Globe* article sums Matt up this way at this point in his life: "The Matt Savage story is rapidly evolving from youthful prodigy with a disability to seasoned performer with a bright future." He is thriving academically, musically and socially, surrounded by other people sharing similar interests and knowledge.

Without doubt Matt has a marvelous musical career ahead of him. He is already far along in that career at age 17. Matt's December 2007 appearance on *NPR*

(National Public Radio) on the *Marian McPartland's Piano Jazz* program contains two 27-minute segments that provide interesting insights into Matt's life at age 14, in his own words, coupled with the pleasant opportunity to hear his outstanding musical artistry, in his own notes. On that program he plays some tunes from his album *Quantum Leap* and he also plays some duet pieces with Marian McPartland.

In the interview portion of the program Matt discusses his autism as he recalls it in his early years, and the success of the auditory integration therapy to deal with his childhood aversion to sound. Ironically, now sound in many ways is the center of his life. About his autism Matt gives this encouraging appraisal: "Most of that is kind of over with. That was a long time ago."

That's the way Matt sums up his autism. His affinity for jazz? He sums that up this way: "What I love about jazz is that you can break all rules and be free." And, without doubt, musically he is "free" and mighty good at what he does.

CHAPTER 15

Flo and Kay: An Unforgettable "Two of a Kind"

Savant syndrome is a rare condition. Even more rare are females with savant syndrome. So the likelihood of finding identical twin sisters with identical savant skills seems most unlikely. Well, meet Flo and Kay.

Flo and Kay are identical twin sisters. Both are autistic and both are premier calendar calculators. Also, both have incredible factual and autobiographical memories. They are the only two such female identical twin savants ever reported.

I met this delightful duo as they stopped in Fond du Lac in April, 2008 for an interview as part of a documentary—*Beyond Ordinary: Flo and Kay, Twin Savants*—being produced about them. They visited me on their way to California (more about the unique purpose of that destination later).

Flo and Kay are in their fifties now. They do look exactly alike and often complete each other's sentences, sometimes replying in unison. They are very polite and gracious. They love interaction with others. Calendar calculating questions for the day of the week for any date past or future are answered with instant responses. Ask them what the weather was like on March 13, 1993 and they will tell you that was the day of the "no name" storm. Ask what they had for dinner on January 10, 1994 and they will tell you it was "pork chops, vegetables and a baked potato." Their reservoir of information regarding music albums, artists and date of release of albums from the 1960s, 1970s and 1980s seems bottomless. For example if you ask who was the performer and on what date were these records released—"Alone Again, Naturally," "Love Will Keep Us Together" and "Disco Lady"— they will answer instantly and accurately.

Flo and Kay were born in 1956 at a time when children with disabilities were often hidden away by families and stigmatized by the public at large. They remember being bullied, ridiculed and called cruel names by their classmates. They also describe an episode where their mother tried to end her life and theirs by turning on gas jets in the oven. Only the intervention by their younger sister interrupted that potentially tragic event.

In the early 1970s the twins began watching game shows on television. They became especially intrigued with the 1973 *$10,000 Dollar Pyramid* show, which eventually morphed into the 1985 *$100,000 Dollar Pyramid* show hosted by Dick Clark. They remember all the questions, answers and when various buzzers sounded from that first show, and all of the shows that followed. They have meticulously kept a diary of what Dick Clark was wearing on each of those shows using their unique color-coding system. If you want to check their memory of what Dick Clark was wearing on a particular day against their written records, you can. Of course they are always right. Remembering all of those programs, questions and answers, bells and buzzers, and what Dick Clark was wearing "is good exercise for the brain. Sometimes we do it so fast that it smells like rubber burning." That is their colorful description of that particular skill.

Dick Clark is their hero. They have accumulated a massive collection of posters, pictures, news clippings and a wide assortment of other Dick Clark memorabilia to which they are very attached.

Following the death of their parents, Flo and Kay moved in with their sister, Jane, with whom they had a very close relationship all of their lives. The twins blossomed in that more accepting and encouraging environment; it was a time of growth and joy. But, sadly, their sister died in 2006. However, their brother had promised their mother that he would always take care of the twins and that they would never have to be in an institution. So they presently live with their brother in an east coast state.

In 1988 another very significant person came into their life. Dave Wagner was an evening news anchor for a Florida television station. The twins became interested in him and his programs. One evening after the newscast, they called Wagner to learn what more they could about him. Wagner was impressed by their massive store of musical knowledge, something which was familiar to him as a former disc jockey. An instant friendship began which has continued to this day. They of course have meticulously documented what shirt, tie and suit Wagner was wearing on each of those broadcasts and have recorded that information in the voluminous such diaries they have kept on all their favourite television celebrities including Dick Clark as mentioned above.

Wagner did several stories about the twins on his station's broadcasts. He also began a video collection documenting some of Flo and Kay's day-to-day lives and various ventures. That has turned into a 13-year video diary of sorts, and it is clips from those years that form the core of the chronological documentary on these two special people.

Flo and Kay's admiration for Dick Clark so impressed Wagner that in 1995 he arranged for the twins to meet their "hero" at Busch Gardens in Florida. The twins dazzled Clark with their knowledge of him and his shows, details he had long forgotten. He in turn dazzled them just by being in his presence. That 25-minute face-to-face meeting with their hero, captured on video, was the highlight of their life to that point. What joy they radiated.

In 2008 Wagner took the twins on a road trip across the United States which became the framework for the documentary. The first stop was to visit Dr. Nancy Isenberg, a behavioral neurologist at the New Jersey Neuroscience Institute. She concluded the twins are autistic, "severely so." She also confirmed their savant calendar calculating skills. Until that time it was assumed that Flo and Kay could only name the day of the week for calendar dates in their lifetime. Instead, they were quickly able to answer, in unison of course, that November 30, 1938 was a Wednesday, a day long before they were born.

Dr. Isenberg asked them whether when they were doing calendar calculating they were somehow actually counting days or whether the answers just naturally come to them. They answered: "Actually it's in our heads. We have a calendar up there. We have a 'micro-chip' up there."

Indeed they do. (I addressed the mystery of calendar calculating which occurs with such regularity in so many savants in Chapter 5.)

The next stop for the twins was in Fond du Lac to determine where they fit on the savant syndrome spectrum. I tested their calendar calculating skills for both common historical events and obscure dates. They were always correct. I tested autobiographical memory for routine day events and it appeared to be very extensive and detailed, although I had no way of verifying such memories. I suppose I could have tested the color-code recollections for a particular celebrity on any particular day, but they did not have those extensive records with them (they are voluminous). Their musical album memory is extensive (I had to prepare some questions rather than rely on my puny repertoire in that area). Again, they were always correct.

We visited my home and spent some time walking the property. Along the way they asked when and where I was born. I didn't think anything particular about that, but, to my surprise, a birthday card arrived from them this year on the exact day.

Based on my visit with these two delightful people there is no doubt about the presence of multiple savant skills and I would place those on the "prodigious" end of the savant spectrum. To my knowledge they are the only two such identical twin female savants ever reported worldwide either in the past or living at present.

In spite of a difficult childhood and adolescence, with the ridicule and scorn of their peers, and the loss of their dear sister after the death of their parents, they remain cheerful and optimistic, full of energy and gentle. I enjoyed my time with them immensely realizing what an uncommon and rare opportunity it was to meet these twins who share the same disability and remarkable ability simultaneously. My positive impressions of these two neat sisters is shared by many others. I know that, because each time the documentary airs, my email box is filled with messages from people who just want to share their warmth and appreciation of these two special souls in some way and the savant website gives them the opportunity to do so.

The highlight of their trip was yet to come after they left Fond du Lac and continued their cross-country journey. Unbeknownst to them at that time was the fact that Dave Wagner had made arrangements for all of them to go to California and once again see their hero, Dick Clark, in person. When the *$100,000 Pyramid* show was taken off the air in 1996, it was a major loss for Flo and Kay. "We were depressed," they told me, "we couldn't sleep and prayed the show would come back." Many days they would sit in front of the TV at the usual time the show formerly played, only to find some disappointing replacement. Therefore meeting Mr. Clark in person again was like a renewal tonic to them. They were bursting with joy at that prospect. Finding his star on Hollywood Boulevard, which they kneeled before almost reverently, was a prelude to the actual home visit with Mr. Clark. And that visit, as the documentary shows, certainly did live up to their expectations.

What is ahead for Flo and Kay in terms of ultimate placement remains to be seen. Their brother is committed to having them remain with him, just as he feels his mother would have wished. Certainly there is no need for any institutional placement at any point in their future lives. But should alternative living arrangements be required in the future, unlike the years in which they were raised as children and adolescents, there are now many alternative living arrangements available such as assisted living, group home, foster home or even supported apartments.

For now, though, Flo and Kay are content with their music, their meticulously kept color-coded celebrity dress charts and, most importantly, each other. It was a treat to meet them, even if only for a brief visit. Fortunately, though, through the present documentary, and other video or print stories that will surely follow, many other people will get to meet these special twin sisters and be touched by their story and abilities, along with their modest nature, just as I was.

Identical twin savants are a rarity indeed. To my knowledge in the case reports of the past 122 years, and in present-day accounts, Flo and Kay are the only two female identical autistic twins with identical savant abilities ever reported. Over that same time span I am aware of only three sets of identical twin males, all presently living, in which the twin brothers both have autistic disorder and both have savant syndrome. In two of these instances, the identical twins are both autistic and both demonstrate identical savant skills. In the third instance, however, while both twins have autistic disorder, they have separate savant skills, one in music and the other in math. Thus identical twin savants represent a very rare circumstance in an already rare condition.

CHAPTER 16

Daniel: "Numbers Are my Friends"

March 14, 2004 was "International Pi" day. That was 3.14 of course. Daniel Tammet, who was 25 years old at the time, says it was a yellow day. That was the day that Daniel Tammet first came to worldwide attention when he recited, from memory, Pi to 22,514 decimal places. It took over five hours and set a new European record. The event, which Daniel named "Pi-in-the-Sky," coincided with Einstein's birthday and took place in front of Einstein's blackboard at the Museum of the History of Science in Oxford, England.

It was a yellow day because just as Daniel perceives every number to 10,000 as having its own separate color, texture and even emotional tone, so does each week day have its own color. Sundays are yellow. International Pi day was a Sunday.

While "Pi-in-the-Sky" launched his worldwide recognition, Daniel's very popular book *Born on a Blue Day: A Memoir of Asperger's and an Extraordinary Mind* provided even greater visibility. Hodder and Stoughton published the first edition in the UK in 2006. I had the privilege of writing the Foreword to that book and Daniel was kind enough, in turn, to write a Foreword to this book. *Born on a Blue Day* was written following a very successful television airing in Europe of a documentary film, *Brainman* (produced by Focus Productions of London). That film has been widely hailed, and has been broadcast often by the Discovery Channel in the United States and now in more than 40 countries. In 2007 *Born on a Blue Day* was published in New York. The two editions have sold over a half a million copies including translations into 20 languages.

In 2009 Daniel's second book—*Embracing the Wide Sky: A Tour across the Horizons of the Mind*—was published and it too has become an instant success. In this book Daniel provides an excellent summary of the scientific work regarding exceptional talent and savant abilities, as well as synesthesia itself. This reader-friendly book provides a very understandable first-hand account of how his mind carries out his exceptional talents, something most persons with savant syndrome are unable to articulate or explain. He states his special abilities are neither a "genetic quirk" nor a "cerebral super-computer." Rather such skills as his are due to unusually rich associative networks in some persons, and a spectrum of such abilities hints at hidden potential within us all.

I met Daniel for the first time in Milwaukee, Wisconsin at the Calatrava-designed Art Museum while filming portions of *Brainman*. Daniel is a very pleasant, polite, soft-spoken and gentle person. He seems preoccupied at times and is quite shy. He is proud, but not boastful, about his enormous abilities, which do exist at a prodigious level. His digit span memory, for example, exceeds that of anyone I have ever interviewed.

The Calatrava building was the ideal place to interview Daniel. Its dramatic setting, rich colors and striking imagery provided the perfect setting. A towering sculpture in part of the building is constructed with a multitude of glass pieces, of all shapes, sizes and colors. That sculpture helped me visualize, in a concrete sense, some of the colorful visual imagery that Daniel was describing to me verbally. And the graceful briese soleil of the museum, as it expanded that morning against a bright blue sky, seemed symbolic of how we are expanding, slowly but surely, our understanding of the human mind and its innermost workings, a research effort to which Daniel now contributes liberally.

But why memorize Pi? Daniel explains in his book that he learned about Pi in school, just as most of us did. He was immediately fascinated by the unique characteristics of Pi and memorized as many digits as he could find in various library books. Then in 2003 his father reminded Daniel that it had been 20 years of being seizure-free since a series of childhood convulsions at about age four. Daniel decided he wanted to do something "to show that my childhood experience of epilepsy had not held me back." So he contacted the National Society for Epilepsy, the largest epilepsy charity organization in the UK, and the fund-raising event for the recitation of Pi was set up and carried out on March 14, 2004 as described above.

In addition to his phenomenal memory capacity, Daniel is also a lightning calculator. If asked to calculate 37 to the power of 4, for example, he will give you almost instantly the correct answer: 1,874,161. Ask him to divide 13 by 97 and he will give you the answer—to over 100 decimal places if you wish. He outdistances the ordinary calculator capacity. So one turns to a computer. Daniel can quickly reach 100 digits on a computer printout, if the answer is that long, and then keep on going. Indeed the only way to see if he is correct is to resort to a computer.

This form of synesthesia, which Daniel describes so vividly and richly in his book *Born on a Blue Day* and in the several documentaries about him, is unique. Daniel sees individual numbers which each have a unique color, form and texture. Some even have an emotional tone. When doing complex computations, the number "images" merge together in a confluence of colors, shapes and textures that provides the final answer. Daniel then simply reads the numbers he sees displayed before him.

And then there is the extraordinary ability to learn an entire new language— grammar, inflection and comprehension—in only one week. The *Brainman* film documents Daniel's immersion in, and then mastery of, the Icelandic language in just seven days. This rapid learning culminated in a live interview on television at the end of the seven days using his newly acquired language in a friendly, animated conversation with his Icelandic TV hosts. They were astonished by the rapidity with which Daniel carried out this task, and by the comprehensiveness and depth of Daniel's quick language acquisition.

Languages, along with numbers, have both been fascinating to Daniel. His native language was English. After reading a teach-yourself book for only a week, he could carry on a conversation comfortably in Spanish. Daniel knows ten languages now, and has been working with creating his own language which he calls Manti. He states that project is a "work in progress."

Daniel maintains a website at www.optimnem.co.uk, which now focuses uniquely on language learning courses.

Daniel was born in London on January 31, 1979. Daniel's synesthesia surfaced after several childhood seizures ultimately diagnosed as temporal lobe epilepsy. Daniel has been given a diagnosis of high-functioning autism, or Asperger syndrome, a condition he writes about openly. Some prominent autistic traits and behaviors were present throughout his childhood and some residual symptoms and obsessive behaviors are still present as an adult. But his very high level of functioning at the present time underscores his observation that he has outgrown some of his autism. Similar progress does occur, fortunately, in some other persons on the autistic spectrum as they grow older. This progress and growth on Daniel's part has created in him a heartfelt life mission—serving as an inspiration for other persons, whether with epilepsy or Asperger's, demonstrating by his own example that such conditions need not interfere with overall development and potential. His mission statement is an empathic one—to make the world a "more welcome" place for persons with such disabilities.

Daniel's books have led to worldwide lecture presentations on better understanding exceptional skills and abilities in whomever they exist, in whatever amount. And what an excellent ambassador he is for a message of enlightenment that mixes science made understandable with in-person inspiration, empathy and optimism.

Daniel's plans for the future include continued help to charities such as the National Autistic Society and the National Society for Epilepsy. His celebrity status provides a great podium worldwide from which to carry out that admirable goal. He also wants to continue to work with scientists and researchers on projects that can study in greater detail his special abilities. And he wants to promote as well different ways of learning, particularly visual learning, which is often so important for better understanding, and teaching, persons with autistic spectrum disorders.

At the present time Daniel is working on a third book, this one a novel focusing on themes of faith and love.

At a very personal level his goals are like most of our own—becoming closer in our intimate relationships, and fostering closer relationships with family and friends as well. He also wants to experience, and relish, those few but precious moments of peace and contentment that he describes in the closing paragraphs of his book. Those are the "heavenly moments", to use his words for being relaxed, at ease and pleasantly convivial.

Daniel says that numbers are his friends. Indeed in his early childhood they seem to be his only friends. But now Daniel is seeking out and making new friends—around the world literally. But friendship is reciprocal and one comes away from his book—or at least I did—with the feeling, through its openness, candor and reaching out, of having made a new friend as well.

The newspapers and magazines of the world carry many interviews of, and insights from, Daniel because of his unique first-hand credential as a prodigious savant coupled with his ability to describe and articulate that remarkable phenomenon. But I was particularly drawn to an account in a February 2009 article in *The Scotsman* which summed up the interviewer's interaction with Daniel this way:

> Yet what is most remarkable about Daniel Tammet is not that one day he could be listed among the great minds of the world—though there is every reason to think that he might be. The truly remarkable thing is the quiet determination by which he has become an ordinary man. Thanks to perseverance, every day he is becoming more and more himself, which might be the hardest thing of all. (Mansfield 2009)

CHAPTER 17

Stephen: "A Rocket of Young Talent"

In October, 2006 a new art gallery opened in London. It was the Stephen Wiltshire Gallery at the Royal Opera Arcade in Pall Mall. There Stephen, a prodigious savant, at age 35, is resident two days a week producing his extraordinary drawings, some paintings and some commissioned work. He is now a world famous artist.

It was 19 years earlier, in February 1987, that the BBC aired a program with several savants titled *The Foolish Wise Ones*. One of those persons was a then 12-year-old autistic boy, Stephen Wiltshire, drawing from memory a remarkably accurate sketch of St. Pancras station, which he had visited for the first time only briefly several hours before. As the camera recorded, he quickly and assuredly drew the elaborate and complicated building exactly as he had seen it with the clock hands set at 11:20, the hour he had viewed them.

There were hundreds of calls and letters to the BBC following that broadcast seeking a source to purchase originals of Stephen's astonishing work. That initial interest and then a sustained demand for the drawings led to the publication of an entire volume of Wiltshire's works entitled *Drawings* (Wiltshire 1987).

In the introduction to *Drawings*, Sir Hugh Casson, former president of the Royal Academy, said of Stephen: "Happily, every now and then, a rocket of young talent explodes and continues to shower us with its sparks. Stephen Wiltshire—who was born with severe speech difficulties—is one of those rockets." He then describes the artistic brilliance further:

> His sense of perspective seems to be faultless... I've never seen in all my competition drawing such a talent, such a natural and extraordinary talent that this child seems to have... Stephen is possibly the best child artist in Britain.

Stephen was born in London on April 24, 1974. He was an extremely withdrawn and almost mute child. A diagnosis of autism was made at age three. He started attending Queensmill, a school in London for children with special needs, at age five. He existed in a world of his own and had many other behaviors, such as rocking or hand flapping, so typically described in autistic youngsters. He was distant, preoccupied, had little or no eye contact and often roamed about classrooms aimlessly, sometimes staring for long times at pictures, then suddenly dashing from room to room. He would absorb himself for long periods of time with drawing on scraps of paper, first animals, then London buses and finally buildings.

Stephen uttered his first word—"paper"—at age six and learned to speak fully by age nine. When he was eight years old Stephen began drawing cityscapes. According to his teachers, he became obsessed with cars and loved to draw London landmarks. He also learnt to read and began to immerse himself for hours in books on architecture and travel.

Stephen was characterized by the headmistress of the special school as having a "gentle personality, humor and curious dignity." Overall he was described as eminently likable and far from detracting from his general development, his art seemingly aided it. While there was some fear that acquisition of language and other skills might, like Nadia, rob him of his genius, that has not been the case at all. Instead, as with Leslie and Alonzo, Stephen's special skills and overall social development progressed simultaneously. The blossoming of his genius continued to coincide with the blossoming of his personality as he grew and developed.

At age ten Stephen drew what he called a "London Alphabet," a group of drawings from Albert Hall to the London Zoo with structures such as the Houses of Parliament and the Imperial War Museum in between. These drawings were formed to teach Stephen an understanding of these letters and to encourage his reading skills. An exquisite sense of perspective is demonstrated in a drawing he titles "Looking Down the Lift Shaft and Stairs," and his drawing of Buckingham Palace is a spectacular example of Stephen's intricacy and accuracy.

One of the influential persons in Stephen's life was Margaret Hewson. She first met Stephen when he was in Queensmill School even before *The Foolish Wise Ones* aired on the BBC in February 1987. After that appearance propelled Stephen to national prominence, Margaret Hewson helped guide the extraordinary journey with Stephen that followed with awe, respect, sensitivity and joy. She travelled with him to Europe, America and Japan and participated in 12 television programs viewed the world over. Together they created four books, one of which topped the *Sunday Times* bestseller list. *Drawings* (1987) was the first book followed by *Cities* (1989) and *Floating Cities* (1991). The latter became a No.1 bestseller in the UK, with remarkable drawings of Venice, Amsterdam, Leningrad and Moscow. His most recent book, *Stephen Wiltshire's American Dream* (1993), was devoted to US architecture and the desert landscape of Arizona.

Until recently, Stephen had concentrated almost exclusively on architecture. He would provide exact, literal renditions of any building, no matter how complex, and in fact he seems to prefer the especially intricate. He views buildings, in person or from a photograph, and retains an exquisitely precise and detailed image in his memory for later recall and drawing. Additionally, he can sense and draw a building, no matter how complex, with a three-dimensional perspective from a two-dimensional photo.

For a long time Stephen's work depicted exactly what he saw without embellishment, stylization or interpretation. He made no notes; impressions were indelibly and faithfully inscribed from a single exposure for later recall and he did his drawings swiftly, beginning anywhere on the page. His remarkable artistic ability was linked to an equally remarkable memory. Through the years there has been a progression and growth in Stephen's art skills. Stephen can still draw buildings with precise detail, window pane by window pane, or produce astonishingly accurate aerial views— encompassing as many as 200 buildings—from a helicopter ride, such as *Tokyo Panorama*. But now his gallery includes drawings such as *Times Square at Night* with all the colorful neon signs and automobile traffic. Or *Piccadilly Circus at Night*, which also shows brilliant color and some improvisation. Like other prodigious savants, Stephen is showing a progression from remarkable literal memory, to improvisation, to creating something entirely new.

Accompanying the progress and improvement in artistic abilities have been gains in language and social skills as well. He is much more comfortable around people, less withdrawn, more animated and more social. The art skills have provided him the "conduit toward normalization" that I have seen in so many persons with savant syndrome. And, importantly, there has been no trade-off of artistic interest, skill or ability for those gains in personal adjustment. Not only has Stephen maintained his astonishing artistic ability, he has also broadened it and is venturing into improvisation and creativity with also sensational skill.

Perhaps the best evidence of that personal and social growth is a drawing first posted in his gallery on February 20, 2007—*Stephen Wiltshire with his Girlfriend*.

Most savants, including prodigious savants, have one single area of expertise. But savants with multiple skills certainly also do exist. During her contacts with Stephen surrounding his spectacular drawing ability, Margaret Hewson discovered Stephen had perfect pitch and encouraged him to have weekly music lessons which continue to this day. Oliver Sacks, in his book *An Anthropologist on Mars* (1995), shares his delightful, and insightful, impressions of Stephen in the chapter on "Prodigies." Having spent considerable time with Stephen, and witnessing the incredible artistic ability that was present, Sacks was very surprised to learn of yet another remarkable ability that Stephen possessed—music.

Stephen always loved listening to music and liked to sing. He was always in tune and enjoyed imitating many well-known singers. When Stephen was 19, he met a music teacher with whom he experienced instant rapport. He began to "play scales, then to sing chords, starting with major triads." As Sacks (1995) describes it, "The idea of thirds, fifths—Pythagorean, numerical sense of musical interval—seemed quite innate in Stephen" (p.238). His teacher remarked, "I never had to teach him." It was obvious, the teacher told Sacks, that Stephen "is possessed of quite extraordinary powers of harmonic identification, analysis and reproduction." In short, Stephen had an innate knowledge of the "rules of music" even without learning or instruction, just as he possessed that same innate knowledge of the "rules of art" earlier. And it came as a surprise even to Stephen's music teacher that Stephen had perfect pitch.

It is interesting, as you will see in my description of Kim Peek in Chapter 10, that this same sudden emergence of musical interest and ability occurred in Kim, at age 50, after he, too, met just the "right" music teacher.

Like all art, Stephen's works are better seen than described. Stephen has a very comprehensive website at www.stephenwiltshire.co.uk. There one can learn more about him and view his gallery directly. Stephen's sister, Annette, and her husband, Zoltan, continue to provide care and encouragement in the gallery and in Stephen's other ventures as well.

The most astonishing examples of Stephen's incredible art skills, coupled with marvelous memory, are in video programs documenting these prodigious abilities. There have been at least three such programs. The first of these was a 2001 BBC program, *Fragments of Genius*, that showed Stephen, after a short airplane ride, producing, in three hours, a drawing that encompassed four square miles of London including 12 major landmarks and over 200 other buildings, which is on the cover of this book.

A 2005 documentary, *Beautiful Minds*, by Colourfield Productions in Dortmund, Germany shows Stephen's three-day, 5.5-yard (5.03 meters) drawing of Rome after a

45-minute flight over that city. Street by street, building by building and column by column, the city is drawn with breathtaking accuracy. Blueprints of the Coliseum, superimposed on Stephen's drawing of it, show a perfect fit.

In October, 2007 I hosted an art exhibit at the Windhover Center in Fond du Lac titled "Windows of Genius: Artwork of the Prodigious Savant." In that exhibit were drawings, sculptures, blueprints, paintings and silhouettes from savant artists around the world. For that exhibit Stephen's London gallery sent me a print of his drawing of Rome at one-third scale. Even at that reduced scale the print was over-powering and drew the immediate attention of everyone who visited the exhibit. It was the highlight of the show.

In April, 2007 Stephen did a similar flyover and subsequent drawing of London which is documented in an hour-long program by Channel Five in its *Extraordinary People* series of programs. Stephen's flight over the Thames lasted only 15 minutes and the London skyline panorama stretched from London Bridge to Canary Wharf encompassing seven square miles of streets, river and buildings. Stephen then spent five days (11 pens and 3 pencils) drawing what he had so briefly seen.

The drawing is incredible in its vista, intricacy, accuracy and beauty. In the film a London aerial photographer who often flies and photographs the same route is astounded at Stephen's accuracy in capturing that scene, as are an architect and a structural engineer regarding the intricate detail and fidelity of the drawing.

This film goes much beyond just the drawing skill of Stephen, however monu-mental that is. Through the memories of family, friends, teachers and others who have known Stephen since he was an infant, Stephen's life is retraced beginning with those early years of mutism and solitude, to his present socially adept, self-confident and self-reliant life. Through clips from some of those earlier films, one can witness the gradual but unmistakable progress in language ability, social comfortableness and increased daily living skills in Stephen. And one can sense the important role that his special artistic skills have played in that overall blossoming process. It is an encouraging and uplifting story in and of itself, but also it serves as an instructive template for using special skills to achieve progress overall in other persons with savant syndrome, whatever their skills and abilities.

Like so many savants, Stephen smiles a lot. He radiates congeniality and con-tentment. He is so proud of what he does, justifiably, and so appreciative of the positive and reinforcing feedback from those who value his artistry. In that way he reminds me of Alonzo, who likewise is so content, so happy and so mellow. For me "mellow" means "relaxed, at ease and pleasantly convivial." If Stephen and Alonzo, with the obstacles they have faced in their lives, can be "relaxed, at ease and pleas-antly convivial"—which is contagious when you are around them—perhaps there is a lesson in that for the rest of us who have had it not quite so difficult.

CHAPTER 18

Ping Lian, Gregory, Richard, George, Jonathan and Some Others: Artwork of the Prodigious Savant

As my contacts with savant artists have grown more numerous through the years, I have accumulated a sizeable collection of their art pieces. I displayed some of those in my home, and some in my office. But as that unique collection grew I felt it deserved a much wider audience. So in fall, 2007 I arranged for an exhibit of this unique collection at the Windhover Center for the Arts in Fond du Lac. It was titled "Windows of Genius: Artwork of the Prodigious Savant." Nearly one hundred pieces from eleven artists were on display. Two of the artists, one from Australia (Ping Lian) and one from Seattle, Washington (Gregory Blackstock), attended in person so visitors to the exhibit could meet them, interact with them and see them at work.

Two of the artists featured in the exhibit—Stephen Wiltshire and Alonzo Clemons—were profiled in seperate chapters earlier in this book. But in this chapter I include some others who participated in the exhibit both to credit their work appropriately, and to use their works as examples of the diversity of style, medium and subjects that exists among savant artists. More information about the particular artists mentioned here, including the opportunity to view their artwork directly, is available on their respective profile postings on the savant website at www.savant-syndrome.com.

The exhibit was an immense success. Hundreds of people of all ages and from all walks of life attended—students from grade school to graduate school; teachers and therapists; workers whether blue collar, white collar or college professors; artists and craftworkers; parents with their children; individuals with disabilities and families of those persons. Through the information posted about the artists along with their artwork and through personal interaction with some of the artists themselves, along with the videotape information and special lectures, the exhibit turned out to be as much an educational event as an art exhibit. The feedback from the general public and the media was positive, copious and most appreciative.

Ping Lian Yeak: "I want to be artist"

With the activity and endurance of the Energizer Bunny, Ping Lian enlivened the "Windows of Genius" art exhibit with his on-site art production, much to the delight of those who had a chance to see him at work. He, his mother and some relatives had come all the way from Australia and Malaysia to Fond du Lac for this event. Now age 15, Ping Lian was not only an artist-in-residence at the exhibit, but also an artist-in-motion throughout the event. Social and communication deficits from his autism are evident, but those are offset by his happy demeanor and the obvious joy he derives from that which he does best—his art.

As a young child Ping Lian had poor fine motor control. To help him with that, his home schooling curriculum included tracing and coloring activities. At age eight, Ping Lian suddenly became obsessed with art, and the transition from tracing to drawing happened almost instantly. One day, after he had finished eating an ice cream cone, he just started drawing the pictures that were printed on the ice cream wrapper. Since that time he has not stopped drawing the fountain of images that flow continuously through his mind.

From simple, childish sketches, Ping Lian's style evolved into a sophisticated level using charcoal, acrylic, watercolor, ink and oil pastels. His work is better seen than described and can be viewed at www.pinglian.com. The website provides much more background on Ping Lian and in the videos section there are two clips of Ping Lian at work at the Fond du Lac exhibit.

Dr. Rosa C. Martinez, whose contribution on "training the talent" with artistically gifted savants is Chapter 26 in this book, also attended the Windhover exhibit and shared this personal impression with me later:

> Watching this young boy create his art was an equivocally amazing experience. Albert Einstein once said "True art is characterized by an irresistible urge in the creative artist." He was speaking about persons like Ping Lian Yeak. Ping Lian possesses this "urge." His demonstration while creating an acrylic painting was astonishing… His paintings tend to encompass hidden aspects or forms, not initially seen or noticed upon first view. His use of color and his creation of intricate lines result in images within images that often appear unlimited on canvas. Each stroke appeared effortlessly calculated requiring measurement, memory, imitation, uniqueness and genius.

Ping Lian's work has also been exhibited elsewhere in the United States, Australia, UK, Germany and Malaysia. Some of his works were featured at the United Nations Headquarters in New York in honor of the inaugural World Autism Awareness Day in April, 2008. He has also been featured in documentaries in the United States, UK, Malaysia, Australia, Scandinavia, Korea and Singapore. A permanent exhibit of Ping Lian's works has been established at the Art Commune in Subang Jaya, Malaysia (Pinglian @ The Art Commune).

The artistic prowess Ping Lian shows provides not only beautiful art for us, but more importantly serves as a source of satisfaction, development and growth for him, helping to minimize whatever limitations spring from his disability. Standing behind and beside each of the savants is a dedicated, patient, loving, determined and perpetually optimistic family which appreciates the special gift in their child, and wishes to share that gift more widely with the world. Ping Lian's mother, along with his siblings, fill that critical role with Ping Lian. They are proud of Ping Lian, and rightly so.

Gregory Blackstock: "an anthropologist of the everyday"

There was another artist present in person at the Windhover exhibit. I knew about Greg's remarkable and unique artwork, which was why I invited him to the exhibit. I was so impressed with him, and his several abilities, that I had written the Foreword to his book *Blackstock's Collections: The Drawings of an Autistic Savant* (Blackstock 2006). I also knew that he was familiar with a number of languages which he had self-learned just from listening to foreign co-workers, or from listening to records in other languages. I guess I had tucked that fact away without much attention to it.

One day at the exhibit I was standing watching Greg at work. Ping Lian's relatives from Malaysia were standing nearby as well, conversing with each other in their native language, as they watched Greg at work. To their astonishment, and mine, Greg joined in on their conversation—in Mandarin Chinese! His ability to learn the rudiments of nearly any language, by osmosis as it were, is but one of Greg's very special talents which include art and music.

Greg, born on January 9, 1946, loves to draw collections of things—birds, fishes, insects, dogs, plants, tools, pianos, drums, bells, cars, tanks, trucks, trains, airplanes, boats, buildings, clothes, kites, clowns, knots, butterflies, fireworks among many others. He often draws these from memory, gathering digital-like images in his mind from the past and assembling them in colorful drawings, done entirely free-hand. At other times he refers to books when he draws, stylizing the animals or objects in his distinct way. The collections are of all sorts of everyday items, leading one newspaper to describe Greg as "an anthropologist of the everyday." Each list is extensive and often exhaustive. His picture-list of tools, for example, has 65 hammers, awls, picks and some tools I have never heard of, carefully placed and meticulously drawn on a page worthy of any tool catalog I have ever seen. The connections he makes among the items on his lists provide evidence of creative, sometimes humorous, associative thinking as well, such as including a diving bell in his drawing of "The Bells."

Greg's lists are impeccably drawn with the precision of a machinist. To those who know him well, it seems that over time his drawings have become increasingly precise and regimented.

I asked Greg if he ever makes any mistakes. He told me that he had gone to Home Depot for some research because he wanted to make a drawing of saws. He then confided in me, apologetically, that he had to go back a second time because he wasn't sure about the exact teeth configuration on one of those saws. But, having seen it a second time, he could then add it to the list. He assured me it doesn't usually take a second visit. (I sometimes forget what I was even going to Home Depot to purchase, let along remember much else about the visit.)

Interestingly Greg will not draw things he cannot correctly name. His cousin once gave him a beautiful book of sea shells and asked if he would be interested in drawing them. He had absolutely no interest in doing so, he told her, because he didn't know their names.

Regardless of what he draws, Greg learns a significant amount of information about his topic and likes to share that with the viewer. He can mimic the call of the bird, describe the use of a tool and provide horticultural information about plants. Greg's drawing of poison ivy, included in his work, "The Notorious Harmful to Man Plants," is comparable to that in a plant field manual and the neatly printed 70-word accompanying text reads like something one might find on a consumer-oriented or first-aid website "Learn to recognize this harmful plant before venturing directly into poison ivy grown areas." And, certainly from the carefully drawn picture in true-to-life color, it will be easy for the viewer to recognize poison ivy in the future.

Greg also is increasingly driven to draw. He has his topics lined up in his head months in advance and he sometimes cannot even wait to finish one piece before he starts on the next. He is rarely distracted by a suggested new topic or even a requested commission, with his standard answer being "Sorry! That will have to wait. I'm just too overloaded with ideas." Greg's music had definitely taken a back seat to art now.

Greg has become a featured artist at Garde Rail Gallery in Austin, Texas, specialists in "Outsider Art." It was his cousin, Dorothy Frisch, Greg's "safety net" and strong advocate, who in 2003 brought his artwork to the attention of owners Karen Light-Piña and Marcus Piña, who immediately fell in love with his unique list drawings.

The Garde Rail Gallery website (www.garde-rail.com) describes Greg thus:

Greg exhibits many of the remarkable traits of the autistic savant; he speaks many languages, is an incredible mimic, and is able to recall events with uncanny precision… It is without doubt in our minds that Gregory Blackstock would be an artist under any circumstance—his autism did not make him become an artist, nor is he an artist because of it… Through his art and his music, Gregory has effectively been able to combat this disability and to meet the challenge with fantastic results… Gregory's drawings are often large, on several sheets of paper pieced together by Greg with tape and glue. Using pencil, crayon, ink and marker, Gregory depicts insects and baskets with incredible precision, straight lines and text executed without the aid of a straight rule. The detail is minute and the shading impeccable.

A unique and coveted product from Greg's inventive mind is the *Standard Time Chart of the World*. Written on a stiff ten-inch square of cardboard in his precise lettering, are all the countries and states of the 27 world time zones—264 countries and the 50 states of the United States. Set in the center of this square is a rotating dial with the 24 hour clock marked off in 15-minute increments. Twist the dial to have the current time pointing to your location, and you can then look up any other location to see what time it is there. It provides a convenient answer to a complex process with striking simplicity. And it is easier to use, and more fun, than many calculators.

Greg is also an excellent musician. He often plays accordion outside of sporting and theater events, usually matching his music to the occasion, such as the university's fight song before the football games or the "Toreador Song" in front of the opera house. Passersby could not possibly know the amazing and complex things going on in the mind of this large, slightly unkempt musician heard whistling the piccolo part while vigorously playing Sousa's "The Stars and Stripes Forever" on his Petosa accordion.

Greg is proud of the creative and distinctive meals he cooks for himself. Concerned about heart disease, he very carefully avoids fats and makes his "cream" soups out of non-fat milk, while blithely adding staggering amounts of salt or sugar to them. His carefully written recipes for "Cream of Mustard Soup—quick method" or "Greg's improved Cream of Spinach Soup" show the same wonderful precision and artistic detail as his drawings.

Greg has been self-supporting most of his adult life and spent nearly 25 years working as a dish-washer at the Washington Athletic Club before retiring with a small pension. He has always been a meticulous bookkeeper of his finances, but he struggles with the concept of "relative value." For example, according to his cousin Dorothy, one of Greg's great pleasures is traveling the nation to visit theme parks and he has been assisted by travel agents in making those arrangements. But when asked about the cost of the plane ticket or hotel, he cannot even guess at the price until he gets the bill. On the other hand, worried about the cost of replacing them, his cousin reports, "he insists on putting his shaving kit, his ever-present Cheez Whiz and jar of Lowry's Seasoning Salt in the hotel safe in case of theft."

Although Greg struggles with the nuances of communication, he is nevertheless a great lover of words and studies the thesaurus with characteristic concentration. Since his visit to Fond du Lac, Greg regularly sends colorful postcards to "Dr. and Mrs. Treffert," which keep us up to date on happenings in his life. It is amazing how he can so meticulously, in still legible handwriting, squeeze so much information into such a small space. My replies are not nearly so neatly written. Greg has been particularly pleased about a video from an *Evening Magazine* television piece which can be accessed on the Garde Rail Gallery website. It is a charming and delightful look into the life of a very gifted and unique man who, at age 64, is happier now than ever before.

The website at www.garde-rail.com and the savant syndrome website provide additional information about him.

Richard Wawro: "with eyes wide open"

Richard, from Edinburgh, Scotland, was a prolific autistic savant artist. He was born on April 14, 1952 and regrettably died in February, 2006 at age 53. But during those 53 years he became one of the world's best known savant artists. He had over 100 exhibitions of his work in the United States and Europe. Notable owners of his work include Margaret Thatcher, who at one point described Richard as "her favorite artist," and the late Pope John Paul II.

Richard began drawing at age three with chalk and a slate board. At age six he entered a center for disturbed children in Edinburgh. There he was introduced to crayons and his talent was immediately apparent; his sole medium remained oil-bound crayon throughout his career. When Richard was age 12, Marian Bohusz-Szyszko of the Polish School of Art in London viewed Richard's art and was "thunderstruck"; he described Richard's work as an "incredible phenomenon rendered with the precision of a mechanic and the vision of a poet."

Because he was legally blind, Richard always drew with his face only inches away from the paper, yet the perspective was maintained in his pictures, no matter the size. He did not sharpen his crayons but used layer after layer to achieve the rich color, deep texture and delicate shadows. A final buffing gave the sheen so characteristic of all his works. Richard loved light. He played with it, experimented with it and mastered it in all of his works.

Like all savants, Richard's work reveals a massive, literal memory. Richard would see a scene, using high-powered binoculars, record and then store it in his mind with digital-camera-like form and fidelity. He would then retrieve the image from his mind at some point later, sometimes years later, and draw the scene with impeccable accuracy. Once viewed, he did not require any further "model."

Richard's father, who was from Poland, through his enthusiasm and pride was an important contributor to Richard's success. The interaction between Richard and his father was a joy and inspiration to watch. I had a chance to witness that first-hand when they both visited Wisconsin at the Medical College in Milwaukee. Richard would work intensely on his drawing, his face always close to the surface no matter how large the picture. When completed that picture would have perfect perspective and proportions. Richard would proudly show the picture to his dad. With a "that's-my-boy" gleam in his eye, Dad would give Richard a vigorous Polish hug, followed by a mini-celebration in which he and Richard would swing their joined hands back and forth with a huge high-five final upward thrust, and a shout of joy. What a celebration! What a compliment! What a reinforcing, self-esteem and confidence building display of love and appreciation! Richard's mother, who also loved him unconditionally, died in 1979. In spite of their closeness Richard did not stop his work upon her death.

Richard had his first exhibit at the Demarco Gallery in Edinburgh when he was 17 years old. His first US show was in 1977. During his lifetime Richard produced over 2600 pictures. With his remarkable memory, he was able to recall where he drew each of those pictures, and the date he did the drawing. While he was capable of exact replication of what he had seen, from time to time he would add his own touches, interpretation or improvisations to some of those images. The colors were bold and deep; the light and shadows engaging.

In 1983 Dr. Laurence A. Becker made a very moving and impressive documentary film about Richard. That film—*With Eyes Wide Open*—won numerous awards.

The film grew out of Dr. Becker's long interest in teaching gifted and talented individuals. In the film some of Richard's autistic and ritualistic behaviors, along with his limited vision, are evident but those limitations are certainly dwarfed by his incredible artistic talent. As Richard's art developed, so did his language and socialization skills. One accomplishment of which he was particularly proud was learning to sign his name to his works. While it would seem that should be a natural skill given his talent in drawing, it took many years for him to be able to do that. His style is so distinctive though that his works would not really require a signature. But he was very proud when he achieved that milestone.

Dr. Becker produced a follow-up film on Richard in 1989—*A Real Rainman: Portrait of an Autistic Savant*. It documents Richard's progress as an artist, and his progress in overcoming some of the earlier obstacles that his autism produced. It also focuses on the relationship between Richard and his brother, reminiscent of the interaction of the brothers in *Rain Man*.

Richard's works, particularly a piece called "King's College Choir," drew a great deal of attention at the exhibit. "King's College Choir" is my favorite. It was done one Christmas Eve and captures the sanctity and emotion of that night such that one can almost hear the choir, not just see it.

Dr. Becker sums it up this way in a brochure he wrote to accompany some of Richard's exhibits in the US, "Richard Wawro, Artist Extra Ordinem":

> To walk into a room at an exhibition and to be surrounded by Richard's pictures is to share in his search for the light. To join, even briefly, with him and to look at a new kind of world through the eyes of one who receives his gift of sight, severely limited as it may be, with eyes wide open, is to rejoice and be glad that his eyes have enabled him to see so much more clearly than we ever imagined before the beauty and wonder in the ordinary world which daily surrounds us.

George Widener: "a mind full of numbers translated to art"

How do you translate a mind full of numbers, calendar dates, census figures, historical facts and lightning calculating into art? George Widener is able to do that. And he has done it very successfully. Currently he continues to draw attention internationally for his exceptional graphic art. For example his work was recently featured in the Orleans Gallery in London and will also be part of an exhibit at the prestigious Jan Krugler Gallery in New York City. His work is handled on an ongoing basis by the Henry Boxer Gallery in London.

At the Windhover exhibit George displayed the largest piece at the show titled "Calendars 21." It was done as mixed media on napkins. It gathered a great deal of attention because of its complexity, intricacy and beauty. The picture depicted days of the week and years of the century in repetitive patterns with arrows pointing to certain months that matched each other. To make the piece a challenge George stated: "I made a mistake on purpose, matching June with a July so people could maybe find it and see it is different from the rest, so they could count calendars also and to make other calendar calculators happy they found the mistake." Some viewers found the mistake, others did not.

George Widener is a multiply gifted savant with skills in the domain of calendar calculating, art and memory. Born on February 8, 1962, it was not until his thirties that he was diagnosed with Asperger syndrome. He is a lightning calculator with a seemingly unlimited range. In 2004 he easily defeated a former NASA scientist, using paper, pencil and formulae (and eventually a laptop computer), in a contest asking questions such as "What day of the week will June 25 be in the year 47,253?" George often uses his interest in calendar numbers and dates to tell people how many days, minutes and sometimes seconds old they will be on their next birthday. He has instant recall of thousands of historical facts and US Census figures which he will sometimes incorporate in his art as well. Mention the "powers of two" and he can reel them off in rapid fire progression up to 20 digits or more.

George graduated from college at age 37 from a special education program for learning disabled persons with a liberal arts degree, *Cum Laude*. George has also been drawing landscapes and portraits which he retrieves from his vast memory. Gradually his art has advanced from literal memory to original, expressive creations which include placing his revered numbers, calculations, calendars, facts, historical data, machine parts and letters into works on paper, often napkins. His work is better seen than described and can be accessed at his website at http://savantartist.com/.

In 1998 George began combining calendar dates with magic squares to create what he calls a Magic Time Square. Using historical events, these can create a calendrical "portrait" of a person. George's magic squares have been recognized by world-class magic square experts from around the world. George is a *Titanic* buff and the Contemporary Center American Folk Art Museum in New York City has added some of his drawings on that subject to its permanent collection.

On his website George emphasizes that the progress he has shown has been by maximizing his strengths, rather than trying to "correct" his weaknesses. I call that "training the talent" and what a compelling and convincing example George Widener is of the success of such a venture. Art historian Roger Cardinal writes in a summer 2005 *Raw Vision* magazine article that George's artworks "alert us to the existence of a distinctive mind, as well as a palpable human presence" (Cardinal 2005, p.46). Well said.

Jonathan Lerman: "a window into his heart"

Jonathan Lerman's charcoal drawings were like a magnet at the "Windows of Genius" exhibit. People were drawn to them because of the emotion expressed so boldly in the faces and eyes drawn in broad strokes on the large portraits. Vivid emotion, faces and eyes are usually not a central theme in art by persons with autism, but in Jonathan's case they are. As his mother describes his drawings: "they are skilled, expressive charcoal drawings that offer us a window into his heart. He brings us to the core of his being and shows us the anguish and triumphs he experiences."

Jonathan, born in 1987, was diagnosed with autism at approximately the age of two. His mother describes him as a normal, happy child who began to "slip away" into autism at age two. Verbal communication skills were very limited.

Autism continued on its course of withdrawal, resistance to change, behavior problems and isolation. But then a marvelous thing happened. In the book *Jonathan Lerman: Drawings by an Artist with Autism* (Rexter 2002), Jonathan's mother and father describe it this way:

> Then one day, when Jonathan was ten years old, we received a phone call. Whenever he was away from home at school we always expected the phone to ring. Usually it was because his behavior was so inappropriate or out of control that his teachers could not handle him. This call, however, was different.
>
> "You have to come down here to see what Jonathan is doing," his aide said.
> "What?" we asked. "Holding the other kids hostage?"
> "No, it's really wonderful," she responded excitedly. "He's drawing—beautifully. You've got to come and see this, now!"
>
> We drove to the school where we looked at Jonathan's work in amazement. A chance encounter with charcoal and pastels revealed the inner thoughts and feelings of a child whose emotions we could only speculate about until then. In that instant, we went from knowing that we had a significantly handicapped child to realizing we had an extraordinarily gifted child. (p.126)

Jonathan had his first solo exhibition at the KS Art Gallery in New York in 1999. An article in the *New York Times* in 2001 by Ralph Blumenthal gave his work national visibility. His work was then featured at the Annual Outsider Art show in SoHo, followed by appearances on the *Today Show, 48 Hours* and other international media.

The text to Jonathan's book was written by critic Lyly Rexer and describes the "full range and astonishing growth of Jonathan's extraordinary talent." The book jacket goes on to describe Jonathan as

> working with the assurance of a Matisse, the speed of a Picasso, and the humor of a born cartoonist… These drawings overturn the stereotype of the so-called savant artist as an unchanging talent sprung to life fully formed. Instead they detail the restless experimentation and rapid growth of an artistic sensibility.

Beyond the art in the book, in an Afterword, Jonathan's parents describe the challenges and satisfactions of raising a gifted child with autism and with special abilities:

to understand, to know, and to love a child with autism takes a belief: that autistic children have many abilities that must be nurtured once we recognize and discover them. It also takes love. In Jonathan's case, love of parents, teachers and friends gave him the opportunity he needed to find a way to communicate. (p.127)

Jonathan's mother believes that her son and many others on the autistic spectrum suffer from silent seizures. She feels that such seizures can go easily undetected and can cause many of the manifestations of what has come to be known as autism. She is currently writing a book called *Autism and Seizures* based on her vast research and the insights of physicians who are coming to understand better this common connection between seizures and autistic disorder.

Jonathan's work can be seen on the KS Gallery website: www.ksartonline.com/jl.html. Also, there is more information about him on the savant syndrome website: www.savantsyndrome.com in the profiles section.

In his text for Jonathan's book, Lyle Rexer describes Jonathan's art epiphany this way:

> we will probably never learn what triggered the first impulse to generate form, or what inspires him to work as he does at breakneck speed. But embodied in his drawings is the trajectory of a gifted graphic artist... I believe the work is bound up with who Jonathan Lerman is and who he is becoming. The teacher might just as well have shouted: "He's being born!" (Rexter 2002, p.6)

And I especially like the quote his parents chose to introduce their Afterword about their son.

> Not all flowers grow straight and true
> And yet,
> They are all beautiful

And some others

Through the savant website more such artists come to my attention regularly. Space doesn't permit mentioning or describing them all. Some paint, some draw and some sculpt.

Wil is a 14-year-old adolescent with autism who makes sensational, colorful cutouts of delightful characters fashioned from construction paper in a most creative way. He holds the scissors in a most unconventional manner, which no one else has been able to duplicate, but nevertheless he manages somehow to cut out perfect circles and any other shapes needed to bring life, and convey emotion, to the characters that convey such happiness and joy in these colorful cutouts. His creations, and more background on him, can be seen on the savant website.

Christophe is unable to use his fingers functionally but, using his hands and some acrylic on paper, canvas and cardboard, he produces beautiful images that are among my favorites. He does not talk, but expresses himself powerfully thorough his paintings which can be accessed on the savant website. His paintings are extraordinary because of the unique style, imagery, color and fluid motion which conveys so much emotion in his fascinating, improbable, mystical characters. He has had exhibits in France, Japan, Italy and the United States.

Seth, who was diagnosed with autism as a child, lived for years in a world of roller coasters, haunted houses and classical music. But a dramatic change came about in 2003, when at age 20 he took an oil painting class at the Cleveland Museum of Art. Seth, who rarely speaks, began then to describe his world in paint. Brilliantly colored canvasses project a permeating sense of joy. His diverse imagery includes many-colored horses, spectacular landscapes, aurora skies, mysterious forests, whales, fish, mythological animals, exotic birds and an iconic imagery of Manhattan.

Seth's story and works have been the subject of a number of television shows such as the *Today* program on regular broadcast stations, as well as on public broadcast networks. There is a very touching and insightful video of Seth titled *A Different Kind of Journey*, which can be accessed on the savant website. That video is a thoughtful and insightful exploration, through the eyes of his mother, an art expert and Seth himself, of a different, more positive view of what "outsider art" means. I especially like the beginning of that piece: *Dedicated to those individuals who dare to be part of the "outside."*

There have been numerous exhibits of Seth's works in the United States and elsewhere. A return to Cleveland, where his art journey began, occurred with his current exhibit "Visions of Galapagos—The Inspiring Works of Seth Chwast" at the Cleveland Museum of Natural History.

My favorite piece of Seth's is *Fantasy Hippocampus*. He is intrigued with the hippocampus—half horse, half man—as a mythical creature. I am intrigued with the hippocampus in the neurologic sense. No doubt that is a meaningless coincidence. But one wonders. Coincidence or not, I was drawn to that piece even before I knew its name. Blue and bold, it captures attention immediately.

More of Seth's enchanting works can be seen on his website at www.sethchwastart.com. That site provides some interesting insights into his world verbally as well through his blog. Welcome to Seth's different kind of journey.

CHAPTER 19

Raymond Babbitt in *Rain Man*: The World's Best Known Savant

Raymond Babbitt is the world's best known savant as a result of Dustin Hoffman's remarkably accurate and sensitive portrayal of savant syndrome in the 1988 movie *Rain Man*. It is a memorable movie about a very memorable savant. It won four Academy Awards, including best actor for Dustin Hoffman and best picture for 1988. I was pleased to have been a technical consultant to that film. That movie, based on its tremendous reception around the world, did more to raise awareness about savant syndrome in its first 101 days in movie theatres than anything that had been accomplished in public education in the 101 years between Down's first description of savant syndrome in 1887 and the screen portrayal of it in 1988. Because *Rain Man* has served as the introduction for so many people to savant syndrome, it is worth looking at some of the effort and activity that led to its creation, its authenticity and its success.

The movie is the story of two men, an abrasive Charlie Babbitt and his brother, Raymond Babbitt, an autistic savant. Their father died leaving $3 million in a trust fund for Raymond's care at an institution where Raymond has spent almost all of his adult life. Charlie wants the money. Charlie traces Raymond to the institution where he lives, discovering once again a brother he did not even remember, since he was just a child when Raymond, then age 18, was placed in long-term care. Charlie was so young at the time that he, in a typical childlike manner, called his brother "rain man" because that's the way the name Raymond sounded to him then.

After this for-the-wrong-reasons reunion at the hospital, a six-day cross-country tour ensues from Cincinnati to Los Angeles in a '49 Roadmaster Buick convertible with a variety of adventures, during which some of Raymond's autistic rituals and savant skills are an asset, and some are an impediment.

By the end of the movie Charlie has changed from referring to his brother as "weird" or as a "retard," to viewing him instead only as different and in many ways very special. There is no six-day cure of autism, and realistically there ought not to be. Raymond returns to the institution at the end of the movie. But in that six-day excursion with each other, both Raymond and Charlie are changed in some notable ways. Raymond has become more self-sufficient and can tolerate some affection; Charlie is spending less time trying to stamp out his brother's odd behavior and is learning more and more to accommodate to it. Raymond's walls of autism have yielded a bit, and Charlie's walls of callousness have yielded as well. They were just different walls.

But in the end, who really changed the most? It was Charlie, not Raymond. The movie leaves that important message for all of us—that as a society we need more to change our stereotypes, and then correspondingly make accommodations for persons with disabilities, rather than always insisting, or requiring, they change to meet our expectations and mandates.

The first version of *Rain Man* was written by Barry Morrow who had earlier written the scripts for the award-winning TV movies *Bill* and its sequel, *Bill II*, in which Mickey Rooney played a mentally deficient person. As described in Chapter 10 on Kim Peek, Morrow had come to Arlington, Texas in 1984 to consult with the National Association for Retarded Citizens (ARC) regarding its public education efforts. Fran Peek was chair of ARC's Communication Committee and Kim had accompanied him to this meeting.

Kim startled Morrow with the sober greeting: "Think about yourself, Barry Morrow!" In the several hours that followed, Kim overwhelmed Morrow with his knowledge of zip codes, authors, books, baseball, boxing, horse racing, maps, geography and many other topics. So touched and inspired was Morrow on this first meeting with Kim Peek, that he wrote the screenplay for *Rain Man*.

It was this October 25, 1986 draft of *Rain Man* which was the initial one sent to me for my reaction and input, because of my interest and involvement with savant syndrome. The executive producer was interested then, and remained so throughout the movie's production, that the story be accurate, authentic, credible and sensitive. On all those parameters, in my view, the studio succeeded marvelously.

Some major revisions

That October 1986 version of the script differed somewhat from the finished product. First of all, that early version had Raymond Babbitt's mental handicap as mental deficiency rather than autism. A variety of persons, especially Dustin Hoffman, felt that the portrayal of an autistic person, with all the typical associated rituals, obsessiveness, resistance to change and relatively affection-less behaviors might make a more interesting character for Raymond Babbitt. A person with autism had never really been portrayed on the screen before as the central character in a movie and this was an opportunity to enlighten the audience about that condition. Also, autism would create an opportunity for more complex interaction between the two brothers.

The change in course to portray autism was a crucial and significant one and, as it turned out, a very successful one. However, it required a major rewrite of the script, changing from the real-life savant model Kim Peek that Morrow had written about, to a new central character. The savant skills remained but the basic disability underlying the savant skills was autism, with all of its own distinctive, difficult and demanding characteristics and features.

The second crucial revision was in deleting some scenes and changing the ending of the movie in order to maintain greater authenticity and believability of the storyline. A January 16, 1989 *Newsweek* article (Ansen *et al.* 1989) describes some of the "scenes you didn't see" including "in a rousing climax, the retarded savant saves Charlie by putting together a motorcycle from a kit and hurtling through the flames that threaten to engulf them. In the heart-rending denouement Charlie and Raymond watch a Dodger game together in the hills above Chavez Ravine, having chosen to live together happily ever after for the rest of their lives" (p.52). The motorcycle scene exaggerated savant skills to the point of unbelievability. Savant syndrome is spectacular in and of itself. The special abilities therein are so remarkable they need not be embellished.

Some moviegoers were disappointed that Raymond returned to the institution at the end of the film. But the "happy ending" in the original script is simply not realistic. There is no six-day cross-country cure for autism. While "living happily ever after" provides a more uplifting ending, it would not be an achievable one. The final script ending was as it should be. Raymond has changed slightly; some tentative closeness has surfaced and one senses the beginning of a transition that could well result in a life outside the hospital some day, but not in six days. As already mentioned, though, Charlie changed during that brief encounter with his brother. The movement toward acceptance, appreciation and love on the part of Charlie for his brother is achievable and believable. I've seen that same welcome change in many persons who have had the good fortune to meet and interact with someone with savant syndrome for the first time.

The movie had a rather tumultuous course to its final production. That scenario is outlined in detail in that same *Newsweek* article about the movie. Other writers became involved, including Ron Bass, who contributed to the final script and is listed, along with Barry Morrow, in the credits of the movie as a co-writer of the screenplay. The movie also went through a number of very well-known directors before Barry Levinson, having just finished *Good Morning, Vietnam* (1987), signed on as director and carried the movie to its completion. In the middle of all that turmoil there was the writers' strike.

There was another critical change, in casting, along the way. According to *Newsweek*, a copy of the script was sent to Dustin Hoffman by his agent with the thought Mr. Hoffman might play Charlie Babbitt in the movie. "But Hoffman is interested in Raymond. He'd seen a *60 Minutes* segment of a retarded savant piano player, and it had moved him to tears. 'So suddenly the script came and I thought, I love him. I want to play a savant'."

And so he did. Dustin Hoffman became Raymond Babbitt, and what a marvelous portrayal it was. With the writers' strike delay, Hoffman had plenty of time to carefully do his homework for the part he very much wanted to do. He watched hours of tapes and movies of savants, both autistic and with other disabilities. He studied scientific papers and manuscripts, talked to various professionals, visited psychiatric facilities and spent time with savants and their families to experience those relationships first hand.

There were three particular individuals Dustin Hoffman met and studied in depth. One was Kim Peek; that meeting is described in Chapter 10. But Kim is not autistic. To learn more about autism, Hoffman met with a young man who was autistic and had a close relationship with his brother, just as in the movie. Hoffman spent a great deal of time with the two of them in their typical day-to-day activities.

Another person Hoffman got to know well was Joseph Sullivan, who is an autistic savant. At that time Joseph was living in Huntington, West Virginia with his parents, Drs. Ruth and William Sullivan. There had been two excellent documentaries filmed about Joseph, a film called *The Invisible Wall* (1967) and another entitled *Portrait of an Autistic Young Man* (1986). Both were projects of the UCLA Behavioral Sciences Media Laboratory. Hoffman carefully studied not only the films themselves, but also many hours of outtakes from those productions. That give him an in-depth look at a most impressive autistic young man and his family.

Joseph is fascinated by, and extremely facile with, numbers. Like other mathematical savants, numbers are his friends. He can do mathematical equations in his head quickly and accurately. When appearing on the *Oprah Winfrey* show in January 1989, for example, it took him only seconds to multiply, in his head, and give the correct answer to the problem $41 \times 385 = 15{,}785$. A second test was even more striking as he correctly gave, in 15 seconds, without paper and pencil, the answer to this problem: $341 \times 927 = 316{,}107$. Joseph is fascinated with license plates and remembers myriads of them only glimpsed at years earlier. He has perfect pitch and, like all savants, has a phenomenal memory. The power of that memory was demonstrated on a *Larry King Live* show when Joseph was given a 36-number grid to study for two minutes. He was able to recall all 36 numbers correctly exactly as they appeared in that grid in 43 seconds.

Joseph has many of the obsessive, ritualistic behaviors seen in autistic persons, and indeed, seen in Raymond Babbitt. In fact Hoffman borrowed one of Joseph's rituals for *Rain Man*: eating cheese balls with a toothpick. In another scene in the movie, a tantrum occurs when the smoke alarm goes off. That was patterned after Joseph's real-life reaction one time to a fire in a wastebasket. The phone number memorization scenes are similar to Joseph's reading and memorizing encyclopedias. Joseph will often incorporate into a stream of languages his favorite license plate number—DT 5252—or become preoccupied with the sound of certain letters and repeat words with those letters over and over such as the sound of "s" in the word "association." These verbalizations are often linked to some kind of characteristic head movements or other repetitive bits of language or sounds. Joseph loves numbers and he loves sounds.

Dustin Hoffman met Joseph in Cincinnati while filming *Rain Man*. Then Hoffman attended a special pre-premiere of *Rain Man* in Huntington, West Virginia on December 10, 1988, just before its official premier in New York City on December 12, 1988. At that event Hoffman stated:

> We just made a film that will play for a month or two, or whatever, in cities around the world, and be put out on cassette and put on shelves and seen once. But you people have Joe in your community for the rest of your lives and I would take that any day of the week. I think that's important. He is a very special person who shines through. This magic he has somehow came through to me. When I first looked at the footage I said "I love that man." And I love you for making him a part of your community. I tried very hard to be myself in this film. But I hope that what emerged was Joe's spirit, because that's what moved me. (Curry 1988, pp.A1, A7)

In his remarkable portrayal of autistic savant, Hoffman is careful to point out that while he had met Kim, Joseph and the other two brothers and got to know them well, he did not seek to imitate them. He used his knowledge about them only to teach himself how he might be if he were autistic. He learned that lesson magnificently.

Raymond Babbitt: a composite savant

While Kim Peek inspired the movie, *Rain Man* is not the story of Kim Peek's life. Raymond Babbitt is a *composite* savant with skills which are patterned on real-life savant abilities, but not occurring in a single real-life individual. The toothpick scene, memorizing the phone book, and calculating square roots, for example, are not fiction or fantasy, they are all drawn from documented savant skills in real individuals, many of whom are mentioned in this book.

It is important to point out that the movie is really about two conditions—autism and savant syndrome. With respect to *autism*, not all persons with autistic disorder are savants. In fact as pointed out in Chapter 1, only one in ten autistic persons have any savant skills, let alone the prodigious abilities of Raymond Babbitt. Dustin Hoffman had some excellent models of autistic disorder in Joseph Sullivan and others he observed in detail. From those observations comes the remarkable replication of autism by Hoffman with its typical characteristics such as obsession with sameness, odd behaviors, stereotyped mannerisms, avoidance of affection, unique use of language, endless repetition, and clinging to ritual.

But superimposed and grafted on to that underlying autistic disorder are the *savant skills* such as memorization, lightning calculating and calendar calculating that Raymond Babbitt demonstrates. Savant skills such as those can occur in a number of conditions other than autism. For the role that Dustin Hoffman carried out so marvelously, then, he really had to learn to portray two conditions—autistic disorder and savant syndrome.

As mind boggling as some of the savant skills are that Raymond Babbitt possesses, they all do exist in real-life Rain Men and Rain Women. The storyline may be fictional in terms of an actual person, but there is a factual basis for what may seem to be preposterous abilities. To the film's credit, it did not stray from the truth for either autism or savant syndrome. It did not have to. Autism is intriguing and striking in its constellation of traits and symptoms, and savant skills are astonishing without need to exaggerate or embellish. Together they make a fascinating story.

Some major messages; some minor caveats

Rain Man opened in December 1988. It was a smashing success at the box office. Filmed on a budget of $25 million, it grossed $42.4 million in its first 18 days and soon reached the $100 million mark, which only a few blockbuster films achieve. It is far beyond that mark now and still counting. The videocassette version was released on August 30, 1989. The box office success was mirrored with four Oscars that the film was awarded, including best picture of 1988.

The film is entertainment, not a documentary. Yet its welcome adherence to credibility is such that it is very informative as well as entertaining, and some important messages come through. First, it portrays the condition of a high-level functioning autistic person both accurately and sensitively. It is clear Dustin Hoffman did his homework and did it well. But it is important to remember that not all autistic persons function at that high level.

Second, the institution where Raymond Babbitt lives is a center for the developmentally disabled, not a mental hospital. That is important because autism is a developmental disability, not a mental illness. Correspondingly, in explaining to Charlie Babbitt the cause of Raymond's disorder, the doctor makes it clear, appropriately, that autism is a biological disorder, not a psychological one. He talks about "damage to the frontal lobes in the fetal stage" and describes some biological defects in Raymond's ability to feel and experience. This is important because for so many years families of autistic persons were inappropriately and inexcusably blamed as if they had caused the condition. The horrendously mistaken term "refrigerator mother" arose from that callous, careless and error-laden theory.

Third, as mentioned earlier, witnessing some tentative and cautious changes in a six-day time span of the movie is more realistic than forging a quick cure for what is a long-term condition. Finally, the storyline points out that in dealing with handicapped persons, whatever the disability, we need to accommodate to their needs and limitations rather than requiring them to make all the changes—to become exactly like us—if they expect to live side by side with us in our communities. By the movie's end, it was Charlie and not Raymond who had changed significantly.

Those are some of the important major messages from *Rain Man*. It enlightens accurately and entertains superbly. Still there are some minor caveats that are worth mentioning because they are important to the families of autistic and other developmentally disabled persons. First, Raymond Babbitt is a high-functioning autistic person. Yet autism is a disorder with a whole range of disabilities within it. While some autistic persons function at such a high level, many others are severely disabled and never reach a level of independent functioning such as seen in Raymond Babbitt. Regrettably, some such persons, even at this point in our knowledge about this disorder, and with the best treatment endeavors and tremendous family support, may still require long-term inpatient care. However, as more and more facilities develop in the communities to meet the special needs of this population, fewer and fewer autistic persons, savant and non-savant, will be relegated to long-term institutional care. Increasingly those persons will be able to live in the community side by side with the rest of us.

A second caveat: Raymond Babbitt not only functions at a high level with his autistic disorder, but also functions at a very high level of savant abilities. As pointed out in Chapter 1, savant skills are also on a spectrum ranging from splinter skills, to talented skills, to prodigious skills. The number of savants with multiple, prodigious abilities at the level Raymond Babbitt demonstrates are very few. Savant skills at that level are exceedingly rare in an already rare condition.

Third, as mentioned above, not all persons with autism are savants, and not all savants are autistic. The possibility exists that some persons could come away from the movie with the impression that since Raymond Babbitt is autistic, that's what all persons with autism are like, special skills and all. That of course is not the case. While it is true one in ten persons with autism do have savant skills at some level, nine out of ten do not.

Autism and savant syndrome, while coexistent in some persons such as Raymond Babbitt, are in fact two separate conditions.

A fine final product

On a scale of one to ten, for me, the movie *Rain Man* is a ten. The writers, producers, directors and Dustin Hoffman wanted the film to be real, accurate, respectful and dignified as it dealt with the delicate topic of handicapped persons. These movie-makers wanted to capture the wonder and essence of autism and savant syndrome but did not want in any way to denigrate or ridicule persons with those conditions. They wanted to portray accurately the essence of autism and the wonder of savant syndrome.

They succeeded.

It was reassuring to see Hollywood so concerned about authenticity and believability when that is often not the case in the movie industry. It was reassuring also to have the writers, directors and actors so open to input from professionals like myself and families such as the Sullivans, or a parent like Fran Peek, who deal with autism in real life on a day-to-day basis.

Few disabilities will ever experience the kind of massive, useful public awareness and education effort carried out in such an empathic, uniformly well received and popular format that *Rain Man* provided for autism and savant syndrome. Hollywood, and all those associated with this film, did their part, and did exceedingly well. Now it is up to us—families, professionals and organizations interested in these special persons—to do as well in maintaining the momentum of interest, inquiry and action begun by this magnificent movie so that a better understanding of both autism and savant syndrome can be propelled further along than ever before.

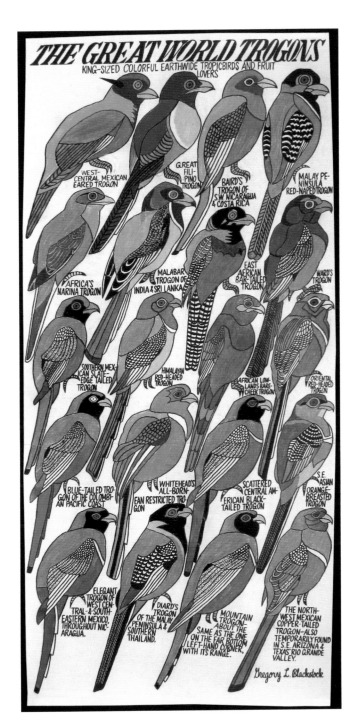

Gregory Blackstock, "The Great World Trogons"

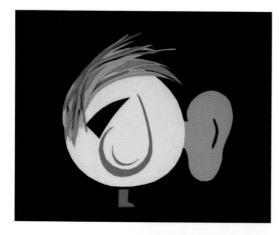

Wil Kerner, "Party Boy"

Wil Kerner, "Pals"

Wil Kerner, "Bird and Boy"

Seth Chwast, untitled

Seth Chwast, "Vision of Galapagos"

Seth Chwast, "Fantasy Hippocampus"

Ping Lian Yeak, "Prosperous Year I (Rooster)"

Ping Lian Yeak, "Happy Fish I"

Ping Lian Yeak, "My Dog II"

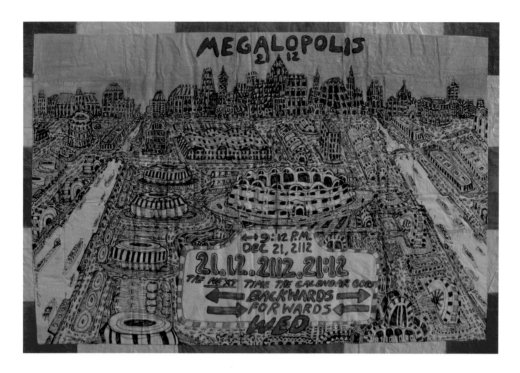

George Widener, "Megalopolis"

Amanda LaMunyon, "Castle on a Cloud"

Richard Wawro, "Benidorm"

Richard Wawro, "King's College Choir"

Alonzo Clemons, "Feeding Time"

Alonzo Clemons, "Bison Calf"

PART THREE

Significant New Dimensions
to Savant Syndrome

CHAPTER 20

"Accidental Genius":
The Acquired Savant

A ten-year-old boy is knocked unconscious by a baseball. Following that traumatic blow he suddenly can perform calendar calculations. He can also remember the weather, along with other autobiographical details of his daily life, from that time forward. An elderly woman who had never painted before becomes a prodigious artist after a dementia process begins and progresses. Another elderly patient with dementia has a similar sudden epiphany of ability, but this time in music. A 51-year-old builder, who had never shown interest or skills in art, abruptly becomes a poet, painter and sculptor following a stroke which he miraculously survived. An eight-year-old boy begins calendar calculating after a left hemispherectomy for intractable seizures. These are examples of what I call the acquired savant, or what might also be called accidental genius.

New reports of acquired savant syndrome continue to come to my attention from the savant syndrome website with regularity. These cases represent the most significant finding regarding savant syndrome in the 122 years since savant syndrome was first described. They forcefully suggest that certain dormant potential resides within each of us in varying degree, perhaps as a backup system, which, except for CNS incident to certain areas of the brain, might not otherwise surface The cases which follow demonstrate that possibility. They also provide evidence that such newly surfaced skills, when present, most often represent a *release* phenomenon of already existing but dormant skills, rather than the development of *new* compensatory abilities.

The real challenge of the acquired savant, if such dormant skills do exist, is how they might be accessed non-intrusively without having to endure a CNS catastrophe.

Before 1996, most of the savants I had met, except for Alonzo Clemons, were persons who were born with autism or some other developmental disability, and in whom some marvelous talent had "exploded" on the scene during infancy or childhood, most often at about age three or four. These are cases of *congenital* savant syndrome (present from birth).

Acquired savant syndrome, in contrast, are instances in which dormant savant skills emerge, sometimes at a prodigious level, after a brain injury or disease in previously non-disabled (neurotypical) persons in whom few such skills were evident before CNS injury or disease. This circumstance, of course, raises the question whether such dormant capacity exists in everyone, only to surface, perhaps as a backup system, when there is such CNS injury or illness.

This chapter summarizes some of these important new cases of acquired savant syndrome and explores the many intriguing implications of such findings.

Alonzo and Orlando: acquired savant syndrome

Alonzo Clemons (described in Chapter 8) is a case of acquired savant syndrome. According to his mother, Alonzo's remarkable sculpting skills appeared after a head injury sustained in a childhood fall. After I met Alonzo in 1984 I began to review the savant syndrome literature to see if other cases of acquired savant syndrome had been reported in the past. Indeed there were several such reports. Minogue (1923) presented a case in which musical genius appeared in a three-year-old child following meningitis. Brink (1980) described the case of Mr. Z., who demonstrated savant skills, behavioral traits and abilities at age nine after a bullet wound to the left brain resulted in a motor paralysis on the right side, along with subsequent muteness and deafness. Following that traumatic brain injury some new special mechanical abilities and other savant skills emerged. Dorman (1991) reported a case in *Brain and Cognition* in which an eight-year-old boy began to show exceptional calendar calculating ability after a left hemispherectomy.

But one of the most dramatic and convincing instances of acquired savant syndrome is provided by Orlando Serrell. At age ten, Orlando was hit on the head by a baseball. Following that, he developed the skill of calendar calculating, an interest and ability he had never shown prior to the head injury. Accompanying that newly acquired skill was the ability to remember the weather for each day of his life post-injury. More recently Orlando discovered his ability for daily recall—where he was and what he was doing on a daily basis in considerable detail. This newly acquired autobiographical memory capability—hypermnesia—is discussed in detail in Chapter 5.

Orlando's acquired savant abilities have been highlighted in a number of documentaries on savant syndrome. *Beautiful Minds* (Colourfield Productions, Germany) provides an in-depth look at both the calendar calculating and autobiographical memory abilities of Orlando when interviewed at the National Institute of Mental Health in Bethesda, Maryland. Orlando maintains a website at www.orlandoserrell. com which contains more background on him and his abilities including a video demonstrating his skills and MRI findings from some imaging studies at Columbia University in New York City.

Acquired savant syndrome in fronto-temporal dementia

In December, 1996 I read a most interesting case report in *Lancet* written by Bruce Miller and colleagues in which they described three patients "who became accomplished painters after the appearance of fronto-temporal dementia" (Miller *et al.* 1996, p.1744). They described one such case in detail, a 68-year-old man with no particular prior art interest or ability, in whom rather spectacular artistic skills emerged as the dementia proceeded.

Miller *et al.* (1998) described two additional patients (now a total of five) with this same type of fronto-temporal dementia (FTD). They likewise displayed new artistic skills in the setting of progressive brain disease. Consistent with the findings in other "congenital" savants reported to that date, in these five older patients, whose artistic skills and abilities emerged after the onset of FTD, the creativity was visual not verbal; the images were meticulous copies that lacked abstract or symbolic qualities; episodic memory was preserved but semantic memory was devastated; and they exhibited intense obsessive preoccupation with art skills. SPECT imaging showed a predominance of *left-sided* brain dysfunction.

Miller *et al.* (1998) hypothesized that selective degeneration of the anterior temporal orbitofrontal cortex decreased inhibition of visual systems involved with perception, thereby enhancing artistic interest and abilities. Such artistic interest and ability was relatively dormant until the FTD disease "released" those hidden abilities through "decreased inhibition of certain more posteriorly located visual systems involved with perception" (p.981). Kapur (1996) used the term "paradoxical functional facilitation" to describe such a "release" phenomenon in which loss of some skills permits the emergence of others. In his article "The key to genius" (2003) Silberman refers to such a disinhibition/release process as "liberating our inner savant from the benevolent tyranny of the left hemisphere" (p.257).

Fronto-temporal dementia accounts for about 25 percent of the presenile dementias and differs from Alzheimer's dementia because in FTD the pathological processes are regional, rather than generalized, and are asymmetric, often affecting the left anterior temporal region, as in these five patients. This article discusses the five patients individually in detail, and also illustrates some of the artistic works that were produced during the progression of the dementia process. Overall Miller *et al.* (1998) conclude that "FTD is an unexpected window into the artistic process" (p.981).

By 2000 Miller had increased the number of his FTD/emergent artistic ability cases to 12. But now this expanded group included some persons with previously dormant musical abilities, instead of art abilities, that had surfaced with progression of the dementia (Miller *et al.* 2000). Even more interesting, however, was the expansion of this research to compare the functional imaging findings (SPECT) on six of the older persons, previously non-disabled, with the imaging findings of a nine-year-old autistic savant artist (DB) (Hou *et al.* 2000). That comparison showed "remarkable parallels" (p.37) between the older FTD patients and this young autistic artist. Both involved loss of function in the *left temporal* lobe of the brain and enhanced function in the posterior neocortex. *The similarities of neuropathology, particularly in the left temporal area of the brain, as seen on SPECT imaging in a nine-year-old autistic savant and these older FTD patients, who share artistic skills in common with very different disabilities, is striking and intriguing.*

Seeley *et al.* (2008) reported a case of a woman, AA, who developed primary progressive aphasia (PPA) in the *left* hemisphere of the brain at age 60. She had done some painting for about 15 years prior to that with a special interest in using her art as a visual depiction of music. She named one of her pieces "Unravelling Bolero." As her PPA began and progressed, however, her artwork changed "unmistakably toward photographic realism, reproducing the world with high surface fidelity. Symmetry and structural detail were emphasized and she often painted natural objects or buildings" (p.41). Structural MRI showed atrophy in the *left* frontal inferolateral cortex (including Broca's area), caudate and hippocampus. Correspondingly there was *increased* grey matter volume "in the *right* posterior regions involved in visual imagery and visuoconstructive ability" (p.45) Postmortem brain analysis was consistent with the imaging findings showing *left-sided* atrophy in the frontal areas particularly and preserved *right-sided* cortex in the parietal areas. These investigators indicated "Her left frontoinsular degeneration was heralded by a blossoming of artistic potential and a penchant for transmodal imagery. 'Liberated' posterior regions showing structural and functional enhancements in AA are thought to support perceptual imagery, translation and integration" (p.48). In this instance the "liberation" from the dominant hemisphere involved left-sided frontal and other deeper structures of the brain compared to Miller's earlier FTD patients where the changes involved anterior temporal areas, again on the left side.

In a different but related vein, Mell, Howard and Miller (2003) raised the question of what would happen to an already accomplished artist with a progressive FTD process, in contrast to the patients above, in whom new talent surfaced. They presented the case of a trained and talented art teacher who, at age 49, at the beginning of a progressive FTD process, changed her style slowly from Western watercolor and traditional Chinese brush painting to highly patterned paintings using Chinese horoscope icons. The "impressive artistic growth," which Mell *et al.* (2003) describe in much greater detail, coincided with a decline in her ability to organize class lessons or grade papers. Paintings became "wilder and freer" in which "intricate designs and patterns of the horoscope figures were replaced by large, intensely colored figures; complex patterning was pushed into the background" (p.1708). Choice of colors changed and "release from the constraints of formal training became clear" (p.1709). Compared to Miller's 12 cases of "new" talent emergence, who generally had asymmetric *left anterior temporal* lobe degeneration, this patient with prior artistic talent, whose style changed so drastically, had predominantly *left frontal* abnormality. Mell *et al.* conclude: *"Asymmetric left hemisphere degeneration may release previously untapped cognitive abilities. Our brain wiring appears to be a major factor in the determination of the nature of our creativity"* (p.1710, italics mine).

Drago *et al.* (2006) carried out other studies on "release" vs. "new" skills which emerged in the setting of FTD. They assigned art judges to assess the artwork of a trained artist with fronto-temporal lobar degeneration (FTLD) during three periods of her life: pre-symptomatic period (18 paintings); peri-symptomatic period, when symptoms were just beginning (6 paintings); and fully symptomatic period (16 paintings). These three time intervals ranged from before symptom onset to eight years after the diagnosis. The judges rated the paintings systematically on six different artistic qualities without knowledge of the patient's clinical diagnosis or when the paintings were produced.

Consistent with the FTD patients described above, this patient showed an increase of some visual artistic skills over time, reflected in technique, *"that might be related to **sparing** and **disinhibition** of the right posterior neocortex"* (Drago *et al.* 2006, p.1285; emphasis mine). However there was a reduction of other aspects of the paintings including closure (completeness of the painting) and evocative (emotional) impact.

"Accidental genius" post-stroke

Lythgoe *et al.* (2005) documented a case in *Neurology* of a 51-year-old builder in London whose poetry and art skills surfaced, for the first time, after a sudden-onset subarachnoid hemorrhage involving bilateral cerebral artery aneurysms. The aneurysms were repaired with coils. Following that, the patient fortunately showed little associated dementia or impaired verbal abilities. CT scans 16 days after admission confirmed that there was no focal injury; however, MRI studies could not be carried out because of the presence of the metal coils. Neuropsychological testing revealed a normal IQ level, some verbal disinhibition, and some mild executive function impairment. The final impression was "mild frontal dysfunction." Lythgoe *et al.* (2005) concluded that "it is possible whatever frontal damage our patient sustained led to a relative disinhibition or paradoxical functional facilitation of these areas" (p.398).

Prior to the stroke, the patient had no particular interest or ability in the creative arts. But several weeks after the corrective surgery, the patient began to "fill several notebooks with poems and verse; he had never written poetry prior to that time.

Following that he began to paint expansively and expressively, spending almost all of his time painting and sculpting" (p.397). Several television documentaries have included segments on this acquired savant story. The London program *My Brilliant Brain* includes an excellent segment on this individual whose paintings and sculptures are better seen than described.

A similar transition occurred in a 35-year-old chiropractor, Jon Sarkin, who had a stroke while playing golf. There was subsequent brain surgery with removal of a portion of the cerebellum. Following that Jon developed an almost insatiable compulsion to draw and paint. Carroll (2006) describes Sarkin as someone who spent "half his life as a linear-thinking pragmatist and the second half as a Bohemian painter. Here is a clear window into the neurological differences that allow a small number of us to transcend the ordinary" (p.31). Sarkin himself puts it this way: "I came to consciousness and things were different right away. Something happened in my brain that made everything different. I don't know what that is and neither does anyone else" (p.31).

Now in his fifties, Sarkin paints continuously and has had his work exhibited at the DeCordova Museum and Sculpture Park's annual exhibit in Lincoln, Massachusetts. He has also had exhibits in West Hollywood, California and elsewhere. An excellent multimedia presentation and special section by Amy Ellis Nutt appeared in the December 5, 2008 edition New Jersey *Star Ledger* describing Sarkin's long journey of discovery. It is available online as well through Sarkin's website at www.aphrodigitaliac.com/sarkin/.

Annoni *et al.* (2005) from the Lausanne University Hospital in Lausanne, Switzerland, noted significant qualitative changes in artistic style in two professional painters as a consequence of minor stroke located in the *left* occipital lobe or thalamus. One of these individuals switched to a more stylized and symbolic art, and the other switched from an impressionist style to a more simplistic, abstract art. In discussing these changes the authors state:

> The artistic changes may have been associated with a direct effect of the infarct. Since the posterior brain regions seem to play a specific role in creative thinking, it is not surprising that a minor lesion in these regions might alter an artist's creative thought and thus his style of painting. Besides, the fact that patients 1 and 2 had *left* hemispheric dysfunction *may provide some support for the theory of right hemisphere functional release.* Different possible cognitive mechanisms may be considered. (Annoni *et al.* 2005, p.800; empasis mine)

Acquired savant skills with other underlying disabilities

Oliver Sacks (1995), in his book *An Anthropologist on Mars*, describes yet another case of "acquired" artistic skills in a person "who had scarcely painted or drawn before," following an illness that included "high fever, weight loss, delirium, perhaps seizures" or some other "neurological condition." The exact nature of the illness remains unexplained. Yet, following that episode, Franco Magnani began painting immaculately accurate scenes from the village of Pontito, where he had grown up, but had left at age 18. This new dawn of painting ability and digital-like memory amazed even Magnani. Sacks quotes him as saying, "Fantastic. How could I do it? And how could I have had the gift and not known about it before?" (p.160).

What makes Magnini's case especially interesting is not just the painting epiphany in his early thirties following illness, but also that his incredible, digital-fidelity recall of the tiny village where he grew up was so exact years after he had left. When compared to present-day photographs of that village, each street, building and archway is reconstructed with breathtaking fidelity. So amazing was the link of exact paintings with documented early memories of village buildings, streets and alleys, that there have been a number of exhibits of his work documenting that digital-like recall. The Exploratorium in San Francisco held an exhibit in 1998 titled "Memory: The Art and Science of Remembering" in which Magnini's work was featured. To demonstrate the remarkable memory involved, his paintings were placed side by side with recent photographs of the same scene. The accuracy, years later in a person with no earlier formal art training, was incredible.

The "halfway savant": acquired savant syndrome with only minor residual trade-off

In acquired savant syndrome there is typically some loss of cognitive or other abilities seemingly as a trade-off for substitution of new savant-like skills. But recently cases have come to my attention in which traumatic brain injury in a neurotypical person was followed by acquisition of new musical, artistic or mathematical skills with only very minor or negligible loss of prior cognitive or other neuropsychological capacity.

Most often these newly available skills are not quite as abrupt in onset or as dramatic in scope as the cases above. Typically the person is functioning very successfully in the work world with a good life adaptation overall. But the fact that they now remember the birthdays of everyone in their workplace, do huge computations in their head without calculators, or never have to look up a phone number of someone they previously had called, for example, or may have some obsessive preoccupations seem somewhat "strange" to them and to others around them. As a result they tend not to share the presence of these skills widely lest they be labeled as "slightly autistic." One person wrote how he keeps these skills quite hidden—"under a bushel"—and another described himself as a "halfway savant."

Space precludes writing about all of these individuals, but one such case will provide an example of the type, and magnitude, of changes reported.

Jim Carollo is 33 years old, and all the quotes below are from our personal correspondence. At age 14 he was in a severe auto accident that killed his mother and a friend. Jim and his sister were both left comatose. Carollo had a severe traumatic brain injury with skull fracture and Glascow Coma Scale score of 3–4. He had "brain swelling with the impact on the right occipital area with contrecoup injury in the left frontal area." For a time he had hemi-paresis on the left with memory loss. Not until about six weeks following the accident, while still in the hospital, did he have real awareness of the injury and begin to understand the outcomes from the wreck. It was only later that he learned of the severity of his injuries and the expectations for survival that had been given. He was not expected to live for a couple of weeks, then not expected ever to walk again or return to school. But he has made a "remarkable recovery," obtained his MBA degree, has regained his strong social skills, and is very active physically. Recovery to this extent was considered very unlikely.

After regaining consciousness, rehabilitation and return to school, he showed an "amazing ability with numbers and mathematics." No such special interest or ability was evident pre-injury. Several months following the accident, geometry came very easy and he received a 100 percent on the Mastery test with no study. Later he passed calculus examinations, never having taken trigonometry, which was a most unusual sequence in his school. While recovering from his injuries he developed a rather complex scheme for applying numbers to letters and simply adds and subtracts the letters in words without referring to the assigned numbers. "I was constantly adding and subtracting letters and words in my head, whether sitting in class, reading a book or running a race." He now has a massive memory for numbers such as high school locker combinations, old and new driver's licenses, credit cards, bank accounts, telephone numbers etc.

> Also, when I graduated with my MBA I decided to read a book on Pi. I never opened it however because many digits were listed on the front. I spent the next two days learning the first 200 digits of Pi, which I still know and I am almost always repeating in my head just like the alphabet/number scheme I created. The *Brainman* video suggested that these special cases tend to like repetition and my whole life is an example of repetition.
>
> Probably 90 percent of the time, I am repeating numbers, letters, or melodies in my mind. Most of the time I am not even aware of those thoughts. While this repetition is occurring, however, I am much more comfortable, as it seems to calm my brain; and I am still aware and paying attention to what is happening around me. That repetition takes my mind off my weakened abilities. I do become aware when that repetition stops, and it usually begins again very quickly.

Following the injury Carollo became focused on logic, organization and structure. This was shown partly by his ease with geometry.

Following the injury Carollo became focused on logic, organization and structure. This was partly shown by his ease with Geometry. Today, those interests are evident in various aspects of his life. He has designed specific routines for completing many of his everyday tasks. He commonly rearranges the items in his life, such as in his home, so that they are well structured and visually aligned. He also spends considerable time focusing on the buildings, tables and various other objects around him, and remarking on their relative structures, alignment and positioning.

> Following the wreck I began designing my life activities so that they were easily remembered and easily repeated. I had methods of doing everything from rearranging the various foods on my plate to following the same patterns and doing most of the same things every day. In situations where I have little guidance, I have difficulty managing my days and can become overwhelmed. Repetition makes dealing with situations much easier and I find I am more comfortable sticking to routines.

Carollo found school to be enjoyable in part because it was so structured and scheduled. He easily feels overwhelmed when facing tasks that are not scheduled or organized, or just facing his life in general. Designing and managing careers, relationships and a social life is very difficult, although he is becoming more productive and getting better at focusing and operating with less routine.

One of his greatest interests before the accident included reading. Following the accident, however, he went all the way through graduate level of school "largely without reading books." For a long time he could not read effectively. He had trouble remembering a sentence from beginning to end, and had difficulty staying focused on the lines of text and the topic being discussed. It became very frustrating, so he just began paying close attention in class. "I was a very good reader before the wreck and spent much of my spare time reading." But that was very problematical for a long time after the accident. It is getting somewhat better but he largely avoids reading. He cannot remember the last time he completed a book.

Carollo had no special interest in math or numbers before the accident. But he was always at the top of his class in most subjects and even was included in some "gifted and talented" classes once a week in an adjacent school. Today he knows that he is quite intelligent and capable, having a graduate degree and scoring between 135 to 150 on a number of IQ tests he has taken. The largest residual defect from the brain injury is short-term memory.

> It is as if I gained a much enhanced memory for numbers after the injury, and my general memory in other areas has been decreased. My memory for my childhood before the accident is tremendous. I can recall details and images of childhood well beyond average. I actually find comfort in those detailed memories because I was not injured at the time and I often rely on those for support and

encouragement. My memory for the events following my brain injury and for recent events is quite poor in comparison. For example, many people know me but I do not even remember who they are. I know I have much ability, but the continual awareness of my deficits seems quite disabling at times.

These abilities sufficiently impressed one of his doctors that she commented in the medical record about Carollo's memorizing 250 digits of Pi which he recited for her. He also described his alphabet/number assignment system and

he demonstrated today how he is quickly able to recite the numbers associated with each letter. His talent with numbers is quite remarkable raising the question as to whether he is a savant. He also denies having any art classes in the past but he sat down and drew a rendition of the Clock Tower downtown. He showed me the picture today and it is quite remarkable for its accuracy.

EEG was abnormal due to left temporal disorganization after hyperventilation. MRI showed mild abnormality surrounding the ventricles and left cerebellum. Neuropsychologic testing showed above average intelligence on most WAIS-R scales. There was some mild cognitive impairment in the area of attention and concentration and specific training exercises were recommended.

I use this case as an example of the type of reports I receive in which persons describe some new, different or unusual abilities, obsessions or preoccupations after head injury, but not at a level that interferes substantially with overall educational, vocational or social adjustment. When these persons see some of the documentaries on savant syndrome, they are motivated to tell their story, often relieved to be able to talk openly about their unusual abilities which they sometimes have kept hidden from others, lest others think they are brain damaged, autistic or just "strange." Carollo, for example, has been discouraged by some persons from focusing on his unusual number and letter talents because "those won't help you in real life." But he wonders how developed those special abilities might be if he did pursue them as he really wishes to do: "My mind has continually fought to pursue those interests as much as I have *hidden* them from others. That is how my brain works. Numbers are not just a hobby for me."

I hope that illustration of cases such as this will allow other persons with similar abilities to be able to exercise them and share them with others free of the need to hide them, lest they be seen as strange or harboring some sort of mental disorder.

Transient "accidental genius"

Finally, another such person was motivated to write to me after having seen some documentaries on savant syndrome describing a most interesting phenomenon which might be called "transient" accidental genius. MP suffered a traumatic brain injury in an auto accident. Following that, MP was experiencing almost continuous dizziness. It was later discovered that he had a "round and oval paralymphatic window fistula in his right ear which allowed the fluid to drain out of the labyrinth" leaving him dizzy nearly 100 percent of the time. Also, about six months after the accident he found himself

> doing tremendously better at Trivial Pursuit, Jeopardy, etc. It seemed I knew just about everything about everything. My friends would come to me and ask questions and somehow I knew the answer. Finally about a year after the accident the fistulas were repaired and so went the "know it all" in me.

According to MP the fistula reopened two more times and

> each of those times about six months later the "know it all" came back. I personally believed that when I was dizzy my brain tried to compensate by rerouting itself a different way thereby going through these stored knowledge areas. However when left with the choice, I chose keeping the fistula repaired.

Summary

"Acquired" savant syndrome or "accidental genius" is the most important new development in the study of savant syndrome since it was first described over a century ago. It is particularly important to note how many such cases include *left* (dominant) *hemisphere dysfunction* with the release of dormant *right* (non-dominant) *hemisphere capacity* (paradoxical functional facilitation) as opposed to development of entirely new skills. In some instances there is a noticeable diminution of certain cognitive or other abilities with the emergence of new skills, (acquired savant) but in other cases only minor, barely significant, detrimental trade-off occurs and these persons continue to function at a very high level overall ("halfway" savant).

This phenomenon of certain abilities being "released" after brain injury in some persons (paradoxical functional facilitation), *particularly if certain areas of the brain are affected,* holds broad implications for buried potential, perhaps, within us all. The challenge of course is how to access that dormant knowledge and skill without some CNS catastrophe. Work to achieve just that is now underway as you will see in the chapters that follow.

CHAPTER 21

"Sudden Genius":
An Epiphany of Talent

The emergence of dormant talent in the acquired savant hints at such buried potential within us all, perhaps as a backup system in case of some central nervous system
injury or disease. And likewise the circumstance of what I call "sudden genius" suggests such dormant potential beneath the surface as well. "Sudden genius" situations
are situations in which normal (neurotypical is the politically correct term these days)
persons have an instant dawning, knowledge and coalition of talent and skill in an
epiphany-like moment where no such total comprehension and mastery of that talent
and skill seemingly existed before. Technically this is not "savant" syndrome, nor
are these persons sudden "savants" because they, unlike savants, whether congenital
or acquired, have no underlying disability. Savant syndrome, by definition, is the
presence of extraordinary ability side by side with some disability. Perhaps some
examples will describe and define this "epiphany" more clearly.

KA: "the most amazing day of my life"
KA is a very bright, 31-year-old man who graduated from Tel Aviv University
Law School and now lives and works in Israel. He has had very high IQ and SAT
(Scholastic Assessment Test: a standardized test for college admissions in the United
States) scores; he has no developmental disabilities. He has had no serious accidents
and has never had a head injury.

His mother was a schoolteacher. His father worked for the government. Dad
always liked to sing and now sings in a group. As a child, KA enjoyed music and
listened to many children's songs, sometimes making up songs of his own. In high
school KA liked tinkering with a MIDI sequencing tool and composed some music

on the computer. He would search for the right place to put down notes manually until they fit what he heard in his head. This seemed to be evidence of his relative pitch, but he had no real grasp of the inner workings of music. He had some limited knowledge of harmony and chords which he called "the background" and he seemed to know it was made up of "happy chords" and "sad chords" along with other chords he didn't understand.

While in the Israeli Armed Forces KA brought a guitar to the base and developed some reasonably good skill in playing chords, but with still no real understanding of music structure or composition. He could play some simple songs from rote memory and was able to distinguish what he called "the happy chord" (major) and "the sad chord" (minor). He had no idea what other more complex chords were; he also played those just from memory. By the end of his military service he was a rather popular "campfire guitarist," but he played, always, from rote memory without a real grasp of music overall. While in Law School KA bought a good electric piano and played it quite often. His ability on the piano remained relatively poor, but he enjoyed playing it nonetheless.

At age 26, while still in school, KA would often visit a local shopping mall near the university. There was a wine store there with an upright piano near it in the mall's lobby. The owners of the mall gave permission for KA to play that piano and he began to do so. After three months there was some very slight, but perceptible improvement in his playing which both he and his friends had noticed.

But then an amazing thing happened as told here in his own words:

At age 26½ I woke up to another nice, regular day—which would turn into the most amazing day of my life. I was sitting at the piano near the wine store just crudely playing the keys, trying to figure out what's what and who's who. I distinctly remember I was attempting to play a certain popular tune by a well-known Israeli singer. I was incidentally playing it in the C major scale—while playing on this scale you almost only use the white keys. I noticed that pressing every other white key, making a triad, made the familiar "sad chords" and "happy chords" which made the background of the song if I found the right chord. As I was attempting to play the melody, I noticed I was only playing the white keys. I asked myself how come? I began to wonder what was going on. I also wondered how come the "happy chords" and "sad chords" have the same shape on the piano, although they are entirely different in character. And why am I almost always playing the white keys, no matter what I do? My head was filled with a critical mass of "why this, why that" riddles, all of which were related to the structure of the music and how it relates to the structure of the piano. I found myself wondering whether there was a system of rules at work here.

The duration of me suspecting something and asking myself "why this, why that," and the strange feeling that followed, lasted about five seconds. Then came the flash.

It is a little hard to describe what went on in my head during this flash. I felt a strange feeling, as in the course of a few short seconds things "came together in my head." I suddenly realized there was a system. However this was only the least of it. Not only did I realize there was a system, I comprehended the system itself and its rules! Among other things, I suddenly (just like that) realized what the major scale was, and what its harmonies were, how they relate to chords which are absolute and have a certain physical shape on the piano and more importantly where to put my fingers on the keyboard in order to play a certain component of the scale, whether harmony or melody. In effect I suddenly realized how the theoretical structure of music relates to the physical structure of the piano.

How I suddenly knew the theory, though, is beyond me. The final ingredient in my gift, I noticed, was the ability to instantaneously and effortlessly recognize the harmonies in songs I knew. Harmony recognition became as involuntary as color perception. Correspondingly came the ability, although a bit less strong, to reproduce melody by either immediately knowing what the note is in the scale (function recognition) or quickly figuring out how high or low the next note is (interval recognition)—a weird mix of involuntary perception and mental calculating.

"Eureka!" I thought. Suddenly I know music. I UNDERSTAND music.

The duration of that eureka moment was well under one second. Amazingly I "learned" a massive amount of music theory in under one second! The whole experience was rather amazing and baffling at the same time. Suddenly at age 26½ after what could best be described as a "just getting it moment," it all seemed so simple. Music was so simple and clear. I could "see" and "feel" music and its components as clearly as I saw colors and felt sensations. I had an intuitive grasp of the structure of music. Without knowing their names—without needing to look at the names—I knew what bass was, what harmony was, what melody was, and what the scale functions were. I could "see" where they fit on the piano and then just had to put my fingers there and press the keys. Even though I have now learned the name for each entity (chord, note, scale, harmony, melody, bass, root, dominant, and so on), I could grasp and manipulate these entities in my head just as well without the need for formal names.

My grasp of harmony then allowed me to find a vast selection of harmonies, much greater than simple major and minor, and not limited to the specific established tonality. I was able to grasp some modulations and "secondary" and "borrowed" harmonies as well.

I started playing with ease every song I knew from memory right there. Suddenly people around the store and my friends stopped what they were doing, looked at me and said: "Whoa. Look at him play!" They, just like me, were amazed at how just a few moments prior I was playing random chords on the keyboard when all of a sudden I started playing like an accomplished pianist. "What in blazes happened to you?" they asked. "I have no clue—I just 'got it'", I replied. I remained there the rest of the evening playing and playing and playing every song that I knew.

After that "Eureka" experience, KA's ability with a guitar also advanced to a whole new level since he no longer had to technically memorize chords for the songs and play them from rote memory. All he had to do, just like on the piano, was memorize the chords of the scale on the guitar and he could instantly play the right harmonies. All he had to do was listen to the song in his head and play along.

In addition to his musical abilities, KA also reports having a heightened ability to recall autobiographical memories. Although apparently still having normal (neurotypical) memory, KA can recall early sporadic memories from as early as age 20 months, and vividly and sequentially remembers most of his life from age three. Furthermore, KA reports that lately he has experienced some interesting mental phenomena, including: often hearing music in dreams (these were very rare before the epiphany, but are now more common); experiencing "strange, unfamiliar emotions," especially before sleep; often feeling "weird" throughout the day; and hypermnesia, often seeing streams of vivid past memories.

Although some of these new experiences started, or became more apparent, at or around the time of the epiphany, whether or not they are connected to it in some way remains to be seen.

KA's ability to reproduce melody instantaneously and accurately also improves as he plays more and more different melodies. According to KA, the more "melody snippets" (two, three or four note melody lines) he has committed to habitual memory and is familiar with, the faster he can recognize them as a whole, as opposed to single notes, thus playing melody much faster. This habitual memory, unlike rote memory, is based on understanding the note's functions, and then learning to recognize lines, rather than single notes.

KA began to search some music theory sites on the Internet trying to learn exactly what might have happened to him in that magic moment. To his amazement, most of what those sites contained regarding music theory he now already knew. He was baffled as to how he could know something he had never studied. Perhaps, he surmised, he was able to derive the "rules of music" in some unconscious way now from all the songs he had heard throughout all of his life. Perhaps he had subconsciously "connected the dots" and "unlocked" something buried within with that Eureka experience. KA wonders whether other people might have that sudden insight stored within themselves as well.

Perhaps we do.

JD: "the music suddenly makes sense"

Following the publication of the story of KA's "sudden genius" on the savant syndrome website I have learned of some other cases including someone who sent me an email stating he had "read the case of the sudden savant and I have similar experiences to report." He went on to describe himself as an accomplished guitar player who plays best with improv and metal, particularly progressive metal. He is a university graduate with an IQ of 135. There is no history or evidence of any disability. He is very content and successful in his work. He prefers to remain anonymous because of his high visibility within his profession, so I will refer to him as John Doe (JD).

JD grew up liking music, but without any special interest in it beyond that. He had recorder lessons as a child but was rather poor on that instrument, usually quickly forgetting the songs that he had rather mechanically learned. But at age 16 and 2 months, a date he remembers precisely, he witnessed a friend playing a current pop-song on an acoustic guitar.

The following day JD dug out a guitar that his mother had and he duplicated what he had witnessed: "Suddenly music made perfect sense to me, like understanding a language." Within three months JD had learned all the common guitar chords and then moved on to where

> I was probably the best (or equal to best) guitarist in the school. But the quantum leap for me was not suddenly being able to play notes on an instrument—it took a few years to build an "impressive" technique, as muscle must develop in the hands and wrists.

Rather it was "*the sudden ability to comprehend music as an almost 3D form.*"

Presently JD can usually play almost anything he hears by ear which he hears internally note for note. Likewise he can instantly harmonize or counterpoint and improvise over in real time as he hears the piece. This musical insight also suddenly gave him the ability to hear accompaniment to a melody, often with bass, harmony and counterpoint just playing along to an external source. This ability was in stark contrast to an inability to compose some harmony to a simple melody in drama class just a few weeks before his sudden musical epiphany. He recalls that stark contrast well.

While JD says he does not have perfect pitch, some days he finds himself tracking the pitch intervals of background sound—"I especially like the tones a vacuum cleaner makes as it ascends in just fifths when the suction increases." He has an obsession with irregular time structures in music, finding the 4/4 of pop music distasteful and preferring the 5/4 and 7/4 rhythmic structures. JD feels his hearing has become more acute and recently began hearing new tones that he discovered, with some research, to be variations on intonation and microtonalities: "*It seems my brain had learned this before my conscious mind identified what it is.*" JD also has the ability to hear about three musical lines simultaneously, sometimes four. His music sometimes triggers a synesthesia "in that I often feel the lurching weight to a bassline and/or the color of a high motif."

TC: "struck by music"

In his book *Musicophilia*, Oliver Sacks (2007) describes a somewhat different kind of "sudden onset syndrome" in a physician who, after being struck by lightning, developed quite suddenly an obsessive interest in music at a level not present before the "bolt from the blue." He has gone on now to be both a performer and composer of some repute. Meanwhile his medical skills remain undiminished.

Sacks begins his book with a chapter he calls "A Bolt from the Blue—Sudden Musicophilia." In it he describes the case of Dr. Tony Cicoria, a 42-year-old orthopedic surgeon who was struck by lightning and who, after an intense near-death experience, remarkably survived and simply "went home." Miraculously there seemed to be no physical residuals. For several weeks there were some mild memory problems, in terms of forgetting names of people familiar to him, but EEG, MRI and neurological examinations were all normal. Cicoria returned to work after several weeks with his surgical skills unimpaired. His memory difficulties disappeared over the next following weeks so that, a month after the "bolt from the blue" his overall functioning was back to the pre-lightning strike level.

But there was one remarkable new happening—"suddenly, over two or three days there was this insatiable desire to listen to piano music." This was unexpected because while Cicoria did have some piano lessons as a child, he really had maintained no such piano playing interest in his later years. In recent times when he did listen to music he much preferred rock.

Along with this powerful desire to listen to piano music, the urge to play classical music came over Cicoria and he started to teach himself once again to play the piano. Simultaneously, as Sacks (2007) describes it, Cicoria began to hear music in his head: "The music was there, deep inside him—or somewhere—and all he had to do was let it come to him. 'It's like a frequency, a radio band. If I open myself up, it comes'" (p.6). Cicoria was "inspired, even possessed by music, and scarcely had time for anything else" (p.6), as Sacks describes that obsession and preoccupation. Nevertheless Cicoria continued his full-time work as a surgeon with no detrimental residual from the lightning strike. He has continued to perfect his performance. Sacks describes a recent concert performance by Cicoria at which he played Chopin's B-flat Minor Scherzo, and one of his own compositions which he had titled Rhapsody, Opus 1. Professional musicians were impressed with the concert which Sacks sums up nicely: "an astounding feat for someone with virtually no musical background who had taught himself to play at forty-two" (p.12).

Granted this musical "epiphany" in Dr. Cicoria was not quite as "sudden" as in KP and JD above. His tremendously heightened musical interest, and then playing ability, occurred in the weeks after, rather than the moments after, the lightning strike. But it was nevertheless a very abrupt change as his brain was reorganizing and preparing, as it were, for his "musicophila."

DA: "knocked into music"

Derek Amato was a 40-year-old corporate trainer when he dived into a shallow pool and suffered a severe concussion. He was in hospital for two days but seemed to have recovered fully without deficit, except for a 35 percent hearing loss. Amato had only "dabbled in music" as a child but never studied music or had any formal training. When he left the hospital he went to visit a musician friend at his home. It was there his "sudden genius" exploded on the scene:

> For some unknown reason I sat down at his piano and began to play. There was no progression. It's not like I started playing "Mary Had a Little Lamb." I just started to play classically structured music, full composition if you will. I ripped off immediately into a very long piece, and I sat there playing for about seven hours straight. Neither of us knew what to think; we were in awe. My friend has known me his whole life, so he just kind of sat there almost in tears. We both were. I was just as shocked as he was.

Amato states that until his accident he had never touched a piano: "I still can't read music or tell you where the notes are. All I know is that the black keys are flat. I don't even know what I'm going to play each time I sit down…but since my accident the notes just pour out of me."

Amato immediately shared this musical epiphany with his mother, who herself played the piano but was well aware that her son had never done so. "You're never going to believe this," he told his mother. "I took her to a local music store and sat down and played. She just sat there and cried."

"Total notation recall," he terms it. If he hears a piece he can play it. If he does "get something in his head" he has to find a piano and immediately play a part of that piece so it remains with him. Once imbedded, it then remains.

Amato has become a professional musician but even to this day cannot read or write music: "The best way to explain it is that I see these black and white structures—like little blocks or squares—and that's what I play. I play with my eyes shut; I don't even have to look at the keys, and I have no idea what is coming next."

Like others with the dawning of such sudden musical genius (such as TC, above), Amato has become obsessed with music: "My mind races all day and all night long. From the moment I get up to the moment I go to bed I think music."

The diving accident and sudden musical epiphany occurred in October, 2006. In 2007 he was selected by a Japanese company to do the soundtrack for a movie and he subsequently did several others for independent film companies. He produced an album of his works—*Full Circle*—and in 2007 was nominated as Independent Artist of the Year by the Association of Independent Artists.

Amato has been interviewed for his story, and has demonstrated his musical ability on a number of national radio and television programs. A particularly detailed and informative such interview occurred with Heather Wallace in Vancouver,

Canada. That interview, and some other video clips of Amato can be accessed on his MySpace site at www.myspace.com/damatoproject.

Amato is now dedicated full time to musical composition and performance. His instrument repertoire has expanded from piano to 6 and 12 string guitars, electric guitars and synthesizers. He is working on new album releases and also devotes some time to charitable causes, including the Shared Journeys Brain Injury Foundation in Fort Collins, Colorado, which is dedicated to helping persons with acquired brain injury achieve independent, successful and productive lives.

Amato is surprised, puzzled and grateful for the gift of music that surfaced after his injury without other deficits. He wonders whether "we all have the possibility of making music" and that the concussion tapped, in him, that possibility. But, nevertheless, as a cautious reminder, he received a beautiful gift one Father's Day from one of his daughters. It was a helmet with the words "No diving" carefully imprinted on it. Maybe she fears another such injury might make that musical gift disappear just as abruptly as it so unexpectedly began.

Summary

"Sudden genius," like the acquired savant or "accidental genius," suggests to me a pool of latent potential of varying size within us all. In the acquired savant some injury or disease in a particular area of the brain is the stimulus to tap that dormant reservoir of talent, and typically the new skills are accompanied by some residual trade-off, major or minor, of some cognitive or memory function. Those persons with sudden genius, in contrast, tap abruptly and unexpectedly into a pool of talent without significant brain injury or disease, and there is no residual trade-off for their new-found abilities. This circumstance, like the acquired savant, also argues, for me, the existence of an inner savant within us all.

CHAPTER 22

"Normal Genius": Dormant Skills Within Us All?

Ordinarily I don't get my information about savant syndrome from late night television. But I was watching the Johnny Carson show one evening some years ago, about the time the movie *Rain Man* was released in 1988. Carson had as his guest a very bright and amiable Cal-Tech graduate student named Scot. Since childhood Scot has had the ability to unconsciously and instantly put the letters in words in alphabetical order in any conversation he might have with someone. Then, if asked, he can recite the conversation back with the words pronounced with their revised spelling. For example the word "Monday" becomes admnoy; "excel" becomes ceelx; "the" becomes eht, and so on. Some words such as ghost, almost, begin or deer are already in alphabetical order in our vocabulary, but those words are really quite few. When sentences or paragraphs are pronounced with all words in alphabetical order, a whole new language is created.

As the program began Carson asked Scot to greet him and some others in his unique language. "Hi, hjnnoy," he began, then greeting "De achmmno" (Ed McMahon) and cdo eeeinnnrssv (Doc Severinsen). Carson then read some newspaper clippings to Scot, which he repeated back in his unusual alphabetized language. Following that Carson read the first sentence of Lincoln's Gettysburg address (30 words) which Scot quickly recited back with the words alphabetized: "foru ceors adn eensv aersy ago, oru aefhrst bghortu fhort no hist ceinnnott, a enw ainnot…" Carson would have done Lincoln's entire speech but he was told by the director he "had to do it fast".

The audience was amazed. Some conversation then followed about savants. Scot indicated that there had been an article about savant syndrome in the Pasadena newspaper the day before his visit to the show. Discussion then turned to Dustin Hoffman's portrayal of an autistic savant in *Rain Man* in which some unusual, seemingly unconscious skills were demonstrated.

Scot explained that he had begun his word alphabetization on a childhood whim, simply wondering what a language would sound like if all the words were required to be in alphabetical order. He tried it out, mastered it and has carried that unusual skill forward to adult life. It serves no particular useful purpose but it is carried out unconsciously and rapidly as a continuing "habit." At the present time Scot retains his ability to alphabetize at will, with no practice required. He completed law school and is licensed as a patent attorney. However he prefers teaching and private tutoring in math, physics, chemistry, law, English and standardized tests which he now does.

The program was very lively and entertaining. Scot is a very engaging and witty person. Scot does not have savant syndrome; he has no disability and in fact he is unusually bright, successful and personable. Actually the term "normal savant" is an oxymoron since a "savant" by definition includes a disability. The politically correct and more accurate way to characterize Scot's unusual abilities would be a "neurotypical person with savant-like skills."

There are other "neurotypical" persons who have savant-like skills carried out in an unusually swift and unconscious matter. As a variation of Scott's skill, a woman from Canada wrote to me describing what she labeled her "eccentric habit." When she hears certain phrases or words, her mind automatically puts the letters in alphabetical order quickly. She then cancels out any letters that repeat and makes a word or phrase from the letters that appear only once. If this word seems to fit or relate to the initial phrase she will write it down. For example, "He is off in his own little world though" becomes "Drug." "What did they say?" becomes "Wise." "Nothing is sure" becomes "Hurt Ego."

There are other complex, but instant, elements to this skill having to do with seeking balance and harmony with letters. For example, her mind will pick up on certain sentences and automatically put the letters in alphabetical order, such as: "Really, you don't have anybody overseas?" This phrase is of interest to her not because the singles make a word or phrase (bhtuv) but because the sentence has such harmony and balance; there are four each of the vowels a, e, o, y, and two each of the consonants l, n, r, s.

This talent began about age eight with a fascination regarding the number of letters per syllable in words and then developed over the years into some of the abilities described above. This woman also learned three languages quickly by immersion in various settings at different times in her life.

She spoke those languages so well, with barely a trace of accent, that she often passed for a native speaker in each of them. There is no impairment accompanying these talents such as autism or any other disability. In our correspondence she was interested, and relieved, to know other neurotypical persons had such skills and she was very willing to volunteer for any studies of such unusual capacities.

A young woman in the United States shared with me an interesting phenomenon in which during conversations, or even with inner thoughts, every word is spelled out in front of her as if projected on to a screen in tickertape-like fashion. Previously, if someone used a word she did not recognize, she would stop and ask them to spell it and she would then store it for future reference. Now if she encounters such new words she will look the word up after the conversation. Like many persons with synesthesia, for example, it was not until she was in high school that she realized that not everyone could "see conversations in their head." Presently this interferes very little in her everyday life except that when in a crowd she not only "sees" the conversation she is directly involved with, but also "sees" surrounding conversations as well to the extent they are picked up. She is a very successful and well-adjusted student, and certainly manifests no disability whatsoever. To the extent any imaging studies have been carried out on her, those have been entirely normal also.

A number of other individuals have written to me describing their particular skills, such as being able to instantly give the number of words, consonants or vowels at the end of each sentence during conversation, or a total of those for the entire conversation. One woman is able to give the total number of "every other vowel or consonant" in such a snippet of conversation. Others assign numbers to each letter in the alphabet (a=1; b=2 etc.) and then hearing a word, instantly compute the total numerical value of the letters added together. This counting occurs unconsciously and the total simply "pops up" automatically.

Others report the ability to do large calculations in their head or to recognize instantly prime numbers in telephone books, house numbers or license plates. Still others remember birthdays of numerous co-workers or even casual acquaintances, startling them with that keen recollection when birthdays roll around.

Perhaps one of the most common of these "super-abilities" in neurotypical persons is the ability to read backward, pronouncing the words as they are spelled backwards. There is an excellent example of this in a young woman interviewed on a National Public Radio program on February 7, 2010. The title of the program is "Meet the backwards speaking girl." There is an audio recording as well as a written transcript at www.npr.org/templates/story/story.php?storyId=123463760. In this interview the young woman reads the preamble to the US Constitution backwards, instantly pronouncing the words as they occur when spelled backwards. In the 13 comments that followed that story four other persons mentioned either they or their child had that same ability, all of them neurotypicals.

On the Children's Unit at Winnebago where I met my first savant, there was a young boy who amazed his teacher and classmates by being able to write the letters "calif" with his left hand and the letters "ornia" with his right hand *simultaneously* on a blackboard. Try that. It's nearly impossible.

I was reminded of him when a note came to me from a woman in Europe— neurotypical, accomplished and in a very responsible position—who is able to write, using both hands, in *two* languages simultaneously. For example she recently opened a convention of an international audience by writing greetings in many different languages on a blackboard. While one hand carefully wrote greetings in one language, the other hand, simultaneously, spelled out greetings in a second language.

In most of these persons the ability has been lifelong, carried over into adult life from childhood, just as some persons carry into adulthood a second language learned as a child, particularly if they were raised in a bilingual family. Quite often many of us may recall some unusual ability, quirk or "habit" which we had as a child—memorizing license plates automobile models, or the ability to recognize autos coming around the corner just by their sound, for example. But then we abandoned those trivial skills as we grew up and put away "childish things." But others, like Scot, have simply continued to use those special abilities and they remain intact. Some have suggested that perfect pitch is an ability which everyone has as a child, but is eventually lost in most persons through disuse. In countries where language depends as much upon pitch as words themselves, however, the incidence of perfect pitch is much higher in everyone because of continual use. In like manner, the child who continues to use a second language while growing up will have that skill when an adult. So it is with these savant-like skills in some neurotypical persons.

There are a number of other savant-like word, musical or mathematical skills in neurotypical persons that have been carried forward into adult life. But what seems cute and amusing in a child can appear to be strange and bizarre in an adult. As a consequence some adults with these abilities simply do not share them with anyone around them lest they be labeled as weird, strange or autistic like *Rain Man*. Instead they simply silently continue to alphabetize, count, measure or compute to themselves. Some do write to me to share their rare "me too" skill after they see some savant documentary or other program where some such skills are depicted. When in response I share with them that there are other individuals with such abilities who are perfectly "neurotypical," they are much relieved. Along that line, Scot was asked on the Carson show if he knew of anyone else who had this unusual skill. Scot said "No" but it would be useful to know if there are others. "Please tell me I'm not the only one," he remarked humorously.

In a similar way some persons with synesthesia, after they discover to their surprise that not everyone "sees" sounds, "tastes" music or "smells" colors, for example, are reluctant to share that unusual phenomenon for the same reasons. But as articles and news reports describe synesthesia as a special ability, rather than something strange or bizarre, more persons are willing to share the fact that they experience this merging of senses. Then, it turns out, synesthesia is not as rare as commonly thought.

Let's hope that pointing out that savant-like skills can exist in "normal" persons without disability or other "trade-off" will be reassuring to other persons who, like Scot, have these unique skills. Then they will be less reluctant to share those skills with others, and might even become rather proud of them.

But the primary significance of the "normal" savant with special skills, and why I discuss that circumstance here, is the fact that such persons, like prodigies or geniuses, are using the same pre-conscious or unconscious circuitry that the savant uses when performing many of his or her skills, as explained in Chapter 3. That same habit or procedural memory circuitry exists in all of us and the normal savant is evidence of that in my view.

Some of these "normal" savant-like skills persist in some persons because they are carried forth from childhood. But most of us lose such abilities, if they were present as a child, because we cease to use them, either because they are not useful as adults, or maybe because they might be seen by others as rather strange. Is it possible, though, that such dormant skills, to the extent they were present as a child, still exist in all of us, reverted now to some obscure spot of storage? Could those be part of an "inner savant" within us all? And if so, how might one tap the circuitry and brain capacity that harbor our inner savant?

We will look at those questions in Chapter 23 on accessing our inner savant.

CHAPTER 23

Accessing the "Inner Savant" Within Us All

Is there an "inner savant"—a little *Rain Man* perhaps—within us all? I believe there is. The acquired savant provides evidence for that. Can it be accessed non-intrusively without CNS catastrophe or other harmful trade-off? I believe it can be, but with several important caveats. Let me summarize how I came to those conclusions.

First, as described in Chapter 3, there is evidence that some savants, because of prenatal, perinatal or postnatal CNS damage, from a variety of genetic, traumatic or disease processes substitute right brain capacity in a compensatory manner for left brain dysfunction. Simultaneously, presumably due to these same injurious processes, savants are forced to rely on preserved, more primitive cortico-striatal (procedural or habit) memory rather than damaged higher level cortico-limbic (semantic or declarative) memory. This combination of *right brain skills* + *habit memory* produces the type of skills and massive memory that *is* savant syndrome. Such right brain capacity and habit memory circuitry exists in each of us. However, because it serves us so well, we have come to prefer, and be reliant on, left brain (dominant) function, including language, logical and sequential thinking, coupled with broader and more facile semantic and declarative memory pathways. Thus right brain capacity and habit memory circuits remain relatively submerged and underused, but nevertheless still present.

Second, cases of "acquired" savant syndrome (see Chapter 20) provide convincing evidence that in some persons, depending on site of injury and underlying talent "pool," dormant savant-like skills and memory can surface following brain injury, stroke or dementia, either as a *compensatory* or *release* phenomenon.

Third, some savants, especially those with severe disabilities, appear to "know things they never learned." None of us starts with a blank disk. Rather, we all come with considerable "factory-installed" software including both knowledge and skills, some of them buried and dormant until accessed and released. Evidence for such genetic memory is as persuasive in prodigies and geniuses, as it is in savant syndrome itself as illustrated by some of the case examples cited earlier.

Fourth, from a number of studies and procedures cited in the section on autobiographical memory, or hyperthymestic syndrome, in Chapter 5, there is evidence for extensive buried or dormant autobiographical memory capacity within us all.

Fifth, as I will point out in Chapter 24, there is ample brain reserve to accommodate such massive, buried skills, knowledge and memory. The human brain capacity to store makes the ever smaller and smaller mass-storage devices, no matter how miniature and how many gigabytes, seem huge and inefficient by comparison.

The overriding question of course is whether such dormant capacities can be accessed without CNS catastrophe and/or detrimental trade-off. Several methods hold promise.

A cognitive approach

In her book *New Drawing on the Right Side of the Brain*, Edwards (1999) summarizes her many years of experience of using drawing, taught systematically just as one would teach a second language, to allow persons to tap dormant right brain function—"visual, perceptual and simultaneous"—so regularly overshadowed by left brain activity—"verbal, analytic and sequential." She had been influenced particularly by Sperry's (1968) work on brain hemisphere specialization. Edwards (1999) was concerned that in the public schools "art" was often seen as only an "enrichment" activity, "valuable, but not essential." Her view, in contrast, was that

> the arts are essential for training specific, visual, perceptual ways of thinking, just as the "3 R's" are essential for training specific, verbal, numerical and analytical ways of thinking. I believe both thinking modes—one to comprehend the details and the other to "see" the whole picture, for example, are vital for critical-thinking skills, extrapolation of meaning, and problem solving. (p.xiii)

Edwards (1999) refers to these two ways of thinking as the "R-Mode" (subdominant, visual, perceptual) and "L-Mode (language dominant, verbal, analytic). By teaching corporate executives, for example, to use more R-Mode thinking their "vision"—seeing the big picture and realizing better some of the "soft" executive side of company dynamics more clearly—can be better balanced with more typical L-Mode analytical, sequential and logical managerial thinking. Both types of thinking are critical to corporate success, Edwards (1999) postulates, and learning to "draw" allows R-Mode thinking to emerge from its more regularly submerged, subordinate position to L-Mode thinking.

Edward's book provides numerous specific instructions and practical exercises. It also provides convincing before, during and after examples as access to R-Mode abilities and thinking is accomplished. One of the final chapters is titled "The Zen of Drawing: Drawing Out the Artist Within." There she states "drawing is a magical process. When your brain is weary of its verbal chatter, drawing is a way to quiet the chatter and to grasp a fleeting grasp of transcendent reality" (p.248). Edwards describes this active, conscious, cognitive shift between the two hemispheres this way:

> First, you draw in the R-mode, wordlessly connecting yourself to the drawing. Then shifting back to your verbal mode, you can interpret your feelings and perceptions by using the powerful skills of your left brain—words and logical thoughts. If the pattern is incomplete and not amenable to words and rational logic, a shift back to R-Mode can bring intuition and analogic insight to bear on the process. Or, the hemispheres might work together cooperatively in countless possible combinations. (p.248)

When teaching high school before she wrote her book, some of Edward's students seemed to "get" drawing very suddenly rather than gradually. They could not explain that sudden transition except to say they "seemed to be seeing things differently." While not as abrupt, it reminded me of some aspects of the "sudden genius" described earlier wherein these persons also very unexpectedly seemed to be seeing things differently in an epiphany-like "Aha" moment.

It also reminded me of a woman who had written to me about a definite "switch" or migration of abilities between left and right brain hemispheres. This woman was a very successful health care professional. She enjoyed playing piano by ear and could play back even lengthy songs after a single hearing. She enjoyed music so much that she decided to leave her profession and pursue a career as a pianist. She entered a conservatory to study formally that which had always come to her naturally. But when she did that, a curious thing happened. As she studied music systematically, her "gift" left her and she found herself playing at a beginner level and now learning music in an entirely different way. Her natural "play by ear" ability migrated to elsewhere in the brain and never returned. She continued to play the piano but now only by reading music. Her experience is consistent with PET studies which have shown that musicians who play by ear show increased localized activity in the *right* hemisphere and those that play by reading music show increased localized activity in the *left* hemisphere. Therefore there is no music center in the brain as such. Rather which brain hemisphere is most active depends on which strategy is being used.

Finally, Rimland (1978b) describes a project in which a graduate student was given the task of consciously and systematically learning how to calendar calculate to see if he could match the skills and speed of the well-known identical twin brothers described by Horwitz and co-workers in 1965. The student practiced day and night and became quite adept at calendar calculating, yet he could not match the skill and speed of the twins for quite some time. But then one day

> suddenly he discovered he could match their speed. Quite to the student's surprise, his brain had somehow automated the complex calculations; it had absorbed the table he memorized so efficiently that now calendar calculating was second nature to him; he no longer had to consciously go through the various operations.

Rimland concluded that this quantum leap in ability took place as the calculating ability migrated from the left brain to the right brain. That was this student's "Eureka" moment.

These examples provide evidence that the left and right brain hemispheres do specialize in certain differential functions. They demonstrate as well that in some instances deliberate cognitive efforts can provide greater access to the typically less dominant right hemisphere of the brain and its special capabilities in a non-intrusive, conscious fashion.

A stroke of insight

Jill Bolte Taylor (2006) provides a unique but in many ways a complementary and persuasive perspective on brain hemisphere specialization and access. In 1996 this Harvard-trained brain scientist had a massive left hemisphere stroke. Her book, *My Stroke of Insight*, provides a very lucid account of the four hours during which she experienced vacillating function between the left side of her brain—more detail oriented, rational, and "attached to the details of my life"—and the right side with a growing "sense of peace" in which she felt "enfolded by a blanket of tranquil euphoria" (p.41). It took eight years for her to heal completely from that time when she was unable to walk, talk, read, write or recall any of her life.

In February, 2008 Taylor gave a talk at the annual TED (Technology, Entertainment, Design) conference, which hosts the best speakers in the United States for an 18-minute presentation. Taylor's is a sensational talk and currently is among the most emailed, and viewed, speeches of that prestigious group (the speech can be accessed at http://blog.ted.com/2008/03/jill_bolte_tayl.php). That speech demonstrates dramatically that not only did Dr. Taylor recover fully from her stroke, but also her experience provided some exceptional insights into right brain/ left brain function, and how to better access "right brain" capacities in a "left brain" world. As the book cover describes it:

> Today Taylor is convinced that the stroke was the best thing that ever happened to her. It has taught her that the feeling of nirvana is never more than a mere thought away. By *stepping to the right of our left brain*s, we can all uncover the

feelings of well-being and peace that are so often sidelined by our own brain chatter. (empasis in original)

Since Taylor is a brain scientist, the book is in itself a valuable primer on brain organization and function. Moreover it also provides a great deal of valuable information, and hope, for stroke survivors and their caregivers. However it is the last several chapters of the book that are particularly pertinent to this section of this book because it provides insight into the fact that one has the "conscious power" to access *both* left and right brain "sets." Taylor states she can

> choose a peaceful and loving mind (my right mind), whatever my physical or mental circumstances, by deciding to *step to the right and bring my thoughts back to the present moment*. (p.147; emphasis in original)

Taylor continues:

> In a world that often feels like it spins dangerously fast, I continue to work very hard to maintain a healthy relationship between what is going on in my right and left minds. I love knowing that I am simultaneously (depending on which hemisphere you ask) as big as the universe and yet merely a heap of star dust. (p.150)

The "conscious power" that Taylor describes is more than just "willpower" in the ordinary sense. Taylor (1999) links right brain/left brain access and cognition to specific brain circuitry and neurophysiology. For example, she states that based on her experience with "losing my left mind, I wholeheartedly believe that the feeling of deep inner peace is *neurological* circuitry located in the right brain. *This circuitry is constantly running and always available for us to hook into"* (p.159; emphasis mine).

From reading the book and listening to her speak, it is clear that Taylor has fully recovered from her stroke. That in itself is impressive and certainly inspirational. But now, as she describes it, she has the new capability to choose more freely and consciously between right brain/left brain, R-mode/L-mode functioning. That in itself is impressive and highly significant. But the fact that such new-found access and "choice" can occur now in Taylor, *without* any detrimental trade-off or disability, is even more significant and encouraging in the search for ways of tapping the "inner savant" within us all. While in her case a stroke provided the impetus for that new-found insight, the kind of conscious choice capability she discovered as a way of accessing the right brain-type skills and traits is not dependent now on some deficit or disability. Rather it would seem to be a conscious mechanism or technique available to anyone, just as meditation, for example, is available to anyone who chooses that technique.

In support of her own observations, in fact, Taylor cites the research by Newberg and D'Aquili (2001) in which Tibetan meditors and Franciscan nuns were invited to meditate or pray while undergoing SPECT imaging. They were to tug on a piece of twine when they either reached their meditative climax or felt united with God. The findings showed that at those moments there was a decrease in the left hemisphere language centers resulting in a lessening of brain chatter. But there was also a decrease in the left posterior parietal gyrus which is an area associated with personal physical boundaries and a sense of personal orientation. Taylor concludes from that research that it

> makes good neurological sense that when my left language centers were silenced and my left orientation association area was interrupted from its normal sensory input, my consciousness shifted away from feeling like a solid, to a perception of myself as a fluid—at one with the universe. (p.136)

A technological approach: rTMS

Snyder and Mitchell (1999), citing the acquired savant cases particularly, hypothesize that "mechanisms for certain savant skills reside equally in all of us but cannot normally be accessed" (p.591). They state that savant skills represent brain processes that occur in each of us regularly but those processes are swamped and buried by more sophisticated conceptual cognition. Therefore the savant-like capacities remain largely at an unconscious level. Autistic savants, they conclude, "have privileged access to lower levels of information not normally available through introspection…we all have the same raw information but just cannot access it, at least on call" (p.587).

In a more recent article, Snyder (2009) says it even more forcefully: "I argue that savant skills are latent in us all… In other words, everyone has the raw information for savant skills, but it requires a form of cortical disinhibition or atypical hemispheric imbalance to be accessed" (p.1399). Snyder uses *low-frequency* repetitive transcranial magnetic stimulation (rTMS) applied to the left anterior temporal area to temporarily *inhibit* neural activity in that localized area of the cerebral cortex (high-frequency rTMS stimulates neural activity; low-level rTMS inhibits neural activity). In three separate studies, summarized in this article, Snyder (2009) has used low-frequency rTMS to enhance certain drawing, proofreading and numerosity skills in neurotypical volunteers. Young, Ridding and Morrell (2004), using a variety of standard psychological tests and tasks specifically designed to test savant skills and abilities, showed that savant-type skills improved in 5 out of 17 participants with rTMS exposure. They concluded that savant-type skills expressions may be possible for some, but not all individuals, just as it appears to be in the disabled populations. Gallate *et al.* (2009) used rTMS to increase literal memory thus providing greater resistance to false memories.

rTMS is an accepted technique in neurology and psychiatry both for diagnostic brain localization studies as well as for treatment of a number of conditions. In October, 2008 rTMS was approved in the United States for treatment of major depression refractory to antidepressant medication as an alternative to electrocon-vulsive therapy. rTMS is a non-intrusive technique. The brain area is targeted with magnetic impulses applied from a cap-like source outside the scalp. The rapidly changing magnetic fields affect electrical activity in the targeted area of the brain. It is a painless procedure with apparently no harmful side effects except for the rare occurrence of an epileptic seizure.

Snyder and others continue their experimental work with this modality. He concedes that the "privileged access" hypothesis remains to be proven and that the empirical evidence that is consistent with the hypothesis is preliminary and requires independent researchers to replicate the findings. But the preliminary findings are intriguing.

Rummaging around in our right hemisphere

Edwards (1999) and Taylor (2006) both point out that it is possible for neurotypical persons to tap right brain/R-mode abilities by conscious effort without detrimental trade-offs. They feel, as I do, that while left hemisphere skills serve us effectively and efficiently, our regular and habitual use of those well-worn paths may keep us from accessing what I refer to as our "inner savant." In my view, portions of that inner savant include: (a) submerged right brain talent; (b) dormant genetic memory; (c) buried autobiographical memory. Cases of acquired savant syndrome demonstrate that access to all three of those components can be triggered by certain CNS injury or disease depending on site of injury and underlying pool of talent.

I am not suggesting that the "inner savant" which lies within each of us houses a potential Picasso, Mozart or Einstein, depending on our buried inclinations and abilities. No doubt talent, whether musical, artistic, mathematical or athletic, is dis-tributed differentially along the lines of the usual bell-shaped curve, just as measured IQ levels, height or certain other physical characteristics are likewise distributed. The type and strength of our "inner savant," whether tapped by CNS incident or conscious effort, will be determined in part by differential genetic endowments dis-tributed over this bell-shaped spectrum.

But whatever that endowment I am convinced that consciously "rummaging" around in our right hemisphere can provide new experiences and release latent abili-ties, sometimes at a prodigious level. By analogy, when I drive from my home to Chicago, I am usually in a hurry so I choose the very familiar route over the inter-state to get me there the fastest. It is not very scenic, but there are multiple, wide lanes so passing is easy and speed limits are high. It's a quick trip (most days). But sometimes on a really nice day I start just a little earlier and take the less traveled side roads along Lake Michigan just for the view. It does take a bit longer, but it is worth it in that it takes me thorough less familiar territory and I see some new sights and learn some new streets. And, with less speed and congestion, it is a more pleasant trip overall.

Others have described to me how much new discovery, joy and appreciation of a marvelous country and its people surfaced when they took a leisurely trip in a motor home over the miles and miles of country they had flown over many times—so efficiently, so hastily, but sequestered and distant really—in the rush to get to the opposite coast.

A January, 2000 issue of *Time* magazine contains an article titled "Careers: Catching their second wind" (Rutherford *et al.* 2000). It describes how so often in retirement persons discover, or uncover, hidden or latent talent. In some instances, such as the renowned American folk artist Grandma Moses, these dormant skills emerge at a stunning, prodigious level. Part of that discovery for some is perhaps simply having the time to follow some lifelong interests, and, with the children through college and the mortgage paid, having some resources to "squander." But Gene Cohen (2000) points out in his book *The Creative Age: Awakening Human Potential in the Second Half of Life* that there are certain neurologic changes in the aging brain that lend themselves not to deterioration, but toward new circuits and pathways consistent with "creativity." Those changes make it easier to shift not just *philosophically*, but *neurologically* as well, from the well-worn left brain/semantic circuits to still intact, but relatively less frequently used, right brain/procedural memory circuits. Grandin (2009) states that:

> Many people have told me that my talks have improved between ages 40 and 60. My ability to think in a less rigid way keeps getting better as I fill up the Internet of my mind with more and more information. I greatly improved socially in my 40s and 50s compared with my 20s. This was due to having more experiences in my memory that provided guidance on how to behave. (p.1438)

And an Associated Press wire report on April 19, 2009 notes that "Rita Levi Montalcini, a Nobel Prize-winning scientist, on the occasion of her 100th birthday said, 'At 100, I have a mind that is superior—thanks to experience—than when I was 20'."

Both Cohen (2000) and Grandin (2009) make the point that whatever the allotment of brain cells might be at any stage of life, it is cumulative life *experiences* that puts accumulated knowledge into perspective producing the "wisdom" so often associated with older age. *This appears to be as much a neurologic process as a psychological one.*

For some persons such insights come gradually, but in other persons the change in mind set and sudden creativity—accessing the "inner savant"—is more abrupt and monumental. I liken those instances to the sudden "I've got it" experience when finally the colored dots on the random dot autostereograms reveal the until-then hidden whale or dinosaur that everyone else seems to have seen sooner than I did. By concentrating, relaxing and seemingly subconsciously aligning one's eyes slightly differently, all of a sudden a whole new three-dimensional image appears, and is sustained.

Some of the persons in Chapters 20 and 21 describe the discovery of their "island of genius" with similar suddenness and clarity. But for most persons, consciously and deliberately "rummaging" in the right hemisphere, as I call it, provides less spectacular and less abrupt abilities. Some pursue an entirely new area of interest and become quite expert "amateur" geologists or anthropologists and are invigorated by a whole new universe of knowledge about those specialties. Others take up mechanics and begin to work with their hands. Some discover a whole new reservoir of empathy which they apply in their volunteer work with hospices.

My "other life" professionally, along with the study of savant syndrome, has been seeing patients on a daily basis. Like most physicians, after a time, one becomes interested in prevention, rather than just treatment, gratifying as successful treatment results can be. So after many years of listening to my psychiatric patients with all manner of predicaments and illnesses, I too began to ponder more about prevention. There is a great deal written about staying well physically—stopping smoking, sensible diet, exercise, sun screen, vitamins and regular check-ups. I call that "rust-proofing people." However, there is not a great deal written about staying healthy mentally. Early in medical school I learned a valuable lesson: "Listen to the patient, he's giving you the diagnosis." And as I listened, embodied in the stories patients were giving me were hints, tips and pearls of prevention. Everything we know about physical health we have learned from the study of disease. And so it is with mental illness. Tips for prevention emerge from the study of illnesses.

So eventually I wrote out a "prescription" for attaining and maintaining positive mental health in a self-distributed booklet titled *Mellowing: Lessons from Listening* (available from www.daroldtreffert.com). That booklet has been very widely disseminated in the United States and other countries through the years just by word of mouth distribution. My definition of positive mental health is summed up in the word "Mellowing"— "being relaxed, at ease and pleasantly convivial." It entails finding a better balance between the *urgent* things and the *important* things in one's life. A better balance as well between what I *do* and who I *am*. Better balancing of *self-esteem* with *other esteem* and being able to "*run for the roses*" and "*smell the roses*" at the same time. Purpose, better communication (talking less/listening more), priorities, problem ownership and perspective are all part of that prescription as well.

I hadn't really thought about how my two interests—savant syndrome and mellowing—really merged together. But when I read Taylor's (2006) account of what she called "nirvana, feelings of well being and peace" as a right brain phenomenon it occurred to me that much of what I write about in *Mellowing* are really right brain antidotes, or offsets, to our left brain hurriedness, "chatter" and propulsion. There is not anything inherently wrong with left brain specialization skills. They serve us well. Rather it is that those L-mode capacities can be usefully balanced, and life enriched, by mixing in R-mode skills, insights and endeavors.

In summary, accessing the "inner savant" in some persons is sudden, dramatic and monumental, especially in the acquired savant. In other neurotypical persons, without injury or disease, it is a more gradual and less sensational process, but equally as important and rewarding. There are a number of ways to gain such access short of CNS catastrophe, some technological, some by deliberate efforts such as meditation or learning to draw, and some by even less structured, less organized ways using conscious reflection or taking a "time-out" from overextended left brain, L-mode "chatter."

In the introduction to this section I mentioned that an "inner savant" does exist in each of us, but there were several caveats in accessing that buried potential. Caveat number one is that, with respect to the acquired savant, whether such abilities surface or not depends on which area of the brain is damaged. Bruce Miller's patients, for example, showed that area most often affected was the left anterior temporal area. Such region-specific neuropathology is why not every person with head injury or dementia (or developmental disability for that matter) demonstrates savant syndrome. Caveat two is that to what extent the "inner savant" skills, once surfaced in any manner, will be spectacular and sensational, or more typical and ordinary, depends somewhat on the talent pool within us, distributed along the usual bell shaped curve of genetic endowment.

But whatever that endowment, average or prodigious, ordinary or spectacular, life can be enriched and in better balance as we pay attention to, and tap, that inner savant within us all. One way to do that is to rummage around a bit more in our right hemisphere. In Chapters 28 and 29 I will suggest some other new ways that might hold promise for expanding and accessing the full potential within us all.

CHAPTER 24

The Bountiful Brain: Half a Brain (or Less) May Be Enough

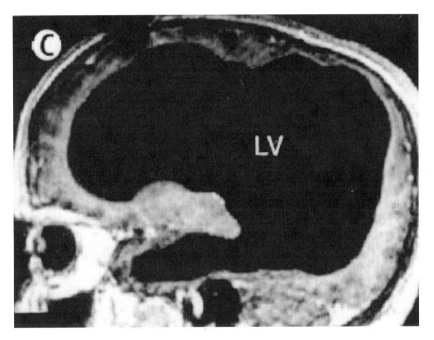

A scan of the man's brain. All of the black in the middle is water and the brain matter is the rim of white along the outside of the skull. (Feuillet, Dufour and Pelletier 2007)

In July, 2007 I was paging through *Lancet* medical journal when the MRI image shown above caught my eye. All that can be seen is a thin layer of cortex with fluid filling what typically is more cerebral cortex and other brain tissue. I wondered what that disability might be. The article was titled "Brain of a white-collar worker."

Feuillet, Dufour and Pelletier (2007) report that this 44-year-old man presented with a three-week history of mild left leg weakness. History revealed that at age six months he had undergone a ventriculoatrial shunt because of hydrocephalus of unknown cause. There had been a shunt revision at age 14 with no cognitive or neurological symptoms since that time.

Neuropsychological testing showed an IQ of 75 (verbal=84; performance=70). The patient was the married father of two children and worked as a civil servant.

As can be seen on the MRI, there is massive enlargement of the lateral, third and fourth ventricle with only a very thin cortical mantle and a posterior fossa cyst. Diagnosis was "non-communicating hydrocephalus with probable stenosis on Magendie's foramen." A ventriculocisternostomy was performed. The leg weakness subsided and neurological examination returned to normal.

It is said we use less than 10 percent of our brain capacity. This brain imaging, showing only a thin layer of cortical tissue in a person functioning perfectly normally, makes one wonder if that 10 percent might be an overestimate. Based on this report, there appears to be rather massive brain reserve and unused capacity available for whatever purpose it might be required and used.

There have been other examples of persons functioning quite normally with marked CNS deficits in terms of brain tissue. Baudoin (1996) reported the case of a woman accountant who had a seizure for the first time at age 30. A CT scan as part of a routine workup showed, surprisingly in view of this woman's overall normal functioning, "a severe porencephalic lesion of around a quarter of the cerebral substance forming a very large ventricle." There was a mild left hemiparesis, a left hemianoposia and a normal neuropsychological test profile except for several mild cognitive defects. In short, this woman was missing at least 25 percent of her brain yet was functioning successfully in her life and career.

The book *Half a Brain is Enough* (Battro 2000) provides similar evidence of reserve capability and plasticity as well. The book tells the story of a boy who had a right hemispherectomy at age three to control his severe epilepsy. Eight years later the boy had developed into a bright child with very minor physical and mental impairment. There was a slight limp when playing or running, but there was no cognitive dysfunction. In school he performed as any child his age in arithmetic and music without evidence of either left or right brain deficits according to the author, himself a distinguished neuroscientist and educator. Battro (2000) looked particularly for evidence of right brain deficits, but except for the mild limp and draftsmanship and handwriting skills somewhat below his age level, there was none. Cognitive spatial ability was preserved and overall this boy performed above average verbally. So perhaps, if the patient is young enough, "half a brain is enough."

These cases (and there are many more) underscore for me the vast availability and plasticity of the brain with plentiful reserve should it be called on for repair, or perhaps, intentional expansion.

PART FOUR

Training the Talent: I've Got a Son or Daughter Who…

One of the sections missing in my *Extraordinary People* book was what might be called a "So Now What?" chapter containing practical advice on "what to do" when one encounters a child or adult with special savant skills. The need for such a chapter has become evident from the many emails or phone calls which I regularly receive from parents which usually begin: "I've got a son or daughter who…" They then go on to describe a child, usually already diagnosed with autism or some other condition, who has shown, amidst the disability, some rather conspicuous savant-like ability in the typical musical, artistic, mathematical or mechanical/spatial areas. They ask about the significance of that special ability and, more importantly, how to approach it. Sometimes the inquiry is from a teacher, grandparent, relative or other caregiver.

They have many questions. Should the special skill be encouraged? Or, should it be discouraged lest it become such a preoccupation or distraction that it overshadows everything else in the child's daily life and learning? Are there any techniques especially useful with such special skills? Are there pitfalls or methods to be especially avoided? Should parents seek out a special teacher or therapist to help "train the talent"? If so, how do they find a qualified person? If there are efforts to encourage other learning, will the special ability, like Nadia's, disappear? How can this special skill be best channeled to a useful outcome?

Just as frequently, however, parents of very young children who do *not* have a diagnosis of autism or other developmental disorder have questions about their child who is reading exceptionally early or shows precocious musical, math or art interest and ability. They have read that such children are sometimes autistic and ask, with some alarm, whether such conspicuous early ability and seemingly obsessive interest might mean their child has some developmental disorder. Other questions follow. How can I tell if my child is autistic? What is the difference between precociousness and savant syndrome? Should I seek a professional evaluation of my child even though he or she seems otherwise developing quite normally?

I am limited to what I can do long-distance in terms of specific in-person evaluation and tailor-made advice. But there are some general principles of the best and most successful approaches to "training the talent," with all of its benefits, that can be shared with these parents or other persons involved with persons with savant syndrome. In the same manner reassurance can be provided to parents of precocious youngsters that not every child that reads voraciously at an early age, or likes to line up railroad cars obsessively, or hums back music exactly after hearing it but once is autistic. The point is precocious children and prodigies do exist; not all such children are on the autistic spectrum. In each individual case it is important to make that distinction.

If there is concern about a diagnosis, I try to put the parent into the hands of a professional person or agency qualified to do the necessary evaluations and make recommendations since, as elsewhere in medicine, the first step in treatment is to make an accurate diagnosis. If the question has to do with where to go next with a special skill, I try to put them in the hands of a professional teacher or therapist who can also help evaluate the type and depth of the skill. And, if it turns out to be a savant skill, this same teacher or therapist can help with "training the talent" and having that special skill act as a "conduit toward normalization" with improved language acquisition, social abilities and daily living skills described earlier.

In this section of the book I hope to answer the "So Now What?" question with some practical advice—"hints, tips and pearls"—from three persons I trust, based on their experience with children with special needs and special skills in the areas of music, art and mathematics.

CHAPTER 25

Teaching Music to the Special Needs Client: A Music Therapist's Approach

Susan Rancer

There are several general principles especially applicable in teaching music to persons with special needs, including savant syndrome. First, many of those persons have perfect or relative pitch which requires special consideration. In my caseload, for example, over 80 percent of my special needs clients typically have either perfect pitch or relative pitch, a much higher percentage than in the general population. If perfect pitch exists in a student, it requires special teaching techniques because traditional music teaching methods can be frustrating and counterproductive to the child with perfect pitch, turning him or her off music education entirely.

Second, the difference between a music therapist and a music teacher is that with a music teacher the child often has to adapt to the teacher's method of *teaching*, whereas with a music therapist the therapist instead adapts to the child's style of *learning*. When I start with new students I have no fixed expectations. I just let them progress at their own rate, letting them lead the way. Sometimes the rhythm is not very crisp and the speed is slow. But each student is doing his or her own best and over time progress occurs. I ask the child to practice the piece three times a week three times each. That seems to work better than using a timer since that device often makes the child feel like he or she has to practice forever. Instead, the 3 x 3 method allows them to count to three and know the end is near. It works well.

I never do recitals.

Tailored teaching techniques for students with perfect pitch

Because so many special needs students, including those with savant syndrome, have perfect pitch, and because tailored teaching techniques are necessary with students who have perfect pitch lest they lose their interest in music entirely, the teacher or music therapist working with these students must know how to recognize and test for perfect pitch, and how to apply those special techniques.

Perfect pitch (also referred to as absolute pitch) refers to the ability to recognize the pitch of a musical tone without an external reference pitch (Baggaley 1974). Perfect pitch can also be described as a photographic memory for sound. People with perfect pitch "feel" music. In some instances they can play a piece after hearing it just once even without formal training. A "tape" in their head picks up the melody and "records" it. As the tape is played back in their brain they try to match it. Rhythm is a part of the process and will also be matched exactly. People with perfect pitch are able to transpose instantaneously. Those with perfect pitch who also have musical training can look at music and "hear" it without playing it, and can "play" their instruments without an instrument actually being present. They are able to name notes from environmental sounds, for example, beeps from machinery, windshield wipers, and rain in a downspout. People who have perfect pitch but have had no formal musical training cannot name the sounds because they don't know the names of the notes; however, they can find the correct pitch on an instrument.

A variant of perfect pitch is *relative pitch*—the ability to identify a pitch if the leading tone is given as a reference point. While perfect pitch is always innate, relative pitch can be either innate or learned. While some people consider perfect pitch and relative pitch to be two distinct phenomena, I consider them to be different levels of the same phenomenon in their innate form, and in this discussion will be referring to perfect pitch and relative pitch in that innate form.

There is some dispute about the frequency of perfect pitch and relative pitch, depending on how precisely it is defined and measured. The generally quoted figure for perfect pitch, however, is 1:10,000 in the general population (Bachem 1955). And there is also a general consensus that perfect pitch is more frequent in musicians, particularly those with early musical training, than in the general population (Sacks 2007). With respect to special populations Leon Miller (1989) devotes an entire chapter in his book to absolute pitch and comments that in the cases of musical savants that had been reported in the literature until that time, perfect pitch was a prominent feature in each of those individuals. The association of musical ability with Williams Syndrome (a disorder caused by chromosonal disorder similar to Down syndrome) has been reported widely, with an increased association of perfect pitch in that population as well (Lenhoff 1998; Levitan and Bellugi 1998; Sacks *et al.* 1995).

In some special needs students, disabilities may interfere with the exhibition of perfect/relative pitch, even though it is present. For example "M" is an 11-year-old girl who is developmentally delayed with severe medical disabilities, including an inability to speak. Nevertheless she shows many of the characteristics of perfect pitch, including perfect rhythm, the ability to pick out songs on numerous instruments, the ability to transpose songs to different keys, along with a high enthusiasm for the music therapy session. Her inability to speak eliminates clues such as singing on pitch, and her eye/hand coordination problems have prevented her from reading music.

"I" is another severely developmentally delayed child, now 16 years old. He is also visually impaired. The only sign of his perfect pitch ability is that when he requests to sing a particular song, he refuses to respond unless it is played in the key of C. Because of his overall low functioning he has been unable to learn to play any instrument, even though music is obviously so enjoyable to him.

Recognizing behaviors that suggest a child has perfect or relative pitch

So given its importance, how does a teacher or music therapist identify perfect pitch in a student? The ear is the dominant force that frequently takes over in those individuals with perfect or relative pitch. When students with perfect or relative pitch read a simple song or a strongly melodious piece of music for the first time, it is automatically processed in the auditory pitch memory bank. By the second time they play it, they have learned it via the auditory memory. This is how their brains process music. The visual learner, in contrast, will read the music again and again without it going into the auditory memory bank. Memorizing comes only after repetitive playing.

Children with perfect or relative pitch will show certain behaviors because of their music processing style. Their eyes and head may drop when playing, or they may seem to look around the room. This behavior will start shortly after they have played a piece for the first time, or even when playing it for the first time, because they are listening to the patterns in the music and anticipating what will come next. They look away from the music because seeing the notes distracts them from listening to it. The visual processing seemingly switches off in these moments, while the brain is concentrating on auditory processing.

After sight-reading a piece, when asked to replay it, some children with perfect pitch become inattentive because they already know how the music sounds. It is already in the auditory memory. They become bored with the repetition. In contrast, for the visual learner, repetition is not boring since there is something new every time the music is read. Until a piece is memorized, the visual learner cannot anticipate what note comes next so there is always something new to discover. Thus note reading for visual learners is stimulating. Auditory pitch learners do not get that stimulation so the repetition becomes mundane.

Another indicator of perfect pitch is a drive to hear the sound, no matter how it is produced. The child is so determined to hear the pitch that is in the head that he or she will play any finger accessible. Fingering therefore tends to be sloppy and the child gets irritated when corrected. And when the child makes a visual note reading error, he or she is compelled to start over at the beginning of a line, or even the beginning of the piece, because he or she must hear the leading tones or melodies to guide him or her through the piece. The leading tones start that "tape recording" in the brain.

Testing for perfect or relative pitch

If a teacher or therapist suspects a child may have perfect or relative pitch, there are methods for testing for both. Since such a high proportion of my special needs clients have perfect pitch, I do routinely test for it. Specific techniques for testing can be found in my booklet *Perfect Pitch & Relative Pitch—How to Identify & Test for the Phenomena: A Guide for Music Teachers, Music Therapists and Parents* (available by email inquiry: Susanrmt@comcast.net; www.susanrancer.com).

How do persons with perfect pitch learn?

Learning occurs, in most people, through use of a combination of auditory and visual cues. *Auditory learning* is done through hearing the spoken language, such as listening to a teacher's verbal explanation, for example. *Visual learning* is done through sight, such as seeing words in a book or writing on the blackboard. Learning for those persons with perfect pitch involves a third process, however: *auditory pitch learning*, which is best defined as a phenomenon by which musical tones are learned solely by hearing them sung or played on instruments. In the absence of perfect pitch ability, auditory pitch learning is not a factor in how students process information. The usual or typical child taking piano lessons learns by reading notes using visual learning. Visual learners cannot learn a song, and then play it, by simply hearing it without substantial training and practice. In contrast, children with perfect pitch can learn a piece and play it almost instantly by simply hearing it, with no visual cues, because they are auditory pitch learners. Even though that is so, however, auditory pitch learning of and by itself does not preclude auditory or visual learning, but it can complicate it if not recognized.

The role of visual learning in persons with perfect pitch

Note reading or visual learning is an essential component of learning to play music, even in persons with perfect pitch, because it helps in developing hand–eye coordination and visual tracking, and increases attention span, fine motor control and motor planning skills. These are all common goals on Individual Education Plans (IEPs) for special needs children. Beyond that, parents frequently report improvement in the child's handwriting, reading and math skills when learning music, especially after note reading skills have begun. And, of course, note reading ability positively affects the musical education itself.

But the presence of perfect pitch complicates learning to read music because, when the playback process involves exclusively the auditory process, it can be so dominant that it takes over the visual (note reading) process. If the teacher or therapist is unaware that the child is an auditory pitch learner, only the auditory skills will develop and the child may never learn to read music properly because students with perfect pitch tend to look for auditory clues, relying on someone to play or sing or even whistle a piece of music. They cannot learn it unless they hear it. Such pure auditory pitch processing left unchecked will continue to hamper the learning of note reading indefinitely if no steps are taken to correct it.

When a student who note reads plays a piece repeatedly, visual learning takes place and note reading ability is reinforced and improved by practice effect. However, in students in whom auditory (perfect) pitch processing dominates, even if the students are able to read a piece through the first time, once they hear themselves playing that piece, the students will never read it again using full visual cues. Therefore, unless visual and auditory pitch processing are balanced, by specific teaching techniques, it is very difficult for the students to make progress, leading to frustration for both student and teacher, and ending, sometimes, with discontinuation of therapy or lessons entirely. A teacher or therapist who is aware of the learning problems involved can shape the teaching to maintain a good balance between visual and auditory pitch learning styles.

A case example can illustrate how such balance in approach can be achieved. "D" has a diagnosis of PDD and was referred after studying with two teachers. He had very strong auditory learning abilities but very poor music-reading skills. Neither teacher had identified him as having perfect pitch and both had difficulty in teaching him. By backtracking to beginning note reading, and carefully balancing visual and auditory pitch learning, "D" was able to learn proficiently. His ear is still a very dominant force in his playing. He often reads a line of a piece and then will suddenly burst out into another song he knows by ear. I have found that the best way to work through this is to let him play his song until he is finished, then go back to the note reading. He simply has to get the song out of his head by playing it before we can proceed with the note reading. I consider this *not* as a behavioral issue, but rather as a characteristic of perfect pitch that I must work around to also teach visual processing effectively.

Achieving balance between visual and auditory learning

When working with perfect pitch students, the therapist or teacher must first stimu-late visual learning and leave auditory learning until later. And when the auditory skill learning is introduced, it must not be taught with the same learning materials as for the visual skills. For example, if you teach "Twinkle, Twinkle, Little Star" by playing the song for them (or even tap out rhythms, or sing the next note) you are stimulating their auditory learning processes. If you then try to teach note reading using this same song, students will play it back by ear, without making any connec-tion to the notes on the page. While you may think they are reading the notes, they are not.

Therefore, to teach visual processing, you would need to use different songs and introduce them to the students without playing them. The students need to read the notes themselves, even though this will stimulate their auditory processing. The auditory processing does come along with the visual, but the visual processing must lead the auditory if these students are to learn note reading.

These students get only one shot at reading a piece, because their auditory sense is so strong. Since the notes go into the auditory memory bank, the students will not need to read that piece again. Because of this, the learning process for reading music takes much longer. Many times teachers mistakenly assume that students are visual learners because they are teaching them visually. But, in fact, the skilled therapist or teacher, with this special population, teaches every child as if they were auditory learners given the high proportion of persons with perfect pitch in this population.

Books recommended for the beginning student

John Schaum's (1967) *Keyboard Talent Hunt,* Books 1 and 2 have been very effective for my beginning piano students. Those books introduce students to piano by using letter names instead of notes. Book 1 starts with the right hand in the "C" position, then goes to the "G" position. Book 2 goes back to the "C" position but uses both hands. It then goes into the "G" position using both hands. By the time students have finished both books, they know their hand positions and the names of the keys on the piano. Their hand–eye coordination as well as the fine motor control and motor planning skills are in place. I call these my "magic books." There is no better way to start a child on a piano than by using this method. They are designed for typically developing four-year-olds.

Transition into note reading can occur next with use of *My Piano Book A,* by Stewart and Glasscock (1985). I use only the first half of this book, which introduces the child to notes "C" through "G" in the right hand. This book has big and colorful notes which makes note reading very inviting. I use this book for about one week and often loan it out to my students.

Next I go into *The Alfred Piano Series* (Palmer, Manus and Lethco 1995), starting with level 1A and moving on to the Lesson Book, the Technic Book, the Recital Book and the Theory Book. If a child is extremely slow, I use the Fun Book for extra reinforcement. These books are excellent for teaching children to be great note readers. A concept is introduced in the Lesson Book, seen again in the Technic Book and then once again in the Recital Book, since reinforcement is the key to getting these children to be good note readers. In those books I skip some of the early pages and go directly to the section where the treble clef is introduced. Then, after about one week, I proceed to the bass clef. Overall the series is very well written and makes the child feel quite comfortable and confident.

Growing up with perfect pitch: the need for special teaching techniques

My own experience provides an example of the need for special adaptation in teaching techniques for *all* children with perfect pitch. I began to play piano in my first grade classroom at age six. I played immediately with two hands, never having touched a piano before. We did not own a piano and I did not have any exposure to one before this classroom. It was like I was hard-wired and knew exactly how to play and which keys to play next. I didn't make mistakes. I simply played whatever song I heard my first grade teacher play in the classroom.

In response to this new-found ability I started piano lessons with a teacher who played all the pieces for me, enhancing my auditory learning skills. I learned the pieces by ear, and identified the songs by their accompanying picture since I wasn't able, as yet, to read the titles. The teacher tried to teach me note reading, but those efforts failed because I had perfect pitch and was able to play everything by ear. Who needs notes?

I soon changed teachers and, *recognizing I had perfect pitch*, that teacher changed teaching techniques in order to teach me to play also by reading notes. But it took several years to make that transition because I seldom practiced my assigned pieces. Instead, I would play pieces I heard on the radio. I did stay with that teacher until the sixth grade, but overall it was a grueling experience for both of us.

As I got older I would listen to the radio and play songs after hearing them just once. In high school I would sit at the piano in the band room and play songs as my friends called them out. Or sometimes they would play new songs to me on the radio and I would immediately play them back because I would then hear the song like a recording in my head and I would simply match it. While people were astonished at something that seemed almost "magical" to them, it simply came as second nature to me.

Later, as an adult, I came to understand that much of my difficulty in learning to note read stemmed from that early reinforcement of my auditory skills without having been first taught visual skills, since my first teacher tried to integrate auditory learning into note reading. In my own teaching now, I have found that if a child with perfect pitch learns note reading without corresponding or competing auditory stimulation from the beginning, learning to note read can be painless and the student is then able to do both.

Some examples of teaching music to children with special needs

"R": a gift that keeps on giving

"R" began music therapy at age 5. He is now 17 and plays piano wonderfully, which provides a great deal of praise and positive reinforcement from family and friends. His diagnosis is high-functioning autism with delayed speech and language. His perfect pitch was immediately apparent when he picked out chords on the omnichord. He can name correctly any note on the piano, black or white. When I play a familiar song on the piano and ask him what the next note is, he will name it instantly. After listening to a "Star Wars" disc on the clavinova, he was able to play the right hand in its entirety without assistance. I then accompanied him on the left hand with the chords. He memorized those chords auditorily, and then played the left-hand chords while I played the right-hand melody.

"R" has gone on to play Mozart, Chopin, Beethoven and Bach. He enjoys starting at the beginning of a sonata album and going to the very end. Setting his own time for the amount he wants to practice, he soon has learned the piece in its entirety. Some sensory issues produce a tendency to "pound" on the notes to get the full sensory impact he desires.

"R" has moved on to improvisation now. He picks up the right hand by ear and brings the words to the song to me. He then asks me to write in the left-hand chords. He then blends right and left hands together in a perfect match. While he can put the chords to melody without help, he prefers to have me do it for him. But I am working now on his being able to do that blending more independently.

"L": a fabulous, unforgiving ear

"L" really exemplifies "perfect" pitch; she insists on it. If my guitar is even slightly out of tune, she will let me know about it. She will also correct me if I change a strum or picking pattern. She will cover her ears if I try to harmonize with her. She will play certain songs, or parts of song, on the piano and sing those as well, in perfect pitch of course. We do holiday songs from year to year and she always remembers in which key we did them and will issue a correction as well if I deviate to a different key.

"L" began reading right-hand letter names with me on the piano, and did very well in the C and G positions. When I started with the left hand, though, it was very difficult for her to do that. Now, several years later, we are starting the right hand again in hopes of integrating the left hand into note reading. This progress has been slow, but some gains are apparent, demonstrating the special adaptations and accommodations that need to be made individually around each client.

"A": musical savants can be creative

"A" was a bright and curious child from the beginning, although she seemed unduly sensitive to sounds of all types which seemed to interfere with her sleeping. If read to as an infant, books with rhyming or rhythmic speech seemed to alert her in such a way as that would also interfere with sleep. She began memorizing songs at a very early age.

When she was 18 months old she was reading books and memorizing them. If bored with that she would begin to develop her own new story to the same pictures. By age 30 months she demonstrated a capacity for photographic memory and auditory memory well beyond her age, although echolalia was also quite noticeable. At age three years, she was given a diagnosis of autistic disorder.

At the present time "A" likes to make up songs and act them out with puppets. She likes to sing a verse and then wait for the therapist to sing a verse, resulting in a round of music including words, sounds, puppets and movement. She loves to improvise and create music. "A" is able to name a key or sound without seeing it played. While she has learned to read musical notes, she prefers to play by ear. However, she also has developed some of her own songs with both unique words and chords.

Sometimes it is said about musical savants that while they are quite spectacular at literal memory and repetition, as a group they are not very creative. "A" demonstrates that simply is not true in all cases, and musical savants can *create* as well as replicate.

About the author

Susan Rancer is a registered music therapist (RMT). She graduated from Eastern New Mexico University in 1974 with a degree in music therapy. She did an internship in music therapy at Norristown State Hospital in Norristown, Pennsylvania. She then began working with children at Killgore Children's Hospital in Amarillo, Texas. In 1980 she began her present private practice of music therapy and music instruction. Almost all of her clients are special needs individuals.

CHAPTER 26

"Training the Talent" in Art and Other Skills: An Educator's Approach

Rosa C. Martinez

Art abilities, sometimes at a precocious level, occur with considerable frequency in savant syndrome. Just as with music or mathematics, "training the talent" in drawing, painting or sculpting can reap remarkable rewards toward better development of language, social and daily living skills overall in persons with savant syndrome while at the same time providing us with the benefit of beautiful artwork itself.

While existing theories seeking to explain savant abilities are as varied as the autism spectrum itself, it is some of the consistent elements of autistic disorder that determine the predilection for certain savant abilities. Three such traits—attention to detail, visual thinking and marvelous memory—are important factors in bringing art ability prominently into the savant repertoire of skills.

Savant art skills are not limited to high-functioning savants only. Rather, artistic savant skills, sometimes at a prodigious level, can exist in severely impaired children or adults and there seems to be little correlation between the level of autistic functioning and the level of artistic sophistication itself. Therefore approaches to persons with savant art skills need to vary considerably depending on overall level of functioning. Further, savant art skills are not limited to persons with autism, they can emerge in the acquired savant as well, as pointed out earlier in this book.

While parents, teachers, therapists and others would quite agree that "training the talent" is the way to proceed, they often have many questions regarding exactly how to carry out that endeavor. This chapter will answer some of those questions based on my 25 years of experience exploring successful education approaches to persons with autistic disorders coupled with my specialized interest in those persons where art ability is the savant skill.

Typical questions directed to me read like the following.

"My four-year-old daughter has a diagnosis of autistic disorder. She displays a high interest in art and makes some very advanced drawings. Where do I go with this particular talent?"

Given that your daughter is very young, the overall goal will be one in which you can nurture her artistic talent while creating high interest learning opportunities in other areas as well. This can be accomplished by incorporating the art topic and abilities across other domain areas. For example, making a color copy of one your daughter's colorful creations, mounting it on a piece of sturdy cardboard, and then cutting it up into puzzle pieces (5–8 medium size pieces or 10–15 smaller sized pieces—dependent upon your daughter's specific skill level) is one way to create a task aiding in the development of fine motor, cognitive and reading skills (by printing words relating to the drawn image directly on the front or back of the artwork) while still providing strong motivation within the one area of particular interest and strength for your daughter. You can further nurture creative prowess by exposing your daughter to activities with clay, paper mache, string art, etc.

To nurture the art ability itself, I would highly recommend introducing different media to your daughter. For example, if she tends to draw using colored pencils or inks, expose her to some acrylic paints, oil paints, even perhaps charcoal or oil pastels. Introduce different types of material to paint on as well (small paper, large paper, boards, walls, ceramics, etc.). Exposure to a variety of media can facilitate overall expansion of her skills, not only by allowing her to experience different textures but also by increasing her awareness of the variety of choices. This provides opportunities to eventually develop a preference of techniques, and also decreases the probability of future satiation with art due to boredom of any given single activity. Also, when possible, enrollment in art classes can prove to be very rewarding. Participation within a group where there are "shared" interests provides for a more enabling environment regarding social opportunities as well.

A book you might find very helpful regarding specific tasks, tools and techniques is *Art as an Early Intervention Tool for Children with Autism* by Nicole Martin (2009). This book addresses some topics more broadly, such as integrating art into early intervention treatment and matching symptoms to style. It also suggest projects especially beneficial to specific skills that "build on strengths" using "painting, drawing, clay modeling, sculpture, found objects, printmaking, collage, mixed media and photography" as the tools of the trade. The author has cleverly outlined a therapeutic approach of art toward "life enhancement" while identifying numerous strategies to strengthen general deficit areas such as abstract thinking and recreational skills.

There are also a number of free resource materials on the Internet that can be very useful. A number of those are listed later in this chapter. One of special interest, though, is SketchUp. This was originally designed for use by professional architects, but quite by accident it was discovered that persons with autism or Asperger's had a special affinity for this program because of their visual thinking. Therefore it provides a remarkable outlet for expressing creativity and developing lifelong art skills. This has since evolved into Project Spectrum, a joint effort between Google, the Autism Society of America and the Lifelong Learning Laboratory of the University of Colorado (http://sketchup.google.com/spectrum.html).

Also, for those individuals who are artistically talented but who *do not* display an "uncanny" memory for detail, one simple technique used to train this ability is "blind drawing." Have the student look at a subject for about five minutes, then remove the subject or turn away from the subject and have the student draw what he or she remembers. When the drawing is completed, compare the subject to the image that was drawn. This "blind drawing technique" is used to "train the artist's eye" to increase memorization beyond an average glance.

At some point you may want to create a defined work space for the artist by perhaps setting up a drawing table or drafting table on which to mount the paper for drawing in order to control the drawing surfaces better. Have all of the supplies organized in the delineated space. Depending upon the types of materials you are using, you may have to consider ventilation and lighting issues when deciding upon a defined space. Some paints have noxious smells, and varied lighting (as when near a window) may become an issue when shading or tones of the artwork being created are important factors.

Eventually you may want to organize and create a portfolio of works which can showcase the talent and be used to present the artwork to gallery owners and potential employers as discussed below. Consider your presentation mediums: slides, transparencies, prints, miniature prints, digital media, and others. Keep in mind that Temple Grandin herself has stated that her "work" and not her "self" were promoted during her initial search of employment opportunities. The *portfolio* was the key.

"I am a parent of a four-year-old boy who was just diagnosed with autism last year. He has begun to show a great talent in art, and he loves his music (specifically the drums). His art has been surprising me and amusing me. His speech is very limited, as he mainly uses echolalia. This is all very overwhelming!"

The message is to "train the talent." Let's hope that when your son is in school, instead of educators limiting or denying him from engaging in activities—utilizing the drums or specific art medium for example—they will understand the importance of nurturing his interests to develop further his overall knowledge, abilities, interests and language. It may prove very beneficial to try to pinpoint the characteristics of his current interests and then apply those characteristics to a wider array of situations and activities. With regard to his speech, it may have surprising results to require some "manding" behavior to request his "art supplies." Speech lessons should focus on having your son mand (request) the "red" paint, the "blue" paint, etc. Given that at this point you have mentioned that his speech is very limited, I would recommend implementing the above with an "errorless" training method. You want to be careful *not* to extinguish his talent in art by requiring that he "request" his art materials. Therefore, in an errorless method, he would receive the items whether the request was made or not, but the experiences are "planted" for whenever he is "ready" to use the language being taught.

"What about formal art training? Is it useful and what might be accomplished?"

Most savant artists begin as "self-taught" artists, simply meaning that they did not initially receive any formal art instruction. The talents are perhaps innate but none-theless untrained. For such artists and emerging artists it is always a good idea to proceed with some professional art education. Whether they enroll in a beginners' art class or attend a course at a junior university, the experience may prove to be very beneficial. At such programs individuals who paint, draw, sculpt or produce art forms from memory or drawings can learn the fundamentals and basics of art.

Although this is not a necessary step in order to enhance the quality of the individuals, art, the enormous amount of information learned can indeed create new avenues of exploration for the talented individual. The following are basic fundamentals that are generally taught in art education programs: color theory, color composition, basic drawing, tracing, copying, basic tenets of size, perspective, depth, illumination, basic shapes and lines, creating tone, wet vs. dry media, matting and framing, and appropriate preparation of a work space.

A formal education within these areas of instruction can help to expand the artist's existing interests beyond his or her initial subject of interest. Below is a list of some of the "relevant" options that could present new opportunities for growth as an artist:

- *Categories*: figure drawing, portrait art, caricatures, mixed media, cartooning, collage, woodworking, and digital media, engraving, photography, computer graphics, architectural design.

- *Media*: pen, ink, watercolor, oils, pastels, acrylics, charcoal, crayons, markers, graphite, chalks, sepia; in addition each of these has its own set of techniques for appropriate application.

- *Types of brushes*: round brushes, flat brushes, fan brush, types of knives (e.g. palette knife).

- *Canvas*: boards, various paper textures, parchment, Bristol boards, hot press, etc.

There is so much to learn and be exposed to! Formal training experiences can result in gains for the savant individual in both practical experience and historical perspective, while also widening the available pool of employment opportunities. Options may include work as an animator, illustrator, painter or cartoonist. Positions may be obtainable in publishing, marketing, motion picture industry, teaching, television, computer software or printing, etc. Freelance or contract work opportunities are also possibilities, as well as self-employment or behind the scenes involvement via online commission opportunities.

Various resources on formal art education training are available through a search on the Internet. Check ratings when possible to obtain legitimate learning aids. Art kits for drawing or sculpting, video art tutorials with toll-free instructional support, as well as interactive online art schools that teach drawing and painting techniques are readily available to sharpen an individual's skills.

"What avenues are available for sharing savant artwork with others?"

There are many avenues one can pursue in order to create further opportunities for exposure and participation of existing art talent and art savant ability. Some suggestions follow on how a parent, educator or mentor can go about exploring possibilities for the artistically gifted individual:

- Search your community for opportunities to enter into group exhibitions.
- Consider featuring artwork in an "outsider" or folk art festival.
- Enroll in art camps.
- Take courses at a local program.
- Enter artwork in a poster contest or art contests.
- Submit a brief bio to autism magazines, mainstream magazines.
- Donate an artwork and associate yourself with foundations and charities.
- Contact autism agencies, galleries, museums.
- Enter the artwork in special art exhibits (e.g. the website http://rcmautismnotebook.com displays artwork of some savants and also offers artists with autism opportunities for participation in special art exhibitions).
- Seek representation through a promoter who can create awareness about your work without the fees of a gallery representative.

- Finally, share the information about the artfully skilled individual by taking advantage of the media and technological advances available for networking. Exhaust (with caution and selectively) such contacts as newspapers, e-blasts, YouTube and newsletters. Be as creative as possible in finding ways to increase visibility and create opportunities for exposure of the individual's works and talents.

"Are there any special considerations for teaching art to persons on the spectrum?"

Some children with autism possess extremely limited attention span and thus are often off-task. Teaching art will require incorporating a very structured setting and a supportive environment to address the specific needs, strengths and deficits of each student individually. In general a rich reinforcement schedule (one that is motivating to the individual) will be necessary to gain the individual's attention. Using a token economy to reward specific task accomplishments will be beneficial toward increasing time on task incrementally.

For younger students, art can be used to develop fine motor skills and increase attention span. For older students, art can aid to develop self-expression, while promoting problem-solving skills, and increasing opportunities for self-empowerment and improved self-esteem. Many parents have attested to improvements in some of the above once their child began creating art independently.

However, given the generally common deficits of autism including eye contact, social awareness, play skills and verbal behavior coupled with commonly encountered troublesome behaviors (self-stimulatory stereotypy, aggression, self-injury) there are various other considerations that are often necessary when teaching art to individuals on the autism spectrum.

Hypersensitivity to certain sensory stimuli is a common occurrence among individuals with autism. The individual may be overwhelmed by certain lights, touch, temperatures, textures or sound and feel over stimulated. This "sensory overload" can result in sensory defensiveness by the autistic individual. Exposure to certain items may cause anxiety and result in a general avoidance of contact with that particular item. Sensory defensiveness may be exhibited as tantrum behavior or withdrawal from the immediate environment (including those people within it). When possible it is best to reduce extraneous sensory stimuli and to strategically create an individualized "working" environment.

Tactile defensiveness which is an extreme sensitivity to anything touching the skin is very often seen with materials such as clay and fingerpaints. This "sensitivity" can be overcome by introducing a behavioral tactic known as *desensitization* (sometimes referred to as graduated exposure therapy). Gradually introducing the art materials which the individual perceives as odious can help the child to become desensitized to the smell, look and/or texture of the art items involved. Whether the defensiveness is to olfactory, visual or tactile stimuli, a desensitization procedure can be implemented to decrease the anxiety produced by initial exposure to such items.

For example, to diminish and overcome tactile defensiveness to clay or finger-paint one can gradually introduce increased amounts of food coloring to regular water and then add paint gradually until the consistency of the water has thickened to that of a fingerpaint. The same procedure can be used with sculpting clays. The idea is to introduce the "offensive" material a little at a time until the individual can accommodate to that which was initially an overload stimulus provoking anxiety. The ultimate goal of a desensitization process is to increase tolerance of the offensive material. This can be very challenging for the individual at first so it is very impor-tant to introduce the changes gradually.

Teaching and learning art should be fun for all. Art classes in schools often use items like sand, sugar, salt (add food coloring!), shaving cream, rice, beans, in order to add texture and interest to the art projects. Any of these items can be used with paints, clays, oils, etc. in order to create bulletin boards, murals, sculptures, etc. An excellent resource for suggestions on activities and inexpensive household materials that can be used to address sensory issues in general is *The Out-of-Sync Child has Fun: Activities for Kids with Sensory Processing Disorder* (Kranowitz 2006).

Individuals with autism are often described as "visual learners" or "visual think-ers." Visual supports can be incorporated into the arts program in the form of pic-tures, logos, photographs, actual three-dimensional objects, written words, and/or symbols used in picture exchange communication systems (Bondy and Frost 2001).

The use of picture schedules can be extremely helpful in promoting independence for setting up an art task or for completion of an art activity. For example, a pictorial sequence of the steps necessary to create a work from start to finish, or a pictorial sequence of a clean-up procedure after painting serve as useful reminders of what to do next. By using picture schedules one can also eventually eliminate the need for instruction or interaction that may not be necessary during a time that should be one of independent creativity and recreation for the individual. The use of task analyses (pictorial or text) for the preparation of the art work space can also be very helpful.

These are just a few ways to motivate and allow the person to eventually proceed with art as independently as possible. A task analyzed approach will more than likely soon become a routine. Given the reliance on predictability in routines for persons with autism, once a routine is established and recalled the visual schedule may no longer be necessary.

Art as a therapy approach is also a recommended and viable option for many children with autism because therapy can target the major deficit areas of autism in treatment sessions. Specific projects, using art, can focus on emotions, abstract thinking, sensory regulation, motor skills and reaching developmental milestones all from a visual perspective. The therapeutic relationship between the therapist and the individual with autism can also help develop social relationships and enhance communication skills. I recently met a parent who very successfully taught his non-verbal son to be able to communicate his emotions and to express himself by enabling him to use his talent in art to create frames of sketches of his daily experiences and feelings. Today, his son is gainfully employed as an animator, and is also able to express himself vocally.

"Can you recommend some inexpensive resources to facilitate training the talent?"

Below is a list of free resources to enhance overall instruction.

Augmentative Communication Devices—Lending Library

Most US states have non-profit foundations which support the lending of resources. Resources range from sensory integration toys, augmentative communication devices, and games or puzzles designed for individuals with disabilities to simple software or low-tech devices. Professionals (and in many states parents) are able to check out a device online and have it delivered to their home or visit designated centers to borrow items.

See www.sandbox-learning.com/default.asp

Boardmaker files

If you have Boardmaker for Windows, you can download these files and print them. They are excellent for communication boards and worksheets and are ready to use.

See www.mayer-johnson.com/products/boardmaker

Spanish Pre-K Special Education Program in Miami-Dade County Public Schools

Download communication boards and picture symbols in Spanish!

See http://prekese.dadeschools.net/BMD/activityspecific.html

Hiyah.net

This website has software for children who want to use the computer but cannot as yet use a keyboard. The downloads include steps to go to the doctor or dentist, get a haircut, and the holidays.

See www.hiyah.net/software.html

Symbolworld.org

This website has story books, nursery rhymes, social stories, etc. totally done in picture symbol format. You can get great ideas to create your own personalized symbol books.

See www.symbolworld.org/stories/index.htm

Picture Planner

You can create activity-based picture schedules with Picture Planner, which is an icon (picture) based scheduling system that assists individuals with disabilities in planning activities by the day, week, or month. Picture Planner uses synthesized speech to provide feedback and aid in accessibility. You can import pictures from any source. Picture Planner also includes a stock library of images.

See www.eugeneresearch.org/picture_planner/intro.html

The TV Teacher (Writing)—ALPHABEATS

This DVD, created by a mom, Susan Ellis, and occupational therapist, Marnie Danielson, uses a multisensory approach to teach children how to write the alphabet.

See www.tvteachervideos.com/index.html

Write-On Handwriting: free demo

The Write-On Handwriting products are developmentally sound; they are supported by research as well as years of experience teaching individuals and groups. Since handwriting is a complex skill, it was essential to incorporate well-recognized developmental components into the handwriting instruction plan. Two key developmental skills are incorporated: the graphomotor function (sequencing pencil movements) and the retrieval memory function.

See www.writeonhandwriting.com/

National Library of Virtual Manipulatives

Includes free downloads in numbers and operations, algebra, geometry, measurement and even data analysis and probability. All levels and downloads are also available in Spanish.

See http://nlvm.usu.edu/en/nav/vlibrary.html

School Arts Support Initiative

In New York City, the School Arts Support Initiative (SASI) is a school-based program designed to help underserved New York City middle schools develop, enhance and sustain instruction in and through the arts. This partnership of the Center for Arts Education (CAE), the New York Times Company Foundation and the New York City Department of Education has resulted in a program of "Teaching Artists" who work with classes on a weekly basis. You may be able to find out what schools or universities may have developed partnerships with an arts program in your state or country.

Conclusion

For young children who show a specific interest in art (whether precocious or savant), it is most important to create further learning opportunities and areas of interest for the child. One must nurture this interest in art by including aspects of the art across as many other domain areas as possible. Whatever the talent, individuals with savant syndrome should be given continued encouragement and enriched opportunities to explore their specific areas of interest.

Grandin and Duffy (2004) recommend that parents and educators focus on "developing emerging talents to their fullest potential." Emphasis should be placed on the individual's strengths. Recent research encourages "training the talent" not only for increases in self-esteem of the individual but also for the attainment of employable skills for the future. Today there is much more awareness of the fact that persons with Asperger syndrome have excellent potential for being good employees given their strengths in attention to details. In addition traits such as punctuality, reliability and less likelihood of socializing during work hours would be considered "assets" to any employer.

Specifically in the area of autistic savants, developing such opportunities may teach autistic spectrum individuals functional and appropriate ways to enjoy leisure time. It can provide them with alternatives to seeking automatic reinforcement through self-stimulatory behaviors by creating and expanding interest in the arts. It can empower student-initiated creativity in a teacher directed environment.

The overall goal is to teach individuals to have fun and be fulfilled while appropriately participating and learning skills that can ultimately be available to them in the natural environment on a daily basis. Given continued encouragement and enriched opportunities to explore other areas using the specific "interest area" as a vehicle can strengthen the individual's ability to express and create. The long-term outcome may be one in which utilizing an individual's strengths and interests results in increased development of overall knowledge and an artist with a great knowledge base.

About the author

Rosa C. Martinez has been working in the field of autism since 1983. She has a BSc in special education from City College of New York, a Master's degree in adolescent autism, a Masters of Philosophy and a Doctorate in Behavioral Disorders from Columbia University. Dr. Martinez is also a board certified behavior analyst. She has managed art exhibits—"Don't 'dis' the Ability"—in New York, Washington, DC and cities in California.

CHAPTER 27

Teaching Autistic Numerical Savants: A Specific Approach that Worked

Peter Lewis

Like music and art skills, advanced mathematical abilities have been consistently reported in the repertoire of savant skills from the earliest descriptions. In the first formal account of savant syndrome, Down (1887) describes several cases "where the power of mental arithmetic existed to an astonishing degree." In his classic chapter on savants, Tredgold (1914) comments on the "extraordinary capacity for arithmetic and calculation" and gives many examples of these special skills. There are many other instances of savants' exceptional mathematical abilities such as "lightning calculating" of addition, subtraction, multiplication, division, prime numbers, squaring, square roots, algebra and geometry problems (Smith 1983; Treffert 2006a).

Critchley (1979) in his description of Fleury, a lightning calculator, shows just how extensive such mathematical abilities can be. Smith (1983) provides this account of Fleury's remarkable skills during 1927 testing at the International Psychical Institute in France:

2 to the 30th power=1,073,741,824 was given as an answer in 40 seconds. Fleury was asked for the values of x and y in $x + y$=707,353,209 where x and y are integers and y had to have four digits. In 28 seconds, he found 891 to the third power + 5,238. In a second such problem, he was given 211,717,440 and came up with 596 to the third power + 8,704 in 25 seconds. When asked, Fleury expressed 6,137 as the sum of four squares. The first answer, given in 2 minutes 10 seconds, was 74 squared + 20 squared + 15 squared + 6 squared. The second

answer was given 10 seconds later: 78 + 6 + 4 + 1 each squared. A third answer was obtained after 1 minute and 20 seconds: 76 + 15 + 10 + 6, each squared. (p.338)

Fleury determined the cube root of 465,484,375 (which is 775) in 13 seconds. He was also a prodigious calendar calculator in both the Julian and Gregorian calendars.

Certainly still today the mathematical savant's remarkable behavior, such as calendar counting, prime number recall, and their uncanny ability to make detailed integer calculations, impresses those who witness it as well. Just as often, it gives rise to the intriguing idea that somehow this extraordinary capability if channeled properly might help autistic individuals achieve progress in their educational and social goals. It raises the question whether these individuals just might be demonstrating a hidden talent or intelligence we all have but is somehow dormant and unused.

As a practical benefit to the mathematical savant, certain educational and socialization efforts tend to transform or spread out narrowly focused numerical abilities into a broader intelligence. This raises the questions of "how much and by what means" can a savant's numerical ability be leveraged to help accelerate his or her progress. Considering how important these skills are to the savant, it is reasonable for there to be some concern these efforts might improve the savant's overall abilities and adjustment at the cost of diminishing the special skills. This has not been the general experience.

There are several books on useful approaches to "train the talent" in savants with music or art skills. There are none I know of for doing the same with mathematical savants. Therefore this account of how an individual savant's mathematical interests and abilities incorporated as part of his general educational program helped this individual progress can be useful as a model for developing ways to help other such individuals.

Engaging and helping Max: the invention of some exercises

Some years ago, I found myself across the kitchen table from a young man aged 15, whose name, for the purposes of this account, will be Max. His family and caregivers consider Max to be a high-functioning autistic (HFA) individual with a longstanding interest in calendars and computers.

At the time of my first meeting, Max was attending a private school specializing in special needs education and receiving Institute for Applied Behavior Analysis (IABA) behavioral therapy. California based, IABA has provided since 1981 a variety of services for individuals with autism, which are best described on their website: www.iaba.com. Max is a generally pleasant young man. While he has made great progress from a combination of a loving family environment, and focused educational and behavioral therapy programs, most people would recognize Max as an autistic individual. What most people would not perhaps understand is that Max is also a numerical savant. Max often demonstrated his fascination with numbers to his family and he was encouraged to develop his interest in various numerical skills. These skills, described below, are not those of a prodigious savant. Instead Max's skills are a more muted form commonly seen in many autistic individuals.

When I first engaged Max in conversation, he wanted to know what year and day I was born. At first, I thought this was just the way autistic individuals communicated with strangers they knew to be family friends. When I told him, Max responded with my correct age in years, months and days. He did nothing more with this information. I am sure if I had told Max the exact time of day of my birth, Max might have changed his answer to include hours and minutes. Aside from obtaining these essential facts, Max initially showed little interest in anything else I had to say or do. While Max's calendar counting ability was to say the least intriguing, I thought perhaps there might be other numerical skills present as well.

I am an engineer and like many of my profession, I feel very comfortable thinking in numbers and seeing the world from a mathematical perspective. So when I found myself alone with Max for a few minutes, I decided on a whim to explore the bounds of his ability. I asked Max if he might be interested in learning a math trick. Max, who had previously maintained his distance from me, drew in very close to me and appeared completely focused. I got the feeling my offer intrigued him as much as his skills did me. My math trick was an explanation of the Ramanujan number, a somewhat famous number, if only among mathematicians and puzzle enthusiasts.

Were it not for a published and often recounted anecdote written over a hundred years ago by Professor G.H. Hardy in his book *A Course of Pure Mathematics* (1993, first published 1908), a conversation he had with the gravely ill Ramanujan, nobody would have known or cared about this number. Ramanujan, arguably the most famous Indian mathematician and indeed one of the world's most important mathematicians, who some say also may have been a savant, asked Hardy why he was late. Hardy complained he was delayed by his cab. Ramanujan asked, "What was the cab's number?" Hardy replied, "1729" and commented he thought the number as boring as his cab ride. Not so, Ramanujan pointed out. This number was a very interesting one, as it happened to be the smallest sum of two different cubed numbers. Soon after, mathematicians began calling this number the Ramanujan number.

Such number oddities or mathematical curios are an enjoyable pastime of math enthusiasts. I did my best to explain this curio, cubic numbers and a little something about Ramanujan to Max. Max's intensely focused demeanor was of someone wanting to convey the impression, "This is my field and here is something I need to know, please continue and leave nothing out." Now I am not sure Max understood cubic numbers or higher math any better when I finished than before I began the discussion. What I did discover was how easy it was to engage and hold his complete attention. I was to find out later that recasting this sort of story to Max is a very effective way to reach him.

Later when I related this encounter to his mother, I learned his family and teachers had known about Max's evident numeric preoccupation for a long time, but aside from encouraging his interest in computers and commenting on his ability to remember dates, could think of little else to do with it. His mother had tried for years with no avail to persuade his teachers to do something productive with Max's skills.

I did some research on autistic individuals and came across accounts of savants. I thought that if the 1729 curio was interesting to the one savant I knew, such things might just be interesting to others. Surely, considering the high percentage of numerical savants among the autistic population, I thought there must be several commercial programs available that took advantage of savant skills. As a courtesy to Max and his family (and to satisfy my own curiosity), I spent a little time reading and searching the web about savants and for educational materials suitable for them.

The birth of Exercise 1 (EX-1)

I did learn some useful things about savants, but much to my dismay, I found there were no commercially or otherwise available educational materials specifically for numerical savants. I decided to do some thinking, look through my library and ask my colleagues for some ideas. After about a month of this, the best I could come up with was a novel game that I later called the "Mystery of the Five Card Decks." This game along with a few simple puzzles and stories became Exercise 1 or EX-1. Max later would refer to this and the two others I created as "EXs." I sent a final draft of EX-1 to Dr. Treffert for comment because I wanted to make sure EX-1 would not do harm. I contacted Max's family and sent them the EX for their approval as well. The family intended that his IABA instructor, who had a long association with Max, would deliver the EX to him.

As I thought Max might not remember me, EX-1 began with a picture of me and his older sister taken in front of his house. The text continued with a display of a 20-digit integer and a question. Did Max think he could memorize this number in five seconds? The next question was did he think anyone he knew could? My text explained that while it might be very easy for him, it would be impossible for most everyone else. I explained that the reason for this is people think in words and not in numbers. Savants like himself love to think in numbers and that is why it is easy for him to memorize 20-digit numbers. This explanation went over very well with Max.

EX-1 continued by showing Max how the 20-digit number is translatable into a word by assigning each pair of numbers to a letter. Included in EX-1 was a strip table that showed how each letter mapped to each number pair. Thus 01 was A, 02 was B and so on. By doing this, Max translated the 28-digit number into the word "transportation," a word he saw every day on his school van.

This was I thought a clever way to introduce the mathematic operation of translation and number to letter codes. My text included simple activities, which asked Max to translate short poems into numbers and numbers into sentences. To the amazement of his family, Max had apparently already learned how to translate letters into numbers himself. Soon his mother took to writing brief notes in numbers to Max, who thought this was very amusing and evidently had no trouble understanding.

The next part of EX-1 began as a question: "Would Max like to solve a mystery using his new math skills?" This led to the mystery of the five decks of cards. In this series of activities, Max explores five decks for differences using the math technique called sampling.

The first deck of cards was an unaltered "correct" deck. The text of EX-1 asks Max to examine the deck of cards closely and count the number of cards, the names of each card and the pattern formed by randomly sampling the deck in five-card hands. For each hand, the EX-1 activity asks Max to mark, with a highlighter marker on a sampling sheet, which cards made up the hand. The sampling sheet has each card's image printed in an ordered grid.

Throughout the activity, EX-1 warns Max repeatedly not to look at the whole deck of cards, but to try to figure out what was wrong with "the bad decks" by looking at only the five cards in the hands. After marking the cards on the sheet, the activity continues with Max shuffling the deck to make a new hand. Each activity's instructions took the form of numerical lists, something Max was quite familiar with from his school and IABA experiences. After several repeats the resulting random patterns gave Max a pretty good idea of what a number deck of cards might produce. At first, Max had some trouble shuffling the cards, but after a while he became comfortable with this new skill.

I sorted the next two decks, called "the bad decks," so that all the red cards were in one deck and all the black cards were in the other. The activity instructions ask Max to repeat his sampling and try to figure out how these decks differed from the first "correct" deck. After some initial confusion, Max came up with the correct answers. He was quite excited about this.

I altered the next two "bad decks" so all of the cards from Ace to seven were in one deck and all the cards from eight to King were in the other. The instructions asked Max to shake the decks to see if he could notice a difference. He responded that the fourth deck did not feel the same as the others. This deck was overstuffed and this intrigued him. Max figured out what was wrong with the fourth deck of cards quickly following the steps and looking at the pattern on the sampling sheet. What happened next was unusual and important.

Max grew confident he knew what was wrong with the fifth deck. Despite being asked repeatedly not to look at the entire card decks, Max decided to cheat. Right after he finished the fourth deck, during a break when his IABA instructor left him alone, Max opened the fifth deck and to his delight, saw his guess was right.

While one expects this "cheating" from many students, one does not expect this from an autistic student. It meant Max had used his new understanding of sampling to make a prediction about something. It also meant by tapping into his interest in math, Max could be encouraged to learn new things. These kinds of positive developments continued throughout the delivery of the EXs. Max's reaction to EX-1 was very positive. I decided to write another. I started with a simple idea and expanded it outward to include other things. Since the single EX-1 picture worked well and helped Max feel comfortable, I decided to use more pictures.

Two more exercises: EX-2 and EX-3

Eventually I created two more exercises, EX-2 and EX-3. These greatly expanded on the basic idea of using math-based mysteries and puzzles in helping improve Max's reading, writing, critical thinking and social skills. I used as source materials *Excursions in Number Theory* by Ogilvy and Anderson (1998) and Newman's *The World of Mathematics* (1956) as well as a variety of other math puzzle books. I took basic information on instructing and handling autistic individuals from *Handbook of Learning Disabilities* (Swanson, Harris and Graham 2005) and *Handbook of Autism and Pervasive Developmental Disorders* (Volkmar, Klin and Graham 2005). Dr. Treffert patiently shared his experience, reviewed the EXs and offered much needed encouragement.

Each EX begins with an overview letter explaining what the EX will contain complete with hints and other things designed to encourage Max to explore the text. I passed on all positive comments I received from his family and IABA professionals and generally added some of my own. All these helped Max feel comfortable about starting a new EX, something he seemed to be unsure about initially but after a time grew very comfortable with.

All mysteries start with simple questions and gradually expand outward into a broader series of questions, skill demonstrations and explanations. Each puzzle can be solved with some form of counting, a basic skill which numerical savants often excel at and are generally comfortable. The puzzles are not trivial however. These puzzles are constructed to simultaneously teach math, reading, general problem solving and reinforce appropriate behavior. The answers to the puzzles are interesting tricks or math facts which Max was encouraged to explain or relate to others.

Using the exercise books

An IABA professional with long experience with Max delivered the EXs. This professional adjusted the delivery of EXs to suit Max's learning style and behavior very effectively. The two latter EXs included feedback from Max's IABA professional, teachers, therapists and parents from the first EX. This greatly improved the EX effectiveness for Max.

Overall the EXs look like a cross between an illustrated storybook and a standard textbook. Throughout, the EXs adopted many of the common textbook features and made as many accommodations to Max's specific needs. For example, because Max liked to redo activities, overhead transparency sheets were inserted over many pages so Max could easily do activities again. Max was encouraged to write on the plastic pages using dry erasable pens. To accommodate his color preferences, the EX text is printed on pastel light green or cream paper using oversized blue or dark green type.

Throughout the EXs, the writing style is conversational. I used colors routinely and symbols like stop signs to alert Max to important concepts. To maintain Max's attention, at regular intervals, I addressed Max by first name and asked simple questions. The IABA instructor periodically refocused Max by asking for responses to these questions and by simply using his name.

The text and the instructor routinely encouraged and praised Max regularly for his work. When appropriate, I also used simple cueing techniques to help reinforce important skills. I used items, such as playing cards, compasses, coins, special dice and rulers, with obvious mathematical aspects as parts of the puzzles. The EX text teaches Max how best to use these items. Throughout the EX, he is encouraged to make predictions or "very good guesses" about what the solution to a puzzle might be. At the end of each EX, Max gets a certificate of completion.

Important features of the EXs are the pictures and brief stories spread throughout the text. The pictures help to introduce a new concept and are part of a deliberate process of evoking Max's positive emotions. Following the ideas used widely to teach autistic individuals social skills, I adapted stories about famous mathematicians from Newman's work. For example, I recast a story of Carl Gauss, the famous mathematician, who as young boy managed to dazzle his classmates by quickly solving a hard problem none of his classmates could. Besides explaining how this problem was solved, I wanted Max to understand how Gauss might have felt. The overall goal was to use math-based stories to help Max understand how other people think and feel about everyday situations.

During the EX delivery, other activities were tried, including tapping into Max's counting skills to learn something about poetry. The activity begins with Max counting lines and words and noticing patterns, expands into an understanding of the poems, and concludes with a confident recitation before his family.

In an effort to foster an interest in newspapers, one activity explains how to play Sudoku. The idea was to get Max to look for puzzles in newspaper and while he was doing this, to use the opportunity to teach him something about newspapers. Max now plays Sudoku quite well and is more comfortable with newspapers.

In EX-3, Max was introduced to Hergé's famous teenage reporter, Tintin, in the graphic novel *The Shooting Star* (Hergé 1978). Here the EX introduces x and y coordinates to Max and uses the concept to work through the picture frames in the

Tintin book. Max's mission is to record the "who, what, why, where, when and how" of each frame in a list and discuss what he thought was happening. This combination of counting and list making appeared to help with his reading comprehension. The clear line artwork in the Tintin books may also have helped. After some initial difficulty, Max caught on and enjoyed reading the story.

In EX-2 and EX-3, the text leads Max to explore rooms in his house and notice number patterns in flowers and trees. On short walks around his neighborhood, Max recorded such numerical data as the number of cars, mailboxes and children he saw on his walks. By carefully examining Google Earth maps, Max learned things about places close to his home and those he had visited on vacations.

These activities always involved some counting, measuring and data recording. The goal is to help him to uncover numerical patterns. In several of the activities, Max writes brief stories or, as they came to be called, "field reports" of his adventures. Partly as a result of these activities, Max's reading, writing and problem-solving skills as well as his confidence improved.

The importance of family support and participation

An integral part of each EX was family participation. At regular intervals, the text asked Max to get the opinions of his parents, caregivers and siblings on the solutions to problems or events described in each EX. Additionally, pictures of family members in familiar settings are found throughout the EXs. Often these pictures include him doing something related to an EX activity. Some of these pictures introduce an activity, while others are woven into puzzles.

As part of the EX, the text asked Max to take additional pictures of himself or his family. Max was aware these pictures were for future EXs; but exactly how these new pictures were to be used was kept as a friendly mystery to Max. Throughout the text he was asked to make "very good guesses" how these pictures might be used in the upcoming EX.

Although he found some of the work hard to complete, Max consistently did his best to complete all the activities and did so very well. This effort was not a scientific study, so there are no precise results to report, but Max did seem to improve his reading, writing, mathematics and problem-solving abilities in part due to his participation. His overall behavior improved and to this day Max often remembers things he did during the EXs and openly expresses his happiness and satisfaction with the EXs.

Some substantial progress

Max graduated from high school in 2008. He is now in the second year of the UCLA Pathways program. The Pathways Program is an experimental program designed in part to help special needs students develop their independence. Max's adjustment to the program has generally been good. He enjoys the positive support of the faculty, residence hall supervisors and other students. It is thought that by paying closer attention to the specific learning patterns of savants, perhaps caregivers and instructors will find new ways to help this population.

About the author

Peter Lewis is a professional engineer with a lifelong interest in mathematics, art and literature. His professional work often involves the management of overseas engineering projects and coordinating the efforts of geographically dispersed project teams. His interest in autism started with his involvement with Max and has steadily grown since. The exercises described above are available from Dr. Treffert on request.

PART FIVE

Our Journey Has Just Begun

CHAPTER 28

New Tools and New Optimism: The Trail Ahead for the *Mind* of the Savant

The years since the late 1980s have provided more insights into savant syndrome and the vast implications it has for better understanding brain function and human potential overall than the 100 years prior. Yet the later years of the twentieth century tended to focus primarily on advances in better understanding and treating cardiac disease, including heart transplants unthinkable in prior times. In that sense those years could be called the "era of the heart." In contrast, without doubt, the years ahead in this twenty-first century will be known as the "era of the brain" with monumental advances on this last, and most impenetrable, frontier of the human body.

The brain is the most complex organ in the body. It is also the most difficult to visualize directly since it sits entirely surrounded by a bony box—the skull—that securely contains and protects it. It cannot be "scoped" like the gastrointestinal, genito-urinary, eye-ear-nose-throat or skeletal systems. Nor can it be easily biopsied like other organs. Certainly CT and MRI scans have been immense improvements over the skull films, which were all that was available when I began my medical career. But even those new images, spectacularly detailed as they are, provide pictures of brain *structure* only. However, so much of CNS neurophysiology and neuropathology is a matter of brain *function*, not brain architecture. Consequently additional techniques have been developed, including functional MRI and magneto-encephalography to monitor the brain "at work." Simultaneously more sophisticated and standardized neuropsychological test batteries have also evolved to permit more precise assessment of brain function using those tools. These are very recent developments in neuroscience and in that sense our voyage into more fully understanding brain function has really just begun. But the voyage ahead, using these recently available tools, and even newer developing technologies, will take us further than we have ever been in the full exploration and utilization of the unique window into the brain that savant syndrome provides.

What's ahead? These are some of my predictions.

Improved imaging and other new technologies

Functional imaging techniques (fMRI, PET, SPECT) certainly hold great promise for better visualizing brain function in any populations studied. But savant syndrome is rare, so carrying out group studies instead of single case investigations has been difficult. As more cases of savant syndrome surface, and as additional interested research teams become involved, studies involving groups of savants, and control subjects for comparisons, will become more frequent.

Furthermore, new techniques have been added to the imaging arsenal. Diffusion tensor imaging (DTI) and diffusion tensor tracking (DTT or "fiber tracking") are methods that measure water flow *in* neurons rather than blood flow *to* those neurons. Measurement of neuronal water flow is more immediate and precise than blood flow and DTI can provide detailed pictures of brain "connectivity" between hemispheres, within hemispheres and between upper level brain function and lower level brain function. Autistic disorder, some have proposed, is perhaps a disorder of connectivity so these new techniques provide a way to assess that dimension of CNS function and dysfunction (Casanova and Trippe 2009). With fiber tracking it is possible to view the actual fibers connecting various areas of the brain rather than inferring connectivity based on blood flow. It is like taking the lid off the computer and viewing the circuits and connections directly. Such studies with savants, prodigies and geniuses thus far are few but certainly many more will follow.

Magnetoencephalography (MEG) measures minute magnetic currents in the functioning brain. It is similar to electroencephalograpy (EEG) except that the skull and soft tissue surrounding the brain affect the magnetic fields much less as measured by MEG than they affect the electrical currents as measured by EEG. Therefore MEG provides more accuracy of the signal because there is less distortion compared to EEG signals. This permits more usable and reliable localization of brain function. MEG can measure "event related potentials" (ERPs), which are very early components of brain activity, reflecting initial, "pre-conscious" stages of mental processing which contrasts sharply with that seen when higher level "executive" functioning is occurring. Birbaumer (1999) compared ERPs of a "human calculator"—a non-autistic arithmetic whiz—to same-age, IQ-matched, healthy controls. Compared to controls, the expert calculator showed "enhanced automatic low level processing" as measured by ERPs.

Studies are now underway with autistic savant calculators to see whether this particular type of early, automatic processing ("without reckoning") is the same as that used by the non-autistic expert calculators. It is my prediction that results will show that savant calculators have access to, and use, the same "pre-conscious" circuitry as expert ("genius") non-savant calculators.

Neuman and co-workers (2009) in Germany have carried out MEG and neuropsychological studies on eight mnemonist savants and eight control subjects which so far suggested a different memory organization in mnemonist savants characterized by its relative independence of general intelligence (personal communication).

One problem in studying savant skills is that it is difficult to play a piano, sculpt or draw in an MRI machine. Yet meaningful comparisons of brain function between persons with savant skills and control subjects need to be done with both groups "at work" rather than at rest. While calendar or lightning calculating do lend themselves to use of screen projections while in an MRI machine, many persons with such savant skills have difficulty following instructions or lying perfectly still for long periods of time. To offset such limitations, there is a new technique called Near Infrared Spectroscopy (NIRS) which measures oxygenated hemoglobin flow in the brain using a non-invasive, easily applied and comfortable skull cap (Bunce *et al.* 2006). This technique is used extensively in the newborn nursery to measure cerebral oxygenated hemoglobin levels while the child is held in his or her mother's arms rather than being in an MRI machine. It also has been used to study cerebral activation during an executive language task as one example of applicability to adults (Jayakar *et al.* 2005). Gratton *et al.* (2007) are using functional NIRS for language mapping in children, adults and special populations. Functional NIRS is not as vulnerable to movement artifact as some other methods of study, so perhaps it will lend itself to brain blood flow monitoring of savants "at work" such as calculating, playing an instrument or sculpting compared to control subjects. The limitation of NIRS is that it measures principally cortical blood flow in contrast to functional MRI, which can measure activity in deeper brain structures.

"Modern day phrenology": a risk and a caution

These newer imaging techniques are extremely useful and promising. However, just as there is the understandable wish on the part of the public and the press to find "the" gene responsible for autism, there is an equal hope, for sake of simplicity, to locate "the" spot on the fMRI scan responsible for all sorts of behaviors, emotions and disorders.

So I put forth this caveat when assessing such imaging studies and reports. Brain function is extraordinarily complex, with intricate interconnections and interaction among the brain areas even with the simplest of tasks. Yet almost daily stories on news networks or in newspapers announce that researchers have now discovered "the" single site of love, lying, guilt, addiction, obesity, sleep, conscience, creativity, success and pleasure, to name a few. There have been efforts in the past to locate the neurological "God Spot" in the brain using imaging techniques. One study regarding such a search was reported in the *Proceedings of the National Academy of Sciences* (Kapogiannis *et al.* 2009). The media headlines regarding that study read "Scientists locate 'God Spot' in human brain," of course, even though the article concludes that while specific components of religious belief are mediated by well-known brain networks, no single "God Spot" exists in the brain. Another study searches for the "seat of wisdom" in the brain (Meeks and Jeste 2009). That study likewise finds no single site of "wisdom" but rather involves various parts of the "old" and "new" brain.

My problem with those "single site" studies, attractive as they are, is a very basic one. How do you create a very specific, delineated, standardized "God" or "wisdom" or "lying" neuronal trigger spot, or how do you identify those abstract concepts precisely enough in qualitative terms, let alone attempting to measure it quantitatively with neuroimaging techniques? Scholars have difficulties agreeing on definitions and parameters of such concepts philosophically so it seems a stretch to locate these to single sites neurologically.

With those studies comes the perpetual hope that having found "the" sleep center or "the" obesity center of the brain, for example, one could attack such well-localized centers with precisely targeted pharmacologic or other methods and cure sleep and obesity disorders.

Not so fast.

Our search to pinpoint complex behaviors to single sites in the brain threatens to become what could be called "modern day phrenology." Instead of measuring bumps on the head and assigning certain functions to those areas, as was done in the distant past, nowadays we look for single brain locations that "light up" with certain stimuli, declaring those to be "the" site for all sorts of functions, dysfunctions and disorders. It is an attractive, but far too simplistic approach. Thus when I speak about right brain/left brain dichotomy for example, I am fully aware the brain is not neatly divided down the middle, even though we use the term "split brain" in certain kinds of research. Rather while it is true that the right brain and left brain do specialize in certain functions, there are still ample cross-connections between those hemispheres, as demonstrated by DTI scans. Certainly attributes such as trust, disorders such as addiction, emotions such as love and processes such as creativity involve multiple areas of brain activity, not single sites.

I am not alone in my concerns. Vul *et al.* (2009) at Massachusetts Institute of Technology and the University of California, San Diego surveyed 55 articles that used fMRI techniques to study emotion, personality and social cognition. They concluded:

> a disturbingly large, and quite prominent, segment of fMRI research on emotion, personality and social cognition is using seriously defective research methods and producing a profusion of numbers that should not be believed...we suspect

that the questionable analysis methods discussed here are also widespread in other fields that use fMRI to study individual differences, such as cognitive neuroscience, clinical neuroscience and neurogenetics. (p.285)

They suggest more rigorous attention to research methodology and statistical analysis before studies are published as a way of dealing with these "impossibly high" correlations in these particular areas of study.

Kriegeskorte *et al.* (2009) at NIMH express similar concern and caution after reviewing 134 articles using fMRI techniques in five top science journals. They found problems with 57 of those articles stemming from the "noise" that fMRI produces in terms of false voxels (three-dimensional equivalent of pixels) and failure to correct for that in analyzing results. They likewise suggest more rigorous peer review of such fMRI articles before publication.

There is no single sleep, guilt, love, appetite, addiction, God, wisdom, pleasure or creativity center in the brain. Those are complex emotions and activities that involve multiple interconnections which can no more be detected and depicted by a single image on an fMRI screen than it can by a single "bump" on the skull. We simply need to remain mindful of that.

Brain computer interfaces: the "man machine"

We all have the fantasy that some day we could walk into a room and turn the lights on just by thinking about it as an electronic-age substitute for the "clapper" to trigger the light switch. While that is not possible yet, I did write portions of this book by speaking into a microphone and having the text magically appear on the computer screen, spell check and all, bypassing the middle man of my often errant finger strokes on the computer keyboard. Will it be possible someday to put on a "thinking cap" and have thoughts go directly to the keyboard and screen in some sort of wireless fashion eliminating even the voice and microphone? The mouse and keyboard already correspond wirelessly with my computer. Why not the brain?

Such technology might not be as far off as it seems. At the Fraunhofer Institute in Berlin, Germany, Krepki *et al.* (2007) – have developed the Berlin Brain-Computer Interface (BBCI) which uses a complex computer hookup that allows persons to control devices by just thinking about doing so, bypassing the normal channels of peripheral nerves and muscles. Such an independent brain–computer interface has direct therapeutic application in persons with amyotrophic lateral sclerosis, or quadriplegia due to high spinal cord level injury, for example.

With this device the patient faces a computer screen wearing an EEG-style brain-cap with 128 electrodes connected to four amplifiers and two computers. Multi-channel scalp EEG recordings analyze Bereitschaftspotential (BP/Readiness potential) which precedes voluntary right or left hand finger movements as detected on the corresponding left and right motor cortex. This method exploits "the BP, i.e., a slow negative EEG shift, which develops over the activated motor cortex during a period of about 1 s prior to the actual movement onset" (p.465). The patient, by imagining movement in his or her hand, produces minute brain potentials that can be picked up and then linked to a communication device which moves a computer cursor to write out a message. The specific mechanism by which this works is described in detail in the above article and one can see the man and machine at work very convincingly and dramatically in the *Beautiful Minds* (Colourfield Productions, Germany) program.

The "man machine" potentially could be very helpful to many persons with paralysis using just thoughts to control devices such as a computer, wheelchair or neuroprosthesis. But already others are suggesting a much wider application for this technology. On March 31, 2009, the Honda Motor Company Research Institute in Japan announced that it had developed a Brain–Machine Interface (BMI) technology which enabled control of a robot by human thought alone. Essentially using the same technology as the "man machine" above, a person wearing an electrode-bearing cap thinks about moving his right arm. There are wires connecting the cap to a human-shaped robot named Asimo and, in response, Asimo moves its right arm by thought control only. At this point the Honda-developed Brain–Machine Interface, using a combination of EEG and NIRS sensors in the human cap, can control certain movements in both arms and legs of the robot but work proceeds on broadening that responsiveness just by thinking about it.

A more intrusive version of this "thought control" approach to paralysis exists as well. Moritz, Perlmutter and Fetz (2008) were able to implant an electrode directly into the motor cortex of a monkey and trace the electrical activity of a *single* neuron in that area. A brain–computer interface was used to translate that single neuron impulse into an electrical stimulus which activated a paralyzed wrist muscle in the animal. The need to implant a sensor directly into the brain makes this a very intrusive procedure, but the fact that a single neuron could be harnessed as a signal that could be transmitted through a brain-computer to a peripheral limb makes this research very pertinent.

There are other forms of "Thought Translation Devices" such as those described by Birbaumer and Cohen (2007). These can provide Internet access to a user with a disability. Other types of assistive technology and devices, some computer based and some not, continue to appear on the scene. An excellent Taiwan-based documentary, *Capturing Dreams in the Dark* (2005), shows a young woman who is brain damaged, visually impaired, paralyzed from the neck down and mute from carbon monoxide injury as a ten-year-old girl. With incredible patience and love her mother used certain cards to teach her daughter to be able once again to recognize letters and numbers. Now this young woman can methodically type her poetry on a computer screen letter by letter, using morse code which she patiently strikes out using her forehead to tap two cushions, one for dots and one for dashes. The device is called a U2 communication board. Her vocational goal? To be a writer. Her dogged determination has already yielded 200 wonderfully sensitive poems.

Such technology will surely continue to be a source of valuable assistance to persons with savant syndrome and many other CNS conditions. The "man machine" and U2 communication boards are but two examples of such assistive devices.

One caveat here: there is no controversy surrounding the use of new technology which permits persons with amyotrophic lateral sclerosis (ALS) or CNS injury to use brain waves to communicate via computer or to be more mobile. But suppose rather than an individual directing thoughts to a computer to activate certain helpful devices, software existed that could reverse that process and "read" a person's thoughts or mind? While the good news might be that such techniques could provide a more reliable method of lie detection (Simpson 2008), the bad news is that this same technology could perhaps provide brain imaging ability capable of detecting what a person is thinking about, if not the direct thoughts themselves.

I will leave the dilemmas of such "reverse thought control" to ethical specialists. I mention that ethical dilemma because in the past, particularly in the early 1960s when electrode implantation was being done to control certain kinds of epilepsy, concerns about the ramifications of "thought control" interfered with progressive research in that area at that time. Now such deep electrode implantation is routinely carried out for treatment of a number of otherwise intractable conditions without impediment of "thought control" concerns.

In my view the likelihood of being able to "read" a person's *specific* thoughts or "mind" with some sort of outside device or equipment, given the complexity of the brain and the relative simplicity of our equipment to fully decipher this intricacy, is really non-existent. It makes for interesting novels and science fiction but I think the brain's complexity and intricacy will adequately preserve us from that kind of intrusion.

Brain plasticity and the death of "neurologic nihilism"

My voyage with savants has changed drastically my more pessimistic view of central nervous system renewal and regeneration that I, along with many of my colleagues, mistakenly harbored based on our earlier training. I particularly like psychiatrist Doidge's (2007) term "neurologic nihilism" to describe this now outdated grim view of brain development and recovery.

Just as all other systems in the body, the brain is continually renewing its cells and neurons to replace those dying. The neurons I use to write this sentence are not the same neurons I used when I wrote my earlier book. Yet somehow not only the neurons, but also the information within those expiring neurons, should be transmitted to the new ones in the renewal process. It is through that continuous production and renewal neuronal process that the brain can change and rewire itself in both congenital and acquired savant syndrome, and likewise in traumatic brain injury or stroke.

Eriksson *et al.* demonstrated as early as 1998 "that cell genesis occurs in human brains and that the human brain retains the potential for self-renewal throughout life" (Eriksson *et al.* 1998, p.1315). Shors (2009) provides an update on neuron renewal and raises the possibility that enhancing neurogenesis might help slow cognitive decline. Since brain cell renewal is a continual process, I too have wondered whether it is possible that Alzheimer's or Parkinson's disease might be not so much a process of excessive or accelerated neuronal death as it is a slowdown in neuronal renewal with a net deficit of neuronal numbers. If that is so—impaired cell renewal rather than accelerated cell death—pharmacologic and other treatment approaches would be very different from those presently based on assumptions about cell death, and might hold more promise. That remains to be seen.

On a likewise positive note, stem cell transplantation may provide clusters of new brain cells on which to build and repair in certain conditions whether neuronal deficits are from slowed renewal or accelerated loss. Such research is already underway.

In short, new knowledge about brain plasticity provides better explanations for the development of exceptional skills in savant syndrome and brings a very helpful new optimism to the treatment of a number of central nervous system illnesses and injuries.

Cognitive enhancement, mind expansion and "cosmetic neurology"

According to popular legend, Ponce de Leon was searching for the fountain of youth to cure his aging. Search for that elixir continues as a multibillion dollar industry worldwide with all sorts of supplements, herbs, tinctures, salves, creams, pills and medicaments. At the same time there has been a comparable search for memory enhancers, IQ lifters, mind expanders and cognitive enhancers. Cognitive enhancement is a legitimate treatment goal in certain CNS conditions involving memory preservation and enhancement in dementia, for example.

But there has also been a desire to use some of these products to "enhance" brain performance in anyone interested. Such "brain enhancers" are also a multibillion dollar industry.

Antipsychotic, antidepressant and anti-anxiety medications have been as dramatic a breakthrough in treating some illnesses in psychiatry as antibiotics have been in the treatment of infectious diseases. The usefulness of some stimulant drugs in the treatment of some persons with Attention Deficit Hyperactivity Disorder (ADHD) can likewise be dramatic. Certain medications in the treatment of Alzheimer's or other forms of dementia can slow the process somewhat or provide some cognitive enhancement at least on a temporary basis. Simultaneously there has been a continual search for the perfect "sleeping pill" for insomnia, the perfect "awake pill" for narcolepsy and the perfect "pain pill," all of which would be free of hazardous side effects or dependency.

While these therapeutic explorations continue, there has also been a perpetual search for legal products that might help anyone interested in being smarter, more awake, more creative, more relaxed or more mentally expanded without harmful side effects or dependency. The hazards of illicit substances such as marihuana, cocaine, LSD, methamphetamine and heroin to seek mind expansion or a mind-altering state are well known. Are there safe and legal cognitive enhancers?

Of course the most commonly used cognitive enhancer is caffeine. Debate is perpetual over benefits and hazards to both general health and cognitive enhancement. Like most products use in moderation is recommended.

With respect to the proven usefulness of *over-the-counter* products, herbs and supplements as cognitive enhancers or dementia preventers, evidence has been, to me, less than convincing. Others will vigorously disagree and provide many testimonials. However, that debate rages over the effectiveness of natural products for prevention and remedy in all manner of conditions and maladies.

Regarding *prescription* medications for cognitive enhancement in "normal" individuals, in my experience that transplantation of purpose from treatment of a diagnosed condition to cognitive enhancement has likewise been less than convincing. Many of the prescription products touted to be the "new, non-narcotic analgesics," for example, turn out, eventually, just like many of the newer sleeping medications, to produce dependency or have other disturbing side effects.

An excellent comprehensive review of what is now being called "cosmetic neurology" appeared in *The New Yorker* in April, 2009 (Talbot 2009). Medications such as Adderall, Ritalin and Provigil are being taken for "off-label" use (the use of prescription drugs for other than medically approved indications) by students, employees, poker players, pilots and many others as "awake pills." To what extent these promote actual "cognitive enhancement" beyond promoting simple wakefulness is debatable and there is some evidence they impede, rather than enhance creativity. After a thorough review of the history of these products, and present-day use, Talbot (2009) concludes:

> The experience that neuroenhancement offers is not, for the most part, about opening the doors of perception, or about breaking the bonds of the self, or about experiencing a surge of genius. It's about squeezing out an extra few hours to finish those sales figures when you'd rather really collapse in bed; getting a B instead of a B-minus on the final exam in a lecture class where you spent half your time texting; cramming for the G.R.E.s at night, because the information-industry job you got after college turned out to be deadening. Neuroenhancers don't offer freedom. Rather, they facilitate a pinched, unromantic, grindingly efficient form of productivity.

Ponce de Leon was a Spanish explorer allegedly seeking to find the Fountain of Youth—the legendary spring that would restore the youth of anyone who drank its waters. The search for the Fountain of Youth—physically and cognitively—is a perpetual one. The search for an easy-to-take "smart pill" fits into that category. But all one can say at this point is that in general, hype and hope outdistance science and results regarding both licit and illicit products. And whether used "on label" or "off label" the same hazards of side effects and dependency apply. There simply is not, as yet, the perfect "smart pill" devoid of those hazards. And I doubt that there ever will be.

Mental gymnastics

Speaking of the search for safe cognitive enhancers, "mental gym" and "memory coach" ideas continue to gain wide acceptance. Based on "the brain is like a muscle" and "steady workouts build brain capacity" reasoning, a wide variety of written materials, tests, mental exercise manuals and computer programs are available for such mental "workouts" for anyone interested. Again, enthusiastic testimonials abound. These are without risk of harm and can be conveniently and liberally applied by anyone and everyone. The availability of the computer-based brain exercise programs has heightened interest and participation in the "brain gym" immensely. Willis *et al.* (2006) reported on a five-year follow-up of 2832 persons living independently in six cities who were involved in formal cognitive training. Results showed that "compared with the control group, cognitive training resulted in improved cognitive abilities specific to the abilities trained that continued for 5 years after the initiation of the intervention" (p.2805).

Such techniques are likewise useful in cognitive rehabilitation after stroke or brain injury, or in Alzheimer or other dementia disorders. Rohling *et al.* (2009) did a meta-analysis of 97 articles which collectively included 2014 individuals who underwent cognitive rehabilitation after brain injury and 870 individuals in a variety of control conditions. They found cognitive therapy was useful and from those results suggested some guidelines: early treatment is best; even older patients age 55 and up can benefit, particularly if the injury is from stroke; and interventions focusing on direct cognitive skills in training specific cognitive domains such as attention and visuospatial processing were particularly effective with more holistic, non-targeted interventions being less effective. Some advocate the use of these mental gymnastics in ADHD or other learning disorders. There are a number of other formal studies underway to demonstrate evidence-based usefulness and effectiveness of cognitive training as a rehabilitation tool.

Multiple intelligences

As I pointed out in earlier chapters, IQ does measure something, using verbal and performance scales, and it has provided a gigantic, standardized database through the years that can be used for a number of useful analyses and projections. But to use IQ as the sole measure of "intelligence" narrows and restricts that definition much too harshly.

Savant syndrome, with its striking "*islands* of intelligence" provided good evidence that a series of intelligences exist within all of us, rather than a single intelligence, and future research will explore and reflect that. Beyond the research lab, teaching methods will evolve to address the multiple types of intelligence, and patterns of learning, that exist in every student body whether housed in special education or regular classrooms. Already there seems to be an acknowledgement that vocational education—more right brain directed—can be as useful and valuable as academic education—more left brain allied—for some students. Indeed there is a recognition now of "non-verbal" learning disorders, for example. Even in the neurotypical student there is general concensus, from experience that some students learn better visually than verbally. The fact is the world can benefit from both types of thinking and it also has plenty of space for the multiple intelligences that are contained within us, and that surround us.

Will an "epidemic" of autism cause an epidemic of savants?

If one in ten autistic persons has savant syndrome, the question of whether there is an "epidemic" of autism becomes pertinent to projections regarding the number of savants in the future. While some of the current increase in the incidence and prevalence of autistic disorder is "relative" due to ever expanding definitions and criteria (diagnostic "creep"), there does seem to be a "real" or actual increase in some measure. But the failure to use standardized criteria for diagnosis, and the failure to separate educational counts from clinical counts, muddy autism prevalence figures in an unintelligible fashion. Beyond that, the increase in autism prevalence needs to be viewed as part of a similar increase in the incidence of other developmental disorders and congenital defects overall which, while elevated, is hardly at an "epidemic" level.

Whatever those numbers, the search for the causes of autism will be an intense one in the coming years. It is important to point out that autistic disorder did not begin with Kanner's description of it in 1944. Dr. Down, in that same 1887 lecture in which he described savant syndrome, also identified a third kind of retardation—which he called "developmental"—to accompany "congenital" and "accidental" categories. In his "developmental" category he described, carefully and correctly, what we now call "autistic disorder" (Treffert 2006b). Using terms such as "world of their own," speaking "in the third person," "automatic movements" and "lessened responsiveness to all endearments of friends," he went on to describe what is unmistakably "early onset" and "late onset" autistic disorder. The fact that he should choose the term "developmental" was a century ahead of its time since we now classify autistic disorder and Asperger syndrome as "developmental disorders."

There is not space here to discuss the prevalence and causes of autistic disorder in any depth. But I have summed up my 50-year view of autistic disorder and these questions on the savant syndrome website in a posting titled "Autism: 52 years later—some common sense conclusions" (Treffert 2008). Suffice it to say here that autistic spectrum disorder did not begin with its first description in 1943. It is not increasing at an "epidemic" level so there will be no flood of new savants. Autism spectrum disorder is not a single condition but is, instead, a group of disorders with a final common path we call autism, in the same manner as mental retardation, for example, is a group of disorders with a common final path we call mental retardation. When we accurately separate autism, into its component subgroups, then we will be able to identify specific causes, preventive strategies and targeted treatments. Etiologies, when all sorted out, will be a combination of genetic *and* environmental factors. I discuss all of this in more detail in the "common sense" posting (Treffert 2008).

Still unanswered questions regarding savant syndrome

In the years ahead there will be ongoing inquiry regarding still unanswered questions about savant syndrome, many of which have been raised in this book. Why is savant syndrome more closely linked to autism than other developmental disabilities? Why the over-representation of calendar calculating, and the triad of mental limitation, blindness and musical genius in savant syndrome? Can genetic memory account for the savant's ability to "know things they never learned" in so many instances? What does the "acquired" savant tell us regarding dormant capacity within everyone? How can such dormant capacity be accessed non-intrusively?

These questions regarding savant syndrome, and many more about brain function and dysfunction overall, will make neuroscience an exciting career path in the years ahead for any "fresh, new explorers" entering the field. Such research has far-reaching implications for better understanding brain function overall, improved treatment for brain disorders and maximizing brain capabilities within us all.

A lingering question in my mind, though, is whether the brain can transcend itself to explain itself fully and entirely. No doubt the brain can ultimately unravel how the kidney, heart, liver, spleen and other body organs work, providing thus all the good that can come from that knowledge preventively and therapeutically. But can the brain transcend itself to explain itself fully or is there a built-in limitation to going outside itself, as it were, to understand itself fully? I think there probably is such a built-in barrier. What do you think?

A savant syndrome registry

I have a folder on my desk labeled "New Savants." It is very thick now and it continues to grow almost daily as reports come to me from around the world, through the savant syndrome website, of more people with savant syndrome. Some reports come from parents, some from teachers or therapists, and some from other clinicians. Most of these are at the splinter skill level, but some are at the talented level and a very occasional case comes along that hints at the prodigious level. Most are children or adolescents and many have autism or Asperger's as the underlying disability. However, some new adult acquired savant syndrome cases are also interspersed in that group of new cases, and other underlying disabilities are represented as well.

I do try to respond to each of those inquiries, and I usually ask for more information, which is always generously provided. Some of the new cases are added to the savant syndrome website and it grows accordingly. To date, though, I have not systematically filed those cases in an easily retrievable "registry" classifying the cases by skill or skill level, age, sex, underlying disability or geographic location. I do intend to do that because such a registry, with appropriate permissions, would be a valuable resource for developing a much larger sample of persons with savant syndrome that could be used to measure the relative number of skills qualitatively and quantitatively, along with many other factors on a whole variety of variables. Indeed when information is sent to me about these new savants, it is often accompanied by a willingness, and eagerness, to be involved in any research projects on savant syndrome.

Such a registry is overdue and there are sufficient new cases now to make it a high priority project.

A savant syndrome institute

One of the impediments to research on savant syndrome, and answering some of the questions above, has been the relative scarcity of persons with savant syndrome, particularly at the prodigious level. Some such persons do reside in the United States, Europe and Australia who we know about. But no doubt there are other such persons not known to us who are living elsewhere in the world including India, Africa, China, Brazil or Russia. The Internet, through the savant syndrome website, has identified both additional persons and the researchers studying them from around the world. The Internet has also provided swifter communication and collaboration between these researchers.

But many case studies of savant syndrome, because of its rarity, are still anecdotal reports. That is not to diminish the value of anecdotal reporting. Many of the great discoveries and advances in medicine have come from single anecdotal reports. But larger samples of persons with savant syndrome could provide a broader base for establishing standardized criteria for savant skills, and uniform definitions of splinter skill, talented and prodigious levels of savant skills rather than the admittedly subjective criteria in use at the present time. And larger samples would allow better comparison of savant skills, and brain function behind those skills, to control groups including persons with other forms of disability, neurotypicals, prodigies and geniuses.

As more cases and additional researchers are identified, this congregate research will accelerate over the coming years. Such larger scale studies are now being carried out on groups of individuals with savant syndrome in some clinics, comparing and contrasting the presence and mechanisms of exceptional skills to other control groups. But more such studies are needed. A savant syndrome registry described above would be a natural resource for identifying persons willing to participate in such expanded studies.

To that end, one of my long-term hopes with respect to understanding savant syndrome better is that there would be established, somewhere in the world, a *Savant Syndrome Institute* (or, even more comprehensively, an *Institute for the Study of Savant Syndrome, Prodigy and Genius*). Such an institute need not be an independent, free-standing building. I don't envision such an institute being a free-standing "building" with its own large, independent staff. Rather it would more likely be housed within an already established neuroscience center, drawing its multidisciplinary staff from various departments to devote some time to the mission and purpose of the institute. Persons with savant syndrome could come to this place for closer study from around the world given the relative scarcity of them in any one location. Many have already volunteered to do so and some foundations have volunteered to help underwrite associated travel, lodging and testing costs. I have yet to determine where such a center might be located, but some universities have expressed preliminary interest. It would be a place where the miles and miles of video footage, file drawers of books, journals, research papers, a "savant registry" and artwork that I have accumulated through the years on savants, prodigies and geniuses could be housed for the use of the "fresh, young explorers"—the neuroscientists of the future—who could come for training and have access to those materials as a baseline of future research.

Given the unique window to the brain that savant syndrome provides, its interface with prodigy and genius, and its broad implications for tapping dormant potential within us all, there really should be such an "institute" somewhere in the world. At the present time there is not.

Since I feel so strongly about that, exploring that possibility is next on my wish list.

The trail ahead is an exciting one

In the decades ahead neuroscience will be *the* leading edge frontier in medical research. It will be an illuminating and exciting trail wherever it leads. Armed with new tools a whole cadre of "fresh, new explorers" will explore neurons, synapses, circuits, specialization and connectivity in the brain in ways heretofore not even possible. Those techniques will provide some useful insights into the marvelous intricacy *of* the brain through the unique window *into* the brain that savant syndrome especially provides. And, since savant syndrome and autism are so closely interrelated, more useful knowledge about the origins of autistic disorder will emerge as well.

Wherever such research is carried out, from it will come not only a better understanding of savant syndrome, but also a better understanding of ourselves and the potential within us all.

CHAPTER 29

Oval Souls on a Round Planet: The Trail Ahead for the *World* of the Savant

In the spring of 2006 I received an unexpected but welcome letter. It was from the first savant I ever met. Remember him? John had memorized the bus system of the city of Milwaukee. He said he was going to be traveling through Fond du Lac on his way to Green Bay with several staff members from the nursing home where he now lives. He wondered if I would be free for lunch.

I gladly accepted the invitation. It's not often the doctor gets the chance to do a 44-year follow-up on a patient.

We met at a local restaurant. I immediately recognized him. He jokingly asked:

"Dr. T, can I have a home pass this weekend?" This was a spirited dialogue we had often back in 1962. I gave him my usual reply: "I'll think about it."

The reason for the trip? John was on his way to the annual meeting of the Wisconsin Association of Home and Services for the Aging to accept the Golden Key Award from that group. The award recognizes the value in a triumph over adversity. The recipient had to be someone who overcame his or her challenges and disabilities with the assistance of a member facility, and who had gone on to have a significant impact on the community.

John's contribution to his community was a column called "Reminiscing," which had become a popular feature in a local magazine called *Renaissance* in the town where he grew up. Drawing on his impeccable memory for detail, John triggered corresponding recollections in his readers about the history of their city. One column, for example, gave the history of the now abandoned M.R.&K. electric inter-urban train that traveled from Milwaukee to Kenosha. He remembered the exact route crossing by crossing and each of the buildings along the way, many now with new purposes. He recalled for the readers "Midway Park is located along the line directly east of where Mulligan's Miniature Golf is today." In another column he described the history of the hospitals and nursing homes in the community. The townspeople loved that column. It brought back so many memories for everyone.

John was so proud to receive his award. A staff member described the scene thus:

> When John stood on stage and accepted his award, many of the assembled group were moved to tears. Most of them were nursing home administrators or nursing directors who knew what an amazing accomplishment this was for someone like him.

John's congressman from the 1st District, Wisconsin wrote a congratulatory letter: "You should be extremely proud to receive such a highly prestigious award." And I was very proud of John also. He ranks very high in my alumni group. Indeed he embodies a triumph over adversity just like so many of the other persons with savant syndrome I have been privileged to meet on this journey.

And what an incredible journey it has been. I have learned a great deal, contributed some and have gotten to know some extraordinary people and their equally extraordinary families and caregivers. I have learned many things of scientific interest to be sure, but just as surely I have witnessed many things of human interest as well. As I said earlier, on this voyage I have learned as much about matters of the heart as I have about circuits in the brain.

Having looked at what's on the trail ahead for research into the *mind* of the savant, let's consider what's ahead on the trail for changing and improving the *world* of the savant.

Increasing inclusion, accommodation and acceptance

Stories of triumph over adversity among persons with savant syndrome, like John's journey above, fortunately are plentiful now. Many of them are in this book. Such triumphs required sustained effort on the part of each savant. But also, standing behind and encouraging each of those special persons was a steadfast family or caregiver, believer and prompter. "Cheerleaders" I call them. But there is a third contributor to those stories of hope and progress—a public which has become much more accepting, accommodating and inclusive of the savant. No more a "private, un-related person, an outsider," savants have been increasingly accommodated, accepted and included in the community at large with respect, appreciation and love.

Welcome "inside" our world. No more an "outsider."

In working with savants all these years I am reminded of a patient of mine some time back. She was a very bright girl but was having problems reconciling her parents' hopes and expectations for her with the somewhat different choices and aspirations she had for herself. She felt her individuality and the unique shape of her psychological "soul" was out of sync with and unappreciated by her parents, relatives, teachers, peers and the world in general. She put it this way:

> Dr. T, I don't know if you believe in God or not. It's not important to me if you do. But to me it's this way. We live on a round planet so we assume that all the other planets are round like the one that we live on. But God looks out over the universe and sees all kinds of planets—round ones, square ones, rectangular ones, oval ones and a whole variety of other shapes. They are not all round as I learned in science class. What happens before you are born is that God sorts your soul out. If you have a round soul He puts you on a round planet; if you have a square soul He puts you on a square planet; and if you have an oval soul He is supposed to put you on an oval planet. In my case He made a mistake. I have an oval soul and He put me on a round planet. The school, my parents and even you, Dr. T., keep trying to file my soul round like everybody else's. I am decomposing in school and when I graduate I'll simply give up my seat to some new starry-eyed cadaver-to-be.

Sometimes it seems as if savants are oval souls on a round planet. And sometimes we do file and scrape and sand a bit on those souls to make them more conform to the shape of our own. That's what Charlie Babbitt did early on in the movie *Rain Man*. But then, gradually we accommodate to, and come to appreciate, as Charlie did, the uniqueness and specialness of the savant-shaped soul. Accordingly we file and scrape and sand less, and encourage and accommodate more. In the process we all change.

There has been a decided, welcome change in acceptance of, and appreciation for, persons with savant syndrome these past 122 years. We see it in treatment programs, schools, the workplace and entire communities. That acceptance and appreciation will continue and even increase in the years ahead.

The story of my patient above with the "oval soul" has a happy ending. This young woman did forge her own path in life very successfully without forfeiting her oval-shaped soul. It was a path different than her parents imagined for her, but now they are very proud and very close to her again. She is eminently happy and satisfied. And so are her parents.

Likewise the savants. The world has better accommodated to the shape of their "souls" and they in turn continue to make some changes in themselves. With that joint effort come many happy endings as well.

There is some controversy regarding the effort to "cure" persons with autism, Asperger or savant syndrome. Some fear that the "cure" will rob those persons of their genius, as allegedly happened with Nadia, and in so doing the world would be robbed of the unique talents and gifts of some very special people. As I pointed out earlier, one doesn't seek to "cure" savant syndrome. Rather one seeks only to channel the special talents and skills—savant syndrome—into useful purposes. To the extent one seeks to "cure" the *underlying* disability—autism, Asperger syndrome or other

CNS disorders—it is only to modify those behaviors and symptoms that grossly interfere with overall adjustment and are a source of distress to both the patient and those around him or her. This can be done without robbing persons of their uniqueness or individuality. Treating the condition the patient has but also respecting fully the patient who has the condition is just the art of good medicine. It is conscientious, respectful bedside manner.

The cruel elitism of "outsider art"

Having said the above, you can understand why I bristle at considering artwork of persons with savant syndrome as "outsider art." To me that term is outdated, elitist, condescending and discriminatory. Alonzo's sculptures are not spectacular because he has some limitations. They stand side by side, and toe to toe, in any gallery with any other sculptor without a "done by a person with a disability" sign attached. The fact that Alonzo lacks formal training, credentials, diploma or degree does not detract from his work. In fact if anything it makes it all the more remarkable. But some critics view savant artists and musicians differently and dismissively because they dare to be "untutored" as if that somehow makes them less valid. At a time when we are trying to include persons with autism or other disabilities "inside" our communities, it is hostile to require that they stay "outside" the art world.

"Outsider art" is meant to be a gentler term for what was originally called *art brut*. That term was born of psychosis and extreme mental dysfunction. And even today it conveys strangeness, isolation and idiosyncrasy. It ought to go the way of "idiot savant" and be thoroughly discarded. It was Dostoyevsky who described the "idiot" as a private, unrelated person and outsider. The savants I have come to know are not "outsiders" in any exclusionary sense, unless it is *we* who exclude them. Likewise with their art.

Cardinal (2009) defines "outsider art" as a

> mode of original artistic expression which thrives on its independence, shunning the public sphere and the art market. Such art can be highly idiosyncratic and secretive, and reflects the individual creator's attempt to construct a coherent, albeit strange, private world. (p.1459)

I would submit that it is not the "outsider artist" that shuns the art world. It is quite the other way around. Many savant artists produce work that is beautiful in its own right—stunning, imaginative, inviting and creative. Why they cannot share equal footing, appreciation and adulation with "real" artists in the opinion of art experts is something I simply cannot understand. But then, I don't like to have wine connoisseurs tell me which wines should taste good to me and are worthy of my appreciation either.

Before I arranged the "Windows of Genius: Artwork of the Prodigious Savant" exhibit in Fond du Lac, which I described in Chapter 18, I did try to interest several art galleries in larger cities in the exhibit. I was told politely but firmly that they "didn't do"

outsider art. But the Windhover Center for the Arts did host the event. The public—
young and old, blue collar and white collar, art connoisseur and art neophyte—all
enjoyed the exhibit judging by the attendance and comments. They appreciated the
artworks, and the artists at work, because they were inviting, interesting, intricate and
meaningful. No one criticized Stephen's drawing of Rome because it only "copied"
what he saw; they thought it amazing. People were struck with the deep emotion
in many of the works; they were not flat and lifeless. Where was the "idiosyncratic,
secretiveness and strangeness"? Frankly I think I have seen more of that recently in the
"real" art museums which proudly display the work of the "insider" artist.

On the trail ahead for the savant artist it is my hope, and prediction, that both
the concept and term "outsider" art will be discarded. As a result, savant artists will be
invited into any gallery worthy of their work on the same footing as "insider" artists.
As we welcome persons with savant syndrome more widely into our communities in
all endeavors, surely that artificial, elitist distinction between credentialed, trained,
"real" artists and uncredentialed, "untutored" savant artists will go the way of the
pejorative term "idiot savant" we so wisely and empathically discarded years ago.

Savant musicians have also had their skills and abilities diminished or marginal-
ized by some critics and "real" musicians. That too is changing. Matt and the other professional musicians in the trio he leads are invited to jazz festivals around the world based
solely on the quality of their music. In 2009 Derek Paravicini had his London debut
concert with Emerald Ensemble Chamber Orchestra. Hikari Oe's CDs of his compositions are played and appreciated worldwide on a par with any other musician.

The years ahead will bring more equal footing receptivity for the art and music
of these genuinely gifted persons.

Innovative, targeted education and employment

Because savant syndrome is relatively rare, classrooms, schools or curriculums specifically dedicated to teaching these "twice-exceptional" (autistic and gifted) persons
have also been quite rare. Donnelly and Altman (1994) noted that increasing numbers of gifted students with autism were being included in "gifted and talented"
classrooms with non-disabled gifted peers. In these settings an adult mentor with
skills in the field of the savant's talent coupled with individual counseling and small
group social skills training were particularly helpful.

Little (2005) provides a very concise historical review of approaches to children
with disabilities and summarizes present-day strategies. She points out that in the
United States alone there are 120,000 to 180,000 learning disabled children with
above average IQ. These children do not fit into programs for the gifted because of
their disabilities and do not fit into resource programs because of their giftedness. In
a special section on "Giftedness and Autism" Little (2005) reinforces the findings of
Donnelly and Altman (1994) of the usefulness of an adult mentor along with the importance of small group social skills training. Parents, and some savants themselves,

have underscored to me the importance of a mentor as well as the beneficial effect of a "friend" program. In these programs peers volunteer to befriend and accompany the savant on a daily basis in a variety of activities. In that way they also learn social skills which can generalize to all sorts of future relationships.

Clark (2001) designed a "savant skill curriculum" using a combination of successful strategies used in the education of gifted children (enrichment, acceleration and mentorship) with autism education (visual supports and social stories). The approach focused on strengths rather than deficits, and centered on interests and abilities that could ultimately be used in a vocational setting. That curriculum was highly successful. It showed gains in behavior, social skills and academic self-esteem. There were improvements in the communication skills of some subjects as well.

Clark now has broadened that program to address educational needs of persons with autism spectrum disorders in a program called "Aspect: A Comprehensive Educational Approach." It now operates in six schools serving over 500 children in New South Wales. The program includes 71 "satellite classes" in mainstream schools which specifically cater to students with Asperger syndrome and high-functioning autism. In those schools persons with savant skills are included in comprehensive educational approaches. The program's critical nine elements, including individualized planning, curriculum and staff, interdisciplinary and family involvement, are described in detail at www.aspect.org.au/our%20services/schools/Aspect_ComprehensiveEduApproach.pdf.

In Australia, as elsewhere, there is a lack of vocational employment for persons with autism or Asperger syndrome when they complete the K-12 curriculum. A program in Denmark run by Thorkil Sonne addressed that void directly. It is a vocational placement service specifically for persons with Asperger syndrome or high-functioning autism. Matches are made between willing employers (trained in the nuances of Asperger's and high-functioning autism) and persons with those disabilities who possess valuable skills. Most of these placements are in the IT area where the skills are often abundant in these prospective employees. I am certain more such programs will develop around the world. Details of this program—Specialisterne—can be accessed at www.apecialisterne.dk. A Harvard Business publication—*Specialisterne: Sense and Details*—provides information about this endeavor as an example of the potential and problems of "social enterprise" programs, such as this one, being contributory and successful in the competitive business world (Austin, Wareham and Busquets 2008).

In the United States the Tailor Institute is dedicated specifically to improving the lives of individuals with high-functioning autism or Asperger syndrome who exhibit areas of giftedness. It is designed to provide these gifted persons on the autism spectrum the tools they need to live and work as independently as possible. Like the program in Denmark, individuals are matched with willing employers who can benefit from the special skills the prospective employee has. Then the Institute provides support services to both employer and employee. More information about that program can be obtained at www.tailorinstitute.org.

The Tailor Institute was set up by Taylor Crowe's father, Dr. David Crowe, who was so impressed by the overall progress in his son who prospered and grew as he developed and shared his special graphic skills more widely. Taylor Crowe is another success story. He graduated from the prestigious California Institute of the Arts with a certificate in character animation, a valuable credential indeed. Taylor has made massive gains also in his general adaptation to life. From a time after late-onset autism when he lost his language ability entirely, Taylor has persevered to where I had the opportunity to hear him present his lecture "The View from Here: My Life with Autism" to 500 speech and language therapists at a convention in Wisconsin. That presentation, given at many autism conventions now, is available on a DVD.

What justifiable pride his dad had in introducing his son to the audience. It was a moving moment. Taylor maintains his own website at www.taylorcrowe.com where one can learn more about his remarkable story.

Discussions about "mainstreaming" versus "special education classes" have broadened considerably now to a general consensus that just as autism and savant syndrome exist over a spectrum of abilities and disabilities, so must the educational and vocational resources reflect a spectrum of settings and opportunities as well. Sometimes "mainstreaming" is best for the whole school day; at other times only portions of the day are more effective. Sometimes special classes or even special schools are the best alternative. A number of private and public schools devoted entirely to education of students with autism or Asperger syndrome have developed in various countries.

Some of those are elementary schools, and some, such as Orion Academy in Moraga, California (www.orionacademy.org) are for high school students with Asperger syndrome. Hope University in Anaheim, California (www.hopeu.com) is a fine arts facility for adults with developmental disabilities and presently has three musical savants among the student body.

Some specialized schools are emerging as well. Soundscape Centre at Redhill College in Surrey, England is the only educational facility uniquely dedicated to the needs and potential of persons with sight loss and special musical abilities, including musical savants.

The trail ahead educationally for savants will see expansion of the numbers and types of programs available for children and adults with special needs. Some will be traditional classrooms with special accommodations to various disabilities; some will be specialized schools for K-12 students designed particularly to deal with autistic and Asperger disorders; some will be schools especially targeted to "twice exceptional" students including savants; and some will be vocational programs matching adults with savant skills with willing employers.

With heightened interest in savant syndrome, and as more stories of success emerge, the trail will be increasingly rich with versatile and inventive resources.

Love is a good therapist too

Having the opportunity to meet and get to know so many of the extraordinary people as I have on this 47-year journey has certainly been the pinnacle. But the opportunity to meet and interact with the families of these special persons has been an immense privilege as well. While we continue to seek more effective treatments for some of the underlying disabilities seen in savant syndrome, these families carry on each day, patiently providing 24/7 or whatever care is needed. More community resources are developing for persons with savant syndrome, making available to the savants and their families more professional and para-professional workers to help with "training the talent" and other strategies to help bring the savant more inside the school, the workplace and the community and be less of an outsider.

That is a welcome development. But through the years, and much contact and correspondence, not only have I been impressed with the love, patience and devotion that parents and other caregivers have for each person with savant syndrome, and its importance, but also I have been impressed with each family's caregiver's ingenuity and individual resourcefulness. As these parents write to me about their "son or daughter who…" their love for that child, no matter how young or how old, or how limited or how gifted, shines brightly through whatever the words. So love is a good therapist too.

I say that because I am continually encouraged by how inventive and ingenious these parents and caregivers are in not only discovering the "islands of genius" that lie within some children, but also discovering and engaging the "islands of intactness" that are also present. And both these "islands" can be gently and lovingly tended and nurtured to whatever full blossom they can attain. Not that professional expertise is unnecessary; it can be very helpful. But sometimes parents, caregivers or teachers "disqualify" themselves as being untrained or uncredentialed and yield only to expertise. But, as I learned a long time ago from listening, sometimes mothers or fathers do know best regarding their child as to what works and doesn't work, and what might work and what might not work.

"Listen to the patient, he's giving you the diagnosis." I learned this from a wise, white-haired professor early in my medical training. It was the most valuable lesson I took away from that training. Certainly I rely on my learning, my reading, my examining and my observing to make diagnoses and come up with treatment plans. But it is the listening to the patient from which I derive the most regarding diagnosis, and it is also the listening that can be so important in treatment as well. For those patients who can't speak for themselves, I learn from listening to those who know them best: the parents or caregivers around them.

If we are to find the causes of autism, we have to blend listening and careful observation with imaging, genomes and all manner of technology. To find out which strategies are best for "training the talent" in the savant to bring it to full blossom— that takes careful listening and personal observation as well, not just double-blind statistical analysis and chi-square statistics.

Unfortunately, there is considerable polarization currently concerning autism spectrum disorders. There are environmental vs. genetic camps regarding etiology. And there are equally polarized camps of traditional medicine vs. alternative medicine with respect to treatment approaches. My hope is that on the trail ahead such polarization will melt, and the feuding cause and treatment camps will merge. That can happen when we listen closely to the evidence without preconceived notions or veiled agendas. Listening closely to what the patient and the parents are telling us, instead of just the experts, is the proper place to start.

"Listen to the patient, he's giving you the diagnosis."

Time to put the brush down

It has been more than two decades since the movie *Rain Man* made "autistic savant" household terms. So much has happened since that time, all of it good, toward better understanding the *mind* of the savant, and being more accommodating to the *world* of the savant, leaving each of those special souls retain its unique, refreshing, extraordinary free-form shape.

There are many success stories regarding savants, many of them described earlier in this book. Some of the musicians and artists have made their mark internationally with works that are truly remarkable, not because they were done by someone with a disability, but rather because they are skilled, creative works in their own right.

Others have had less sensational impact, but their skills have provided useful roles or employment like the middle-aged fellow I met on one of the Oprah shows. He had memorized all the zip codes in the United States and worked in the post office as what must have been the world's fastest human mail sorter.

Then there was the young man who had memorized the Chicago Transit Authority, Pace and Metro routes and was employed as a "travel information specialist" by the Regional Transportation Authority of that city. Persons lost or stranded in the systems could talk to him by telephone—a human voice rather than endless push-button menu options—to get explicit directions for "help" to get to the proper station and correct train or bus to take them to their destination. Sometimes he would handle as many as 200 calls on an eight-hour shift. His ability to memorize maps and schedules made him a natural for that job. While other travel information specialists needed to access requested information by computer, this man had internalized the information and could produce it faster than the computer could. This "man with a map in his head" was assisted in finding that position by the Marriott Foundation through its "Bridges...From School to Work" program.

Sara, for whom "coding just flies," is the president of a very successful Mid-West computer consulting firm she founded. Sara describes her swift programming skills as "pattern recognition" which allows her to identify the pattern the original programmer used and then build on it. She can detect flaws in software at a glance by spotting irregularities in coding patterns which she sees as a "printout" in her head. She can do coding in five or six hours that it would take others several days to complete. She, like Temple Grandin, is an intensely visual thinker and memories are encoded in images, not words. Her attention to detail obsessiveness spills over to the written word because rules-based English language was a "must learn" subject as a child and she cannot read a report without circling all the misspellings and grammatical mistakes.

Computer-related positions are ones at which high-functioning persons with autism often excel. Sara certainly is an example of such a successful match. These days she enjoys sharing her story with others on the spectrum, including high school or other students at various levels. They come away from her presentations inspired by her achievements. But they are also comforted by the fact that they are not alone in dealing with the day-to-day problems that persons with autism or Asperger syndrome encounter because of their disorder. Simultaneously they are reassured that such problems are not incompatible with a successful adjustment in the work world.

So many similar uplifting stories, new cases and new research findings continue to come to my attention daily from around the world. My file of "new savants" is getting thicker and thicker. I would like to share all of those stories because they are so encouraging and exciting. But like an artist doing a painting, at some point you have to "put the brush down" and declare the work complete. So it is with this book for now.

I started this chapter with a success story, and I want to end with several others because they demonstrate how far we have come as a society in accepting and appreciating the special persons that savants truly are. They also demonstrate how neatly and nicely the valuable skills the savant has can contribute mightily and meaningfully to the world overall. In the coalition of those forces whatever gap exists between "our" world and "their" world slowly disappears leaving all of us truly respecting and deeply valuing each other whatever the shape of our individual souls.

Trevor Tao: from autistic child to research scientist

Trevor Tao was diagnosed with autism at age two. He began talking at age three. In 1981, at age four he was the first autistic child in South Australia, perhaps all of Australia, to be successfully integrated into a regular kindergarten setting. By age five he was attending a regular school. The concept of integrating autistic children into mainstream schools was new at that time and his successful educational experience was the subject of a book, *The Opening Door* by Jean Bryant (1993), Trevor's first teacher.

And a successful educational experience it was. In 2006 Tao received a PhD in applied mathematics from the University of Adelaide. His thesis was on image analysis: "An Extended Mumford-Shah Model and Improved Region Merging Algorithm for Image Segmentation." Since 2006 Tao has been working as a research scientist at a government agency in Australia.

Tao is also a prodigious musical savant, which is how I first learned about him. An article titled "Miracle on Parkgate Place" by Armstrong (1989) in *The Australian Magazine* details Tao's extraordinary musical abilities at age 11. After hearing Dvorak's *New World Symphony* for the first time, Tao played the first movement back flawlessly on the piano, even though this is not a piece for the piano but rather is written for an entire orchestra. Tao's father had encouraged his son, at age eight, to take up formal musical training believing it would help broaden his overall development including socialization. His father was right about the music. "Training the talent" did help with skill development overall, including the socialization opportunities that came with interacting with other musicians and concert performances. He won many prizes in piano competitions and music composition.

Tao's father also encouraged him to take up chess for the same reasons. He was exceptional at that skill too, representing Australia at the International Chess Olympiad in 1994. He also represented Australia at the International Mathematical Olympiad in 1995. Tao feels that the overseas travel helped in overcoming some of his earlier autistic fears and handicaps.

Tao agrees that these special savant skills were important in his overall development:

> Looking back, I think my parents and teachers had deliberately encouraged me to accompany others in music or concerts, and play chess at matches or tournaments, so that I could socialize with more people. This strategy had definitely helped, and it had also made me more confident about myself, as I kept winning prizes in both music and chess. (personal communication)

Tao's mother of course has also been a vital force in his development. She had taught mathematics and science subjects in high school but gave up her career to accept the full-time challenge that Tao presented as an autistic child. Tao gives credit as well to his brothers "in helping me to grow up as a normal child." And indeed sibling interaction and support is so often a vital contributor to better interactive and social skills. One brother, like Tao, also has a PhD in mathematics; in 2006 he was awarded the prestigious Fields Medal in mathematics and currently is a professor of mathematics in Los Angeles. His other brother is a software engineer at Google.

It is a long route from autism to research scientist. But Tao's journey demonstrates that with proper opportunities educationally with both special and general skills, such a successful transition can occur. It also demonstrates the vital role the family, including siblings, can play in providing sustaining encouragement, support and love. And, as in so many other instances of persons with savant skills, a particularly observant, empathic and skilled teacher or therapist, like Anne Sullivan with Helen Keller, discovers and seizes the opportunity that special skills present toward engagement and progress.

Tao sums up his life now in three words: "LIFE IS GOOD." He lives with family. He has a secure research job where he can use his mathematical skills. He has other hobbies such as cryptic crosswords, Bridge, GO and Scrabble. He uses his music skills as well. In 2008 Autism Association of South Australia asked him to compose music for a DVD documentary on autism and he did so. It gave him the chance to meet some professional people in the film industry to broaden his socialization even further.

Tao describes his life as a journey which opened doors "from the dark room of autism to a bright world of normal life. Dad told me that the most important thing in life is happiness, and I think I have plenty," Tao says today.

For him, and the rest of us as well, "That's as good as it gets."

Don't you agree?

Amanda: "a dream unfolds"

We all have dreams for our lives. And so do savants. A person whose life dream is slowly unfolding in a spectacular and satisfying way is Amanda LaMunyon.

Amanda has Asperger syndrome. She is now 14 years old. She began reading at age four. She had a difficult time in school. She could repeat all the rules but had a hard time adhering to them. She simply couldn't sit still. Amanda's mother thought that maybe a spark of artistic talent, which had surfaced from time to time, might provide a way for Amanda to express herself. Mother sought out a teacher for Amanda, a very gentle, patient woman with a sweet smile who admitted she had never taught a seven-year-old girl; her students were mostly adults.

At that first session, when her mother came to pick her daughter up, both Amanda and the teacher were covered with paint. Amanda led her mother to some paintings she had done—some watermelons. And the teacher exclaimed: "This girl can paint!"

And paint she can. Amanda has won many awards for her artwork. She also loves to sing and not only sings songs, but paints impressions of them as well. She also writes poetry.

Her artwork, her singing and her poetry can all be accessed on her website at www.amandalamunyon.com.

Once tapped, Amanda's special skills, as with many other savants, served as a means of communication, expression and outlet. Self-confidence and self-esteem flourished and she became more outgoing instead of retreating into, and remaining inside, her "world of autism" as she describes it in frequent presentations to peers and adults.

A special opportunity helped Amanda immensely. She was enrolled in the Duke University Gifted and Talented program which enrolls gifted and talented children from throughout the United States. The fact that her gifts and talents were accompanied by Asperger syndrome did not exclude her from that important program, nor should it. One of Amanda's paintings provided the cover for *Girls Under the Umbrella of Autism Spectrum Disorders* by Ernsperger and Wendel (2007). Her story, paintings and poems have appeared in many newspapers, magazines and television stories.

All of this provided sufficient confidence and poise that she entered the National Miss Pageant Oklahoma. She was in the top five in talent and acting and was first runner-up in best resume. She has received a number of state and national awards for community service in fund-raising efforts for autism research and other children's health projects. The most meaningful of those awards, for Amanda, was the 2008 Wendy F. Miller Recognition award from the Autism Society of America given to that person nationwide with autism who demonstrates exceptional dedication, effort or achievement.

In May, 2009 Amanda received another award, this time competing with all middle level school students from throughout the United States. Each year ten young students are selected for recognition in the Prudential Spirit of Community and Scholarship Awards program based on their outstanding achievements in community service and school success. Five high school students and five middle level school students from throughout the United States are selected for this honor. In 2009 Amanda was one of the five such outstanding students and volunteers at the middle school level to receive this prestigious award. The award noted that Amanda "performs at charitable events, sells cards and prints of her paintings to raise money for sick children, and draws upon her experience with autism to educate others about the disorder."

In May, 2009 Amanda also represented Oklahoma in the US National Teenager competition. She placed fourth and won the Citizenship award (a $10,000 scholarship) and the Directors award. She graduated from eighth grade in 2009 and moved on to high school. She intends to continue to bring visibility to concerns about autism generally, but particularly wants to focus on providing information on overcoming challenges on an individual basis. And what a marvelous example and role model she is for both those initiatives.

One of Amanda's poems is called "A Little Secret." The secret is her Asperger syndrome, hardly visible in all the effort and honors above. The poem ends this way:

> How do I know so much about Asperger's Syndrome?
> I know because I have it.
> Some say it is a disability
> But I am a girl with dreams.
> I will take what God has given me.
> Along with the challenge and use it
> To fulfill the purpose he has for me.
> Let me say to you,
> If you know someone who seems a little different
> Look for something good.

It will be there.
It may be just "a little secret" waiting to be told
A dream waiting to unfold.

For Amanda the good news is that the particular dream for her life, like any teenager who dreams, is unfolding in an unimpeded fashion in a world much more knowledgeable, accepting and appreciative of persons with special needs and special gifts. And there is even more good news. Her "secret" doesn't have to be a secret any longer. Her achievements, and their recognition on a parallel with any other teen her age, is gratifying evidence of that.

How far Amanda, and we, have come in making the "secret" less cloistered and more open by discovering, nurturing, appreciating and celebrating the *strengths* in these extraordinary people.

★   ★   ★   ★   ★   ★

I do not know what I may appear to the world; but to myself
I seem to have been like a boy on the seashore, and diverting
myself in now and then finding a smoother pebble or prettier
shell than ordinary, while the great ocean of truth lay all
undiscovered before me. (Sir Isaac Newton)

I used that quote in my first book, but it still seems so apt. In the intervening years I have found more "smoother pebbles"—extraordinary people—with their uniquely shaped souls, and I continue to be fascinated and inspired by them. The "ocean of truth" about them, while still large, has yielded some to more recent discoveries and more will follow.

For me it has been an incredible journey that has piqued my interest, taught me much, expanded my interests, and has taken me into some areas of thought and discovery I might never have ventured into before. I hope recounting this journey does the same for you.

This voyage has prompted me to look for, and nurture, human potential in whomever it is found and in whatever form or quantity it exists, including that within ourselves. It has reinforced what a mighty power unconditional love, belief and optimism can be in discovering and bringing to full blossom not only "islands of genius" but also "islands of intactness" however hidden or secret they might be. It has humbled me to realize how little we know about that most marvelous organ in the body—the brain—with its baffling intricacy as well as its still untapped possibilities. But it has inspired me as well to know that now, with the new tools we have available to explore this vast "ocean" of neuroscience, the "fresh, new explorers" on the way will, in the decades ahead, take us further than we have ever been in better understanding both the brain and human potential.

References

Annoni, J.M., Devuyst, G., Carota, A., Bruggimann, L. and Bogousslavsky, J. (2005) "Changes in artistic style after minor posterior stroke." *Journal of Neurology, Neurosurgery and Psychiatry 76,* 797–803.

Ansen, D., Reese, M., Crichton, S. and Foote, J. (1989) "Who's on first?" *Newsweek,* January 16, 52–56.

Austin, R.D., Wareham, J. and Busquets, J. (2008) *Specialisterne: Sense and Details.* Boston, MA: Harvard Business Publishing.

Bachem, A. (1955) "Absolute pitch." *Journal of the Acoustical Society of America 27,* 1100–1185.

Baggaley, J. (1974) "Measurement of absolute pitch." *Psychology of Music 22,* 11–17.

Baron-Cohen, S. (2002) "The extreme male theory of autism." *Trends in Cognitive Sciences 6,* 248–254.

Barr, M.W. (1898) "Some notes on echolalia, with the report of an extraordinary case." *Journal of Nervous and Mental Diseases 25,* 20–30.

Battro, A.M. (2000) *Half a Brain is Enough: The Story of Nico.* Cambridge: Cambridge University Press.

Baudoin, D. (1996) "Curious dissociation between cerebral imaging and clinical findings." *Lancet 347,* 965.

Birbaumer, N. (1999) "Rain Man's revelations." *Nature 399,* 211–212.

Birbaumer, N. and Cohen, L.G. (2007) "Brain–computer interfaces: Communication and restoration of movement in paralysis." *Journal of Physiology 579,* 621–636.

Blackstock, G.L. (2006) *Blackstock's Collections: The Drawings of an Artistic Savant.* New York: Princeton Architectural Press.

Boddaert, N. (2003) "Perception of complex sounds: Abnormal pattern of cortical activation in autism." *American Journal of Psychiatry 160,* 2057–2060.

Bolte, S. and Poustka, F. (2004) "Comparing the intelligence profiles of savant and nonsavant individuals with autistic disorder." *Intelligence 32,* 121–131.

Bondy, A. and Frost, L. (2001) *A Picture's Worth: PECS and Other Visual Communication Strategies in Autism.* Bethesda, MD: Woodbine.

Breathnach, C.S. and Ward, C. (2005) "The Victorian genius of Earlswood: A review of the case of James Henry Pullen." *Irish Journal of Psychological Medicine 22,* 151–155.

Brill, A.A. (1940) "Some peculiar manifestations of memory with special reference to lightning calculators." *Journal of Nervous and Mental Diseases 92,* 709–726.

Brink, T.L. (1980) "Idiot savant with unusual mechanical ability: An organic explanation." *American Journal of Psychiatry 137,* 250–251.

Bryant, J. (1993) *The Opening Door.* Stepney, South Australia: Swift Printing.

Bunce, S.C., Izzetoglu, M., Izzetoglu, K., Onaral, B. and Pourrezaei, K. (2006) "Functional Near-Infrared Spectroscopy." *IEEE Engineering in Medicine and Biology Magazine 25,* 4, 54–62.

Butterworth, B. (1999) *What Counts: How Every Brain is Hardwired for Math.* New York: Free Press.

Cardinal, R, (2005) "The Calendars of George Widener." *Raw Vision 51,* 42–47.

Cardinal, R. (2009) "Outsider art and the autistic creator." *Philosophical Transactions of the Royal Society 364,* 1459–1466.

Carroll, L. (2006) "The science of art." *Neurology Now 2*, 6, 31–33.

Casanova, M. and Trippe, J. (2009) "Radial cytoarchitecture and patterns of cortical connectivity in autism." *Philosophical Transactions of the Royal Society B 364*, 1433–1436.

Chandler, K. (2004) "People who remember things they never learned." *Australian Journal of Parapsychology 4*, 1, 2–31.

Charness, N., Clifton, J. and MacDonald, L. (1988) "A Case Study of a Musical Mono-savant: A Cognitive Psychological Focus." In L.K. Obler and D.A. Fein (eds) *The Exceptional Brain: The Neuropsychology of Talent and Special Abilities.* New York: Guilford Press.

Clark, T.R. (2001) *The Application of Savant and Splinter Skills in the Autistic Population through Curriculum Design: A Longitudinal Multiple-replication Case Study.* Unpublished doctoral dissertation, University of New South Wales, Sydney, Australia.

Cohen, G.D. (2000) *The Creative Age: Awakening Human Potential in the Second Half of Life.* New York: HarperCollins.

Cowan, R. and Frith, C. (2009) "Do calendrical savants use calculation to answer date questions? A functional magnetic resonance imaging study." *Philosophical Transactions of the Royal Society B 364*, 1417–1424.

Critchley, M. (1979) *The Divine Banquet of the Brain.* New York: Raven Press.

Curry, J. (1988) "Hoffman hits home." *The Herald-Dispatch*, December 12, A1, A7.

DeBlois, J. and Felix, A. (2005) *Some Kind of Genius: The Extraordinary Journey of Musical Savant Tony DeBlois.* Emmaus, PA: Rodale.

DeLong, R. (1999) "Autism: New data suggest a new hypothesis." *Neurology 52*, 911–916.

Doidge, N. (2007) *The Brain that Changes Itself: Stories of Personal Triumph from the Frontiers of Brain Science.* New York: Viking.

Donnelly, J.A. and Altman, R. (1994) "The autistic savant: Recognizing and serving the gifted child with autism." *Roeper Review 16*, 252–256.

Dorman, C. (1991) "Exceptional calendar calculating ability after early left hemispherectomy." *Brain and Cognition 15*, 26–36.

Down, J.L. (1887) *On Some of the Mental Affections of Childhood and Youth.* London: Churchill.

Drago, V., Foster, P.S., Trifiletti, D., Fitzgerald, D.B. *et al.* (2006) "What's inside the art? The influence of frontotemporal dementia in art production." *Neurology 67*, 1285–1287.

Dubischar-Krivec, A.M., Neumann, F., Poustka, C., Braun, N., Birbaumer, N. and Bolte, S. (2008) "Calendar calculating in savants with autism and healthy calendar calculators." *Psychological Medicine 38*, 1–9.

Duckett, J. (1976) *Idiot Savants: Superspecialization in Mentally Retarded Persons.* Doctoral dissertation, Department of Special Education, University of Texas – Austin.

Edwards, B. (1999) *The New Drawing on the Right Side of the Brain.* New York: Jeremy P. Tarcher/Putnam.

El-Hai, J. (2001) "One smart bookie." *Atlantic Monthly 287*, 5, 44–49.

Eriksson, P.S., Perfilieva, E., Bjork-Eriksson, T., Alborn, A.M. *et al.* (1998) "Neurogenesis in the adult human hippocampus." *Nature Medicine 4*, 1313–1317.

Ernsperger, L. and Wendel, D. (2007) *Girls Under the Umbrella of Autism Spectrum Disorders.* Shawnee Mission, KS: Autism Asperger Publishing.

Escalant-Mead, P., Minshew, N. and Sweeney, J. (2003) "Abnormal brain lateralization in high functioning autism." *Journal of Autism and Developmental Disorders 33*, 539–543.

Feuillet, L., Dufour, H. and Pelletier, J. (2007) "Brain of a white collar worker." *Lancet 370*, 262.

Gallate, J., Chi, R., Ellwood, S. and Snyder, A. (2009) "Reducing false memories by magnetic pulse stimulation." *Neuroscience Letters 449*, 1151–1154.

Gardner, H. (1993) *Frames of Mind: The Theory of Multiple Intelligences.* New York: Basic Books.

Garst, D. and Katz, W. (2006) "Foreign accent syndrome." *The ASHA Leader 11*, 10–11.

Gazzaniga, M.S. (2000) *The Mind's Past.* Berkeley, CA: University of California Press.

Geschwind, N. and Galaburda, A.M. (1987) *Cerebral Lateralization: Biological Mechanisms, Associations, and Pathology.* Cambridge, MA: MIT Press.

Gillespie, J. (1964) "The Egyptian Copts and their Music." Available from http://tasbeha.org/ or www.copticchurch.net/ (accessed November 5, 2009).

Giray, E.F. and Barclay, A.G. (1977) "Eidetic imagery: Longitudinal results in brain-damaged children." *American Journal of Mental Deficiency 82*, 311–314.

Gnothi Sauton oder Magazin der Erfahrungsseelenkunde als ein Lesebuch fur Gelehrte und Ungelehrte, edited by K.P. Mortiz. Berlin: Nylius, 1783–1793.

Goddard, H.H. (1914) *Feeble-Mindedness.* New York: Macmillan.

Grandin, T. (1996) *Thinking in Pictures: And Other Reports from My Life with Autism.* New York: Vintage.

Grandin, T. (2006) *Thinking in Pictures: And Other Reports from My Life with Autism*, 2nd expanded edn. New York: Vintage.

Grandin, T. (2008) *The Way I See It.* Arlington, TX: Future Horizons.

Grandin, T. (2009) "How does visual thinking work in a mind of a person in autism? A personal account." *Philosophical Transactions of the Royal Society B 364*, 1437–1442.

Grandin, T. and Barron, S. (2005) *Unwritten Rules of Social Relationships: Decoding Social Mysteries through the Unique Perspective of Autism*. Arlington, TX: Future Horizons.

Grandin, T. and Duffy, K. (2004) *Developing Talents: Careers for Individuals with Asperger Syndrome and High Functioning Autism*. Shawnee Mission, KS: Autism Asperger Publishing.

Grandin, T. and Johnson, C. (2005) *Animals in Translation: Using the Mysteries of Autism to Decode Animal Behavior*. New York: Scribner.

Grandin, T. and Scariano, M.M. (1986) *Emergence Labeled Autistic*. Novato, CA: Arena.

Gratton, G., Fabini, M., Gagnon, L., Valois, K. *et al.* (2007) "Near-infrared spectroscopy as an alternative to the Wada test for language mapping in children, adults and special populations." *Epileptic Disorders 9*, 241–255.

Gray, C.R. and Gummerman, K. (1975) "The enigmatic eidetic image: A critical examination of methods, data, and theories." *Psychological Bulletin 82*, 383–407.

Gurder, J. and Coleman, J. (2006) "Foreign accent syndrome." *Journal of Neurolinguistics 19*, 5, 341–430.

Hamani, C., McAndrews, M.P., Cohn, M., Oh, M. *et al.* (2008) "Memory enhancement induced by hypothalamic/fornix deep brain stimulation." *Annals of Neurology 63*, 119–123.

Hamblin, D.J. (1966) "They are idiot savants—wizards of the calendar." *Life 60*, 106–108.

Hardy, G.H. (1993) *A Course of Pure Mathematics*, 10th edn. Cambridge: Cambridge University Press.

Hauser, S.L., DeLong, G.R. and Rosman, N.P. (1975) "Pneumographic findings in the infantile autism syndrome." *Brain 98*, 667–688.

Hergé (1978) *The Shooting Star (The Adventures of Tintin)*. New York: Little, Brown.

Hermelin, B. (2001) *Bright Splinters of the Mind*. London: Jessica Kingsley Publishers.

Hermelin, B., O'Connor, N. and Lee, S. (1987) "Musical inventiveness of five idiot-savants." *Psychological Medicine 17*, 685–694.

Hermelin, B., O'Connor, N., Lee, S. and Treffert, D. (1989) "Intelligence level and musical improvisation ability." *Psychological Medicine 19*, 447–457.

Hill, A.L. (1977) "Idiot savants: Rate of incidence." *Perceptual Motor Skills 44*, 161–162.

Hill, A.L. (1978) "Savants: Mentally Retarded Individuals with Special Skills." In N. Ellis (ed.) *International Review of Research in Mental Retardation*. New York: Academic Press.

Hoffman, E. (1971) "The idiot savant: A case report and review of explanations." *Mental Retardation 9*, 18–21.

Hoffman, E. and Reeves, R. (1979) "An idiot savant with unusual mechanical ability." *American Journal of Psychiatry 136*, 713–714.

Horwitz, W.A., Deming, W.E. and Winter, E.F. (1969) "A further account of the idiot savants: Experts with the calendar." *American Journal of Psychiatry 126*, 160–163.

Horwitz, W.A., Kestenbaum, C., Person, E.I. and Jarvick, L. (1965) "Identical twins—'idiot savants'—calendar calculators." *American Journal of Psychiatry 121*, 1075–1079.

Hou, C., Miller, B., Cummings, J., Goldberg, M. *et al.* (2000) "Artistic savants." *Neuropsychiatry, Neuropsychology and Behavioral Neurology 13*, 29–38.

Howlin, P., Goode, S., Hutton, J. and Rutter, M. (2009) "Savant skills in autism: Psychometric approaches and parental reports." *Philosophical Transactions of the Royal Society B 364*, 1359–1357.

Jayakar, A., Dunoyer, C., Rey, G., Yaylali, I. and Jayakar, P. (2005) "Near infra-red spectroscopy to define cognitive frontal lobe functions." *Journal of Clinical Neurophysiology 22*, 415–417.

Jung, C.G. (1936) "The Archetypes and the Collective Unconscious." In *The Collected Works of C.G. Jung*, translated by R.F.C. Hull. Bollingen Series XX, Volume 9.i. Princeton, NJ: Princeton University Press.

Kanner, L. (1944) "Early infantile autism." *Journal of Pediatrics 25*, 200–217.

Kapogiannis, D., Barbey, A., Su, M., Zamboni, G., Krueger, F. and Grafman, J. (2009) "Cognitive and neural foundations of religious belief." *Proceedings of the National Academy of Sciences 106*, 4876–4881.

Kapur, N. (1996) "Paradoxical functional facilitation in brain-behavior research." *Brain 119*, 1775–1790.

Keeler, W.R. (1958) "Autistic Patterns and Defective Communication in Blind Children with Retrolental Fibroplasias." In P. Hoch and J. Zubin (eds) *Psychopathology of Communication*. New York: Grune & Stratton.

Kerbeshian, J. and Burd, L. (1986) "Asperger Syndrome and Tourette Syndrome: The case of the pinball wizard." *British Journal of Psychiatry 148*, 731–736.

Kranowitz, C.S. (2006) *The Out-of-Sync Child Has Fun: Activities for Kids with Sensory Processing Disorder*. New York: Perigee.

Kriegeskorte, N., Simmons, W.K., Bellgowan, P.S. and Baker, C.I. (2009) "Circular analysis in systems neuroscience—The dangers of double dipping." *Nature Neuroscience 12*, 535–540.

Krepki, R., Curio, G., Blankertz, B. and Muller, K. (2007) "Berlin brain-computer interface—the HCI communication channel for discovery." *International Journal of Human-Computer Studies 65*, 460–477.

Kyle, Clason (1978) "'Blind Tom': slave-born pianist a sensation." *Ledger-Enquirer*, April 23.

LaFontaine, L. (1974) *Divergent Abilities in the Idiot Savant*. Doctoral dissertation, School of Education, Boston University, Boston, MA.

Lenhoff, H.M. (1998) "Insights into the musical potential of cognitively impaired people diagnosed with Williams Syndrome." *Music Therapy Perspectives 16*, 22–36.

Levitan, B.J. and Bellugi, U. (1998) "Musical ability in individuals with Williams Syndrome." *Music Perception 15*, 357–389.

Lewis, C. (2008) *Rex: A Mother, her Autistic Child, and the Music that Transformed their Lives*. Nashville, TN: Thomas Nelson.

Little, C. (2005) "A Closer Look at Gifted Children with Disabilities." In S.K. Johnson and J. Kendrick (eds) *Teaching Gifted Students with Disabilities* (Gifted Reader Series). Austin, TX: Prufrock.

Luria, A.R. (1968) *The Mind of a Mnemonist*. New York: Basic Books.

Luszki, W.A. (1966) "An idiot savant on the WAIS?" *Psychological Reports 19*, 603–609.

Lythgoe, M., Pollak, M., Kalmus, M., deHaan, M. and Khean Chong, W. (2005) "Obsessive, prolific artistic output following subarchnoid hemorrhage." *Neurology 64*, 397–398.

Ma, D.Q., Jaworski, J., Menoid, M.M., Donnelly, R.K. *et al.* (2005) "Ordered-subset analysis of savant skills in autism for 15q11-q13." *American Journal of Medical Genetics Part B: Neuropsychiatric Genetics 135B*, 38–41.

Maenner, M.J., Arneson, C.L. and Durkin, M.S. (2009) 'Socioeconomic disparity in the prevalence of autism spectrum disorder in Wisconsin.' *Wisconsin Medical Journal 108*, 253–255.

Mansfield, S. (2009) "Daniel Tammet Interview: Wide Sky Thinking." *The Scotsman*, February 14.

Marshack, A. (1991) *The Roots of Civilization*, 2nd edn. London: Moyer Bell.

Martin, N. (2009) *Art as an Early Intervention Tool for Children with Autism*. London: Jessica Kingsley Publishers.

Meeks, T.W. and Jeste, D.V. (2009) "The neurobiology of wisdom: A literature overview." *Archives of General Psychiatry 66*, 355–395.

Mell, J.C., Howard, S.M. and Miller, B.L. (2003) "Art and the brain: The influence of frontotemporal dementia on an accomplished artist." *Neurology 60*, 1707–1710.

Miller, B.L., Boone, K., Cummings, L.R. and Mishkin, F. (2000) "Functional correlates of musical and visual ability in frontotemporal dementia." *British Journal of Psychiatry 176*, 458–463.

Miller, B.L., Cummings, J., Mishkin, F., Boone, K. *et al.* (1998) "Emergence of artistic talent in frontotemporal dementia." *Neurology 51*, 978–982.

Miller, B.L., Ponton, M., Benson, D.F., Cummings, J.L. and Mena, I. (1996) "Enhanced artistic creativity with temporal lobe degeneration." *Lancet 348*, 1744–1745.

Miller, L.K. (1989) *Musical Savants: Exceptional Skill in the Mentally Retarded*. Hillsdale, NJ: Lawrence Erlbaum Associates.

Miller, N., Lowit, A. and O'Sullivan, H. (2006) "What makes acquired foreign accent syndrome foreign?" *Journal of Neurolinguistics 19*, 385–409.

Minogue, B.M. (1923) "A case of secondary mental deficiency with musical talent." *Journal of Applied Psychology 7*, 349–357.

Mishkin, M. and Petri, H.L. (1984) "Memories and Habits: Some Implications for the Analysis of Learning and Retention." In L.R. Squire and N. Butters (eds) *Neuropsychology of Memory*. New York: Guilford Press.

Monrad-Krohn, G.H. (1947) "Dysprosody or altered 'melody of language'." *Brain 70*, 405–415.

Monty, S. (1981) *May's Boy: An Incredible Story of Love*. Nashville, TN: Thomas Nelson.

Moritz, C.T., Perlmutter, S.I. and Fetz, E.E. (2008) "Direct control of paralyzed muscles by cortical neurons." *Nature 456*, 639–642.

Naidoo, R., Warriner, E.M., Oczkowski, W.J., Sevigny, A. and Humphreys, K.R. (2008) "A case of foreign accent syndrome resulting in regional dialect." *Canadian Journal of Neurological Sciences 35*, 360–365.

Neumann, A., Dubischar-Krivec, A., Braun, C., Bolte, S., Low, A., Poustka, F. and Birbaumer, N. (2009) "The mind of the mnemonists: An MEG study of autistic memory savants." ,Poster presentation for Society for the Annual Meeting of the Society for Psychophysiological Research, Berlin, Germany October 21–24.

Newberg, A. and D'Aquili, E. (2001) *Why God Won't Go Away*. New York: Ballantine.

Newlandsmith, E. (1931) "The ancient music of the Coptic Church." A lecture delivered at the University of Oxford, May 21, 1931. Available at www.coptic.org/music/oxford.htm (accessed November 5, 2009).

Newman, J.R. (1956) *The World of Mathematics*. New York: Simon & Schuster.

Nirenberg, M. (1968) "Genetic memory." *Journal of the American Medical Association 205*, 1973–1977.

Nurcombe, M.D. and Parker, N. (1964) "The idiot savant." *Journal of the American Academy of Child Psychiatry 3*, 469–487.

Nurmi, E.L., Dowd, M., Tadevosyan-Leyer, O., Haines, J., Folstein, S. and Sutcliffe, J.S. (2003) "Exploratory sub-setting of autism families based on savant skills improves evidence of genetic linkage to 15q11-q13." *Journal of the Academy of Child Adolescent Psychiatry 42*, 856–863.

Ockelford, A. (2007) *In the Key of Genius: The Extraordinary Life of Derek Paravicini*. London: Hutchinson.

Ockelford, A. and Matawa, C. (2009) *Focus on Music 2: Exploring the Musicality of Children and Young People with Retinopathy of Prematurity*. London: Institute of Education, University of London.

Ockelford, A., Pring, L., Welch, G.F. and Treffert, D.A. (2006) *Focus on Music: Exploring the Musical Interests and Abilities of Blind and Partially-Sighted Children with Septo-optic Dysplasia.* London: Institute of Education, University of London.

Ogilvy, C.S. and Anderson, J.T. (1998) *Excursions in Number Theory.* New York: Dover.

Palmer, W.A., Manus, M. and Lethco, A.V. (1995) *Alfred Piano Series.* Van Neys, CA: Alfred Publishing.

Parker, E.S., Cahill, L. and McGaugh, J.L. (2006) "A case of unusual autobiographical remembering." *Neurocase 12,* 35–49.

Peek, F. (1996) *The Real Rain Man: A Father's Inspiring Account of Kim Peek.* Salt Lake City, UT: Harkness.

Peek, F. and Hanson, L. (2008) *The Life and Message of the Real Rain Man: The Journey of a Mega-savant.* Port Chester, NY: National Professional Resources.

Penfield, W. (1978) *Mystery of the Mind.* Princeton, NJ: Princeton University Press.

Phillips, A. (1930) "Talented imbeciles." *Psychological Clinics 18,* 246–255.

Pinker, S. (2003) *The Blank Slate: The Modern Denial of Human Nature.* New York: Penguin.

Powell, D. (2006) "We are all savants." *Shift: At the Frontiers of Consciousness 9,* 14–17.

Restak, R.M. (1984) *The Brain.* New York: Bantam.

Rexter, L. (2002) *Jonathan Lerman: Drawings by an Artist with Autism.* New York: George Braziller, Inc.

Rife, D.C. and Snyder, L.H. (1931) "Studies in human inheritance, VI: A genetic refutation of the principles of 'behavioristic' psychology." *Human Biology 3,* 547–559.

Rimland, B. (1964) *Infantile Autism: The Syndrome and its Implication for a Neural Theory of Behavior.* New York: Appleton-Century-Crofts.

Rimland, B. (1978a) "Savant Characteristics of Autistic Children and their Cognitive Implications." In G. Serban (ed.) *Cognitive Defects in the Development of Mental Illness.* New York: Brunner/Mazel.

Rimland, B. (1978b) "Inside the mind of the autistic savant." *Psychology Today 12,* 3, 68–80.

Rimland, B. and Fine, D. (1988) "Special Talents of Autistic Savants." In L. Obler and D.A. Fine (eds) *The Exceptional Brain.* New York: Guilford Press.

Roberts, A.D. (1945) "Case history of a so-called idiot savant." *Journal of Genetic Psychology 66,* 259–265.

Rohling, L.R., Faust, M.E., Beverly, B. and Demakis, G. (2009) "Effectiveness of cognitive rehabilitation following acquired brain injury: A meta-analytic re-examination of Cicerone *et al.*'s (2000, 2005) systematic reviews." *Neuropsychology 23,* 20–39.

Rubin, E.J. and Monaghan, S. (1965) "Calendar calculation in a multiple-handicapped blind person." *American Journal of Mental Deficiency 70,* 478–485.

Rush, B. (1789) *American Museum 5,*62–63.

Rutherford, M., August, M., Matthieussent, D., DeQuine, J., Gunn, E and Savaiano, J. (2000) "Careers: Catching their second wind." *Time Magazine* January 31.

Sacks, O. (1989) *The Man Who Mistook His Wife for a Hat.* New York: Harper & Row.

Sacks, O. (1995) *An Anthropologist on Mars: Seven Paradoxical Tales.* New York: Knopf.

Sacks, O. (2007) *Musicophilia.* New York: Knopf.

Sacks, O., Schlaug, L., Jancke, Y. and Steinmetz, H. (1995) "Musical ability." *Science 268,* 5211, 621–622.

Saloviita, T., Ruusila, L. and Ruusila, U. (2000) "Incidence of savant syndrome in Finland." *Perceptual and Motor Skills 91,* 120–122.

Sano, F. (1918) "James Henry Pullen, The Genius of Earlswood." *Journal of Mental Science 64,* 251–267.

Sarason, S.B. (1959) *Psychological Problems in Mental Deficiency.* New York: Harper and Brothers.

Scheerer, M., Rothmann, E. and Goldstein, K. (1945) "A case of 'idiot savant': An experimental study of personality organization." *Psychology Monograph 58,* 1–63.

Seeley, W.W., Matthews, B.R., Crawford, R.K., Gorno-Tempin, M.L. *et al.* (2008) "Unraveling Bolero—Progressive aphasia, transmodal creativity and the right posterior cortex." *Brain 131,* 39–49.

Selfe, L. (1977) *Nadia: A Case of Extraordinary Drawing Ability in an Autistic Child.* London: Academic Press.

Sequin, E. (1866) *Idiocy and its Treatment by the Physiologic Method.* New York: William Wood and Company.

Shors, T.J. (2009) "Saving new brain cells." *Scientific American 500,* 3, 47–54.

Silberman, S. (2003) "The key to genius." *WIRED Magazine* December 12, 226–228, 255–258.

Simpson, J.R. (2008) "Functional MRI lie detection: Too good to be true?" *Journal of the American Academy of Psychiatry and the Law 36,* 491–498.

Smith, N. and Tsimpli, I.-M. (1995) *The Mind of a Savant: Language, Learning and Modularity.* Oxford: Blackwell.

Smith, S.B. (1983) *The Great Mental Calculators.* New York: Columbia University Press.

Snyder, A.W. (2009) "Explaining and inducing savant skills: Privileged access to lower level, less-processed information." *Philosophical Transactions of the Royal Society B 364,* 1399–1405.

Snyder, A.W. and Mitchell, D.J. (1999) "Is integer arithmetic fundamental to mental processing? The mind's secret arithmetic." *Proceedings of the Royal Society B 266,* 587–592.

Southall, G.H. (1999) *Blind Tom, The Black Pianist-Composer.* Boston, MA: Scarecrow Press.

Sperry, R.W. (1968) "Hemisphere disconnection and unity in conscious awareness." *American Psychologist 23*, 723–733.

Steel, J.G., Gorman, R. and Flexman, J.E. (1984) "Neuropsychiatric testing in an autistic mathematical idiot-savant: Evidence for nonverbal abstract capacity." *Journal of the American Academy of Child Psychiatry 23*, 704–707.

Stevenson, I. (1974) *Xenoglossy: A Review and Report of a Case*. Charlotte, VA: University Press of Virginia.

Stewart, J. and Glasscock, B. (1985) *My Piano Book A*. Van Neys, CA: Alfred Publishing.

Swanson, H.L., Harris, K.R. and Graham, S. (eds) (2005) *Handbook of Learning Disabilities*. New York: Guilford Press.

Sylva, B. (2001) "A song in her heart." *The Sacramento Bee*, January 18, E1, E5.

Talbot, M. (2009) "Brain gain: The neuroenhancer revolution." *New Yorker* April 27, 32–43.

Tammet, D. (2006) *Born on a Blue Day: A Memoir of Asperger's and an Extraordinary Mind*. London: Hodder & Stoughton. Also published 2007, New York: Free Press.

Tammet, D. (2009) *Embracing the Wide Sky: A Tour across the Horizons of the Mind*. New York: Free Press.

Tanguay, P.E. (1973) "A tentative hypothesis regarding the role of hemispheric specialization in early infantile autism." Paper presented at the UCLA Conference on Cerebral Dominance, Los Angeles, CA.

Taylor, J.B. (2006) *My Stroke of Insight: A Brain Scientist's Personal Journey*. New York: Penguin.

Terry, T.L. (1942) "Fibroplastic overgrowth of persistent tunica vasculosa lentis in infants born prematurely." *American Journal of Ophthalmology 25*, 1409.

Thioux, M., Stark, D.E., Klaiman, C. and Schultz, R.T. (2006) "The day of the week when you were born in 700 ms: Calendar computation in an autistic savant." *Journal of Experimental Psychology 32*, 1155–1168.

Tredgold, A.F. (1914) *Mental Deficiency (Amentia)*. New York: William Wood.

Treffert, D.A. (1970) "The epidemiology of infantile autism." *Archives of General Psychiatry 22*, 431–438.

Treffert, D.A. (1988) "The idiot savant: A review of the syndrome." *American Journal of Psychiatry 145*, 563–572.

Treffert, D.A. (1989) *Extraordinary People: Understanding "Idiot Savants."* New York: Harper & Row.

Treffert, D.A. (2006a) *Extraordinary People: Understanding Savant Syndrome*. Lincoln, NE: iUniverse.

Treffert, D.A. (2006b) "Dr. Down and developmental disorders." *Journal of Autism and Developmental Disorders 36*, 965–966.

Treffert, D.A. (2008) "Autistic disorder 52 years later: Some common sense conclusions." Available at www.savantsyndrome.com (accessed November 5, 2009).

Treffert, D.A. and Christensen, D.D. (2005) "Inside the mind of a savant." *Scientific American 293*, 6.

Twain, M. (1869) Quoted in *Archangels Unaware*. Available at www.twainquotes.com/archangels.html (accessed November 5, 2009).

Viscott, D.S. (1969) "A musical idiot savant." *Psychiatry 32*, 494–515.

Volkmar, F.R., Klin, P.R. and Graham, S. (eds) (2005) *Handbook of Autism and Pervasive Developmental Disorders*. Hoboken, NJ: Wiley.

Vul, E., Harris, C., Winkelman, P. and Pashler, H. (2009) "Puzzlingly high correlations in fMRI studies of emotion, personality and social cognition." *Perspectives on Psychological Science 4*, 274–290.

Wallace, G.L., Happe, F. and Giedd, J.N. (2009) "A case study of a multiply talented savant with an autism spectrum disorder: Neuropsychological functioning and brain morphometry." *Philosophical Transactions of the Royal Society B 364*, 1425–1432.

Williams, C. (1958) "Retrolental fibroplasias as associated with mental defect." *British Journal of Ophthalmology 42*, 549–557.

Willis, S.L., Tennstedt, S.L., Marsiske, M., Ball, K. *et al.* (2006) "Long term effects of cognitive training on everyday functional outcomes in older adults." *Journal of the American Medical Association 296*, 2805–2814.

Wiltshire, S. (1987) *Drawings*. London: J.M. Dent & Sons.

Wiltshire, S. (1989) *Cities*. London: J.M. Dent & Sons.

Wiltshire, S. (1991) *Floating Cities*. New York: Summit.

Wiltshire, S. (1993) *Stephen Wiltshire's American Dream*. London: Michael Joseph.

Young, R. (1995) *Savant Syndrome: Processes Underlying Extraordinary Abilities*. Unpublished doctoral dissertation, University of Adelaide, South Australia.

Young, R., Ridding, M. and Morrell, T. (2004) "Switching skills on by turning off a part of the brain." *Neurocase 10*, 215–222.

Appendix: Books About Savant Syndrome and Books By or About Specific Savants

Books about savant syndrome

Hermelin, B. (2001) *Bright Splinters of the Mind*. London: Jessica Kingsley Publishers.

Howe, M. (1989) *Fragments of Genius*. London: Routledge.

Miller, L.K. (1989) *Musical Savants: Exceptional Skill in the Mentally Retarded*. Hillsdale, NJ: Lawrence Erlbaum Associates.

Treffert, D.A. (2006) *Extraordinary People: Understanding Savant Syndrome*. Lincoln, NE: iUniverse.

Books about specific savants

Bryant, J. (1993) *The Opening Door*. Stepney, South Australia: Swift Printing (the story of Trevor Tao).

Cameron, L. (1998) *The Music of Light: The Extraordinary Story of Hikari and Kenzaburo Oe*. New York: Free Press.

DeBlois, J. and Felix, A. (2005) *Some Kind of Genius: The Extraordinary Journey of Musical Savant Tony DeBlois*. Emmaus, PA: Rodale.

Lewis, C. (2008) *Rex: A Mother, her Autistic Child and the Music that Transformed their Lives*. Nashville, TN: Thomas Nelson.

Monty, S. (1981) *May's Boy: An Incredible Story of Love*. Nashville, TN: Thomas Nelson.

Ockelford, A. (2007) *In the Key of Genius: The Extraordinary Life of Derek Paravicini*. London: Hutchinson.

Peek, F. (1996) *The Real Rain Man: A Father's Inspiring Account of Kim Peek*. Salt Lake City, UT: Harkness.

Peek, F. and Hanson, L. (2008) *The Life and Message of the Real Rain Man: The Journey of a Mega-savant*. Port Chester, NY: National Professional Resources.

Rexter, L. (2002) *Jonathan Lerman: The Drawings of a Boy with Autism*. New York: George Braziller.

Selfe, L. (1977) *Nadia: A Case of Extraordinary Drawing Ability in an Autistic Child*. London: Academic Press.

Smith, N. and Tsimpli, I.-M. (1995) *The Mind of a Savant: Language, Learning and Modularity*. Oxford: Blackwell (the story of Christopher Taylor).

Books by specific savants

Blackstock, G.L. (2006) *Blackstock's Collections: The Drawings of an Artistic Savant*. New York: Princeton Architectural Press (Foreword by D.A. Treffert).

Grandin, T. (2006) *Thinking in Pictures: And Other Reports from My Life with Autism*, 2nd expanded edn. New York: Vintage.

Grandin, T. (2008) *The Way I See It*. Arlington, TX: Future Horizons.

Grandin, T. and Johnson, C. (2005) *Animals in Translation: Using the Mysteries of Autism to Decode Animal Behavior*. New York: Scribner.

Grandin, T. and Scariano, M.M. (1986) *Emergence Labeled Autistic*. Novato, CA: Arena.

Tammet, D. (2006) *Born on a Blue Day: A Memoir of Asperger's and an Extraordinary Mind*. London: Hodder & Stoughton. Also published 2007, New York: Free Press (Foreword by D.A. Treffert).

Tammet, D. (2009) *Embracing the Wide Sky: A Tour across the Horizons of the Mind*. New York: Free Press.

Wiltshire, S. (1987) *Drawings*. London: J.M. Dent & Sons.

Wiltshire, S. (1989) *Cities*. London: J.M. Dent & Sons.

Wiltshire, S. (1991) *Floating Cities*. New York: Summit.

Wiltshire, S. (1993) *Stephen Wiltshire's American Dream*. London: Michael Joseph.

Subject Index

Author Index

153.9

LRC